THE CAMBRIDGE
COMPANION TO
RENAISSANCE HUMANISM

The beginning of Book I of Virgil's *Georgics*: MS London, British Library, King's 24, f. 17ʳ. The script is attributed to the famous Paduan calligrapher Bartolomeo Sanvito, who may also have been responsible for the illuminations. The manuscript was made *c.* 1490 for the apostolic protonotary Lodovico Agnelli, later to become archbishop of Cosenza.

THE CAMBRIDGE
COMPANION TO
RENAISSANCE HUMANISM

EDITED BY
JILL KRAYE
Warburg Institute

Published by the Press Syndicate of the University of Cambridge
The Pitt Building, Trumpington Street, Cambridge CB2 1RP
40 West 20th Street, New York, NY 10011–4211, USA
10 Stamford Road, Oakleigh, Melbourne 3166, Australia

© Cambridge University Press 1996

First published 1996

Printed in Great Britain at the University Press, Cambridge

A catalogue record for this book is available from the British Library

Library of Congress cataloguing in publication data

The Cambridge companion to Renaissance humanism / edited by Jill Kraye.
        p.   cm. – (Cambridge companions to literature)
    Includes bibliographical references (p.   ) and index.
ISBN 0 521 43038 0 (hardback). – ISBN 0 521 43624 9 (paperback)
    1. Humanism. 2. Renaissance. I. Kraye, Jill. II. Series.
                CB361.C26   1996
        001.3'094'09024–DC20   95–9469 CIP

ISBN 0 521 43038 0 hardback
ISBN 0 521 43624 9 paperback

CONTENTS

ix

ILLUSTRATIONS

CONTRIBUTORS

WARREN BOUTCHER is a Lecturer in the School of English and Drama at Queen Mary and Westfield College, University of London. He is the author of an article on Montaigne's visit to the Vatican Library (*Michigan Romance Studies*, 1995, ed. John O'Brien) and of *Montaigne's 'Essais' in Early Modern Europe* (forthcoming, Oxford University Press).

CLARE CARROLL is Associate Professor of Comparative Literature at Queens College and The Graduate Center, City University of New York. She is the co-editor of *An Annotated Edition of Richard Beacon, Solon His Follie* (Binghamton, 1995) and the author of *Orlando furioso, a Stoic Comedy* (forthcoming, Medieval and Renaissance Texts and Studies).

MARTIN DAVIES is Head of Incunabula at the British Library and editor of *The Library*. He is the author of *Columbus in Italy: An Italian Versification of the Letter on the Discovery of the New World* (London, 1991) and *Aldus Manutius, Printer and Publisher of Renaissance Venice* (London, 1995) and the co-editor of *Vergil: A Census of Printed Editions 1469–1500* (London, 1992).

ANTHONY GRAFTON is Dodge Professor of History at Princeton University. He is the author of *Joseph Scaliger*, 2 vols. (Oxford, 1983–93) and *Defenders of the Text: The Traditions of Scholarship in an Age of Science, 1450-1800* (Cambridge MA, 1991) and the editor of *Rome Reborn: The Vatican Library and Renaissance Culture* (Washington DC, 1993).

ALASTAIR HAMILTON is Professor of the History of the Radical Reformation at the University of Amsterdam and the C. L. Thijssen-Schoute Professor of the History of Ideas at the University of Leiden. His publications include *The Family of Love* (Cambridge, 1981); *William Bedwell the*

Arabist 1563–1632 (Leiden, 1985); and *Heresy and Mysticism in Sixteenth-Century Spain: The Alumbrados* (Cambridge, 1992).

JAMES HANKINS, Professor of History at Harvard University, is the author of *Plato in the Italian Renaissance*, 2 vols. (Leiden, 1990) and numerous articles on the intellectual history of the Renaissance.

CHARLES HOPE is Senior Lecturer in Renaissance Studies at the Warburg Institute. He is the author of *Titian* (London, 1980) and is preparing an edition of sources and documents about Titian.

KRISTIAN JENSEN is Head of the Bodleian Library Incunable Project. He is the author of *Latinskolens dannelse* (Copenhagen, 1982) and *Rhetorical Philosophy and Philosophical Grammar: Julius Caesar Scaliger's Theory of Language* (Munich, 1990).

JILL KRAYE is Lecturer in the History of Philosophy at the Warburg Institute. Associate editor of *The Cambridge History of Renaissance Philosophy* (Cambridge, 1988) and one of the joint editors of *The Uses of Greek and Latin: Historical Essays* (London, 1988), she has also written various articles on the influence of classical philosophy in the Renaissance.

JOSEPH LOEWENSTEIN chairs the English Department at Washington University in St Louis. The author of *Responsive Readings: Versions of Echo in Pastoral, Epic, and the Jonsonian Masque* (New Haven, 1984), he is currently completing a book on Renaissance intellectual property.

ELIZABETH MCGRATH is Curator of the Photographic Collection at the Warburg Institute and co-editor of the *Journal of the Warburg and Courtauld Institutes*. She is the author of *Rubens: Subjects from History*, Corpus Rubenianum 13 (forthcoming, Harvey Miller).

PETER MACK is Senior Lecturer in the Department of English at Warwick University. He is the author of *Renaissance Argument: Valla and Agricola in the Traditions of Rhetoric and Dialectic* (Leiden, 1993), the editor of *Renaissance Rhetoric* (London, 1994) and the co-editor of *England and the Continental Renaissance: Essays in Honour of J. B. Trapp* (Woodbridge, 1990).

MARTIN L. MCLAUGHLIN is University Lecturer in Italian at the University of Oxford and a Student of Christ Church. He is Italian editor of *The Modern*

Language Review and author of a forthcoming book on literary imitation in the Italian Renaissance.

NICHOLAS MANN is Director of the Warburg Institute and Professor of the History of the Classical Tradition at the University of London. He has worked for many years on Petrarch and aspects of his interest in the ancient world.

MICHAEL REEVE, Professor of Latin at Cambridge and Fellow of Pembroke College, has edited Longus' novel *Daphnis and Chloe* (Leipzig, 1982) and Cicero's speech *Pro Quinctio* (Leipzig, 1992). Besides contributing to L. D. Reynolds, ed., *Texts and Transmission* (Oxford, 1983), he has studied the humanistic phase in the textual transmission of many classical Latin authors.

PREFACE

For many years now, Renaissance humanism has been a topic of widespread interest to students and scholars in a variety of fields. Numerous publications in this area, however, are written with an audience of specialists in mind. It is often assumed that readers have a solid knowledge of both ancient and Renaissance culture and that they can comfortably handle Latin and Greek; furthermore, a large number of essential monographs and articles are written in foreign languages. Access to the most up-to-date and thorough studies has therefore been denied to those who lack the requisite background and linguistic skills, even though they have the desire to learn about this subject. One of the aims of the present volume is to help remedy this situation by providing accessible treatments for an English-speaking readership of some of the major issues in Renaissance humanism. In pursuit of this goal, all quotations from classical and foreign languages have been translated, and an attempt has been made to present even the most challenging material in a manner which can be readily grasped by students and non-specialists.

A further aim in producing this book is to counter the view that Renaissance humanism was a narrowly philological enterprise, concerned only with the technicalities of classical scholarship and with a definable curriculum consisting of grammar, rhetoric, poetry, history and moral philosophy. These subjects are discussed at length in the volume; but equal stress is laid on the role of humanism as a broad intellectual and cultural movement, which contributed to, or at any rate engaged with, disciplines such as biblical studies, political thought, art, science and all branches of philosophy. In addition, instead of locating humanism solely within the period from the beginning of the fourteenth century to the end of the sixteenth, as is customary, considerable attention has been devoted to its medieval antecedents and, in particular, to its survival into the seventeenth century and beyond. A final objective is to highlight the complex interaction between the Latin-based and vernacular cultures of the Renaissance, documenting in detail the impact which humanism had on literature, with particular attention paid to Italy and England.

In order to make the volume as useful as possible to students perhaps encountering Renaissance humanism for the first time, a guide to further reading has been provided which includes only material either written in or translated into English. Those readers who want to pursue subjects in greater depth will find more detailed bibliography, including works in foreign languages, in the notes to individual chapters. One potential difficulty in a book such as this, which covers several centuries and ranges over many countries, is that the cast of characters is so large that it can become unmanageable. To alleviate this problem in the least obtrusive way, a biographical index, giving dates and brief identifications of the figures mentioned in the volume, has been provided instead of the chronological table usually found in the Cambridge Companions to Literature.

The secret of making a good movie, according to some directors, is all down to the casting. Certainly, I feel that my most valuable contribution as editor of this volume is having brought together a superb team of scholars from both sides of the Atlantic; all experts in their own fields, they have been willing to make their expertise available to a wide audience. My own editorial, not to say scholarly, endeavours have benefited beyond measure from daily access to the library of the Warburg Institute, an extraordinary intellectual resource for the study of Renaissance humanism, as for all aspects of the survival and transmission of ancient learning and culture to the modern world. Together with its august neighbour, the British Library, it constitutes an ideal centre for anyone working in this field.

Jill Kraye

Map 1   Western Europe to Byzantium: centres of medieval and early Renaissance classical scholarship

xvii

Map 2   Italy: centres of medieval and early Renaissance classical scholarship

I

The origins of humanism

NICHOLAS MANN

Any account of the past is necessarily coloured by the preconceptions, the aspirations and, above all, the knowledge or ignorance of the scholar who produces it. The terms and concepts that historians use to order and explain the objects of their inquiry are neither fixed nor value-free, but are evolving and often highly subjective elements in that process of revealing the past that gradually leads us to a better understanding of it. Labels such as Dark Ages or Renaissance, which are affixed to whole periods of European history, while they are convenient for the purposes of historiographical exposition, may tell only part of the truth about those segments of the past that they purport to characterize. The more we learn about the period following the decline of Rome, the less dark and uncultured it appears; the more we inquire into what was reborn in the fourteenth and fifteenth centuries, the more we become aware of vital continuities with the past.

The history of humanism exemplifies both those continuities and a sense of renewal. The term itself owes its origin to the Latin *humanitas*, used by Cicero and others in classical times to betoken the kind of cultural values that one would derive from what used to be called a liberal education: the *studia humanitatis* constituted the study of what we might now think of as 'arts' subjects – language, literature, history and moral philosophy in particular. Even if Cicero was not widely read in the Middle Ages, he and his terminology were well known to certain fourteenth-century scholars (notably Petrarch, who regarded him as his favourite author); by the following century, the *studia humanitatis* were firmly enshrined in the university curriculum. The term *umanista* was used, in fifteenth-century Italian academic jargon, to describe a teacher or student of classical literature and the arts associated with it, including that of rhetoric. The English equivalent 'humanist' makes its appearance in the late sixteenth century with a very similar meaning. Only in the nineteenth century, however, and probably for the first time in Germany in 1809, is the attribute transformed into a substantive: humanism, standing for devotion to the literatures of ancient Greece and Rome, and the humane values that may be derived from them. The concept to which this volume is dedicated is thus a relatively new one, even if, as this first chapter will attempt to show, the activity to which it relates has a long and honourable pedigree, and was being practised for centuries before anyone thought of giving it a name.[1]

For the purposes of the present discussion, a working definition of humanism is clearly necessary, notwithstanding the misgivings expressed above about the value of historiographical labels. But it is precisely because it was originally an activity and not a concept that we can with confidence advance a description that will justify devoting an entire volume to it. Humanism is that concern with the legacy of antiquity – and in particular, but not exclusively, with its literary legacy – which characterizes the work of scholars from at least the ninth century onwards. It involves above all the rediscovery and study of ancient Greek and Roman texts, the restoration and interpretation of them and the assimilation of the ideas and values that they contain. It ranges from an archaeological interest in the remains of the past to a highly focused philological attention to the details of all manner of written records – from inscriptions to epic poems – but comes to pervade, as we shall see, almost all areas of post-medieval culture, including theology, philosophy, political thought, jurisprudence, medicine, mathematics and the creative arts. Grounded in what we would now think of as learned research, it rapidly found expression in teaching. And in this way it was to become the embodiment of, and vehicle for, that very classical tradition that is the most fundamental aspect of the continuity of European cultural and intellectual history. This chapter will endeavour to trace the main features of that continuity from its apparent beginnings in the ninth century to the end of the fourteenth century – a period in which scholarly interest was focused largely, but by no means exclusively, on Roman culture and Latin literature.

That these beginnings were only apparent, and that they themselves rested upon the uncharted scholarly efforts of an earlier age, themselves no doubt relying on still earlier attempts to keep the spirit of Rome and its texts alive, may be demonstrated by a minute but symptomatic instance of the survival of a classical text, *De chorographia* of the first-century geographer Pomponius Mela. We know that Petrarch acquired a copy of this rare work at Avignon in the mid-1330s, and although we do not possess his manuscript, a number of those derived from it preserved his annotations to the text and transmitted the results of his erudite labours to later scholars. The copy from which Petrarch was working was almost certainly a twelfth-century one, and at all events clearly descended from a ninth-century manuscript made at Auxerre and annotated by the Carolingian teacher Heiric. He in turn owed his knowledge of *De chorographia* to a sixth-century miscellany of texts assembled by Rusticius Helpidius Domnulus at Ravenna, which had since late antiquity been an important cultural centre. In this case – and it is not unique – we can therefore trace a direct line of textual descent from Rome to the Renaissance, a line constructed by scholarly activity of a kind characteristic of humanism.

Heiric's activity at Auxerre is exemplary of what is known as the Carolingian Renaissance, a surge of scholarship that took place in the eighth and ninth centuries in which many features of later humanistic practice can be observed. Auxerre was but one of the great monastic centres where during Charlemagne's reign the production of books flourished and important libraries were formed; others include Tours, Fleury and Ferrières in France, Fulda, Hersfeld, Corvey, Reichenau and St Gall in Germanic areas, Bobbio and Pomposa in northern Italy. Heiric was an influential scholar and teacher, to whom we owe the transmission of a number of classical texts besides that of Pomponius Mela, and notably fragments of Petronius. He was a pupil of Lupus of Ferrières, who was the greatest scholar of the ninth century and in effect the first classical philologist. Not only did he build up a substantial library, but he made every effort to acquire further manuscripts of texts that he already possessed, so that by comparing them he could correct and augment his own copies. More than a dozen surviving manuscripts, including works by Cicero, Valerius Maximus and Aulus Gellius, are annotated in Heiric's hand and bear witness to his philological skills. Five or six centuries on, manuscripts such as these were to provide the Italian humanists with the primary material for their recovery of the classics.

A quite different aspect of the Carolingian period, but one which also to some extent foreshadows the revival of learning that was to come later in Italy, was the need generated by a centralized regime for educated administrators outside the narrow sphere of the monasteries. Charlemagne's solution was to summon the head of the greatest school in Europe at York to advise him on educational matters in 782. Alcuin brought with him from England an effective pedagogical method, based on the reading of classical texts, and a significant consequence of his advice was the imperial edict establishing schools not only in monasteries but also for the secular clergy attached to the cathedrals. These schools, whose aim was perhaps no greater than to guarantee the spread of basic literacy, none the less helped to create a literate class outside the monasteries and, in generating an increasing need for books, widened the circle of readers for the texts that they contained.[2]

Even if with the decline of Charlemagne's empire the flourishing literary culture that had accompanied it at its height did not survive, the pattern which it had established for the spread of education to cities was to be of the greatest significance. Major monasteries continued to be centres of scholarship and book-production, and to promote interest in classical literature. The outstanding example is the Benedictine mother-house of Monte Cassino, to whose activity, especially in the eleventh century under Abbot Desiderius, we owe some magnificent manuscripts and the survival of a number of key texts. But the future was with the courts, the cathedral schools and the cities. During the twelfth century, classical literature underwent a new revival, this time labelled as the twelfth-century Renaissance; at the courts and in the cathedral schools (some of them destined to become universities) of southern Italy and Sicily, of Spain, of Bologna and Montpellier, of northern France and Norman England, scholars turned their knowledge of the classics not only to literary ends but also to more practical and above all secular ones. In addition to men of letters and philosophers, society needed lawyers, doctors and civil servants, and for them the study of the writings of antiquity assumed the role of professional training. The range of texts available had not only expanded considerably in the field of literature, grammar and rhetoric, but now included Latin translations of Greek scientific and philosophical texts: medical treatises, Euclid, Ptolemy and some works of Aristotle.

It is a measure of the degree to which twelfth-century French culture was permeated by classical material that even vernacular literature came to bear its traces. In the last decades of the century three romances – the *Roman de Thèbes*, *Eneas* and the *Roman de Troie* – and many shorter texts were directly based upon material reaching back to antiquity. The growth in production during the same period of *florilegia*, anthologies of excerpts from classical authors, confirms the impression that their writings, or parts of them at least, were reaching an increasingly wide, though not always scholarly, audience.[3]

One of the outstanding scholars of the age, John of Salisbury, may stand as an illustration of the embryonic state of humanism. He had been educated at Chartres and Paris in the early twelfth century and certainly possessed an impressive, if somewhat patchy, knowledge of Latin literature (some of it no doubt derived from *florilegia* rather than the original texts); he praised eloquence and defended liberal studies in his *Metalogicon*; he was skilled at deploying his knowledge of examples drawn from ancient history to illustrate the moral judgements that he brought to bear on contemporary problems. Yet he shows no signs of an awareness of the ancient problem of the relationship between rhetoric and philosophy, nor of

4

a deeper understanding of the works from which his examples were derived: they served as ornamentation to his argument rather than as a fundamental part of the thinking behind it. He was an excellent Latin stylist, but as a result of being a grammarian rather than a philologist. In short, he was typical of the best kind of medieval classicist: broadly familiar with, but still only an armchair traveller in, the terrain that the humanists were later to explore in depth and make their own.[4]

The factors that prevented the kind of classical reading that was done by a John of Salisbury from developing into fully-fledged *studia humanitatis* were endemic in a society, such as that of northern France, in which the Church and its needs dominated. Canon law (the body of ecclesiastical rules imposed by authority in matters of faith, morals and discipline) and the new logic of Aristotle were the mainstay of the education of clerics, and within the confines of scholastic theology, pagan literature could hardly come into its own. Indeed, scholasticism was later to be regarded by some as the very antithesis of humanism, though such a view greatly oversimplifies the issues. In contrast to the largely agrarian and feudal society of countries north of the Alps, however, a quite different and predominantly urban civilization had developed in Italy. In the city-states of the north in particular, the needs of civic administration and commerce were to prove stronger than those of the Church; educated laymen, lawyers and civil servants in particular emerged as the new literate class.

Whereas in France the study of classical texts – which was to continue well into the fourteenth century – tended to remain rooted in grammar as a tool for understanding and sometimes imitating Roman writers, in Italy it developed along different lines and particularly in the direction of rhetoric as a skill for contemporary life. The study of what in classical times had been the art of public speaking had by the twelfth century in Italy become the *ars dictaminis*, the art of letter-writing; those who practised it, the *dictatores*, applied their knowledge to the needs of their patrons and the legal profession. They were not initially classical scholars in any profound sense, but rhetoricians who drew upon ancient models to achieve eloquence in the writing of letters and speeches; yet they held positions of influence as teachers, secretaries or chancellors to rulers and communes, and were consequently involved in, and influential upon, affairs of state. We can see in *dictamen* one of the roots of humanism, reaching deep into the past: the letter, thanks above all to Petrarch, was to become one of the most favoured and versatile literary genres of the Renaissance, encompassing private and political discourse, scholarly and philosophical enquiry, and all manner of literary enterprises.

Another main root of humanism which may be observed in thirteenth-century Italy, closely entwined with, and sometimes inseparable from, the activities of the *dictatores*, was the study of Roman law in its philological and practical aspects. Indeed, as early as the ninth century there are traces of notaries at the royal palace at Pavia applying the *Corpus iuris civilis* (the sixth-century codification of Roman law compiled at the behest of the Emperor Justinian) to contemporary situations, anticipating by some 400 years the figure of the legally trained civil servant as the typical learned layman who was to play such an important part in civic life. In the rapidly developing independent communes of the north, the role of lawyers in economic and political affairs was crucial. From at least the twelfth century onwards, and notably at the University of Bologna, there had been a revival in legal education. The glossing and interpretation of the great texts of Roman law, the *Code* and the *Digest*, with a view to applying them to current legal problems, combined with an awareness of historical origins no doubt reinforced by the presence of many physical remains of antiquity, helped to give a sense that the civilization of the past was still alive, and this in turn led to curiosity about that civilization.[5]

The lawyers who studied legal texts and adapted the precepts of Roman law to the needs of a fundamentally different society thus also became interested in other aspects of their classical heritage, and in particular in history and moral philosophy; they even resorted to the recreational writing of Latin verse. Lovato Lovati is the earliest figure who exemplifies these tendencies. Lovato gathered around him in Padua a group of like-minded men whose scholarly activities justify one in regarding that city as one of the earliest centres of proto-humanism. A notary and subsequently a judge, he was familiar with a remarkable range of classical texts, many of them extremely rare at the time, including Seneca's tragedies and lyric poets such as Catullus, Tibullus and Propertius. He almost certainly encountered some of them at the Benedictine Abbey of Pomposa and in the Chapter Library of Verona, both of them renowned as repositories of the writings of antiquity. He was also a skilled interpreter of epigraphs and showed a passionate antiquarian concern for Padua's past when in 1283–4 he identified an early Christian sarcophagus that had been dug up during building works as containing the remains of the mythical Trojan founder of the city, Antenor. It is significant of the cultural climate that it was agreed to incorporate this supposedly glorious relic of the city's ancient past into a monument of supposedly classical style bearing a Latin inscription composed by Lovato himself.

Yet however revealing this episode may be, it does not do justice to his scholarship. Lovato's real achievements, or such as survive today, were his

Latin verse epistles, bearing the traces of his reading of the classical poets, and a remarkable short commentary on Seneca's tragedies, the fruit of his own careful reading of the texts and in effect the first brief treatise on classical metrics. In these works we perceive in embryonic form three of the features that were to mark the later development of humanism: an appetite for classical texts; a philological concern to correct them and ascertain their meaning; and a desire to imitate them. These features mark, to a greater or lesser degree, a number of other minor figures in Lovato's Paduan circle, above all his nephew Rolando da Piazzola and Geremia da Montagnone, compiler of one of the most successful of medieval *florilegia*, the *Compendium moralium notabilium* ('Anthology of Noteworthy Examples of Virtuous Behaviour'), or *Epitoma sapientie* ('Epitome of Wisdom') in the 1505 edition, containing a vast range of carefully identified excerpts from classical and medieval authors.[6]

The most significant of Lovato's pupils, and the key figure in this scholarly revival, was the lawyer, politician and patriot Albertino Mussato, who came to be known, as diplomat and man of letters, far beyond the bounds of his native city. He too was widely read, and his reading bore fruit in his Latin verse, much of it in a polemical vein; he wrote a defence of poetry and a history, *De gestis Henrici VII Cesaris* ('The Deeds of Emperor Henry VII'), modelled on Livy. Above all, he was noted for his verse tragedy *Ecerinis*. It was not just that this was the first play to have been composed in classical metre since antiquity, in imitation of Seneca; it was also a work with a powerful political message, telling of the fall of the tyrant of Padua Ezzelino da Romano and warning against the dangers of domination by the ruler of Verona, Cangrande della Scala. In recognition of this work of poetry and patriotism, Mussato was crowned with laurels in 1315 by his grateful compatriots. For the Florentine humanist and chancellor Coluccio Salutati, writing eighty years later, this coronation was no doubt one of the reasons why he placed Mussato among the forebears of Petrarch in his survey of the restorers of learning.[7]

Recent research has rescued from oblivion a number of other minor figures in and around Padua in the late thirteenth and early fourteenth centuries. They were generally lawyers by training, and their enthusiasm for classical culture was shown by their interest in links with antiquity (such as an epigram by Benvenuto dei Campesani of Vicenza celebrating the return to Verona of her long-lost son Catullus) and by their emulation of classical letter-writing or historiography. Verona itself, no doubt in part because of its remarkable Chapter Library, can be seen as another cradle of humanistic activity. Giovanni Mansionario, for example, drew upon manuscripts that he found there to compile, between 1306 and 1320, a *Historia imperialis*, which shows a distinct ability to compare and evaluate historical sources critically. He also devoted a study to showing that the Pliny who was well known in the Middle Ages as the author of the *Natural History* was not the same as the Pliny who wrote a collection of letters, but that there had been two men of that name in antiquity. Also at Verona, Cangrande's chancellor Benzo d'Alessandria composed a vast historical encyclopedia, the *Cronica* (1313–20), based on a very wide range of classical texts, many of which he had himself unearthed during his travels. The search for texts, like the critical acumen shown by Mansionario, are clear signs of the progress that scholarship was making.

Such progress appears, in Padua, Vicenza and Verona at least, to amount almost to the development of a common literary and aesthetic ideal: the rediscovery of classical texts and through them the assertion of links, sometimes mythical, with Roman civilization; and the restoration of classical genres and styles of writing. Elsewhere in Italy, the evidence for some kind of classical revival is much more tenuous, seeming often to depend on isolated individuals. One such was Giovanni del Virgilio, appointed to teach Latin poetry at the University of Bologna in 1321, who appears to have limited himself to Virgil and Ovid, but whose Latin poems addressed to Mussato and Dante included one of the earliest eclogues in Virgilian mode. There were in addition in Florence a number of scholars active in the revival and imitation of classical literature, including Francesco da Barberino and Geri d'Arezzo, who is placed on a par with Mussato by Coluccio Salutati;[8] but there was at this period no sign of a concerted interest in the culture of antiquity.

There are two other centres of learning in the fourteenth century, however, which deserve particular mention in the context of the present discussion. The first is the Angevin court of Naples, one of the earliest places in Italy to witness a revival of Greek, to which we shall return in the final part of this chapter. The other, closely in contact with the Angevin court, most especially during the reign of King Robert I (1309–1343), is the papal curia at Avignon. For the first three-quarters of the fourteenth century, the so-called 'Babylonian captivity' of the popes there – the result of pressure exerted by the powerful kings of France – meant that it became the diplomatic and cultural centre of the western world. The papal library gradually acquired an important collection of classical texts; the curia, as a focal point of patronage, attracted scholars and men of letters from all over Europe, providing employment for cultivated lawyers and *dictatores*. Perhaps the single most illustrious intellectual figure to emerge from the Avignonese milieu was Petrarch (Francesco Petrarca), often considered to be the father of humanism and certainly the outstanding scholar and creative writer of his generation.[9] It is in his activities and in his writings that we perceive the fulfilment of all the various scholarly tendencies that we have so far observed; yet it is also clear that without the preparation of the terrain that we have witnessed his achievements would not have been possible.

His father, a Florentine notary, was exiled from his native city a few months after Dante in 1302 – both men were conservatives who fell victim to a shift of power in favour of the radicals – and sought employment at the papal curia. Not surprisingly, he wanted his son to have a legal education, sending him to Bologna for six years when he was sixteen. But by Petrarch's own account his father's intentions were foiled, for from an early age he developed a passion for the classical authors, reading everything that he could lay his hands on, and in particular the works of Cicero and Virgil. From the former he was to learn that mastery of rhetoric and style which was to raise him above the level of the *dictatores*, and from the latter a love of poetry that was to shape his whole literary life. In his early legal and rhetorical training we see the reflection of the Paduan notaries of Lovato's day; like them too, Petrarch was to remain in the secular world and to serve political patrons as politician and diplomat.

He spent the first half of his life in or around Avignon, principally in Vaucluse a few miles away. He thus had access not only to patronage and to the cultural and intellectual milieu of the curia, but also to books: those in the papal library and those brought to Avignon by others. However much he came to resent the business of the curia and the iniquities of the papal city as time went by, it was in a sense an ideal centre in which to conduct his first philological enterprises and from which to travel in search of others.

It was doubtless at Avignon that he supervised the preparation of a Virgil manuscript for his father around 1325, and certainly there that, a dozen years later, he had a frontispiece added to it by the Sienese artist Simone Martini. It was also at Avignon, aided by manuscripts found there or brought there, that he was able to piece together and restore the text of Livy's *History of Rome*, combining an incomplete thirteenth-century copy of the third decade with a copy of the first, much of which he transcribed in his own hand, and finally a copy of the fourth decade brought to Avignon from Chartres by Landolfo Colonna. By about 1330 he had succeeded in assembling the most complete text of Livy then known and was able to recognize what the shape of the original must have been. But in addition he was able considerably to improve the text, collating that of each of the decades with other manuscripts. His notes and corrections to the third decade are particularly valuable, since they record the variants of a manuscript which was probably also provided by Landolfo Colonna, but is now lost, and which descended from a quite different branch of the tradition. Although there is no real evidence of critical reflection on Petrarch's part as to the relative merits of the various sources that he was comparing, there can be no doubt as to either his philological zeal and acumen or his enthusiasm for classical literature.[10]

This enthusiasm is reflected in his search for new texts, first manifested in a journey to the north in 1333, when he found a manuscript of Cicero's forgotten *Pro Archia* in Liège, and one of Propertius in Paris, stemming from the thirteenth-century scholar Richard of Fournival. Both these texts he studied assiduously and transmitted to posterity with his annotations and emendations, as he did also with *De chorographia* of Pomponius Mela (mentioned above); one clear benefit of Petrarch's humanism is his particular contribution to the tradition of classical texts which he had himself inherited from earlier generations of scholars. Much subsequent scholarship would have been impossible without his intervention, and it is indeed probable that we owe the very survival of certain texts to his discoveries and his labours.

He was of course not alone in his enthusiasm, and the history of the restoration of Livy probably owes as large a debt to Landolfo Colonna as it does to Petrarch; yet the active search for manuscripts of classical texts clearly points to the development of what was to become a major humanist activity of subsequent generations of scholars, starting with Petrarch's friend and disciple Giovanni Boccaccio. Its most immediate consequence was that Petrarch's personal library grew rapidly. We know from a list that he made of his favourite books in the late 1330s that by then it already contained a high proportion of classical texts (including fourteen by Cicero); by the time of his death it had become the largest collection of Roman literature in private hands and included a number of works which Petrarch had himself discovered.[11]

Although this precious library was dispersed, many books from it have survived – perhaps most significantly the Virgil mentioned above, now in the Ambrosian Library in Milan, and Petrarch's copy of Livy, in the Harleian collection of the British Library.[12] It is in the margins of such manuscripts as these that we see Petrarch's dialogue with ancient authors at close quarters: his annotations to Virgil's poems and to Servius' commentary upon them reveal a close eye for points of prosody and history, and a dense network of cross-references to the writings of other classical authors. As a result of his remarkably wide knowledge of them, he was frequently able to correct Servius' interpretations and even (in a later letter) to prove that Virgil's account of the love of Dido and Aeneas was historically incorrect, since she lived some 300 years after Aeneas' death.[13] Petrarch's notes and emendations to Livy's text bear witness to his concern to get not only the words but also the facts right. His close familiarity with every detail of it furnished him with a remarkable knowledge of Roman history, which he deployed to correct other writings, such as St Jerome's translation of the chronicle of Eusebius. To such sources he added his personal observations upon the monuments of Rome, visited in 1337, and even the study of coins. The quality of his historical scholarship was such as to enable him to identify certain buildings (such as the Septizonium, the ruins of which were part of the monastery of San Gregorio al Celio) and to point out that the comic poet Terence (Terentius Afer) had traditionally been confused with a different Terence (Terentius Culleo). His brief biography of Terence became attached to the majority of later humanist manuscripts of the comedies. He was even called in to act as expert consultant to the Emperor Charles IV in 1361 and was able to demonstrate, by reference to historical, stylistic and linguistic features, that a document claimed by Rudolf IV Habsburg to be a privilege granted by Julius Caesar and Nero, justifying his claim that Austria was an independent sovereign state within the Empire, was a forgery.[14] Scholarship was thus put to the service of the state.

On the other hand, Petrarch did not get everything right. He failed to observe many details of the monuments he visited in Rome, ascribing, for instance, the Ponte Sant'Angelo to Trajan, despite the name of Hadrian clearly inscribed upon it; he, like Lovato, believed that the tomb of a freedman named T. Livius discovered in Padua in the early fourteenth century was that of the great Livy himself. In this instance we may perceive an element of political naïvety on Petrarch's part: the wish to re-establish the continuity with ancient Rome proved stronger than the critical sense which might have revealed the error. To this same naïvety may be attributed his unquestioning admiration and support for Cola di Rienzo, a Roman notary with pronounced antiquarian tastes who attempted to restore the ancient republic. Cola was involved in a series of popular uprisings in Rome in the 1340s, which culminated in his nomination first as rector and then as tribune of the city, and finally his knighthood in a ceremony which included ritual bathing in the font of Constantine and, on 15 July 1347, his solemn coronation as 'Tribunus Augustus' on the Capitoline Hill. Petrarch was apparently dazzled by Cola's passion for, and exploitation of, all that he himself held dear: the Roman ideal as refracted through inscriptions, monuments, coins and Livy's history.[15] No matter that the ideal was flawed, or indeed that Cola's revolution burned out almost as quickly as it had flared up, causing severe embarrassment to the pope and indeed to Petrarch himself. The restoration of the ancient world in its capital city, then sadly neglected in the absence of the papacy, was a goal to which he was even prepared to sacrifice the most prestigious of his own literary projects, the writing of an epic poem, *Africa*, celebrating the Roman virtues of Scipio Africanus.

It was probably this project which earned Petrarch his laurels in a ceremony, which – if we are to believe all that he tells us about it – also had strong connotations of classical revival: after a searching oral examination by King Robert in Naples, he was crowned with laurels on the Capitoline by a Roman senator on Easter Sunday 1341 and made a speech, based on a Virgilian text, in which he dwelt at length upon the importance of the poetic art.[16] Both in the ceremony and the defence of poetry, there was very likely some conscious echoing of Mussato's example; Petrarch was also aware that in ancient times both emperors and poets had been honoured by coronation. At all events, the renewal of an interest in poetry, and indeed in writing Latin verse in good classical style, is a typical humanist concern. In the case both of his *Africa*, conceived in imitation of the *Aeneid*, and of his *Bucolicum carmen* ('Eclogues'), strongly influenced by Virgil's *Eclogues*, not only the fact of writing such classicizing works, but also the intimate details of the way in which he sought to imitate his models without copying them too closely, are characteristic of the peculiarly Petrarchan blend of the intensive scholarly study of antiquity and the rewriting of that antiquity in new and substantially original form.

Petrarch is best known today for his vernacular poetry and above all for the great cycle of sonnets, the *Canzoniere*, in which he celebrates his love for a fictitious lady named Laura.[17] Even there, the influence of the Roman poets is evident. But it is obviously his Latin works that most clearly establish his reputation as a humanist. The precise historical foundations for the epic poem already mentioned were laid in his *De viris illustribus* ('On Famous Men'), which drew in particular on Livy and Suetonius, and contained the lives of important Roman figures, especially those, which he frequently reworked and expanded as his own knowledge grew, of Scipio Africanus and Julius Caesar. *Rerum memorandarum libri* ('Memorable Matters'), on the other hand, in response to the *Factorum et dictorum memorabilium libri IX* of Valerius Maximus, provided numerous examples of the Christian virtues drawn from Roman history.

Petrarch's letters deserve special attention. He must have been collecting them, as he wrote them, from early adulthood onwards; but in 1345 he was inspired, by finding a manuscript of Cicero's *Ad Atticum*, his letters to his friend Atticus, in the Chapter Library of Verona, to begin to shape them into a collection, the *Rerum familiarium libri* ('Letters between Friends'), which he continued to reorder and to refine until the late 1350s. What he then published (although he continued to revise it until 1366) was in effect the first humanist *epistolario* (letter collection), owing its form and its conception to Cicero – and a great deal of its contents to Petrarch's admiration for the Roman statesman – and to his careful cultivation of the image of himself that his letters projected. Certain of them, and in particular ones addressed to Boccaccio, deal specifically with the topic of *imitatio* which was to become crucial to the next generation of humanists. Petrarch describes the impact of classical literature on him and his profound acquaintance with it. He sets out his views on the legitimacy of drawing material from the great writers of the past, but at the same time on the need to do so in a way which is neither servile nor too visible: the writer may follow in another man's tracks, but not exactly in his footsteps. The resemblance to be achieved is not that of portrait to sitter, but of a son to his father: *similitudo non identitas*. The image is borrowed from Seneca; it is symptomatic of Petrarch that even in theoretical discussion he never moves far from the practice. Indeed, he goes so far as to discuss precise practical examples of passages in his *Bucolicum carmen* where he had detected verses that echoed too closely for his taste their Virgilian, Ovidian or Horatian models, and which he changed to good effect.[18] Some of these statements have a self-satisfied ring and are not so much the matter of everyday letter-writing as the substance of polemical and even didactic treatises addressed to those whose interests were closest to his own. Of all Petrarch's genera-tion, Boccaccio was probably the man who most closely shared his passion for seeking out manuscripts of rare classical works and writing in imitation of them. He too wrote a work of partly classical history, as well as an immensely influential handbook on the pagan gods; he was also Petrarch's accomplice, as we shall shortly see, in the first significant attempts to revive the study of Greek.

The concern which we have observed with both the form and the content of the writings of antiquity is reflected in the most idiosyncratic and somehow medieval way in the major treatise of Petrarch's maturity, *De remediis utriusque fortune* ('On the Remedies for Both Kinds of Fortune') of 1366. This moral encyclopedia, providing remedies for the undesirable effects of good fortune and consolation for the blows of ill fortune, is modelled upon Cicero's *Tusculan Disputations* and takes the form of a series of dialogues between a Stoically-minded Reason and the four emotions (condemned by the Stoics): Joy and Hope, Sorrow and Fear. It contains an enormous amount of explicitly classical material: more than 500 examples drawn from antiquity and a great deal of implicit quotation of Roman writers. It might be seen as the peak of Petrarch's literary achievement, and yet it is a work without synthesis. There is no systematic moral-philosophical thread running through it other than a conventional

Christian scorn for worldly goods, and consolation for adversity in the tradition of Boethius. The classical material therefore loses its sting; the Stoic echoes of Cicero and Seneca disappear in a mass of material reinforcing more orthodox views. What Petrarch does not achieve here, in what was to be internationally his most popular work for at least two centuries, is any kind of philosophical renewal which might lead us to regard him as the founder of the deeper vein of humanism that goes beyond the mere reading and using of texts.[19]

The only work in which he explicitly addresses a philosophical topic is his polemical *De sui ipsius et multorum ignorantia* ('On His Own Ignorance and That of Many Others'). Written in 1367, it was a rejoinder to four Aristotelians who had said that Petrarch was a good but uneducated man. He first berates the learned ignorance of his accusers, and thereby the doctrines of scholastic philosophy, which may teach you the truth, but cannot induce you to love it. He then defends the cause of the kind of learning, the *studia humanitatis*, to which he had devoted his life, claiming that the study of literature, and in particular classical literature, makes a man good. He thus reunites the causes of rhetoric and moral philosophy. His most powerful example is of course Cicero, whom he portrays as a proto-Christian. With *De ignorantia* we come full circle: to the writer who first inspired him and who provided him throughout his career not merely with texts to study but with a literary and ethical model for his own life and works.[20]

We may in the end judge that Petrarch was not entirely an innovator, but that he depended upon the efforts of earlier generations to prepare the ground for the kind of scholarship at which he excelled, and that he was therefore part of a continuing tradition. We should none the less recognize the immense impetus that he gave to that tradition by the extraordinary breadth of his learning, by his real sense of the historical distance that divided his age from that of Rome, by the much improved Latin and the influential writings that he bequeathed to posterity and by the new prestige that he attached to his role as scholar. That imitation of the classics which he both preached and practised, and which was embodied in his coronation with laurels *all'antica* in 1341, was responsible for giving Renaissance humanism its first real impulse – and its good name.

There is one essential component of the growth of humanism which has so far escaped our attention, and that is the revival of the study of Greek. A significant portion of Greek scientific writings, and in particular much of the work of Aristotle, had been translated into Arabic and had found its way to the Latin west via north Africa and Spain, where many translations into

Latin were made between the eleventh and thirteenth centuries. But the Greek language itself was virtually unknown in Italy (and indeed in the rest of Europe) in the early fourteenth century, even though it continued to be spoken, in a vernacular form, in Sicily and the southernmost parts of the peninsula, and despite regular trade contacts between Venice and Byzantium. There was consequently no tradition, such as the one that we have witnessed for Latin literature, of continuous study.[21]

There are fragmentary pieces of evidence suggesting that in Padua towards the middle of the century certain teachers and lawyers possessed Greek manuscripts and even understood them; there are likewise signs that during the reign of King Robert I, the Angevin court of Naples was a centre for the translation into Latin of Greek texts contained in manuscripts in the royal library amassed by Charles I of Anjou (who conquered the Kingdom of Sicily in 1268) and his successors. At one point Robert had no fewer than three translators working for him, including a Calabrian, Niccolò da Reggio, to whom we owe versions of various of Galen's medical writings. It was, however, another native of Calabria, a Basilian monk by the name of Barlaam, who had spent some time in Constantinople but had transferred his allegiance to the Latin Church and moved to King Robert's court, who was the first man to make any significant impact on the humanists whom we have so far discussed.

It appears that he was sent on a diplomatic mission to the papal curia at Avignon by King Robert in 1342 and spent some time teaching Greek there that summer. Petrarch, with characteristic enthusiasm for all things classical, took private lessons with him for some months until Barlaam departed to take up a bishopric in Calabria for which his new pupil had recommended him. This brief episode cannot be said to have made an enormous impression on Petrarch, since when early in 1354 he received a manuscript of Homer as a gift from Nicholas Sygeros, a Byzantine envoy to Avignon (whom he had met in Verona in 1348), he found that he could not read it. This did not prevent him from asking Sygeros to send him works of Hesiod and Euripides, nor did it inhibit his search for other copies of Homer. We know that he inspected, but rejected, one in Padua towards the end of 1358, and that at much the same time he made the acquaintance there of another Calabrian and pupil of Barlaam, an apparently most unpleasant man by the name of Leonzio Pilato.[22]

The following March Boccaccio paid a visit to Petrarch in Milan, during which they discussed Petrarch's *Bucolicum carmen* and some of the questions of *imitatio* which were to give rise to the letter mentioned earlier. They also spoke of Pilato, and as a result Boccaccio persuaded him, when he stopped at Florence on a mission to Avignon, to stay there and teach Greek with a stipend from the Florentine authorities. The year 1360 thus marks the first known official teaching of Greek in an Italian city. Although it is not clear how long Pilato stayed in Florence, his time there left tangible traces in the form of translations of some of Homer and about 400 lines of Euripides' *Hecuba*, commissioned by Boccaccio, and of some of Plutarch's *Lives*, done at the request of Coluccio Salutati.

Pilato's subsequent activity is ill-documented, but he certainly stayed with Petrarch in Venice for about three months in 1363, and they were joined by Boccaccio for part of the time. That summer, he decided to return to Constantinople, inveighing against Italy and the Italians; it was not long, however, before he was inveighing against Constantinople and its inhabitants and planning to return to Italy. He died in a shipwreck on his way back in 1365. That spring, Petrarch had made enquiries of Boccaccio about a particular passage in the Homer translation; towards the end of the following year he finally received his copy of the complete *Odyssey* and *Iliad* in Latin and had fair copies of them made by his amanuensis Giovanni Malpaghini two years later.

These contacts, deriving from the Angevin court, were at best hesitant beginnings in the history of the recovery of Greek. Pilato's translations were literal to a fault and taxed Salutati severely when he tried to put parts of Homer into better Latin. So did another text that he tried to improve a few years later: a plodding half-Greek version of Plutarch's treatise on anger made in Avignon by the archbishop of Thebes, Simon Atumano, in 1373.[2] It was in fact only later, and direct from Byzantium, that the first real scholars came, initially as envoys in the context of increasing diplomatic activity between Constantinople and the west in the face of the growing threat of Turkish domination over the Greek empire. Thirty-seven years after Pilato's false start, a Byzantine diplomat called Manuel Chrysoloras came to Florence on business and instituted there a regular series of lectures on Greek which were to last for several years.

It was a feature of his teaching that the old style of word-by-word rendition which had so bedevilled the literary translations of Pilato and Atumano (and which may have owed something to a desire for accuracy thought appropriate to scientific texts) was to be abandoned in favour of versions which had literary merit in Latin. In pursuit of the better understanding of Greek, Chrysoloras also composed a grammar book, the *Erotemata* ('Questions'), which was to be the first of its kind to be printed in the late fifteenth century and which clearly enjoyed a considerable success not only among Chrysoloras's pupils, but also among such later leading humanists as Erasmus.

It is thus 1397 which has to be seen as a key date in the history of humanism and even of European culture. Chrysoloras numbered among his pupils some of the most outstanding scholars of the new generation, notably Leonardo Bruni and Guarino of Verona. With them, and the advent of the fifteenth century, Greek regained its status as part of the *studia humanitatis*, and humanism may be said to have entered a new phase.

NOTES

1 Two rather different approaches to the historiographical problems surrounding the terms 'humanism' and 'Renaissance' are to be found in W. K. Ferguson, *The Renaissance in Historical Thought: Five Centuries of Interpretation* (Cambridge MA, 1948) and P. Burke, *The Renaissance* (London, 1964); see also Burke's chapter, 'The spread of Italian humanism', in A. Goodman and A. Mackay, eds., *The Impact of Humanism on Western Europe* (London, 1990), pp. 1–22; C. Trinkaus, *The Scope of Renaissance Humanism* (Ann Arbor MI, 1983); and M. McLaughlin, 'Humanist concepts of Renaissance and Middle Ages', *Renaissance Studies*, 2 (1988), 131–42. On the terms 'humanism' and 'humanist', see P. O. Kristeller, 'Humanism', in C. B. Schmitt, Q. Skinner and E. Kessler, eds., *The Cambridge History of Renaissance Philosophy* (Cambridge, 1988), pp. 113–37.

2 There is an excellent brief account of the scholarship of the Carolingian period in L. D. Reynolds and N. G. Wilson, *Scribes and Scholars: A Guide to the Transmission of Greek and Latin Literature*, third edition (Oxford, 1991), ch. 3; see also Trinkaus, *Scope*, pp. 4–6.

3 On the twelfth-century Renaissance, see C. H. Haskins, *The Renaissance of the Twelfth Century* (Cambridge MA, 1927); M. de Gandillac and E. Jeauneau, eds., *Entretiens sur la renaissance du 12ᵉ siècle* (Paris, 1968); C. Brooke, *The Twelfth Century Renaissance* (London, 1969); R. L. Benson and G. Constable, eds., *Renaissance and Renewal in the Twelfth Century* (Oxford, 1982), esp. pp. 1–33. On the Old French *romans d'antiquité*, see A. Fourrier, *L'Humanisme médiéval dans les littératures romanes du XIIᵉ au XIVᵉ siècle* (Paris, 1964).

4 See Gandillac, *Entretiens*, pp. 53–83; Brooke, *Twelfth Century Renaissance*, pp. 53–74.

5 On the role of *dictatores* and lawyers in this context, see R. Weiss, *The Dawn of Humanism in Italy* (London, 1947), pp. 3–5; P. O. Kristeller, *Eight Philosophers of the Renaissance* (Stanford, 1964), pp. 147–65; Kristeller, 'Humanism', pp. 127–30; Trinkaus, *Scope*, pp. 9–11; R. G. Witt, 'Medieval Italian culture and the origins of humanism as a stylistic ideal', in A. Rabil, ed., *Renaissance Humanism: Foundations, Forms, and Legacy*, 3 vols. (Philadelphia, 1988), I, pp. 29–70; J. E. Seigel, *Rhetoric and Philosophy in Renaissance Humanism* (Princeton, 1968), ch. 6.

6 On the Paduan and other early humanists, see, in addition to the works mentioned in the previous note, R. Weiss, *Il primo secolo dell'umanesimo* (Rome, 1949), esp. ch. 1, and his *The Renaissance Discovery of Classical Antiquity*, second edition (Oxford, 1988), pp. 16–29; N. G. Siraisi, *Arts and Sciences at Padua: The Studium of Padua before 1350* (Toronto, 1973),

pp. 42–55; the chapters by G. Billanovich, R. Avesani and L. Gargan in *Storia della cultura veneta*, 6 vols. (Vicenza, 1976–86), II, pp. 19–170.

7   In a letter of 1 August 1395 to Bartolomeo Oliari; see Coluccio Salutati *Epistolario*, ed. F. Novati, 4 vols. (Rome, 1891–1911), III, p. 84: 'the firs cultivator of eloquence was your compatriot Mussato of Padua'. On Mussato see M. T. Dazzi, *Il Mussato preumanista 1261–1329: l'ambiente e l'oper* (Vicenza, 1964).

8   In the letter quoted in the previous note, immediately after the mention o Mussato, Salutati, *Epistolario*, III, p. 84, says: 'there was also Geri d'Arezzo, th greatest imitator of the orator Pliny the Younger'.

9   The standard short biography of Petrarch is E. H. Wilkins, *Life of Petrarch* (Chicago, 1961); see also M. Bishop, *Petrarch and His World* (Bloomington 1963); for an introductory study which pays some attention to his humanism and has a bibliography of texts and studies, see N. Mann, *Petrarch* (Oxford 1984). See also Trinkaus, *Scope*, pp. 6–7, 11–15.

10 See the account of Petrarch's philological work in Reynolds and Wilson, *Scribe. and Scholars*, pp. 128–34.

11 On Petrarch's favourite books at Vaucluse, see P. de Nolhac, *Pétrarque e l'humanisme*, second edition, 2 vols. (Paris, 1907), II, pp. 293–6; on th subsequent history of his library, see M. Pastore Stocchi, 'La biblioteca de Petrarca', in *Storia della cultura veneta*, II, pp. 536–65.

12 Both manuscripts are available in facsimile: MS Milan, Biblioteca Ambrosiana S.P. 10.27, in Petrarch, *Vergilianus codex*, ed. G. Galbiati (Milan, 1930); M London, British Library, Harley 2493, in Giuseppe Billanovich, *La tradizion del testo di Livio e le origini dell'umanesimo*, 2 vols. (Padua, 1981), II: *Il Livi del Petrarca e del Valla*.

13 Petrarch, *Seniles* IV.5, in his *Opera* (Basel, 1554), p. 872; English translation i Petrarch, *Letters of Old Age. Rerum senilium libri I–XVIII*, trans. A. S Bernardo, S. Levin and R. A. Bernardo, 2 vols. (Baltimore, 1992), I pp. 139–51, at 147.

14 Petrarch, *Seniles* XVI.5, in his *Opera*, pp. 1,055–8; translated in Petrarch *Letters of Old Age*, II, pp. 621–5.

15 On Petrarch's knowledge of Rome, and his relations with Cola di Rienzo, se Weiss, *Renaissance Discovery*, pp. 32–42.

16 See E. H. Wilkins, *The Making of the Canzoniere and Other Petrarchan Studie* (Rome, 1951), pp. 9–69; the speech that he made on that occasion is translate by Wilkins in his *Studies in the Life and Works of Petrarch* (Cambridge MA 1955), pp. 300–13.

17 For a good parallel text edition of the *Canzoniere*, see Petrarch, *Lyric Poems* ed. and trans. R. M. Durling (Cambridge MA, 1976).

18 See Petrarch, *Le familiari*, ed. V. Rossi, 4 vols. (Florence, 1933–42); and i English translation: Petrarch, *Letters on Familiar Matters. Rerum familiarium libri*, trans. A. S. Bernardo, 3 vols. (Albany NY, 1975; Baltimore, 1982–5). Th letters particularly concerning the question of imitation are *Familiares* I.8 XXII.2; and XXIII.19.

19 *De remediis utriusque fortune* was Petrarch's most popular work and i preserved in hundreds of manuscripts. It was first printed in 1474 and may b consulted in Petrarch, *Opera*, or in English translation: Petrarch, *Remedies fo*

Fortune Fair and Foul. A Modern English Translation of De remediis utriusque fortune, trans. C. H. Rawski, 5 vols. (Bloomington, 1991). For a brief account of Stoic attitudes expressed in it, see N. Mann, 'Petrarch's role as moralist in fifteenth-century France', in A. H. T. Levi, ed., *Humanism in France at the End of the Middle Ages and in the Early Renaissance* (Manchester, 1970), pp. 6–15.

20 Petrarch, *De ignorantia*, in his *Opere latine*, ed. A. Buffano, 2 vols. (Turin, 1975), II, pp. 1,025–151; English translation in E. Cassirer, P. O. Kristeller and J. H. Randall, Jr., trans., *The Renaissance Philosophy of Man* (Chicago, 1948), pp. 49–133.

21 On the revival of Greek, see Weiss, *The Dawn*, pp. 19–20; Kristeller, 'The medieval antecedents', pp. 157–9, and his 'Renaissance humanism and classical antiquity', in Rabil, *Renaissance Humanism*, I, pp. 5–16, at 10–14; Reynolds and Wilson, *Scribes and Scholars*, pp. 146–9; G. Di Stefano, *La Découverte de Plutarque en occident* (Turin, 1968), especially ch. 1.

22 On relations between Petrarch, Barlaam and Pilato, see Wilkins, *Life of Petrarch*, pp. 33–4, 162–4, 169, 190–2, 200; and N. G. Wilson, *From Byzantium to Italy: Greek Studies in the Italian Renaissance* (London, 1992), pp. 2–7.

23 On this translation, see Di Stefano, *Découverte*, chs. 2–3.

2

Classical scholarship

MICHAEL D. REEVE

In 62 BC Cicero defended in court a Greek poet, Archias, whose citizenship had been challenged. The version of his speech that he later circulated expatiates on the service that poets render to the state by conferring immortality on heroes and thereby encouraging public spirit. Even historians, he says (*Pro Archia* 24), achieve less: Alexander the Great took many on his campaign, and yet, when he came to the tomb of Achilles near Troy, he exclaimed: 'lucky young man, to have had your prowess advertised by Homer!' – and he was right, because without the *Iliad* the tomb would have closed not only over his body but over his name.

William of Malmesbury, who died about 1143, tells the same story about Alexander.[1] Had he read it in Cicero's speech for Archias? Though the Latin literature of republican and imperial Rome spans over 600 years (from about 200 BC to the early fifth century), not a single autograph survives; and the poems of Virgil, the plays of Terence and Livy's account of the war against Hannibal are unusual in being preserved by manuscripts even as old as the fourth or fifth century, written for collectors not obviously affected by the conversion of the empire to Christianity. After that, the historical record dwindles until the end of the eighth century, when Charlemagne created a successor to the Roman empire in the west and ruled it from the lower Rhine. In ways hard to trace, monastic and royal libraries then began to acquire old manuscripts, not least of pagan texts, and to make copies, usually in a new script that modern printers have inherited with little change. For most classical Latin texts, therefore, surviving copies begin in the ninth century or later, and up to the end of the thirteenth most of them come from northern Europe. By the twelfth century some texts, among them speeches of Cicero's, could be found in many libraries. Of the speech for Archias, however, only two manuscripts older than the fourteenth century survive, one written about 1030 at the abbey of Gembloux in Belgium, the other about 1150 for the abbey of Corvey in north-west Germany.[2] William of Malmesbury never visited the

Continent. In fact, his wording shows that he read the story about Alexander at second hand in St Jerome, who opens his life of Hilarion with it.[3]

Not far into his twenties, Petrarch left Italy and attached himself to the papal court at Avignon. From there in 1333 he visited Paris and Liège, and at Liège he discovered the speech for Archias, which he copied out in his own hand. Eighteen years later, when a Florentine friend offered him more speeches of Cicero's, he thanked him with a copy of *Pro Archia*, which he describes in his covering letter (*Variae* 45) as 'a speech full of wonderful compliments to poets'. There speaks the first poet since Statius to be crowned on the Capitol, who in the address that he composed for the occasion in 1341 quoted Cicero's view that poets are born by divine favour, not made (*Pro Archia* 18).[4] The manuscript at Liège is lost, and so is Petrarch's copy, but Petrarch's copy can be shown to lie behind all but one of the later manuscripts. Some preserve in their margins notes that he entered in that copy.[5] When Cicero uses the phrase *litterarum lumen*, 'the light of literature' (§ 14), Petrarch writes *lumen litterarum* alongside and draws a sketch of a lamp or candle. When Cicero says that many cities claimed Homer as a citizen (§ 19), Petrarch adds that Homer was also reputed to have been an Egyptian because he came from Thebes, a famous city in Egypt; and he gives as his authority the second book of Chalcidius' commentary on Plato's *Timaeus* (his own copy survives). When Cicero says that Greek poets can achieve greater glory than Latin because Greek is read almost everywhere but Latin just in its own narrow domain (§ 23), Petrarch writes 'not what he usually says about Greek'. When Cicero says that even philosophers who write books about indifference to glory put their name in the title (§ 26), Petrarch quotes a passage from the *Tusculan Disputations* where he says the same (I.34). When Cicero says that virtue wants no reward for its efforts but glory, without which in this short life we have no reason to exert ourselves (§ 28), Petrarch writes alongside 'be careful, though'. At several points he marks a word in the text and writes an alternative in the margin, and two of these alternatives, *togati* for *locati* in § 27 and *quantum* for *quanto* in § 31, appear in all modern editions; they are almost certainly conjectures that he made himself.

Historians debate the meaning and origin of the term 'humanism'. A recent investigator has concentrated on the phrase *studia humanitatis*, 'cultural pursuits', which he finds attested in two passages of Cicero's speeches, *Pro Murena* 61 and *Pro Caelio* 24, and then in many Italian writers from Coluccio Salutati in 1369 to the middle of the fifteenth century.[6] In Italy, however, no one read *Pro Murena* at all, or *Pro Caelio* in a form that included the word *studio* in § 24, until Poggio Bracciolini in

1415 sent to Florence an old manuscript from Cluny. Surprisingly, a passage from the exordium of *Pro Archia* has been overlooked (§ 3):

> ... in this case I beg you to grant me a concession that suits the defendant and puts you, I hope, to no inconvenience: as I am representing a poet of supreme distinction and a man of great learning, in a court where such devotees of literature are gathered, where the jury possesses such humanity, and where this of all magistrates is presiding, allow me some latitude to speak about cultural and literary pursuits [*de studiis humanitatis ac litterarum*] ...

Petrarch marked the passage. Salutati had the speech by 1370, when he sent a correspondent a copy in his own hand, and no speech provided him with more quotations in his letters; a reworking of a passage from it (§ 16) brings to a stirring conclusion his most often cited recommendation of *litterarum studia* and *humanitatis studia*.[7] If it is true that Italian humanists had no expression closer to 'classical scholarship' than *studia humanitatis*, then *Pro Archia* provided classical scholarship in the Renaissance with its charter of foundation.

Labels and slogans, however, simplify and mislead. In Petrarch's attention to *Pro Archia* eight elements can be distinguished:

1. he discovered the speech
2. he liked it because it extolled poetry
3. he used it in works of his own
4. he marked details in it, sometimes because related things had struck him elsewhere in his reading of ancient literature
5. he adjusted its text
6. he spoke of his discovery in correspondence that he put into wider circulation
7. he put the speech itself into wider circulation
8. such was his prestige both as a writer and as a collector that after his death *Pro Archia* became one of many texts in his library that were sought out for copying.

Confronted with a biographical medley like this in a period remote from the one that they study, classical scholars of today aim by the shortest route for the manuscript that Petrarch discovered. Impatience with the other seven elements, however, breeds misjudgements. Some editors of Catullus have believed that after line 10 of *Poem* II in a 'very ancient manuscript' Alessandro Guarino had seen a 'huge fragment' otherwise unknown, but by *fragmentum* he meant 'gap'. Recent editors of Cicero's speech *Pro Plancio* unwittingly include in § 88 a phrase jotted down by Petrarch to clarify an elliptical transition.[8] Many editors have been deceived by manuscripts copied from printed editions or by manuscripts that incorporate so many layers of collation and conjecture that they seem to have drawn on valuable sources now lost. Sixteenth-century scholars have been accused of inventing manuscripts when by *codex* they meant a printed book. The only protection against such misjudgements is familiarity with the language and procedures of humanists. The other seven elements therefore deserve a closer look.

The most obvious result of the last two is that over 200 manuscripts of *Pro Archia* survive even today. From two that happened to be available in 1471 the speech went into print at Rome and Venice, and since then most readers have read it in print rather than in manuscript; but modern editors have worked their way back through the humanistic manuscripts to Petrarch's copy of 1333. This turning back of the clock has been accomplished by progressive refinement of methods already employed by Petrarch, methods seen at work in his annotation and adjustment of the text: collecting evidence is fundamental to scholarship, and the need to improve corrupt texts, though not limited to classical scholarship, arises more often when the texts have been copied by a long succession of people with different interests, different knowledge and different habits of script.[9]

No more than his use of the text, it may be objected, does his annotation always amount to classical scholarship. Modern scholars may have written monographs on the language of vituperation in ancient Rome, but when Jean Jouffroy marked the most colourful insults in his copy of Cicero's attack on Piso, he was intending to use them.[10] When Leonardo Bruni showed that Florence had been founded not by Caesar but already by Sulla, he was bent on giving the Florentine republic a republican rather than an autocratic origin (Lorenzo Valla retorted that Sulla was an utter villain and the first tyrant at Rome).[11] When Panormita (Antonio Beccadelli) listed classical poets who had defended licentious verse, and respectable figures who had composed it, he was responding to Poggio's reception of his *Hermaphroditus* (1425–6): even Virgil, Poggio said, had composed *Priapea* in his youth, but Panormita too should grow up.[12] When in 1440 Lorenzo Valla exposed the Donation of Constantine, which provided documentary support for the secular power of the papacy,[13] his employer Alfonso of Aragon was at war with Pope Eugenius IV over Naples. More generally, classical rules and models for composing speeches, letters, histories or poems helped people whose civic careers brought regular demands for such compositions; classical philosophers, poets and historians furnished moral precepts and examples in abundance, most of them entirely compatible with Christianity; and good writers inspired other good writers.

Three further things make classical scholarship in the Renaissance hard to isolate. One is that many of the people who took a critical interest in classical texts had no employment in a university or library and therefore no professional commitment to scholarship. Another is the incorporation of scholarly concerns in literary works. Panormita's *Elegy* to Giovanni Lamola, written in 1427, includes the form *retulit*, picked out in an autograph by three forms of highlighting. It rests on a corruption in Lucretius, *De rerum natura* VI.672, *retulerunt* for *tetulerunt*, as emerges from a copy of Lucretius that he later annotated: 'RETVLIT, with the first syllable short, which I followed in my *Elegy*.'[14] Most of Petrarch's works have such a texture; and as though every chapter in the *Miscellanea* (1489) of Angelo Poliziano (Politian) were not learned enough, the preface is a web of sophisticated allusion to novelties. The third difficulty is that Italian humanists never defined quite so narrow a field as classical scholarship. Petrarch's list of his favourite books, compiled no later than 1343, includes nothing medieval except an astronomical tract and two works of reference,[15] Salutati finds no stylistic merit in any writer between Cassiodorus and Dante,[16] and Valla holds that no one after Boethius wrote proper Latin;[17] but they none of them draw any distinction of principle between pagan and Christian writers, and Valla worked on the text of the New Testament. Cosimo de' Medici, who acquired books of Salutati's and collaborated closely with one of the main Florentine collectors, Niccolò Niccoli, appears to have had a partiality for Cicero and classical historians; but he took care to stock the new library at San Marco with works that complemented Niccoli's largely classical bequest.[18] General distaste for the Middle Ages also left room for disagreement about when they began. The most ambitious historical work of the fifteenth century, Flavio Biondo's *Decades* (1437–42), is a history of Italy to his own day from the capture of Rome by the barbarians in AD 410, which he saw as the beginning of its decline – a century before Boethius and Cassiodorus.[19] In his survey *Scriptores illustres Latinae linguae* ('Eminent Latin Writers', 1437) Sicco Polenton maintained that after Juvenal Latin poetry fell into slumber for a millennium.[20] Inevitably, the boundary depended on one's field of interest. The Florentine reformers of script at the beginning of the fifteenth century followed not ancient models but manuscripts written in Carolingian minuscule (lower-case letter forms), especially Italian manuscripts of the eleventh or early twelfth century.[21]

Modern students of the Renaissance have their own reasons for concentrating on all these differences and concluding that it is anachronistic to look for classical scholarship in what they take to be the modern sense. Even the published works of many humanists are bulky, and not everyone reads Latin with ease, let alone the blocks of unparagraphed, strangely punctuated and often misprinted Latin published in editions of the fifteenth or sixteenth century.[22] Moreover, classical scholarship may not be the main interest of those who do make the effort. Consequently, pronouncements about the aims of humanists tend to reflect at best the more sweeping of the pronouncements that they made themselves. In their turn, many of these have a certain artificiality, especially if they occur in prefaces or other places where tradition obliged writers to justify their activities.

In fact, the literary legacy of the Renaissance includes a vast amount of material that contributed to the reconstruction of classical antiquity whether it was designed to do so or not, and much of it can hardly have served any purpose beyond the advancement of knowledge. Its circulation, however, was patchy and to some extent governed by literary conventions. Material intended for circulation happens to include many pieces of external evidence like the reference to *Pro Archia* in Petrarch's correspondence; but even Petrarch, who covered his copies of ancient texts with variants taken from other copies and with conjectures of his own, has left in his voluminous works not a single discussion of any textual or interpretative problem. He put together and partly wrote, for instance, a manuscript of Livy, now MS Harley 2493 in the British Library, which later came into the hands of Valla.[23] His adjustments and other annotations far outnumber Valla's, but it was Valla in 1447 who issued a set of corrections to Books XXI–XXVI.[24] Valla had a polemical purpose. Incompetently in his opinion, Panormita and Bartolomeo Facio had corrected the manuscript of Books XXI–XXX that Cosimo de' Medici presented to King Alfonso of Naples. They may never have thought of issuing their corrections, and Valla, who knew them from the manuscript itself, could have impressed Alfonso by entering his own alongside; but he wanted a wider triumph. Open discussion of textual problems had ancient precedent, for instance, in Servius' commentary on Virgil, and one Colmán in a letter preserved in a ninth-century manuscript diagnoses unmetrical variants in copies of Sedulius's *Carmen Paschale*;[25] but the frequency of such discussions in the second half of the fifteenth century, after their absence through the Middle Ages despite constant emendation of texts, marks a big step towards what the modern world understands by classical scholarship.

What then of the remaining element, Petrarch's liking for *Pro Archia*? Without it, his discovery might have led nowhere. Some works of classical literature owe their survival to responses like it. Furthermore, responses different from ours may open our eyes.

After Petrarch's response, *Pro Archia* soon met with others that went further. Within thirty years of his death in 1374, Antonio Loschi, secretary to the duke of Milan, wrote a commentary on eleven speeches of Cicero's that had passed through his hands. In his introduction to *Pro Archia* he mentions the praise of poets in 'this relaxed and very fine speech' but goes on to ask why Archias' citizenship had been challenged if he had aroused no hostility or resentment or anything of the kind; 'the speech gives no answer, and I do not recall reading one elsewhere'. When he proceeds to analyse the speech with techniques learnt from Quintilian,[26] he remarks that the praise of poets is largely irrelevant.

Petrarch's discovery of *Pro Archia* is one of the earliest in a succession of discoveries that by the 1570s had transformed the canon of classical Latin literature.[27] Up to about 1520, most of them were either made or instigated by Italians, but many were made outside Italy. Just as Petrarch at Avignon profited from international contacts and opportunities for travel, so later scholars who attended ecclesiastical councils or took up diplomatic or secretarial posts abroad learnt how to exploit even distant libraries. In 1433 Giovanni Aurispa brought to the Council of Basel from Mainz a manuscript of twelve speeches addressed to emperors, among them one that the Younger Pliny addressed to Trajan in AD 100; Aurispa told a correspondent that he had never read anything more delightful. The text needed improvement, however, and a corrector whose name it embarrassed a recent editor not to know emended numerous passages 'with admirable shrewdness'.[28] He has recently been identified as Tommaso Parentucelli, better known as Nicholas V, the humanist pope who planned a library at Rome to rival the ancient library at Alexandria.[29] In 1426 he had discovered at Nonantola a sixth-century copy of Lactantius; between 1439 and 1443 he drew up for Cosimo de' Medici a list of works that a good library ought to contain; and in 1451 he sent Enoch of Ascoli as far north as Denmark in search of manuscripts. Enoch returned with a disappointing haul, but appropriately enough it seems to have included Tacitus' monograph on Germany and his life of his father-in-law Agricola, who as governor of Britain had sailed round Scotland.

Discoveries are an untidy subject. They were not always preceded by systematic search or followed by immediate diffusion; they did not always happen when they might have done; they sometimes went unannounced or were not announced by the actual discoverers; and 'discovery' is not altogether easy to define.[30]

Salutati made one discovery by accident: when he wrote to Milan for a copy of Cicero's correspondence with Atticus, which Petrarch had discovered at Verona in 1345, he received instead a copy of his miscellaneous correspondence, *Ad familiares*, which Petrarch never knew. Some of the texts new to Poggio between 1415 and 1429 had probably been discovered by others, such as the French humanists Nicholas of Clamanges and Jean de

Montreuil, and many hardly circulated before he retired from papal service to Florence in 1453. An anonymous poem of condolence addressed to Augustus' wife Livia on the death of her son Drusus in 9 BC first appears in a manuscript of 1469 probably written at Padua, and nowhere is anything more said about its discovery than what Giovanni Calfurnio says in an edition printed at Venice in 1474, that 'it was found recently'. In 1423 Poggio asked his Florentine friend Niccoli to return two texts that he sent him from Britain when he was serving as secretary to Cardinal Beaufort: the pastoral poems of Calpurnius and a piece of Petronius. About 1360, however, a manuscript of Calpurnius had already come to Petrarch's notice at Verona, and two descendants of it survive, one of them written by a friend of Boccaccio who like both Petrarch and Boccaccio wrote pastoral poems himself. As for Petronius, the transmission of his novel is full of twists and turns. A French manuscript of the twelfth century in which excerpts from Petronius follow the agricultural writer Palladius had arrived in Italy by the fourteenth, and one of its Italian owners, the Venetian Francesco Barbaro, corresponded regularly with Poggio and Niccoli about their discoveries; but there is no sign that anyone in Italy ever turned the pages beyond Palladius, and it was Poggio's manuscript of the same excerpts that put them into circulation. In the very year of Poggio's letter to Niccoli, a scholar from the Veneto copied out another piece of Petronius that Poggio had found, this time at Cologne Cathedral: the *Cena Trimalchionis*. His copy is the only one extant. Why no other descendants of Poggio's manuscript survive is a total mystery; but no descendants of this copy survive because it rapidly migrated to a cultural backwater in Dalmatia, where it resurfaced only about 1650. Meanwhile, in the 1560s, French scholars had discovered new excerpts from Petronius in manuscripts about whose date and contents they are infuriatingly uninformative.

Faulty texts, especially texts with obvious gaps, were one of the things that spurred humanists to explore libraries, just as in the ninth century Lupus of Ferrières badgered correspondents for fuller copies.

Between Tuesday (*dies Martis*) 1 September 1388 and Tuesday 2 March (*mensis Martius*) 1389 Paolo di Bernardo of Venice copied out the first decade of Livy, 'largely martial in content', and added at the end:

> This work should greatly appeal to anyone, but I must be honest and say that it is not a model of editorial polish, because I do not believe that any such can be found at present. What I will make bold to say is that it is less corrupt than many others that I have seen in my time both here and elsewhere. To produce this copy, I used as many exemplars as I could, and with the aid of these and my own feeble brain I put a certain amount of sweat into a springclean.[31]

Some years after he had copied out a defective text of Cicero's longest treatise on oratory, *De oratore*, Poggio found another manuscript in the neighbourhood of Strasbourg; but as he had no means of checking on the spot whether it had a fuller text, and no wish either to spend days of his own time copying it out or to pay a scribe for the purpose if it might turn out to have the same text as before, he contented himself with noting the beginning and end of each distinguishable section so that he could make the comparison at home. To stay with *De oratore*, by losing the end of Book I and the beginning of Book II the most productive medieval manuscript lost the transition from one to the other and left readers guessing where it occurred; at what is now known as II.26, an annotator of the early fifteenth century wrote: 'I have found Book II starting here in a very old manuscript, reasonably, I think, because below he says "yesterday" and "yesterday's discussion", and furthermore Quintilian cites some passages that occur below as from the second book.'[32] In fact, his arguments are better than his palaeography can possibly have been.

Splicing copies in this way, and transferring readings from one to another, have been dubbed 'contamination' by modern editors who practise it on every page. They would defend themselves by pointing out that their *apparatus criticus*, the collection of notes at the foot of the page, explains what they have done, whereas the humanists not only had rudimentary criteria for preferring one manuscript to another, or one reading to another, but left no record of their procedure and indeed lacked any system for referring to their manuscripts at all, or even for distinguishing between variants and conjectures; furthermore, modern editors are forced to choose between variants, whereas the humanists frequently left them to fight it out.

Well before the end of the fifteenth century, however, some humanists were on the way to solving these problems. In a manuscript of Cicero's *Verrines* written about 1400 a hand identified by someone not much later as Bruni's writes this at the end, perhaps as an instruction to a scribe about to copy from it: 'This book was correctly written at the outset but later corrupted by someone who meant to correct it but corrupted it; so accept the original text and reject the corrections.'[33] Giovanni Pontano collated an eleventh-century manuscript of Ovid's *Remedia amoris* with another, and beside the variant at 131, which he noted at the foot of the page, he wrote: 'the text above is right in my opinion'.[34] A scribe who copied out in 1407, probably at Milan, the poem *Culex*, ascribed by the manuscripts to Virgil, and added at the end that he had taken it 'from a very old exemplar in a script almost unknown these days', had some reason to believe that old manuscripts were better than recent ones, and so did Bernardo Bembo, who called his ninth-century copy of the same poem *antiquissime antiquitatis reliquiae* ('a relic of extreme antiquity').[35] Broadly they were right, whatever they meant by 'very old' and whether or not they were good judges of age. One of the texts most studied about 1400, especially by Gasparino Barzizza and his pupils at Padua and Pavia, was Cicero's *De oratore*, which they knew to be seriously incomplete; so that the complete text discovered in 1421 at Lodi, near Milan, created immediate demand. As early as 1428 Giovanni Lamola bemoaned one result:

> This venerable relic of extraordinary age has been treated quite disgracefully by the people who have handled it and have taken the text now in general circulation from that uncorrupted exemplar. Failures of understanding, erasures, alterations, additions – they have many to answer for ... For my part, I applied all the care, intelligence and skill that I myself and some like-minded experts on antiquity could muster to bringing everything back into line with the original text and noting in the margin at each point the contributions of those wordmongers, those barbarian monsters. I also took pains to reproduce the entire appearance of the old manuscript down to the smallest dot, even where it went off the rails as old manuscripts do, because I would rather go off the rails in such company than share the sanity of our conscientious friends.[36]

On the other hand, a manuscript of Florus written by Lamola has recently been identified, and he can be seen to have produced a veritable edition.[37]

Naming manuscripts, an important contribution to accountability, served only a temporary purpose unless they had come to rest in an institutional library, but many older manuscripts had, and new foundations like the public library of San Marco at Florence helped more to do so.[38] Petrarch refers to a manuscript of St Ambrose in the archives of Sant'Ambrogio, Milan (*De vita solitaria* II.11). Towards 1400 someone found an alternative ending to Terence's *Andria* in a chained manuscript at San Domenico, Bologna, and two of the scribes who copied it name their source. Later in the fifteenth century an Italian scholar interested in two problematical passages of Vitruvius consulted a manuscript at Mons Blandinius, Ghent, and noted on his own copy that the *Blandinianus codex* had just the same readings.[39]

All such efforts, however, pale beside the work of someone who called himself *homo vetustatis minime incuriosus* ('a man far from averse to studying antiquity') – the Florentine humanist Angelo Poliziano. Though he published no edition, he has the following achievements to his name:

1. he was the first scholar to make a thorough collation of an ancient manuscript, the fifth-century manuscript of Terence then owned by Pietro Bembo and his father Bernardo
2. he collated several other manuscripts still valued by editors

3. when he collated more than one manuscript on the same printed copy, he distinguished their readings by giving each a symbol
4. he identified his manuscripts by naming the owner and adding details about their history or appearance
5. he surmised that a manuscript of Statius' *Silvae* written in 1417 lay behind all others in circulation, and he proved that manuscripts of Cicero's *Ad familiares* and Valerius Flaccus' *Argonautica* with their leaves in the wrong order lay behind others that he had seen
6. he confirmed his argument about Valerius Flaccus by recognizing the hand of Niccoli in the misbound manuscript
7. he found in Suetonius' life of Nero criteria for identifying an autograph, which he applied to the ancient copy of the *Digest* (the Emperor Justinian's main corpus of Roman law) known as the Florentine *Pandects*[40]
8. he came more and more to distinguish between variants and conjectures.

The fifth of these achievements was part of his wider concern with the authority of evidence, seen for instance in his contention that all writers after Herodotus who regarded the Greek alphabet as imported from Phoenicia by Cadmus were following Herodotus.[41]

In Poliziano's time the idea of a received text, a vulgate, was beginning to take hold. Giannantonio Campano, the second editor of Livy (Rome, 1470), expresses religious reverence for Livy's work and welcomes the advent of printing, which will duplicate a responsibly produced text and do away with the errors of individual scribes. Galeotto Marzi warns Lorenzo de' Medici that civilization will collapse if people are allowed to alter the text of Virgil, the Bible, Aristotle, Thomas Aquinas, title deeds or histories.[42] For every tirade against wilful tinkering, however, one can find a boast like Franciscus Puteolanus's in the second edition of Statius' *Silvae* (Parma, 1473), that he had improved the text of Catullus and *Silvae* in over 3,000 places. While some saw that printing hundreds of copies gave editors new and dangerous power, others welcomed a common point of reference such as the wide circulation of identical copies might provide. Already by 1535 the intellectual laziness of treating a familiar text as a good text had gone far enough to provoke trenchant words from the Bohemian scholar Sigismundus Gelenius in the edition of Livy that he prepared jointly with Beatus Rhenanus:

> So before immediately objecting that we are doing away with the received text, people should consider what we have done away with and what we have put in its place. In my opinion, what should count as the received text is the text received over 1,000 years ago, rather than the text that has slipped into

use in recent years by the grace of inattentive typesetters and extended its influence from one day to the next by reproduction in large numbers, while scholars have either turned a blind eye or had other things to do.[43]

In the same edition, indispensable to modern editors for its use of two important manuscripts now lost, Rhenanus complains that no one can be bothered to inspect manuscripts any more. Fortunately scholars all over Europe soon proved him wrong.

Improving texts is only one aspect of coming to understand them. Who was the author? When and why did he write this work? What does this strange word mean, or this strange piece of Latin? What story is he alluding to here? Does he mean what he says or is there a hidden meaning? Who is right about a particular matter, this author or that one?

Medieval readers often jotted answers to such questions in their manuscripts, and some medieval scholars produced continuous exposition of classical texts, for instance the rhetorical handbook *Ad Herennium* (attributed to Cicero) or the satires of Persius and Juvenal.[44] Humanists did nothing fundamentally new in the field of commentary until the 1470s, when Domizio Calderini set a fashion of tackling selected problems rather than going systematically through a text and inevitably repeating things that commentators had said before.[45] On the other hand, the volume of classical literature that might shed light on an obscure passage grew enormously with the new discoveries, so much so that annotators can often be dated and sometimes localized by the texts from which they draw their explanatory or comparative material.

As readers outnumbered writers, annotations may spring surprises. At I.2.15–16 Propertius mentions Phoebe and Hilaira, the daughters of Leucippus who took the fancy of Castor and Pollux, and the annotator of a manuscript probably written at Rome in the 1450s tells a story about them on the authority of 'Urbanus, an ancient commentator on Book VI of the *Aeneid*';[46] a briefer version of the same story, again told on the authority of Urbanus, appears in the margin of a roughly contemporary Ovid.[47] No commentary on Virgil is known to survive under the name of Urbanus. Servius does cite an Urbanus, and Book VI of the *Aeneid* mentions Castor and Pollux; but Servius does not cite Urbanus on that passage and nowhere tells the story. Where did the annotators find it?

Some texts quickly became works of reference. Carolingian scholars had used the dictionary of Nonius Marcellus, 'a diet for pioneers and enthusiasts',[48] but it did not circulate widely again until the fifteenth century. Alongside the title *Monobiblos* in a manuscript of Propertius that he wrote in 1427, Panormita noted 'or *Elegies* according to Nonius Marcellus', a title or description buried away in Nonius' entry on the verb *secundare*.[49] Niccoli combed Nonius for references to missing works of Cicero.[50] Pontano's working copy of Plautus has the name of Nonius in the margin oftener than any other.[51] The dictionary is alphabetically arranged, but in those days, before anyone had drawn up an index of authors cited, the only way of finding relevant citations was to read through it. Humanists read many works that modern scholars only consult.

Sometimes humanists were moved to raise doubts about authenticity. One scribe who copied out the alternative ending of Terence's *Andria* from the manuscript at Bologna added: 'but I do not think Terence wrote it, because neither the style nor the content fits what precedes'. A speech written as if by Cicero and transmitted as his from at least the ninth century, *On the Eve of Exile*, drew from someone about 1400 the comment: 'anyone who says Cicero composed this speech is telling an untruth'. No strictly classical text received such a methodical demonstration of spuriousness as the Donation of Constantine, which Valla demolished with a battery of historical and linguistic arguments.[52]

Of the more discursive scholarly genres, the humanists inherited from both antiquity and the Middle Ages a rich tradition of biography. Two forms dominated: encyclopedias modelled ultimately on St Jerome's *De viris illustribus*, and single biographies of writers, usually compiled as part of an introduction to copies of their works.[53] The most enterprising of humanistic biographies are Petrarch's unfinished *De gestis Cesaris* ('Caesar's Career'); Bruni's *Cicero novus* ('New Cicero') and life of Aristotle;[54] and Sicco Polenton's *Scriptores illustres Latinae linguae* ('Eminent Latin Writers').[55] Bruni's were made possible by something that overshadows all other advances in the Renaissance and more than anything else entitles it to that name: the return of Greek to western Europe.[56]

At no time had it been completely absent. Native speakers of Greek inhabited parts of southern Italy (they still do); traders and diplomats needed it; some scholars in every century from the ninth to the fourteenth did serious work on Greek literature, none more than Robert Grosseteste, Bishop of Lincoln from 1235 to 1253 and the first Chancellor of Oxford University, who produced what has been called the first ever critical edition of a Greek text (the corpus attributed to Dionysius the Areopagite) made by a westerner;[57] and somehow a monk in Alsace about 1190, Johannes de Alta Silva, came to include in his cycle of Latin stories, *Dolopathos*, versions of Homer's story about Odysseus' escape from the Cyclops' cave and Herodotus' about the Egyptian who got away with burgling a pyramid.[58] In fourteenth-century Italy, Niccolò da Reggio translated medical works by Galen for Robert of Anjou, King of Naples, decades before Boccaccio set a Greek from southern Italy, Leonzio Pilato, to work translating Homer. Even this latter venture, however, dissatisfied its sponsors and led nowhere.

Coluccio Salutati admired Cicero for being both a distinguished statesman and a distinguished writer. In 1392–3, as we have seen, he acquired both sets of his correspondence, and the manuscripts that he received from Milan both survive. He must have found them frustrating. Steeped in Greek literature and surrounded by Greek culture, Cicero enlivened them with Greek phrases and quotations, which generations of scribes could do no more than reproduce uncomprehendingly by copying the curves and strokes as faithfully as possible. Salutati would not have been able to follow these snippets of Greek even if they had been flawlessly transmitted. In the margins, however, an elegant Greek hand has written them out as correctly as their garbled form allows, dividing the words and adding accents, and someone has put Latin translations above them. Palaeographers have matched the Greek hand with the signature of Manuel Chrysoloras, who according to a later report 'restored the Greek letters' in a manuscript of Cicero's *Ad Atticum*. In 1390 Chrysoloras had led an embassy from Constantinople to Venice. Roberto Rossi of Florence met him there, and in 1395 Rossi's acquaintance Jacopo Angeli da Scarperia set off for Constantinople to study Greek with him. In 1396 the University of Florence invited him to come and teach Greek grammar and literature for ten years, and the letter of invitation, which alludes to the *Aeneid* and twice quotes Cicero, was surely written by the chancellor himself, Salutati. Before setting out the terms of the contract, it steers a nice course between superiority and deference:

> Our forebears always had the greatest reverence for learning and knowledge. In consequence, though there was once no university established in the city, Florence has to her name in both single and successive generations many experts in a variety of disciplines, whose memory burns bright in their literary works and their widespread reputation. In our own time we have seen the great benefit of adding Greek scholarship to such accomplishments. 'The Romans, lords of the world', of whom we are not the meanest part, confessed through the mouth of their greatest authors that from the Greeks they received all aspects of knowledge: the verdict of our own Cicero confirms that we Romans either made wiser innovations than theirs by ourselves or improved on what we took from them, but of course, as he himself says elsewhere with reference to his own day: 'Italy is invincible in war, Greece in culture.' For our part, and we mean no offence, we firmly believe that both Greeks and Latins have always taken learning to a higher level by extending it to each other's

literature. This conviction, and the wish that our younger generation should be able to drink from both springs and add Greek to Latin for the enrichment of their knowledge, led us to resolve that we should appoint an expert in both languages to teach Greek here and to confer both a useful service and a signal distinction on that great centre of excellence the University of Florence.

In February 1397 Chrysoloras arrived. A later chancellor, Bruni, recalled the significance of the event for his own career: teachers of law abounded, but no one in Italy had known Greek for 700 years, and here was a heaven-sent and unique opportunity of meeting Homer, Plato and Demosthenes, and steeping himself in the wonderful things that they had to impart.[59] Chrysoloras's grammar, *Erotemata* ('Questions'), found its way to many a desk either in its original form or in Guarino's adaptation. Greek manuscripts began to reach Italy in large numbers and Greek texts to be translated. When Constantinople fell to the Turks in 1453, many Greeks found refuge in Italy, and more manuscripts came with them. As late as the 1490s, Lorenzo de' Medici sent Janus Lascaris off to collect yet more, and he returned with some 200.[60]

Much in Greek culture had been mediated by Latin literature, and thanks to such Latin writers as Cicero, Horace and Servius, some of their Greek predecessors, for instance Plato, found a red carpet laid out for them. At first it was chiefly these, together with Greek historians of Rome, that attracted attention. Many translators seized on Plutarch's lives, and Roman lives came first, among them the life of Cicero, so useful to Bruni. In the first fifteen years after 1397, there were two notable exceptions: Ptolemy's *Outline of Geography*, written in the second century AD and later illustrated by maps, and a fourth-century work, St Basil's essay *To the Younger Generation on Making Good Use of Greek Literature*. Chrysoloras himself began a Latin translation of Ptolemy, completed in 1409 by Jacopo da Scarperia. In 1418, at the Council of Constance, Cardinal Fillastre of Reims commissioned a copy for his cathedral; in his note of presentation at the end he wrote: 'please look after it properly, because I think it is the first copy in France'.[61] Basil's essay did for Greek literature very much what *Pro Archia* had done for literature in general, and it had the further advantage of being written by a Christian for other Christians and so providing an answer to Christian attacks on pagan literature like Giovanni Dominici's *Lucula noctis* ('Firefly') of 1405. Bruni's translation, made by 1403, survives in over 300 copies.[62]

A second wave of largely historical translations followed in the pontificate of Nicholas V, no doubt prompted by his plans for a grand library in Rome. It included Valla's translation of Thucydides, whose speeches set one of the stiffest tests in the whole of Greek literature. He could have found equally stiff tests among the poets, whose idiom, metre and sometimes dialect pose problems enough even without the degree of corruption that Aeschylus for one has suffered; but on the whole, in Latin as well as Greek, poetry took second place to prose – Virgil to Cicero, for instance, in the eyes of Bruni– until the latter half of the century.[63] Even then, preference went to Greek poets imitated by Latin poets and especially to Virgil's models, Homer, Hesiod and Theocritus.

Very few Latin translations of Greek works have been properly edited, for obvious reasons: they are of no use to editors of the Greek text unless the translator used an important manuscript now lost, as Valla probably did for Thucydides, and students of humanism seldom need to go beyond a broad view of the translator's approach or competence. Consequently not enough is known about either the scale or the pattern of their diffusion. Lucretius' poem on the universe, discovered by Poggio in 1417, gives a much fuller account of Epicurean materialism than the largely hostile summaries in Cicero's philosophical works, and some fifty descendants of Poggio's copy survive; but Diogenes Laertius in his *Lives of Philosophers* devotes a whole book, the tenth and last, to Epicurus, and though few humanists read it in Greek, Ambrogio Traversari completed a Latin translation in 1433.[64] How many manuscripts of the translation survive? Incidentally, Traversari omitted the poems.

Italians had little use for Greek as a living language, and at first they contented themselves with exploiting Greek literature either in the original or in translation for what it could tell them about Latin literature. About 1462 Cristoforo Landino spotted that Persius took the theme of his fourth satire from Plato's *First Alcibiades*.[65] In 1482 and 1504 the Florentine humanist Bartolomeo Fonzio lectured on the *Argonautica* of Valerius Flaccus, and his working copy, a printed edition (Bologna, 1474), makes detailed use of Valerius' main source, the *Argonautica* of Apollonius, on which he had acquired material from the Byzantine scholar Andronicus Callistus.[66] Here again Poliziano goes much further. His notes, for instance on Ovid's *Fasti*, cite an astonishing range of Greek as well as Latin writers; and work done on the poetess Sappho by Giorgio Merula and Domizio Calderini in connection with the Ovidian *Letter from Sappho* led him to assemble an impressive collection of fragments and *testimonia*.[67] A rare poetic text cited not only in his notes on *Fasti* but also in his *Miscellanea*, Nonnus' *Dionysiaca*, 'was accessible in MS Laur. 32.16, written *c.* 1280 in a hand that would have tested Politian's palaeographical knowledge to the limit'.[68] Impressive erudition can also be seen in the corrections to Pliny and Pomponius Mela published in 1493 by his Venetian contemporary Ermolao

Barbaro.[69] Erasmus's discursive treatment of ancient proverbs, his *Adagia* of 1500, attained the same range and depth only in later editions.[70]

By 1500 nearly all the Greek literature that survives today had reached Italian libraries, and between 1495 and 1515 Aldus Manutius at Venice put most of it into print; but native Italians did almost nothing for the improvement of texts, and only Marsilio Ficino's commentaries on Plato and the Neoplatonists merit a place in the history of their interpretation.[71] Poliziano alone had the flair and experience that might have led him to achieve more, but he died at forty, a year before Aldus printed his first edition, and the best critic that Aldus employed was a Cretan, Marcus Musurus, just as the best critics of the previous generation were expatriate Greeks: Theodore Gaza, Cardinal Bessarion, Andronicus Callistus. Amongst western Europeans, Greek scholarship first made progress in France, where its greatest monument, the dictionary of Robert and Henri Estienne, appeared in 1572.

One of the earliest contributions to classical scholarship made in the Italian Renaissance combined epigraphy and local pride. Someone at Padua unearthed an inscribed slab on which the first word written out in full was the name Livius. Convinced that it marked the tomb of their compatriot Livy, the Paduans displayed it in the monastery of Santa Giustina, and whoever wrote the brief life of Livy that appears in a number of fourteenth-century manuscripts, possibly the Paduan jurist Lovato Lovati at the end of the thirteenth century, appended a sentence about the discovery.[72] Then or later, the lettering was gilded; and in 1350, when Petrarch addressed a letter to Livy (*Familiares* XXIV.8), he signed it 'in the city where I now live and you long ago were born and buried, in the porch of the maiden Giustina and face to face with the slab from your tomb'. In 1413 Sicco Polenton excitedly announced the discovery at Santa Giustina of Livy's bones in a lead coffin.[73] Neither modern biographers of Livy nor the learned compilers of the *Corpus inscriptionum Latinarum* disclose who pricked these bubbles.[74]

On journeys to the eastern Mediterranean, especially in 1435–7 and 1444–8, Cyriac of Ancona drew Greek monuments and recorded inscriptions. His notebooks, however, are mostly lost, and their reconstruction from later copies is more than usually hazardous; nor did he write up any results or conclusions.[75]

Collections of inscriptions, often illustrated with sketches of the objects that they were inscribed on, interested not just historians but also architects like Giovanni Giocondo of Verona, who combined a practical career with the study of classical antiquity. Best known to classicists for discovering in Paris the Younger Pliny's correspondence with the Emperor Trajan, he sold his services as architect and engineer to kings of France and the Republic of Venice, and when he designed the Pont-de-Notre-Dame in Paris and supervised its construction, he used machinery and methods described in Vitruvius' treatise on architecture, which he edited in 1511, 'with illustrations and an index so that it can now be read and understood', after consulting 'no small number of old copies, found not just in one area or city but in many'. Two years later he edited Frontinus' treatise on the aqueducts of Rome. The first edition, published at Rome about 1487 together with Vitruvius, rested on a very corrupt manuscript, and it was Giocondo who first printed a better text. The source of the improvements, a manuscript written in the 1430s for Pietro Donato, Bishop of Padua, has corrections in Giocondo's hand. A fascinating miscellany, it includes a collection of inscriptions, and Giocondo compiled another, in which he distinguished between those that he had seen himself and those that he had found reported.[76]

In the 1130s Geoffrey of Monmouth composed an ambitious and entertaining *Historia regum Britanniae* ('History of the Kings of Britain') from Brutus, great-grandson of the Trojan refugee Aeneas, to the death of Cadwallader in AD 689. It was a huge success. One of many manuscripts written before the end of the twelfth century came into the hands of a humanist who recorded his reaction: 'Though I have put unprecedented effort into reading through all the literature that I have anywhere encountered, nowhere have I found anything so replete with fictions and frivolities. The contents of this book outdo the wildest fantasies induced by drink or delirium.'[77] From anyone other than Biondo, Blondus Flavius as he called himself, the claim of unprecedented effort would be an idle boast. Between 1444 and his death in 1463, he produced four historical works of immense learning. Three of them he dedicated to popes, the first of whom, Eugenius IV, had been forced in 1434 to abandon Rome for Florence; and the sorry contrasts that the dilapidated Rome of those days presented, on the one hand with the new splendours of Florence, on the other with the ancient glories of its own empire, demanded both explanation and rectification. When Eugenius returned to Rome in 1443 and the long overdue revival of the city seemed to have begun, Biondo responded with *Roma instaurata* ('Rome Restored', 1446), an architectural and topographical reconstruction of ancient Rome from classical writers, inscriptions and the surviving monuments. Every Lent, he says, 40,000 or 50,000 pilgrims come flocking to Rome and are thrilled to see the old palaces, the amphitheatres, the baths and the aqueducts, and to learn what they were and what they meant; 'set in a firm foundation, then, the glory of Roman majesty still thrives, and in blissful reverence, under no compulsion and with no clash of arms, much of the world bows its head to the name of Rome'.[78] Did he regret one of those phrases when he came to survey the institutions of ancient Rome and dedicated *Roma triumphans* ('Rome Triumphant', 1459) to Pius II, who planned a crusade against the Turks?

In much of his work, Biondo sets out to explain the present. A typical passage of *Roma instaurata* deals with aqueducts (II.98–101). Poggio had discovered Frontinus' treatise at Montecassino in 1429, and Biondo cites a number of passages, among them Frontinus' own eulogy of Rome, before passing to the Elder Pliny and later sources. Why did so little survive of such massive structures? Some say the Goths destroyed them, some blame the ravages of time; but both explanations are wrong. Read Cassiodorus, and you will see that Theodoric, who had no lack of public spirit, wrote to the Romans from Ravenna about an opportunity of supplying the suburbs with water; and the elements cannot have been responsible, because sections are still intact in unpopulated countryside. No: the system of upkeep described by Frontinus lapsed, and people over the centuries have appropriated the masonry.[79]

After dedicating to Nicholas V in 1453 his historical geography of Italy, *Italia illustrata* ('Italy Illustrated'), Biondo revised it as opportunity arose, for instance when he saw a fragment of the fourth-century historian Ammianus Marcellinus, probably one found at Hersfeld by Enoch of Ascoli towards 1455. Poggio had brought to Italy a ninth-century manuscript from Fulda, and Biondo possessed one of its progeny, on which he collated the Fuldensis itself and made emendations hitherto ascribed to later critics. The fragment, however, was independent, and Biondo took from it a new passage of Book XVI, on ribbon development along the Via Flaminia from Rome to Ocriculum. Incidentally, his collation of the Fuldensis confirms what other evidence already suggested, that despite his vast reading in Latin he knew little Greek: he did not restore the Greek from the Fuldensis in passages left blank in his own manuscript.[80]

The fragment of Ammianus was not the first important manuscript of which Biondo obtained an early view. He enters the scholarly stage in a subscription appended to a copy of Cicero's *Brutus*:

> The exemplar went no further. Two leaves are torn out, though in my opinion only a few words are missing, certainly not leaves.
>
> I wrote this *Brutus* at Milan from 7 to 15 October 1422 from a very old exemplar recently found at Lodi, which contained Cicero's works *De inventione*, *Ad Herennium*, *De oratore*, *Orator ad Brutum* and *Brutus de claris oratoribus*.[81]

This was the manuscript that provoked Lamola's outburst.[82] In fact Biondo did not copy the whole of *Brutus* from it, but he marks the point where he switched to it.

In 1435 Biondo had occasion to draw on *Brutus* and the work that preceded it in the old manuscript, *Orator*, when he addressed to Bruni his first venture in historical research, a short monograph *De verbis Romanae locutionis* ('On Roman Vocabulary').[83] It describes a debate that took place in the antechamber of Eugenius IV amongst Bruni, Biondo and four other papal secretaries. Bruni maintained that the Romans had used two languages, one colloquial, like the vernacular of later ages, and the other literary; even the greatest orators spoke in the colloquial language and used the literary language only for their published versions, as could be seen from what they say about revision. That Cicero revised most of his speeches for publication Biondo accepts on the evidence of Asconius Pedianus' commentary and a letter from Cicero himself to Trebatius, but he argues from the criticisms of some orators in *Brutus* that what Cicero calls the *sermo vulgi*, ('the language of the masses'), was unpolished Latin, not the vernacular. In *Roma triumphans* he returned to the difference between the version delivered and the version published in order to cite further evidence: a letter from Pliny the Younger to Tacitus about Cicero's practice (I.20) and a letter from Cicero about Brutus' (*Ad Atticum* XV.1a.2). The inference that he represents Bruni as drawing from such evidence nicely illustrates the very different uses to which the same material can lend itself at different points in the history of scholarship: alterations that Cicero may have made to his speeches before publication have been much discussed in the last century without reference to the fifteenth-century debate, but no issue of linguistic history has arisen again.

The Latin language created other controversies, often fuelled by the reappearance of ancient texts.[84] Spelling, vocabulary, grammar, idiom, all came under scrutiny, and the results, widely diffused in practice even among people who had not read much of the latest theory, are best seen in correspondence between Italian humanists and scholars outside Italy who had not yet caught up: already in 1352–3, for instance, between Petrarch and Johann von Neumarkt,[85] or in the 1460s between Donato Acciaiuoli and the Spanish historian Alfonso de Palencia.[86] Biondo complimented Bruni on displaying Ciceronian eloquence to a greater degree than anyone since Lactantius, but meaner spirits later objected to every word or expression that broke an ancient rule or had no ancient parallel.

Medieval scribes had reduced *ae* and *oe* first to *ę* and then to *e*; but as Angelo Decembrio says in his *Politia litteraria* ('On Literary Refinement'), dedicated to Pius II in its final version of the early 1460s, it matters whether a foreign ruler demands from the Romans justice, *aequum*, or his horse, *equum* (VII.74–5). A scribe who wrote out Cicero's version of Aratus' astronomical poem about 1400 took over from his exemplar, probably an old manuscript that Cyriac of Ancona later saw at Vercelli, all its worst habits of spelling, such as *gemali* for *hiemali* ('wintry') and *adienibus* for *a genibus* ('from the knees').[87] Half a century later many scribes go to the other extreme of writing *cum* in its oldest attested form, *quom*, which even recent scholars have sometimes taken as a sign of access to venerable exemplars. Manuals of spelling, *De orthographia*, were produced by Gasparino Barzizza and Giovanni Tortelli, and the latter, librarian to Pope Nicholas V, perhaps worked with an eye to standardizing the spelling of the manuscripts that would be written for the new library, especially manuscripts of new translations;[88] his manual also serves more broadly as an encyclopedia of things Greek. Not many of their proposals can have caused such alarm as Poliziano's announcement in 1489 (*Miscellanea* I.77) that to judge from an ancient manuscript written in capitals Virgil was actually Vergil.

In the hands of Lorenzo Valla the close study of language became a devastating weapon. We have already met two examples, in his work on Livy and the Donation of Constantine; and 500 years before a modern grammarian remarked that 'the attempt of the early Greek philosophers to think out an explanation of what the world was made of, and how it had reached its present stage, broke down because the vehicle of their thought had not yet itself been subjected to scientific investigation',[89] Valla argued that much of scholastic philosophy was built on misuse of Latin, such as forming nouns in *-itas* from nouns instead of adjectives. His *Elegantiae* (1441–9) launches a linguistic campaign with a grandiose metaphor drawn from Livy V: not by writing history, translating from Greek, or composing speeches or poems, can we drive out the invading Gauls and restore Rome to freedom; Valla himself will muster an army and hurl himself first into the fray; who will be the new Camillus, the new saviour of Rome? Fifty-nine editions in sixty-five years must count as a victory. In a survey astonishing for its comprehensiveness and analytical skill, he swept away the superficialities that contented Isidore of Seville and his medieval successors and described the language of classical writers at first hand: 'there will be nothing in this work that anyone has said before'. 'I should point out that Cicero nowhere uses *et* for *etiam* as later writers do from Virgil on, as in *natus et ipse dea* ("he, too, son of a goddess")' (II.58): a simple point, but Valla had almost every page of Cicero that survives today, and he needed to read them all first. Grammar, syntax and idiom do not exhaust his coverage: modern critics who think they have invented the topic of closure should glance at his chapter 'On expressions that suit the end of a work' (III.85).

Three aspects of Valla's crusade are still with us: his methods of analysis, the primacy that he assigned to grammar and his plea for a return to classical standards. For the first no one has reason to be anything but grateful. Tortelli, the dedicatee of the *Elegantiae*, made one application of the second in a quotation from Quintilian (I.4.5): 'unless grammar lays a firm foundation for the budding orator, whatever you build on it will collapse'. The controversial side of this view can be seen in the difference between the English term 'scholarship' and the Continental descendants of *philologia*: unlike *klassische Philologie* or *filologia classica*, classical scholarship has as much room for Biondo as for Valla. The third aspect was the one that Valla did least to justify. Though he recognized that new things demanded new words, his plea for a classicizing purge resembles a plea that modern Americans should revert to the language of Gibbon and Burke. Not all his followers have been as harmless as editors of classical texts who still write prefaces in what they hope will pass for classical Latin, and part of the harm has been to give the impression that classicists lay down the law and oppose change. It would be anachronistic, however, to object that he ignored or arbitrarily condemned the processes of change in a living language, because he shared the view contested by Biondo that Latin had never been anyone's first language. Just as the humanists had to rediscover classical antiquity, so modern scholarship has to rediscover the humanists.

NOTES

1 William of Malmesbury, *Polyhistor*, ed. H. T. Ouellette (Binghamton, 1982), p. 49, lines 212.
2 L. D. Reynolds, ed., *Texts and Transmission: A Survey of the Latin Classics* (Oxford, 1983), pp. 85–6. See this volume wherever I mention details of transmission without giving a reference.
3 St Jerome, *Vita S. Hilarionis*, Patrologia Latina 23 (Paris, 1883), col. 29. I owe the observation to Neil Wright.
4 C. Godi, 'La "Collatio laureationis" del Petrarca', *Italia medioevale e umanistica*, 13 (1970), 127, at 14, 17. For the most up-to-date material on Petrarch, see M. Feo, ed., *Codici latini del Petrarca nelle biblioteche fiorentine* (Florence, 1991).
5 I quote from the earliest: MS Vatican City, Biblioteca Apostolica Vaticana, Vat. Lat. 9305, ff. 46^r–50^r.
6 E. Petersen, ' "The communication of the dead": notes on the *studia humanitatis* and the nature of humanist philology', in A. C. Dionisotti, A. Grafton and J. Kraye, eds., *The Uses of Greek and Latin: Historical Essays* (London, 1988), pp. 57–69.

7   Coluccio Salutati, *Epistolario*, ed. F. Novati, 4 vols. (Rome, 1891–1911), I, p. 134; III, p. 330; IV.2, index IV, 'Autori classici e medievali', *s.v.* Cicero, *Pro L. Archia*.

8   S. Rizzo, *Il lessico filologico degli umanisti* (Rome, 1973), pp. 237–8 (and cf. ix); and her 'Apparati ciceroniani e congetture del Petrarca', *Rivista di filologia e di istruzione classica*, 103 (1975), 5–15, at 11–13.

9   E. J. Kenney, *The Classical Text: Aspects of Editing in the Age of the Printed Book* (Berkeley, 1974); S. Timpanaro, *La genesi del metodo del Lachmann*, second edition, reprinted with corrections and additions (Padua, 1985).

10 MS The Hague, Koninklijke Bibliotheek, 75 C 63, ff. 37$^{\rm v}$–45$^{\rm r}$.

11 E. B. Fryde, *Humanism and Renaissance Historiography* (London, 1983), pp. 13–14; L. Barozzi and R. Sabbadini, *Studi sul Panormita e sul Valla* (Florence, 1891), p. 75.

12 Panormita, *Epistolarum libri V* (Venice, 1553), ff. 79$^{\rm r}$–83$^{\rm r}$.

13 Lorenzo Valla, *The Treatise on the Donation of Constantine*, trans. C. B. Coleman (New Haven, 1922).

14 J. L. Butrica, *The Manuscript Tradition of Propertius* (Toronto, 1984), p. 91 n. 11.

15 W. Milde, 'Petrarch's list of favorite books', *Res publica litterarum*, 2 (1979), 229–32, in the footsteps of B. L. Ullman, 'Petrarch's favorite books', in his *Studies in the Italian Renaissance*, second edition (Rome, 1973), pp. 113–33.

16 B. L. Ullman, *The Humanism of Coluccio Salutati* (Padua, 1963), p. 95.

17 Lorenzo Valla, *Dialecticae disputationes*, in his *Opera* (Basel, 1540; reprinted Turin, 1962), p. 644 (preface). Cf. M. L. McLaughlin, 'Humanist concepts of Renaissance and Middle Ages in the Tre- and Quattrocento', *Renaissance Studies*, 2 (1988), 131–42.

18 B. L. Ullman and P. A. Stadter, *The Public Library of Renaissance Florence* (Padua, 1972); A. C. de la Mare, 'Cosimo and his books', in F. Ames-Lewis, ed., *Cosimo 'il Vecchio' de' Medici, 1389–1464* (Oxford, 1992), pp. 115–56.

19 D. Hay, 'Flavio Biondo and the Middle Ages', *Proceedings of the British Academy*, 45 (1959), 97–125.

20 Sicco Polenton, *Scriptorum illustrium Latinae linguae libri XVIII*, ed. B. L. Ullman (Rome, 1928), pp. 125, lines 17–22, 128 line 31–129 line 1.

21 B. L. Ullman, *The Origin and Development of Humanistic Script* (Rome, 1960); E. Casamassima, 'Per una storia delle dottrine paleografiche dall'umanesimo a Jean Mabillon', *Studi medievali*, ser. 3, 5 (1964), 525–78, and his 'Literulae latinae', in S. Caroti and S. Zamponi, *Lo scrittoio di Bartolomeo Fonzio* (Milan, 1974), pp. ix–xxxiii. Many works by A. C. de la Mare include relevant material, for instance 'New research on humanistic scribes in Florence', in A. Garzelli, *Miniatura fiorentina del Rinascimento 1440–1525: un primo censimento*, 2 vols. (Florence, 1985), I, pp. 393–600, at 396–7.

22 Hay, 'Flavio Biondo', 101–2, explains why the most important works tend to be available only in the most outdated editions. There are also difficult editorial problems, often caused by authorial revision.

23 Giuseppe Billanovich has published a facsimile, *Il Livio del Petrarca e del Valla* (Padua, 1981).

24 Lorenzo Valla, *Antidotum in Facium*, ed. M. Regoliosi (Padua, 1981), pp. 327–70.

25 R. Sharpe, 'An Irish textual critic and the *Carmen paschale* of Sedulius: Colmán's letter to Feradach', *Journal of Medieval Latin*, 2 (1992), 44–54.

26 C. J. Classen, 'Quintilian and the revival of learning in Italy', *Humanistica Lovaniensia*, 43 (1994), 77–98.

27 R. Sabbadini, *Le scoperte dei codici latini e greci ne' secoli XIV e XV*, 2 vols. (Florence, 1905–14), reprinted with an introduction by E. Garin and additions and corrections from an annotated copy of the author's (Florence, 1967). My article 'The rediscovery of classical texts in the Renaissance', in O. Pecere, ed., *Itinerari dei testi antichi* (Rome, 1991), pp. 115–57, does not give a systematic account but includes some bibliography. For the period after 1493 there is no adequate treatment, but see L. D. Reynolds and N. G. Wilson, *Scribes and Scholars*, third edition (Oxford, 1991), p. 139.

28 *XII Panegyrici Latini*, ed. R. A. B. Mynors (Oxford, 1964), p. x.

29 I owe the information to Antonio Manfredi, who will shortly publish it in *Studia classica Iohanni Tarditi oblata*.

30 Reeve, 'Rediscovery', pp. 115–18. Kenney, *Classical Text*, pp. ix–x, mentions his 'discovery' of G. Pasquali's *Storia della tradizione e critica del testo* (Florence, 1934).

31 MS Paris, Bibliothèque nationale, lat. 5727, f. 106^r.

32 MS London, British Library, Add. 19586, f. 64^v.

33 MS Florence, Biblioteca Medicea Laurenziana, Strozzi 44, f. 104^v.

34 F. Munari, *Il codice Hamilton 471 di Ovidio* (Rome, 1965), pl. IV.1.

35 M. D. Reeve, 'The textual tradition of the *Appendix Vergiliana*', *Maia*, 28 (1976), 233–54, at 243, 245 n. 58.

36 Guarino of Verona, *Epistolario*, ed. R. Sabbadini, 3 vols. (Venice, 1915–19), I, pp. 641–2 (*Ep.* 455, lines 143–72).

37 M. D. Reeve, 'The transmission of Florus and the *Periochae* again', *Classical Quarterly*, 85 (1991), 453–83, at 475–7.

38 Ullman and Stadter, *Public Library*.

39 M. D. Reeve, 'Two manuscripts at the Escorial', forthcoming in the proceedings of a conference held at Madrid in September 1991.

40 V. Fera, *Una ignota Expositio Suetoni del Poliziano* (Messina, 1983), p. 224, quoted by N. G. Wilson, *From Byzantium to Italy: Greek Studies in the Italian Renaissance* (London, 1992), pp. 110–11.

41 A. T. Grafton, 'On the scholarship of Politian and its context', *Journal of the Warburg and Courtauld Institutes*, 45 (1977), 150–88.

42 Butrica, *Propertius*, pp. 60–1 n. 22.

43 Livy, *Decades tres*, 5 vols. (Basel, 1535), I, p. 5.

44 A *Catalogus translationum et commentariorum* is in progress, with seven volumes published between 1960 and 1992; it was begun by P. O. Kristeller and is currently edited by Virginia Brown.

45 Grafton, 'Scholarship of Politian', 152–6.

46 MS El Escorial, Real Biblioteca, g III 12, f. 2^r; I owe my knowledge of it to Trinidad Arcos Pereira and María Elisa Cuyás de Torres.

47 MS Vatican City, Biblioteca Apostolica Vaticana, Vat. Lat. 1595, f. 39^r, on Ovid, *Heroides* XVI.327–30; I owe my knowledge of it to Gemma Donati and Silvia Rizzo.

48 L. D. Reynolds, 'Nonius Marcellus', in Reynolds, ed., *Texts and Transmission*, pp. 248–52, at 252.

49 MS Vatican City, Biblioteca Apostolica Vaticana, Vat. Lat. 3273, f. 1ʳ.

50 P. A. Stadter, 'Niccolò Niccoli: winning back the knowledge of the ancients', in R. Avesani, M. Ferrari, T. Foffano, G. Frasso and A. Sottili, eds., *Vestigia: studi in onore di Giuseppe Billanovich*, 2 vols. (Rome, 1984), II, pp. 747–64, at 757.

51 R. Cappelletto, *La 'lectura Plauti' del Pontano* (Urbino, 1988), index, *s.v.* Nonio.

52 See n. 13 above.

53 See the introductions to G. Bottari's edition of Guglielmo da Pastrengo's *De viris illustribus et de originibus* (Padua, 1991) and W. Braxton Ross's forthcoming edition (posthumous, alas) of Giovanni Colonna's *De viris illustribus*.

54 For English translations of these two biographies, the former composed *c.*1415 and the latter *c.* 1429, see *The Humanism of Leonardo Bruni: Selected Texts*, trans. G. Griffiths, J. Hankins and D. Thompson (Binghamton, 1987), pp. 184–90, 283–92.

55 See n. 20 above.

56 Wilson, *From Byzantium to Italy*. See also K. J. Dover, ed., *Perceptions of the Ancient Greeks* (Oxford, 1992): ch. 5, 'The medieval west' by A. C. Dionisotti, and ch. 6: 'The Renaissance', by P. Burke.

57 A. C. Dionisotti, 'On the Greek studies of Robert Grosseteste', in Dionisotti, Grafton and Kraye, eds., *Uses of Greek and Latin*, pp. 19–39, at 29–30.

58 Johannes de Alta Silva, *Dolopathos*, ed. A. Hilka (Heidelberg, 1913), pp. 73–5, 49–57. That such stories had circulated orally for centuries is a romantic fantasy.

59 Reeve, 'Rediscovery', pp. 134–7, where I re-edit the Latin text of the invitation to Chrysoloras.

60 S. Gentile, 'Lorenzo e Giano Lascaris: Il fondo greco della biblioteca medicea privata', in G. C. Garfagnini, ed., *Lorenzo il Magnifico e il suo mondo* (Florence, 1994), pp. 177–94.

61 Reeve, 'Rediscovery', pp. 137–40.

62 L. Schucan, *Das Nachleben von Basilius Magnus 'ad adolescentes'* (Geneva, 1973), pp. 62–76, 235–42.

63 C. Dionisotti, *Geografia e storia della letteratura italiana* (Turin, 1967), pp. 177–99, at 186–8.

64 A. Sottili, 'Il Laerzio latino e greco e altri autografi di Ambrogio Traversari', in Avesani, ed., *Vestigia*, II, pp. 699–745; M. Gigante, 'Ambrogio Traversari interprete di Diogene Laerzio', in G. C. Garfagnini, ed., *Ambrogio Traversari nel VI centenario della nascita* (Florence, 1988), pp. 367–459.

65 R. Cardini, *La critica del Landino* (Florence, 1973), p. 173 n. 50, from MS Milan, Biblioteca Ambrosiana, I 26 inf., f. 213ʳ.

66 G. Resta, 'Andronico Callisto, Bartolomeo Fonzio e la prima traduzione umanistica di Apollonio Rodio', in *Studi in onore di Anthos Ardizzoni*, 2 vols. (Rome, 1978), II, pp. 1,055–131.

67 Angelo Poliziano, *Commento inedito ai Fasti di Ovidio*, ed. F. Lo Monaco (Florence, 1991). For other recently published notes of Poliziano's, see my review, *Classical Review*, 107 (1993), 153–6.

68 Wilson, *From Byzantium to Italy*, p. 180 n. 15.

69 Ermolao Barbaro, *Castigationes Plinianae et in Pomponium Melam*, ed. G. Pozzi, 4 vols. (Padua, 1973–9); V. Branca, 'Ermolao Barbaro and late Quattrocento Venetian humanism', in J. R. Hale, ed., *Renaissance Venice* (London, 1973), pp. 218–43.

70 M. M. Phillips, *The 'Adages' of Erasmus: A Study with Translations* (Cambridge, 1964).

71 J. Hankins, *Plato in the Italian Renaissance*, 2 vols. (Leiden, 1990), I, part IV. There is no mention of Ficino, however, in R. Kraut, ed., *The Cambridge Companion to Plato* (Cambridge, 1992).

72 Giuseppe Billanovich, *Tradizione e fortuna di Livio tra medioevo e umanesimo* (Padua, 1981), pp. 310–31.

73 Ullman, *Studies*, pp. 53–77, at 53–9.

74 In a work of 1684 reprinted by A. Drakenborch in his edition of Livy, *Historiarum ... libri qui supersunt omnes*, 7 vols. (Leiden etc., 1738–46), VII, pp. 27–80, D. G. Morhof gave the credit to his contemporary Marquard Gude. See Drakenborch, VII, pp. 12 n. 1, 35.

75 E. W. Bodnar, *Cyriacus of Ancona and Athens* (Brussels, 1960), pp. 17–72; for a sample of the *Commentaria*, E. W. Bodnar and C. Mitchell, *Cyriacus of Ancona's Journeys in the Propontis and the Northern Aegean 1444–1445* (Philadelphia, 1976).

76 On Giocondo, see L. Ciapponi, 'Fra Giocondo da Verona and his edition of Vitruvius', *Journal of the Warburg and Courtauld Institutes*, 47 (1984), 72–90, and her 'Agli inizi dell'umanesimo francese: Fra Giocondo e Guglielmo Budé', in O. Besomi, G. Gianella, A. Martini and G. Pedrojetta, eds., *Forme e vicende: per Giovanni Pozzi* (Padua, 1988), pp. 101–18; Reeve, 'Two manuscripts'.

77 MS Vatican City, Biblioteca Apostolica Vaticana, Vat. Lat. 2005, f. 69; cf. Flavio Biondo, *Scritti inediti e rari*, ed. B. Nogara (Rome, 1927), p. cvii n. 131.

78 Biondo, *Scritti*, pp. c–ci, from the closing sentences of *Roma instaurata*.

79 Poggio covers similar ground in his dialogue *De varietate fortunae*, now edited and annotated by O. Merisalo (Helsinki, 1993). In general, see A. T. Grafton, ed., *Rome Reborn: The Vatican Library and Renaissance Culture* (Washington DC, 1993), pp. 87–123; the first five chapters of this sumptuous volume are all relevant to classical scholarship.

80 R. Cappelletto, *Recuperi ammianei da Biondo Flavio* (Rome, 1983), pp. 26 n. 30, 95, 102.

81 MS Vatican City, Biblioteca Apostolica Vaticana, Ottob. Lat. 1592, f. 58^v, illustrated by E. Chatelain, *Paléographie des classiques latins*, 2 vols. (Paris, 1884–1900), I, pl. XXa.

82 See n. 36 above.

83 Biondo, *Scritti*, pp. 115–30; M. Tavoni, 'The 15th-century controversy on the language spoken by the ancient Romans: an inquiry into humanist concepts of "Latin", "grammar", and "vernacular"', *Historiographia Linguistica*, 9 (1982), 237–64; S. Rizzo, 'Il latino nell'umanesimo', in A. Asor Rosa, ed., *Letteratura italiana* (Turin, 1982–), V: *Le questioni*, pp. 379–408, at 401–8, and her 'Petrarca, il latino e il volgare', *Quaderni Petrarcheschi*, 7 (1990), 7–40. Besides contributing to this debate, the works of Cicero's discovered at Lodi in 1421 'clearly shape the writing of literary history in the second half of the

century': so M. L. McLaughlin, 'Histories of literature in the Quattrocento', in P. Hainsworth, V. Lucchesi, C. Roaf, D. Robey and J. R. Woodhouse, eds., *The Languages of Literature in Renaissance Italy* (Oxford, 1988), pp. 63–80, at 77.

84 W. K. Percival, 'Renaissance grammar', in A. Rabil, ed., *Renaissance Humanism: Foundations, Forms, and Legacy*, 3 vols. (Philadelphia, 1988), III, pp. 67–83; P. L. Schmidt, 'Die Wiederentdeckung der spätantiken Grammatik im italienischen Humanismus', *Studi italiani di filologia classica*, 85 (1992), 861–71; Rizzo, 'Il latino', pp. 379–408.

85 S. Rizzo, 'Il latino del Petrarca nelle *Familiari*', in Dionisotti, Grafton and Kraye, eds., *Uses of Greek and Latin*, pp. 41–55.

86 Reeve, 'Rediscovery', pp. 131–2.

87 M. D. Reeve, 'Some astronomical manuscripts', *Classical Quarterly*, 74 (1980), 508–22, at 510 n. 11.

88 I thank Silvia Rizzo for sharing with me ideas that she has not yet published about how Nicholas V, Valla and Tortelli conceived the new library. See also Grafton, *Rome Reborn*, pp. 3–45.

89 E. C. Woodcock, *A New Latin Syntax* (London, 1959), p. xix.

3
Humanism in script and print in the fifteenth century

MARTIN DAVIES

There was no humanism without books. They were the prime material on which the movement was founded and the natural medium through which it was transmitted. All humanists were consumers, and usually also producers, of books in manuscript. Many humanists first gained a reputation by seeking out and accumulating books. Humanists early associated themselves with the printing press when it came into being in the mid-fifteenth century and provided authors, editors and market for its products. Some, pre-eminently Erasmus, so thoroughly harnessed the great power of print that they were able to project themselves on to a European stage. In a less controlled way, this had happened a century and more before with the manuscript diffusion of the works of the early Italian humanists. Throughout the Renaissance, secular and ecclesiastical princes with cultural pretensions built themselves up with libraries as much as any other trappings of civilization. A book was often the vehicle of an alliance between culture and power, in the form of translations or dedications of original works, commissioned or unsolicited.

The common bond of humanism, uniting many disparate strands of interest, was the study, absorption and imitation of the classics, and the common style was a classicizing humanistic Latin. What was distinctive about the humanistic book? In the first place, it was a new manner of the preparation and writing of manuscripts: new in that it turned against current practice in these matters, but backward-looking in its attempt to recover classical virtues of clarity and purity. There were plenty of early humanists in the monastic and mendicant orders, and many humanists became academic teachers; but in origin and essence the movement stood apart from the traditional centres of book production in the religious houses and universities. We owe humanistic script and book production, and hence many features of books today, to a group of secular students of the classics in Florence at the end of the fourteenth century.

The origins of the humanistic reform of script, like so much else in the history of humanism, go back to Petrarch. Already in the mid-fourteenth century he was calling for a radical clarification of current handwriting. The Italian book-hands of his day had not taken on the intricate and angular 'woven' appearance of Gothic hands north of the Alps, but even so Italian Gothic scripts shared in the increasing ambiguity and artificiality of handwriting. The tendency towards regularity and uniformity had led to tight pages, heavily bounded by ruled frame lines. There was often too little space between the lines and the letters closely abutted one another, many of the rounded characters being joined together in conventional fusions. The general effect of artistic balance and neatness was bought at the price of legibility: many of the minuscule (lower case) letters were difficult to distinguish from others, and letters with ascenders or descenders scarcely occupied more vertical space than those without.

To Petrarch, such writing was more the work of painters than scribes, appealing from a distance but fatiguing to follow closely, 'as though it had been designed for something other than reading'. He advocates instead a script that is 'pure and clear, which lends itself spontaneously to the eye, and in which no mistakes of an orthographical or grammatical kind may be found'. In another place he protests against a different vice of contemporary hands (here he is thinking more of university textbooks): their excessive smallness and extreme abbreviation.[1] In an earlier letter to Boccaccio, Petrarch had commended the 'majesty, harmony and sober decoration' of an eleventh-century manuscript of St Augustine which still exists.[2] Petrarch himself never adopted this style of writing, a large and clear late Carolingian minuscule. But a later generation took up his advocacy of reform, the group associated with the chancellor of Florence at the turn of the fourteenth and fifteenth centuries, Coluccio Salutati.

Salutati's own hand shows a clear desire for increased legibility in the tracing and disposition of individual letters, even if the actual letter forms remain essentially Gothic. But Coluccio's 'pre-antiqua' hand, as it has been christened, also made some experimental returns to features of Carolingian minuscule which were to become emblematic of humanist script: upright *d*, long *s* at the end of words, greatly reduced abbreviation and reintroduction of the forgotten ampersand (as against other medieval signs for *et*). It is really only with the earliest, unsigned manuscripts of Salutati's protégés Niccolò Niccoli and Poggio Bracciolini, dating from around 1400, that we can speak of a fully formed humanistic script: a round, upright, formal book-hand characterized by spaciousness, avoidance of abbreviation and of fusion of letters, and reformed spelling. The letter forms mentioned above are used along with others (not necessarily all present in a single specimen) such as an upright *r* where Gothic script would use a rounded one, uncial *a* with a distinct bowl, an early medieval upper case letter now used as a minuscule, where Gothic typically used a single-compartment *a*, the sequences *st* and *ct* joined in ligatures, and (most distinctively) minuscule *g* with two bowls joined by a stroke, just as in our modern roman type. These minuscule characters were allied to a range of upper case letters (majuscules) derived from ancient Roman inscriptions, at first with an unsteady admixture of Gothic or medieval uncial capitals. The revival of the diphthongs *oe* and *ae*, often rendered as an *e* with a cedilla, and such spellings as *mihi* ('to me') and *nihil* ('nothing') for medieval *michi* and *nichil*, may be reckoned as the particular contribution of Niccolò Niccoli, who had a known interest in such minutiae.

This was the style of writing (see figure 3.1, for a mid fifteenth-century example) which soon became known as *litterae antiquae* or *lettera antica*, in modern terms *humanistica rotunda* or *formata*. It looked back not directly to antiquity but to the first great revival of antiquity in Carolingian times, and specifically to Italian manuscripts of the eleventh and twelfth centuries; as early as 1395 Salutati asked a friend for a manuscript of Peter Abelard in 'antiqua littera', and he cannot have supposed that Abelard (d. 1142) was anything other than a late medieval author. By the standards of the time, the libraries of both Salutati and Niccoli were disproportionately rich in older manuscripts of this sort, evidence of their common desire to reach back to a purer tradition of the texts they studied: as more and more texts were sought out for acquisition and copying, the more frequently must the humanists have come across these older, 'more classical' types of handwriting. It is still an open question whether the earliest humanists really believed that the ancients too had written in this style.[3]

More than the reform of handwriting was involved. In layout, ruling and decoration, older models were sought in a deliberate and programmatic rejection of current techniques of book production. Nearly all humanist manuscripts are written in well-spaced long lines rather than the two or more columns frequent in Gothic manuscripts. The majority are on vellum carefully ruled with a hard point, the writing (in prose texts) extending to an even right margin by 'justification', another trait passed on to print. For decoration the earliest humanists again passed back over the Gothic centuries to the simple and sober white vine-stem initials found in late Carolingian manuscripts. In humanistic work they are generally confined to the beginnings of individual books within a text. Borders too were at first very simple, typically consisting of vine-stem decoration added to one or two margins of the very first page of the text. The whole effect is chaste, not showy, harmonious not fussy.[4]

Humanistic script was used for humanistic texts, pre-eminently the Latin

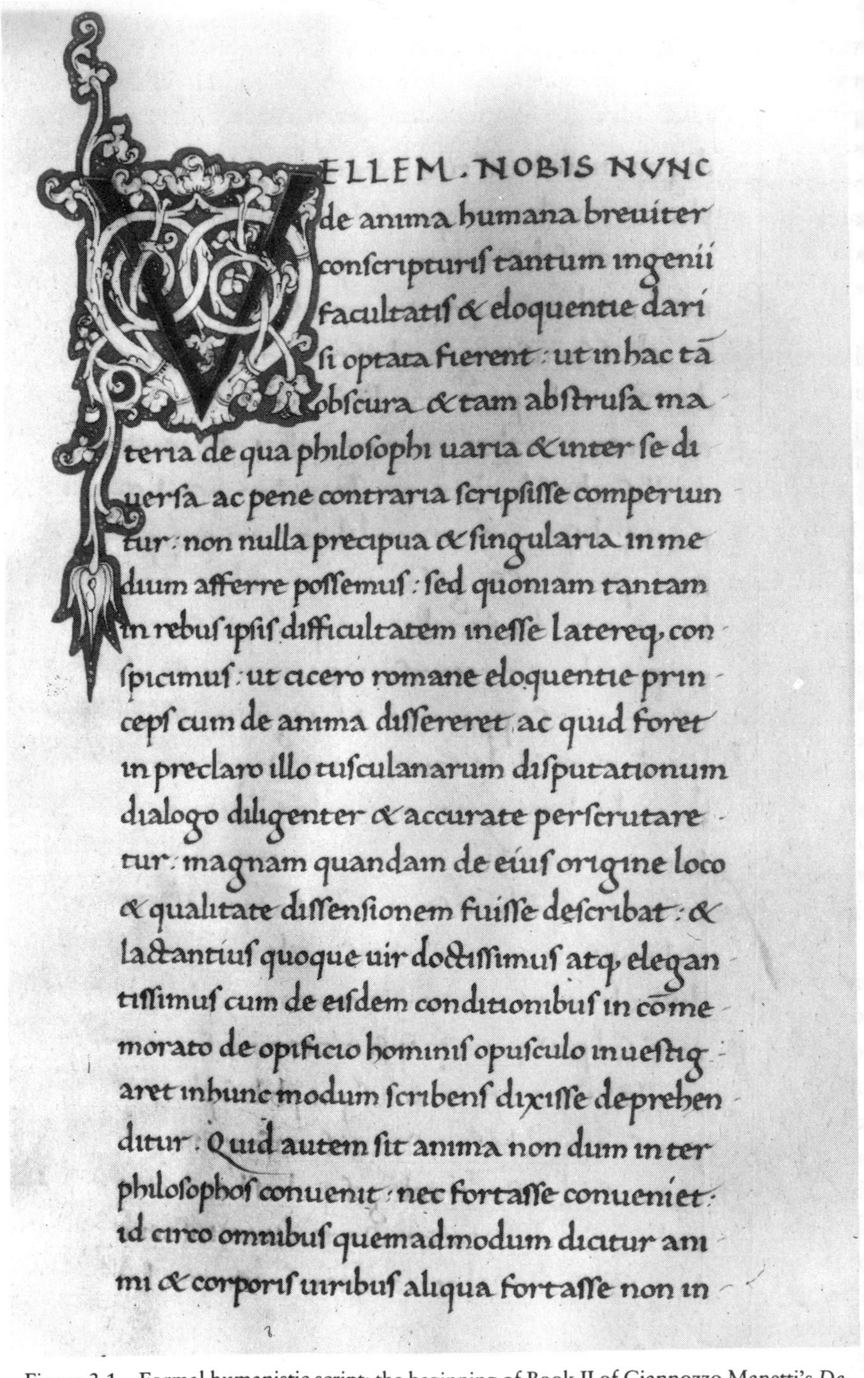

ELLEM · NOBIS NVNC
de anima humana breuiter
conscripturis tantum ingenii
facultatis & eloquentie dari
si optata fierent: ut in hac tā
obscura & tam abstrusa ma
teria de qua philosophi uaria & inter se di
uersa ac pene contraria scripsisse comperiun
tur: non nulla precipua & singularia in me
dium afferre possemus: sed quoniam tantam
in rebus ipsis difficultatem inesse latereq̃ con
spicimus: ut cicero romane eloquentie prin
ceps cum de anima dissereret ac quid foret
in preclaro illo tusculanarum disputationum
dialogo diligenter & accurate perscrutare
tur: magnam quandam de eius origine loco
& qualitate dissensionem fuisse describat: &
lactantius quoque uir doctissimus atq̃ elegan
tissimus cum de eisdem conditionibus in cōme
morato de opificio hominis opusculo inuestig
aret in hunc modum scribens dixisse deprehen
ditur: Quid autem sit anima non dum inter
philosophos conuenit: nec fortasse conueniet:
id circo omnibus quemadmodum dicitur ani
mi & corporis uiribus aliqua fortasse non in

Figure 3.1   Formal humanistic script: the beginning of Book II of Giannozzo Manetti's *De dignitate et excellentia hominis*, copied by the Florentine scribe Gherardo del Ciriagio in 1455. MS London, British Library, Harl. 2593, f. 25ʳ.

texts of classical and patristic antiquity and increasingly of the humanists themselves. Works of professional interest to philosophers, lawyers and physicians continued to be written and read in close columns of Gothic script. Vernacular texts with their own strong traditions were seldom written in humanistic script before the second half of the fifteenth century, and not often then. A humanistic manuscript was intended to suggest its contents by its look: old wine in new bottles, or the very latest vintage in stylish new dress.

We shall never be able to chart the precise roles in the 'invention' of humanistic script played by Salutati, Poggio and Niccoli, though the identification of the early formal hand of the last has given him increased prominence in recent years. What is certain is that it was Poggio who most thoroughly developed the script in the first decade of the fifteenth century. The Florentine bookseller Vespasiano da Bisticci, looking back from the 1470s, mentioned that Poggio had been a very fine writer of 'lettera antica' and had written for money in his youth (presumably before he left Florence for Rome and a career in the papal curia in 1403).[5] It was the example, and sometimes the direct instruction, of Poggio that led to the rise of a class of professional scribes trained in the humanist script. By the time of the inventory of the Medici library in 1418, where almost half the manuscripts are described as being in 'lettera antica', this style – the visible expression of a cast of mind – was well on the way to sweeping the field in the production of plain but elegant classical texts. A professional such as Giovanni Aretino could become for some years the scribe of choice for the Medici brothers, Cosimo and Lorenzo, as they forged the amalgam of power and culture that has brought them such a good press.

It seems to have been the adoption of manuscripts and libraries in this new mould by the governing class of the Italian cities that secured the long-term future of the humanistic book. Of course, poor students, and scholars of all sorts, continued to write out books for their own use in hands which might differ hardly at all from traditional gothic styles. There were always, too, local variations and approximations in the handling of formal humanistic script. But the cachet very soon achieved by the work of Poggio and his followers in the libraries of such influential collectors as the Medici of Florence made it possible for booksellers and stationers to devote large numbers of scribes to the production of these highly finished volumes. The story is well known of how Vespasiano organized (as he tells us) 45 scribes to copy out 200 manuscripts in less than 2 years when Cosimo de' Medici wanted to furnish the Badia of Fiesole with a library. The Badia library was formed on the basis of a list of books desirable in any library which had been drawn up by the humanist Tommaso Parentucelli.[6] A similar case arose in the 1470s when Vespasiano was entrusted with the rapid building up of a great princely library (which still survives almost intact in the Vatican), that of Federico da Montefeltro, Duke of Urbino. And amid these large-scale transactions the humanists continued to transcribe, buy, sell and above all discuss manuscript books for their own use and delight: the letters to Niccoli of Poggio at Rome and of the monk Ambrogio Traversari at Florence are full of passages relating to books ancient and modern, and how the one might become the other. We can be sure that the great majority of new manuscripts were in the formal humanistic script, or in the neat, sloping humanistic cursive – essentially a rapid version of the same script – which was to develop into italic.

In more elevated circles, there arose an element of competitive acquisition, as princes of church and state hastened to build up classical libraries, from scratch or as accretions to existing collections. Such acquisition was a badge of their power as patrons of culture and had definite publicity value. They bought humanist books and commissioned humanist works and translations in the same way that they hired humanists to dance attendance on them, to write their letters or their lives. As Pope Nicholas V, Tommaso Parentucelli was to be responsible for the foundation of what became the greatest of all Renaissance libraries, the Biblioteca Apostolica Vaticana.[7] But there were many parallel feats of collection building – by the Este at Ferrara, the Sforza at Milan, the Aragonese kings of Naples and others.

With the elevation of status of the humanist manuscript as an object of patronage went an increasing elaborateness of production. Simple vine-stem initials at the beginning of a book became larger and more ornate, attracting borders in the same style or in floral or knotwork patterns, in bright colours and gold, at first on one side only but increasingly on two, three or four sides of the text. Arms, or empty wreaths to take them, began to be regularly added to the lower border, often supported by putti. The second half of the fifteenth century also saw, more or less concurrently with the rise of print, the introduction of elaborate title medallions listing the contents of a book opposite the first page of the text. Another late development, of Paduan origin, was an opening page set within an architectural frame which could accommodate all sorts of classical motifs and illusionistic devices. Initial capitals were often faceted in a style modelled on ancient Roman inscriptions which was inspired by Felice Feliciano and Andrea Mantegna. The climax of Renaissance book decoration is really reached with hand-finished printed books, the incunabula of the 1470s and 80s. We are a long way here from the chaste simplicity of the early Florentine manuscripts. But even these late and luxurious productions are recognizably of classical and humanist inspiration: rich decoration is typically confined to the frontispiece, beyond which the text speaks for itself. In general, humanists themselves were not interested in pictures but in texts.

The key point is that such activities and developments were possible at all: they rested on a highly literate urban society with a highly organized book trade – Vespasiano was only the most famous of the Florentine *cartolai*, or stationers. For the first time (outside, perhaps, the narrow case of textbooks at large universities) booksellers and stationers were able to arrange the production of popular texts in the sure knowledge that they would sell. Production, in other words, began to precede demand, as it does today, and books could be made for sale on a speculative basis. The most popular author in Renaissance manuscripts is Leonardo Bruni, chancellor and historian of Florence. Vespasiano, who knew him, tells us that Bruni was in the pleasant position of being able to walk around the city and find his own works being copied everywhere he went.[8]

Looked at from the viewpoint of the supporting structure of trade rather than the means of production, these are the conditions of print. As it happened, the invention of printing had no connection with humanism of any sort (if we except the fact, incidental and apparently without immediate consequence for Italy, that the humanist Enea Silvio Piccolomini, later Pope Pius II, is our sole witness to the Gutenberg Bible in the making, in late 1454).[9] But the ready adaptation of the humanists, as of all literate classes of Italian society, to the innovation from the north, and the overall pre-eminence of Italy itself in early printing, are marks of the receptivity which long exposure to an active trade in books had brought. The *cartolaio* remained in the centre of the picture even with the arrival of print: he could organize paper stocks, find the large capitals sums needed to support the initial investment in men and materials while sales were awaited, supply workers for the hand-finishing of books and above all give access to networks of distribution which were, and are, essential for any successful publishing enterprise.

Some ten years after Enea Silvio saw the first fruits of Gutenberg's invention (and the technique was at first a closely confined secret), printing arrived in Italy with two German clerics. Conrad Sweynheym and Arnold Pannartz were part of the diaspora from Gutenberg's city of Mainz consequent upon political upheavals there in 1462. They set up their presses in the Benedictine abbey of Subiaco, some fifty miles east of Rome, where the first books were issued in 1464–5. Why they came to Subiaco is not known, but it is reasonable to suspect the involvement of the German churchman and philosopher, Cardinal Nicholas of Cusa (Cusanus), who had long been familiar to humanist circles in Italy. By the account of Giovanni Andrea Bussi, who had been his secretary from 1458 until the cardinal's death in 1464, Cusanus had always desired that the new method of multiplying books should be brought from Germany to Rome.[10]

Cusanus may well have seen in this 'sacred art' a means of disseminating more accurate and uniform texts for divine service, a cause we know to have been close to his heart. But of course there was no need to restrict one's output to any particular class of book – all early printers, naturally with individual bias and frequent miscalculation, printed whatever they thought would find a market. Sweynheym and Pannartz did not in fact print service books, nor indeed any law or scholastic theology, staples of early production elsewhere.[11] The character of their press was from the outset resolutely humanistic. This was signalled both by the texts they chose to print (classical and patristic, for the most part) and the form in which they printed them. The books appeared at first in a rather rough approximation to humanistic script, subsequently improved to something like the modern roman typeface when the printers moved to Rome in 1467. The two Germans also put themselves to the trouble of having two successive founts of Greek type cast in order to give the proper look to Latin books incorporating Greek quotations. Just as Gutenberg had modelled his layout and types on current gothic manuscript models (having no other), so Sweynheym and Pannartz attempted to reproduce the sort of books acceptable to cultivated Italian taste. This naturally also involved the hand-finishing which Italian buyers expected – book and chapter headings written in red, hand-painted initials at major divisions of the text, vine-stem borders on the first page and so on – often carried out in the printer's office. The humanist accent of the production of Sweynheym and Pannartz became more pronounced when they engaged Cusanus's old secretary to be their press editor. Bussi's prefaces, in one of which he speaks of Cusanus's hopes for printing, form one of the most fascinating set of documents of early printing.[12]

What had changed and how was the change perceived? We have an almost immediate reaction to the impact of print from the pen of one of the leading humanists of the day. Leon Battista Alberti, papal secretary and in the modern phrase 'universal man', tells us in his autobiography that he was in the habit of enquiring of all sorts of scholars, artists and craftsmen about their professional secrets. In the preface to another work, *De cifris* ('On Secret Writing'), written about 1466, he reports a most interesting conversation with another papal courtier which has every appearance of verisimilitude. Sitting in the Vatican gardens, they fell to talking about the remarkable German invention which enabled as few as 3 men to make 'by impression of characters' 200 copies of a given book in a 100 days.[13] This sort of calculus rapidly became a commonplace in early notices on printing, and we can suppose it is how Sweynheym and Pannartz introduced themselves and their work.[14]

The vast change of scale inherent in the new technology obviously had very great consequences for the economic operation of the book trade. But Italian scholars were not slow to see the advent of the press in terms of what it could do for their own works and reading matter. A humanist such as Francesco Filelfo, who had spent much of his long life copying out texts by hand, rejoiced in the new availability of books and sought to buy the earliest products of the Roman press.[15] From the point of view of the consumer, greatly increased numbers of books meant not only easier access to the texts in demand – many an earlier humanist letter is devoted to finding out just where a text might be had for copying – but also cheaper access. As Bussi proclaimed in his prefaces, learned works were now within the reach of poor students for the first time. He sent out priced lists of the books printed by Sweynheym and Pannartz to correspondents by way of advertising; one of them finished in the hands of the Nuremberg humanist and physician Hartmann Schedel, an indication of the reach of the international book trade.[16] Thanks to his good connections, with the Medici in particular, the Florentine scholar Angelo Poliziano had access to priceless manuscript treasures from the past; but when he wanted a text on which to enter collations, or simply to read, he would buy a printed book – convenient, legible and cheap.

Apart from considerations of price, a printed edition had the additional merit (generally speaking) of uniformity throughout all its copies, many hundreds at a time, which encouraged precise and systematic reference in a way not possible with manuscripts. In this way the Venetian humanist Ermolao Barbaro could key his entire series of textual corrections of the Elder Pliny, made in the early 1490s, to the 1472 Venice edition of the *Natural History* (figure 3.2).[17] Standardization of reference, and ease of actually finding one's way around a text with printed headlines, chapter sections, foliation and eventually pagination, were important advances for scholarship. None of these devices was unknown to the manuscript world, but in the nature of the case they were sporadic, inconsistent and individual in their application.

Standardization of the texts themselves was another important consequence of print. Outside very circumscribed situations, such as official textbooks of the major universities, it was impossible for central authorities to control the dissemination of accurate texts in the Middle Ages. Print gave texts fixity, for good or ill. The process of comparing manuscripts of a given work tended to result in a conflation of two or more streams of textual tradition which then became the intellectual property of an individual or

CAII PLYNII SECVNDI NATVRALIS HISTORIAE LIBER .I.

CAIVS PLYNIVS SECVNDVS NOVOCOMENSIS DOMITIANO
SVO SALVTEM.   PRAEFATIO.

IBROS NATVRALIS HISTORIAE NO-
uitium camœnis quiritium tuorum opus natum
apud me proxima fœtura licentiore epistola narrare constitui tibi iucundissime imperator. Sit.n.
hæc tui præfatio uerissima:dum maxio consenescit
in patre. Náq; tu solebas putare esse aliqd meas
nugas:ut obiicere moliar Catullum conterraneu
meum.Agnoscis & hoc castrese uerbum. Ille eni
ut scis:permutatis prioribus syllabis dunusculii
se fecit:q uolebat existiman a uernaculis tuis:&
famulis. Simul ut hac mea petulantia fiat:quod
proxime nó fieri questus es:i alia procaci episto-
la nostra:ut in quædam acta exeat. Sciantq; omnes:q ex æquo tecum uiuat:impium.
Triumphalis & censorius tu sextumque consul ac tribuniciæ potestatis particeps. Et
quod iis nobilius fecisti:dū illud patri pariter & equestri ordini præstas præfectus præ-
totii eius:omniaq; hæc reipub. Et nobis quidem qualis in castresi contubernio? Nec
quicq mutauit in te fortunæ amplitudo in iis:nisi ut prodesse tantundem posses: &
uelles. Itaq; cum cæteris in ueneratione tui pateant omnia illa:nobis ad colendum te
familiarius audacia sola superest. Hanc igitur tibi imputabis:& in nostra culpa tibi
ignoscens. Perfricui faciem:nec tamen profeci. Quando alia uia occurris ingens. Et
longius etiam submoues ingenii facibus. Fulgurat in nullo unq uenis dicta uis eloquentia. Tibi tribuniciæ potestatis facūdia. Quáto tu ore patris laudes tonas? Quáto fratris amas? Quantus in poetica es? O magna fœcunditas animi. Quéadmodū
fratrem quoq; imitareris:excogitasti. Sed hæc quis posset intrepidus æstimare?subi-
turus ingenii tui iudicium:præsertim lacessitum? Neque enim similis est conditio
publicantium:& nominatim tibi dicantium. Tum possem dicere:quid ista legis imperator? Humili uulgo scripta sunt: agricolarum: opificum turbæ: deniq; studioru
ociosis. Quid te iudicem facis? Cum hanc operam condicerem:non eras in hoc albo.
Maiorem te sciebam:q ut descensurum huc putarem. Præterea est quædam publica
etiam eruditorum reiectio. Vtitur illa &.M. Tullius extra omnem ingenii aleam po-
situs. Et quod miremur:per aduocatum defeditur. Hæc doctissimum omniū Persiū
legere nolo. Lælium Decimum uolo. Quod si hoc Lucilius qui primus cōdidit stili
nasum:dicedum sibi putauit. Si Cicero mutuandū:præsertim cum de repub. scribe-
ret:quanto nos causatius ab aliquo iudice diffidimus? Sed hæc ego mihi nunc patro-
cinia ademi nuncupatione. Quáplurimū refert:sortiatur ne aliquis iudicet:an eligat.
Multumque apparatus interest apud inuitatum hospitem & oblatum. Cum apud
Catonem illum ambitus hostem:& repulsis tanquam honoribus ineptis gaudentem:
flagrantibus comitiis pecunias deponerent candidati:hoc se facere:pro inocétia:quod
in rebus humanis summū esset:profitebát. Inde illa nobilis.M.Ciceronis suspiratio.
O te fœlicem.M.Porti a quo rem improbam petere nemo audet. Cum tribunos ap-
pellaret.L.Scipio Asiaticus:iter quos erat Gracchus:hoc attestabat:uel inimico iudici
se approbare posse. Adeo summum quisq; causæ suæ iudicem facit:quæcunq; eligit:
Vnde prouocatio appellatur. Te quidem in excelsissimo humani generis fastigio po-
situm summa eloquentia summa eruditione præditum religiose adiri etiam a salutá-
tibus scio. Et ideo immensa præter cæteras subit cura ut quæ tibi dicátur:cum digna

Figure 3.2   Roman type: the *Natural History* of Pliny the Elder, printed in 1472 at Venice by
Nicholas Jenson. This is a copy printed on vellum and illuminated by hand. British Library,
C.2.d.8, f. 4ʳ

small circle. With the appearance of printed books a *de facto* standard was set up to which scholars and students everywhere could bring correction or commentary. This was not so much by design as the outcome of ordinary human sloth. It was very much easier to reprint an existing edition than to set one up afresh from a manuscript, if only because the high cost of paper made accurate calculation of the length of a book a matter of vital concern to printers. The popular classical and patristic texts therefore tended to consolidate, not without exceptions or editorial interventions, into a vulgate text or *textus receptus*, received, that is, by the community of scholars at large. It was still possible for distinct strands of text to descend in parallel series of editions, but this is not generally the case, or not for very long, for works in which humanists took an interest. It is also true that many an early edition, or editor, proclaims a thorough revision of the text in hand which investigation shows to be at best wishful thinking, at worst imposture.

This power of the press to impose a measure of uniformity was felt from the beginning to be double-edged. The hasty correction which a hard-pressed editor such as Giovanni Andrea Bussi was obliged to carry out, very often on the first manuscript that came to hand, permitted corrupt texts to be put into wide circulation.[18] Even worse, an already corrupt text could become the vehicle of wilful emendation on the part of the editor. It was precisely this that provoked another papal curialist, Niccolò Perotti, Archbishop of Siponto, to attack Bussi's editing as early as 1471 and to call for centralized overseeing of texts issued at Rome. He says that he had thought the advent of printing was an inestimable boon to mankind until he set eyes on Bussi's 1470 edition of Pliny and realized that men of slight learning were now in a position to publish whatever they liked in hundreds of copies, without any sort of editorial responsibility or control. He proposes as a remedy that the pope should appoint a competent scholar (he thinks of himself) to supervise texts printed at Rome.[19]

Perotti himself, when Bussi ceased working for Sweynheym and Pannartz to become the papal librarian, got the chance to turn his hand to preparing editions for the same firm in 1473: his own work found no kindlier reception with a number of fellow humanists than Bussi's had with him. His Utopian scheme for control of the press came to nothing, but it did point up a troublesome aspect of the new invention. There were voices raised on the other side. Bussi saw his task as getting the material into print, and then correction of outstanding difficulties could follow as a sort of communal enterprise. Years later, in the Greek Theocritus of 1496, the Venetian printer Aldus Manutius took a similar complacent (or resigned) line, to the effect that something is better than nothing, and a text once printed can at least find many correctors where a manuscript can only receive occasional and individual emendation. This, of course, is true in the long run.

By the time of Aldus many humanists had long been closely associated with the press, as authors, editors and even printers (like Aldus himself, Felice Feliciano at Pojano, Bonaccorso da Pisa and Alessandro Minuziano at Milan). When in the late 1440s Filelfo had wanted to distribute fine copies of his *Satires*, he had had to organize a number of scribes to write out each manuscript. To have his translation of Xenophon's *Cyropaedia* attain wide circulation in 1476 he had only to hand a single manuscript – of course, corrected by the author – to the printer.[20] The scholars who came to hold university posts as professors of rhetoric – Domizio Calderini at Rome, Giorgio Merula at Venice, Filippo Beroaldo at Bologna and then Paris – seem to have encountered no difficulty in finding publishing outlets for their own writings (Poliziano had regular printers of his works on both sides of the Apennines, at Florence and Bologna) and for the classics upon which they commented. There was a steady demand for the staple schoolroom authors of antiquity, though some firms, notably Sweynheym and Pannartz at Rome and the first Venetian printers, suffered by over-estimating the rate at which the market could take up their products in this line. Many of these editions, perhaps most, came equipped with authoritative humanist commentary, the format soon falling into a small number of standard designs derived from manuscript models. And even if there was no commentary, there was still apt to be room for letters, poems, author's lives – small humanist adornments which gave employment to authors and pleasure to readers. Nearly 200 editions of Virgil and over 300 editions of Cicero in the fifteenth century alone, in an average print run of perhaps 500 copies, will give an idea of the scale of production and of the opportunities which print opened up.[21]

Reports of the death of the manuscript in the Renaissance have been greatly exaggerated, as are reports of the death of the book in our own.[22] There are probably as many manuscripts of the second half of the fifteenth century as of the first, and overall the (extant) production of that century outweighs in numbers all previous centuries put together. From the point of view of the humanist scholar, there were always works (if only one's own) which were either not available in print or not obtainable when they were: there are hundreds of manuscripts of the period copied from printed editions, and texts in Greek were very uncommon in print before the end of the century. Necessarily, one still relied on hand-copying.

From the point of view of professional scribes, the effect of the coming of print was to drive their products up-market. With the cutting of Nicholas Jenson's first roman fount in 1470, humanist handwriting was fixed in type of a beauty and regularity which few scribes could match (figure 3.2). Besides that, incunabula of the 1470s and 1480s, Venetian ones in particular, were often illuminated and decorated to a standard as high as that in any contemporary manuscript work.[23] By the 1490s this phase of extravagant illumination of printed books had waned, as printers found compelling economic reasons to enhance their books with cheaper wood-cuts. But these too were often the work of artists of the first rank working within the traditions of Veneto classicism, such as the unknown master who illustrated the famous *Hypnerotomachia Poliphili* (Venice, 1499), published by Aldus Manutius. Such developments left scribes to concentrate on luxury productions: dedication copies, copies for princely libraries, books bespoke and handmade. Yet even at the top end of the market, as at all lower levels, printed books were used alongside manuscripts indifferently, as variant forms of the same thing. Neither the Medici collections nor the extraordinary Italianate library of Matthias Corvinus in Hungary scorned the handsomest printed books of the day. Federico da Montefeltro, we are often told, felt it would be a matter of shame to have his library at Urbino sullied by print.[24] We seldom hear what research has now revealed, that Federico's library contained printed books alongside the luxurious vellum codices which for Vespasiano were the only books worth having.[25]

By the end of the fifteenth century the raw material of humanism – the written word – was available in manuscript and print in greater quantity and more cheaply than ever before. The worlds of the scribe and the printer were not separate but interacted in close and complex ways: many scribes became printers; illuminators might work for both equally; printed books adapted or adopted manuscript models and techniques. One such case may stand finally as an emblem of this interaction and its relation to humanism.

Successive refinements of the humanistic cursive hand had brought about towards the end of the century a special type of luxurious manuscript, usually containing a plain classical text (often poetry), without commentary, small in format and written in the neat but informal sloping hand ultimately derived from that of Niccolò Niccoli. The supreme master of this script and of this sort of book – not at all the style of dress in which incunable editions of the classics appeared – was the Paduan Bartolomeo Sanvito (see frontispiece). Sanvito worked for the Venetian noble Bernardo Bembo, among others, and some of his books for Bembo survive. In the preface to his Virgil edition of 1514, addressed to Bernardo's son, the humanist and vernacular author Pietro Bembo, Aldus Manutius remarks that it was the sight of books such as these in Bernardo's library that had given him years before the notion of his series of octavo classics. These were close and sympathetic renderings of the plain-text cursive manuscripts of Sanvito. For this class of literature and for printed books, they were novel in design, format and type – the Aldine italic. Thenceforth, from 1501 onwards, italic type and octavo format became the chief means by which classical literature was spread through Europe, not indeed primarily for scholars but for a cultivated public now open to the humanist message, in Latin, Greek and the vernacular.

The contributions of Aldus Manutius to European culture are manifold, his publication of the vast Greek Aristotle (1495–8) and of the *Opera* of Poliziano (1498) chief among them. The Aldine Greek types brought about something signally lacking up to that point, a distinctively humanist style of presentation of Greek texts.[26] Aldus combined in one person the figures of humanist-scholar and printer-publisher, thus setting the stage for the great scholar printers of the next century, the Frobens and the Estiennes. Behind all his varied and not always successful enterprises lay a simple, and for centuries very powerful idea: the humanist conviction that good letters lead, under God's guidance, to good men.

NOTES

1 B. L. Ullman, *The Origin and Development of Humanistic Script* (Rome, 1960), p. 13, quotes these passages (both dating from 1366) from Petrarch, *Familiares* XXIII.19.8 and *Seniles* VI.5.

2 MS Paris, Bibliothèque nationale, lat. 1989.

3 Coluccio Salutati, *Epistolario*, ed. F. Novati, 4 vols. (Rome, 1891–1911), III, p. 76, quoted by Ullman, *Origin*, p. 14. We have no humanist statement on what exactly they meant by *litterae antiquae* as applied to handwriting. The term itself was inherited from the fourteenth century where it was opposed to *litterae modernae*, Gothic script. For discussion of the semantic range (indicating Carolingian or humanistic scripts indifferently) see S. Rizzo, *Il lessico filologico degli umanisti* (Rome, 1973), pp. 117–22, and her article 'Gli umanisti, i testi classici e le scritture maiuscole', in C. Questa and R. Raffaelli, eds., *Il libro e il testo* (Urbino, 1984), pp. 223–41.

4 For a compact summary of the main features of humanist book production and decoration, see A. Derolez, 'Le livre manuscrit de la Renaissance', in *El libro antiguo español. Actas del segundo coloquio internacional* (Madrid, 1992), pp. 177–92.

5 Vespasiano da Bisticci, *Le vite*, ed. A. Greco, 2 vols. (Florence 1970–6), I, pp. 539–52, at 539–40 ('Vita di meser Poggio fiorentino').

6 Vespasiano da Bisticci, *Vite*, II, pp. 167–211, at 183 ('Vita di Cosimo de' Medici'). What is impressive is not so much the speed of copying as the highly centralized character of the process. For Parentucelli's *canon*: *ibid.*, I, pp. 35–81, at 46–7 n. 7 ('La vita di Nicolao P. P. V').

7 See A. Grafton, ed., *Rome Reborn: The Vatican Library and Renaissance Culture* (Washington DC, 1993).

8 Vespasiano da Bisticci, *Vite*, I, pp. 463–84, at 478 ('Vita di meser Lionardo d'Arezo').
9 See J. Ing, *Johann Gutenberg and his Bible* (New York, 1988), p. 67.
10 See most recently J. Röll, 'A crayfish in Subiaco', *The Library*, ser. 6, 16 (1994), 135–40. The connection of Cusanus with the enterprise of Gutenberg himself is unsubstantiated but hazarded by N. Barker, *Aldus Manutius: Mercantile Empire of the Intellect* (Los Angeles, 1989), pp. 13–14. The Spanish cardinal Juan de Torquemada may also have played a part in inviting the printers to Subiaco, where he was commendatory abbot.
11 The works of Nicholas of Lyra and Thomas Aquinas which Sweynheym and Pannartz printed are to be classed as Bible commentary rather than scholastic philosophy.
12 Conveniently gathered together with a substantial introduction in Giovanni Andrea Bussi, *Prefazioni alle edizioni di Sweynheym e Pannartz, prototipografi romani*, ed. by M. Miglio (Milan, 1978); see pp. 4–5 for the passage on Cusanus, which occurs in the preface to Jerome's *Letters* of 1468.
13 See Leon Battista Alberti, *Dello scrivere in cifra*, ed. A. Buonafalce (Turin, 1994), pp. 27–8. Alberti's interlocutor was Leonardo Dati, who happens to have owned an extant Subiaco book, Augustine's *City of God*, finished on 12 June 1467. Dati's copy in the Bibliothèque nationale in Paris mentions his purchase (the first of its kind known in Italy) of the book 'from the Germans themselves [now, in November 1467] living in Rome, who are accustomed not to writing but "printing" (*formare*) books of this sort without number': *Catalogue of Books Printed in the Fifteenth Century now in the British Museum* [hereafter *BMC*] (London, 1908–), IV, p. 2.
14 Compare the interesting preface of Nicolaus Gupalatinus to Johannes Mesue, *Opera medicinalia* (Venice, 1471), expounded by M. A. and R. H. Rouse, 'Nicolaus Gupalatinus and the arrival of print in Italy', *La Bibliofilia*, 88 (1986), 221–47.
15 L. A. Sheppard, 'A fifteenth-century humanist: Francesco Filelfo', *The Library*, ser. 4, 16 (1935), 1–26.
16 See Miglio in Bussi, *Prefazioni*, p. lvi, and the whole chapter on 'Il prezzo dei libri', pp. lv–lxiii; cf. also 'Il costo del libro' in *Scrittura, biblioteche e stampa a Roma nel Quattrocento. Atti del 2° seminario ... 1982*, ed. M. Miglio (Vatican City, 1983), pp. 323–553. A similar priced list exists sent by Bussi to the Milanese envoy at Rome, Nicodemo Tranchedini. Hartmann Schedel had been trained in Italy in the humanities and medicine: he bought humanist manuscripts and printed books alike, many of which still survive, and he was later responsible for a world history, the famous *Nuremberg Chronicle* printed in 1493.
17 Ermolao Barbaro, *Castigationes Plinianae et in Pomponium Melam*, ed. G. Pozzi, 4 vols. (Padua, 1973–9). The work was first published in Rome, 1492–3; no manuscripts of it are known.
18 Compare (as Kenney himself does) C. Bühler, *The Fifteenth-Century Book* (Philadelphia, 1960), p. 41: 'The invention of the press came at a time exactly suitable for its advent' with E. J. Kenney, *The Classical Text. Aspects of Editing in the Age of the Printed Book* (Berkeley, 1974), p. 1: 'From the point of view of the editor of texts it can be said ... that the new invention could hardly have come at a worse moment.'

19 See M. C. Davies, 'Making sense of Pliny in the Quattrocento', *Renaissance Studies*, 9 (1995), 239–55. The broadcasting of corruption by the press was a common theme from Merula to Erasmus and beyond: see M. M. Phillips, *The 'Adages' of Erasmus: A Study with Translations* (Cambridge, 1964), p. 73.

20 Though it must be said he was sadly dissatisfied with the result: Sheppard, 'Filelfo', 14–15.

21 A lengthy analysis of classical and humanist printing in fifteenth-century Italy is given in the introduction to *BMC*, VII, pp. x–xix (by Victor Scholderer). See also Scholderer's 'Printers and readers in Italy in the fifteenth century', in his *Fifty Essays in Fifteenth- and Sixteenth-Century Bibliography*, ed. D. E. Rhodes (Amsterdam, 1966), pp. 202–15.

22 On the first point, scribal publication continued for centuries in specific circumstances. On the second, all the authors in this present volume have composed their chapters on a computer and submitted their work on disk; the book has been computer typeset, and matters of distribution and sale will be firmly guided by computers. The result is a printed book in codex form and roman type which a humanist of 500 years ago would have no difficulty in recognizing. And so it seems likely to continue for some time yet.

23 Some of the best work of both sorts is amply illustrated in the exhibition catalogue edited by J. J. G. Alexander, *The Painted Page: Italian Renaissance Book Illumination* (London, 1994), though this does not deal exclusively with books we can associate with humanists; see especially Lilian Armstrong's contribution, 'The hand-illuminated printed book', pp. 163–208.

24 The story comes from Vespasiano da Bisticci, *Vite*, I, pp. 355–416, at 398 ('Vita del signore Federico, duca d'Urbino'); pp. 385–99 are taken up with the account of the creation of what Vespasiano regarded as a model humanist library.

25 See A. C. de la Mare, 'Vespasiano da Bisticci e i copisti fiorentini di Federico', in *Federico di Montefeltro: lo stato, le arti, la cultura*, 3 vols. (Rome, 1986), III, pp. 81–96, at 96 n. 80.

26 The Aldine types crystallized a particular strand of contemporary Hellenic calligraphy into a standard for hundreds of years. For the background see the amply illustrated book by P. Eleuteri and P. Canart, *Scrittura greca nell'umanesimo italiano* (Milan, 1991).

4

The humanist reform of Latin and Latin teaching

KRISTIAN JENSEN

Despite the many changes which were made during the Renaissance, humanist Latin represented a development of both the forms and the functions of medieval Latin. Latin was the language of the educated and of, if not the ruling, at least the governing classes. Not knowing Latin demonstrated that one did not belong to these social groups. In the Middle Ages, Latin was the international language of secular and ecclesiastical administration, of diplomacy, of liturgy and of the educational institutions where students were prepared for positions in these spheres. Interest in Latin was motivated by practical concerns. Official correspondence in Latin was the most important task of those engaged in church and secular administration. The *ars dictaminis*, or art of letter-writing, had been a central feature of late medieval education in Italy, but less so north of the Alps, where university education was directed towards theological rather than legal training. In post-medieval Italy, Latin retained all these functions, and the art of writing letters and composing orations remained important aspects of Latin education.

In no area were prestige and presentation of greater importance than in matters of state. International affairs were transacted in Latin through the exchange of letters and through orations delivered by envoys. Humanist Latin emerged in the fourteenth and early fifteenth centuries in Italy among men in the highest ranks of ecclesiastical or civil administration. Chancellors of Florence, such as Leonardo Bruni and Poggio Bracciolini, both of whom had also served as secretaries to the pope, were prominent exponents. The power of this new style of Latin diplomacy was exalted (with some exaggeration) by a humanist of the next generation, Enea Silvio Piccolomini, later Pope Pius II; he reported that Duke Giangaleazzo Visconti of Milan was frequently heard to say that Coluccio Salutati's writings had done him more harm than 1,000 Florentine horsemen.[1] Prestige was what humanist educators in Italy aimed to enable their students to achieve for their employers or their patrons.

Although humanist education and humanist Latin drew in part on French learning, they essentially grew out of Italian traditions and needs, and from Italy spread throughout Europe. Since knowledge of Latin was a sign of status, the more advanced one's command of the language, the greater the social cachet attached to it. The standard by which the achievement was to be measured was in no doubt: the superiority of the Latin written by the great authors of the classical past – Cicero, Terence, Virgil, Horace and Ovid – had been central to the curriculum of medieval schools and remained so in humanist schools, although the list of authors who were frequently read was extended. The claim made in Italy that the new Latin emulated the best ancient Latin was generally regarded as justified.

The international political function of Latin as a language of power is clearly expressed in the introduction to Lorenzo Valla's *Elegantiae linguae Latinae* (1441-9), a title which is perhaps best translated as 'Advanced Idiomatic Latin'. There he describes how, although the Roman empire had perished as a political force, in a deeper and truer sense it still survived: 'To us belongs Italy, to us belongs France, to us belong Spain, Germany, Hungary, Dalmatia, Illyricum and many other nations. For the Roman empire is found where the Roman language holds sway.'[2] He emphasizes Roman supremacy by using the phrase *lingua Romana*, as against the normal *lingua Latina*. Valla's *lingua Romana* could lay claim to superiority over all of learned Europe because it was not filled with the unclassical expressions and syntax introduced by invading hordes of barbarians; it was instead, as he sets out in detail in the book, the accomplished and polished language of ancient – and modern – Rome. This is partly to be understood in connection with Valla's contention that there was an unbroken linguistic tradition in Rome: even the Italian vernacular now spoken by the people of Rome was distantly related to the colloquial Latin of the ancient Roman masses.[3] Valla's linguistic empire was ostensibly unattached to any political entity. He even dissociated it from the ancient Roman empire: the subject peoples had had good reason to reject its laws and decrees, which to them were merely tools of oppression; but while they had rejected the political dominion of Rome, they had retained the benefit of the Roman language. Nevertheless, Valla's programme was not merely to establish humanist Latin as the international language but to give priority to the Latin of papal Rome – a programme which, not coincidentally, would facilitate a career for himself at the papal curia.

It is easy to detect an anti-imperial attitude in Valla's words. The Holy Roman Empire derived its political legitimacy from a supposed continuity of power transferred from the ancient empire of Rome. Valla's definition of proper Latin was an attack on this political heritage. Anti-imperial and therefore anti-German propaganda is frequently found in Italian humanist circles in the fifteenth century. Its motivation was partly political – imperial troops interfered directly in the affairs of Italian city states, culminating with the Sack of Rome by the German emperor's troops in 1527 – and partly economic. The controversy concerning the transfer of capital from Germany to Rome through ecclesiastical dues, which was to become a central issue in the Reformation, was already perceived as a serious problem in the fifteenth century. The specific form given to anti-imperial propaganda was often that of reminding Germans of their barbarian forebears, who were responsible for the destruction of ancient civilization. What clearer sign of their continued barbaric nature than their barbarous Latin? Thus, in addition to the function of humanist Latin as an indication of personal social status, and its role in the political rivalries between Italian states, it carried a clear political message of Italian cultural supremacy over the rest of Europe – despite the political realities.

German authors were painfully aware of this line of attack. Johannes Santritter, a German settled in Venice, complained that the astronomical works of his compatriot Johannes Regiomontanus had not had the reception in Italy which they deserved. He explained the Italians' failure to appreciate Regiomontanus's writings by their hatred of everything German. This hatred was put down to envy of the technically competent Germans, who had invented printing and who championed all the practical sciences. Only in one area did Italians have the advantage: Germans had not yet learned to write Latin as elegantly as they did. 'But even in Italy proper Latin was once forgotten', wrote Santritter, 'and I hope that it will not be long before eloquence, the queen of all things, will attain perfection in our country as well. Our Roman empire shall not long be deprived of the language which is its own. The Roman language (*lingua Romana*) shall rejoice in rejoining its own empire.'[4] We hear an echo of Valla's words in the phrase *lingua Romana*, but his argument has been turned round to claim the Roman language for the Holy Roman Empire. The point, none the less, was conceded that the proper form of Latin was that used by Italian humanists. Similarly, when Dietrich Gresemund, a well-educated son of a Mainz patrician family, went to Padua to study law in the 1490s, he had an unhappy time. His friends could only accept him by maintaining that his good qualities proved that he was not a real German. Gresemund could usually console himself by his sense that the attacks were unjustified; when, however, the Italians laughed at his Latin, he had to admit that they were right.[5]

By the late fifteenth century, Italian superiority on the cultural and linguistic level was well established. The main goal of educational reformers throughout Europe was to achieve the same command of classical Latin as that which was found in Italy. If they failed to compete, they would lose their best students. Jakob Wimpfeling, who promoted reform in German schools from around the end of the fifteenth century, explained in his book, *Isidoneus Germanicus de erudienda iuventute* ('A Doorway to Learning for German Youth', *c.* 1497), why it was imperative for good Latin to be taught in Germany: 'To foreigners we seem barbarians, because the few Germans who get a good education spend their lives on grammatical trivialities ... If the need were to arise, they would be unable to receive a distinguished foreign visitor with an elegant speech or to address them courteously.'[6] In another work, *Germania* (1501), Wimpfeling warned the burghers of Strasbourg that reform of their school was essential if they wished their young men to be able to compete and obtain high positions in the administration of the Church or the Empire or to be able to undertake diplomatic functions for their city. Here again we see that a career either in civil or ecclesiastical administration or in diplomacy was the goal of the educated members of the higher strata of society.

The allure of Italian education was by no means confined to Germany. 'I am purposid', wrote an early sixteenth-century Englishman, 'to leue my cuntre and go in-to italie and that oonly for the desire of latyn and greke, for thought I can fynd here in ynglonde that can thech me, yet by-cause I thynke I can lerne better ther than her I haue a gret desire to goo thether.'[7]

In the years before 1430, Guarino of Verona composed a Latin grammar for pupils just beyond the elementary stages of education, who had already learned how to decline nouns and conjugate verbs. The topics with which his textbook dealt, and the way in which it dealt with them, show the continuity between humanist Latin grammar and the elementary Latin taught in the late Middle Ages. Guarino's chief reform was a significant reduction in technical vocabulary: he stressed the desirability of brevity and simplicity as principles for grammatical instruction. After Guarino, many other Italian writers composed grammars and, aided by the opportunities offered by the invention of printing, some of these works were widely distributed throughout Europe. They differ in matters of detail, some being more prone to retain aspects of late medieval terminology, others less so; but all are basically similar in their approach to the topic.

In a textbook first published in the mid-1480s, an anonymous Low German author, in a chapter entitled 'Complaint that schoolboys are made to spend too much time on obscure, long-winded and useless aspects of grammar' recommended an approach modelled on that used in Italy:

Italian teachers have this praiseworthy habit with boys whose education is entrusted to them: as soon as they have learned the most elementary grammar they are immediately set to work on the best poet, Virgil, and the comedies of Terence and Plautus. They study the *Epistulae ad familiares*, *De amicitia*, *De senectute*, *Paradoxa Stoicorum* and other works by Cicero. This is why they outshine all other nations in writing rich and elegant Latin ... Little boys need a few brief rules which will lead them rapidly to their goal.[8]

This sums up an outsider's view of the reasons for the success of Latin teaching in Italy. Medieval grammatical textbooks were considered to be too complicated. This criticism was two-pronged. Partly it was directed against normative grammars, where rules were laid down: for instance, the *Doctrinale* (1199), a popular grammar in verse by the Frenchman Alexander de Villa Dei. Alexander's rules were obscurely phrased in poor verse; in addition, they were often incorrect according to the new standard set by humanists aspiring to imitate classical authors. Alexander's grammar became a symbol of the bad Latin taught in the Middle Ages.[9] In Italy, national considerations here too played a role. The author of a Latin grammar printed in Venice in 1480 expressed his frustration that until recently Italians had been compelled to learn Latin – their own language – from the works of barbarian foreigners.[10]

The other aspect of grammar which was condemned was the theoretical approach found in many medieval works. Perhaps the most severely criticized was the Danish author Martinus de Dacia, who came to symbolize a speculative, philosophical approach to grammar. Martinus was a *modista*, that is, he was engaged in the study of how words refer to the world (the *modi significandi*); he therefore viewed language as a logically explicable structure. Neither normative nor descriptive, modist grammar set out a philosophy of meaning. But the grammatical terminology created by the *modistae* for philosophical purposes was also employed by normative grammarians. This link between philosophy, especially logic, and the description of Latin was fiercely resisted by humanists. For them, the sole aim of grammar was to teach Latin usage. The study of grammar therefore had no value in itself: grammar was a tool, and as such it should be dealt with as succinctly as possible.

Francesco Priscianese, author of a Latin grammar first published in Rome in 1540, declared that modern languages could be learned without any great effort, whereas Latin and Greek could only be acquired at the cost of much sweat and labour. It took a long time, and most of those who began ended in failure. This was because both ancient and more recent grammarians of Latin and Greek had been inclined to teach their pupils grammar rather than language.[11] The tendency to organize the material in grammars without a view to the needs of the teaching process was frequently criticized. But while this complaint was often repeated, no thorough attempt at finding a solution was made by any humanist grammarian. The very hostility of humanists to the theoretical approach to grammar made it difficult for them to develop a radically new concept of their own. Like the grammars produced by their late medieval predecessors, the textbooks written by humanists continued to be based on ultimately philosophical considerations of the structure of language rather than being organized around a clear notion of which aspects of grammar might be more conveniently taught before others.

In *De ratione studii* ('On the Method of Study', 1511), Erasmus gave advice as to the best textbook of Latin grammar:

> There is not much difference to detect among contemporary Latin grammarians. Niccolò Perotti seems the most accurate, yet not pedantic. But while I grant that grammatical rules of this sort are necessary, I want them to be as few as possible, provided they are good. I have never approved of the approach found among run of the mill grammarians who spend several years inculcating such rules in their pupils.[12]

Niccolò Perotti's *Rudimenta grammatices* ('Elementary Grammar', 1468) was the most widely diffused humanist Latin grammar of the late fifteenth century. Much longer than that of Guarino, it is chiefly distinguished from earlier works in the genre by its exclusion of many words and types of construction which derived from medieval, as opposed to classical, Latin, and by its provision of extensive discussions of classical words which had not previously found their way into elementary grammars. Much of the information contained in Perotti's grammar would appear to us to belong properly in a dictionary. In this respect he followed his late medieval predecessors. But there was a difference. Vocabulary which had been in general use in late medieval Latin was now subjected to careful historical and philological scrutiny.

In the later Middle Ages it had been commonly accepted that words achieved their meaning by social convention. While a theoretical link could be established between the things referred to by words and the mental processes which lay behind the meaning of words, phonetic structures bore no logical relation to the objects which they signified. The consequence of this was that linguistic correctness depended on the consensus of users; so words could be made up when convenient, and language could be manipulated for the purposes of those who employed it. Late medieval Latin is characterized by highly flexible rules for creating new words. Philosophers, theologians and lawyers all devised a vocabulary and a phraseology specific to their disciplines. The deviation of philosophers from classical usage (*usus*) was attacked by Valla in his *Repastinatio dialectice et philosophie* ('Reworking of Dialectic and Philosophy', three versions, produced from the 1430s to 1457).[13] While humanists agreed that usage determined linguistic correctness, contemporary Latin usage had no normative value in their eyes. Only the usage of ancient authors was acceptable, whereas that which had grown up in the various scholastic disciplines seemed to humanists to rest on the mistaken assumption that language could be created by an act of rationality. The concept of usage thus became linked to the concept of authority (*auctoritas*): knowledge of linguistic correctness was to be derived from ancient texts. The proper meaning of words was now to be firmly based on the usage current in classical times.

Much of the effort of humanist grammarians was directed towards purifying the Latin language of words which could not be found in classical authors. The aim was to banish medieval neologisms and replace them with classical equivalents. In the absence of a thorough lexicography of ancient Latin, this was no easy task and largely depended on an individual's assimilation of the classical idiom through extensive reading and memorization of approved authors. Even more difficult was the eradication of the unclassical use of classical words.

The demand for a precise understanding of classical usage was not merely antiquarian. Schoolteachers responded to the needs of men engaged in professions where the correct understanding of classical texts was essential. Physicians, for instance, were required to understand the Latin terminology found in the Elder Pliny's *Natural History* in order to ensure that they had an accurate knowledge of the medicinal proprieties of plants or minerals. Lawyers needed to understand the exact meaning of classical words in order to provide correct interpretations of the law – the section of the *Digest* (the main corpus of Roman law, compiled under Emperor Justinian) entitled 'On the Meaning of Words' became the basis of humanist legal education.

Perotti's *Rudimenta grammatices*, in the version which he himself produced, laid down rules for a more classical Latin than that presented in the textbooks of his medieval predecessors. In subsequent editions, however, late medieval constructions and words which Perotti had excluded or even explicitly rejected were reinstated as prescribed usage. A similar tendency can been observed in relation to Perotti's description of the correct style for a humanist letter, which was explicitly directed against the recommendations of medieval letter-writing manuals. In later editions of his work, we find that his rules were reversed, and phrases and forms rejected by him were once again advocated.

The establishment of a proper understanding of the ancient Latin vocabulary was a central concern for Valla in his *Elegantiae*. This book was not, however, a viable tool for teaching classical usage to schoolboys. His information was too descriptive and insufficiently normative; moreover, the work itself was too long and too expensive. Compendia based on Valla's treatise were soon made in order to provide small reference books on the meaning and proper construction of words. As in the case of Perotti's grammar, these compendia did not invariably prescribe the sort of Latin which Valla himself had proposed. This is certainly true of those compiled in Italy;[14] and across the Alps the distance between Valla's Latin and that found in works claiming to be based on him was even greater. One grammar first published in Basel around 1485 purports to be an adaptation of Valla but in reality bears no relationship to any of his works.[15] We are therefore confronted with a discrepancy between claims to follow the new humanist model of Latin and a practice which turns out to be rather different.

There were many reasons for this reluctant adoption of the new linguistic norms, despite declarations of support for their underlying principles. Part of the explanation is to be found in the difference between the types of school where Latin was taught. While mastery of Latin could help gain access to influential positions because of the importance attached to presentational skills, the foundation on which these skills were built was often laid in humble schoolrooms by humble schoolteachers. Some Italian masters, Guarino for instance, ran private boarding schools for pupils from the ruling élite. Humanist education was initially reserved for pupils at such institutions; only gradually did it penetrate into less exclusive schools. For municipal schools, cities usually hired teachers whose status was not particularly high, whose qualifications were not always the best and whose remuneration was slight. The comprehensive reform of the Latin language attempted in the foremost humanist schools was emulated, with varying degrees of success, by modest teachers of students with lower social ambitions.

A second explanation of this conservatism is the commercial nature of the publication of school texts. Wimpfeling, in his *Isidoneus*, blamed greedy printers for attempting to sell outdated textbooks.[16] Their greed would not, however, have been satisfied had they not catered for a market. Conversely, a printer would be reluctant to embark on the speculative publication of a revolutionary textbook which ran the risk of not being accepted by a sufficiently large number of teachers. Schools, moreover, were dependent on the books which were at their disposal. Even in a wealthy book-producing centre like Nuremberg this could be a problem: in 1511 a newly appointed schoolmaster explained that the grammar which had previously been in sole use was the only printed textbook available.[17]

In the third place, schools are by nature conservative institutions. Teachers teach what they themselves have been taught. Furthermore, they are subject to the demands of parents who worry that untried modern methods might put their children at a disadvantage. Giovanni Sulpizio, in a grammar written around 1475, made it clear that parents were the greatest obstacle to a reform of the curriculum: 'What is the use of it all if parents insist that their children are brought up on Alexander [de Villa Dei]? Our corrupt values are the misfortune of our children. Alas, I could weep and cry out in protest.'[18] In 1511 a Netherlandish author, Hermannus Torrentinus, mentioned objections even to modifications of Alexander's grammar. Those who remembered how they themselves had sweated over Alexander's obscure rules demanded that youngsters should be put to the same hard work and not be corrupted by an easy life.[19]

While the conservatism of parents, teachers and educational institutions was an important factor, the slowness with which the new linguistic norms were assimilated was also influenced by the fact that Latin was still a living language. Words were not merely learned from books, grammars and commentaries but also from the spoken language, where unclassical words of long standing could not be easily expunged. This underlines the element of continuity between late medieval and humanist Latin and also highlights the difficulty of radically reforming a language which is part of an ongoing tradition.

Although progress towards the widespread adoption of a more classical Latin was hampered by conservatism, grammar books and other newly written school texts played a role in the gradual reform of the language by increasingly describing and prescribing a classically based vocabulary. Some grammars were structured almost like dictionaries: they abandoned the systematic description of types of verbal construction and instead listed verbs alphabetically, with an indication of the construction after each verb. Nevertheless, rules of grammar and of classical usage were not taught through manuals alone, nor was it thought possible to do so, if only because many aspects of classical Latin grammar found no place in humanist grammars.

It was a commonplace that the brevity of grammatical instruction provided by humanist grammars enabled pupils to leave manuals behind and progress to the reading of ancient authors. Since the theory behind grammar was found to have no value in itself, a quick move on to practice was desirable. Further grammatical instruction and further acquisition of a classical vocabulary were to be gained through the meticulous examination of ancient texts.

This sounds more straightforward than it actually was, for ancient authors had not written their works with the teaching of Latin as a foreign language in mind. Classical texts were not graded by difficulty, and no work was written with complete beginners in mind. For elementary reading, a group of eight texts had been much used in the late Middle Ages. These are often found together in manuscripts and printed books and are known collectively as the *auctores octo*. They are all texts with a moralizing tendency; but, from a humanist point of view, none of them was notable for elegant Latin. Of the eight works, two – the *Disticha Catonis*, morally uplifting verses attributed to Cato, and a Latin translation of a collection of Greek fables ascribed to Aesop – survived as school texts well into the sixteenth century, even in schools which aspired to humanist ideals of Latinity. The others disappeared from the curriculum in Italy before the advent of printing and, towards the end of the fifteenth century, even in northern Europe. Another collection of moral sayings in verse, organized alphabetically and known as the *Proverbs*, had gained a wide readership because it was erroneously thought to be by the philosopher Seneca. Erasmus published it in 1514, pointing out that the ascription to Seneca was false. Thereafter, it soon fell out of use in schools.[20]

Humanists could not, however, do without elementary introductory texts. One of the *auctores octo* was an anonymous text, *Facetus*, which prescribed manners for schoolboys. In a more humanist curriculum this work was often replaced by Giovanni Sulpizio's versified set of instructions on good table manners.[21] Classical works were still read after texts composed for introductory purposes. First published in 1500, Erasmus's *Adagia*, a collection of moral sayings, was used in schools much like the *Disticha Catonis*. Erasmus also composed a collection of phrases for use in daily conversation, *Familiarium colloquiorum formulae* (1518), organized by topic; these were later reworked into little dialogues or *Colloquies* (1522–33), widely adopted in schools.[22] Erasmus and others who wrote in this genre aimed at teaching colloquial Latin by describing humdrum, daily events and thus providing pupils with a vocabulary for their everyday needs.

Later in the curriculum classical works were introduced. Many texts read in humanist schools had also been common in late medieval syllabuses. As with the more elementary texts, classical authors were chosen for their moral as well as their linguistic qualities. Terence's comedies, school texts throughout the Middle Ages, retained their position as one of the most frequently read works in schools. Plautus, the other surviving Roman writer of comedies, was also studied, but to a lesser extent. He belonged to an older generation than Terence, and his language did not reflect the usage which students were supposed to imitate, although his comedies were a marvellous source of colloquial Latin. Plautus' comedies were also generally thought to be less edifying than those of Terence, which could – with some good will – be read as exhortations to sexual continence, marital fidelity, obedience to one's parents and other secular virtues.[23]

The letters of Cicero to his friends (*Ad familiares*) also became a central part of the curriculum. Relatively unknown until the 1490s, they were probably the single most important addition to the basic canon of school authors. Like the comedies of Terence, they were important because they displayed a classical Latin which, although polished, was, if not colloquial, at least informal. Cicero's orations and works on moral philosophy, particularly *De amicitia*, *De senectute* and *Paradoxa Stoicorum*, were read at a higher level, partly for their moral content, but mainly because they provided an excellent pattern to follow in linguistic and stylistic matters. By contrast, Seneca's letters, another body of philosophical texts, were not regarded as desirable models for imitation; however, on account of the widely diffused spurious correspondence between him and St Paul, Seneca acquired the status of an honorary Christian.[24] Some classical works were read at a more advanced level as textbooks of rhetoric: most frequently the Pseudo-Ciceronian *Ad Herennium* and Cicero's *De oratore*; the *Institutio oratoria* of Quintilian, on the other hand, the complete text of which was rediscovered by Poggio in 1416, never became part of the curriculum.

Humanists often emphasized the importance of historical works in the syllabus, deploring the bad old days when ancient historians had not been read in schools. While the *Factorum et dictorum memorabilium libri IX* of Valerius Maximus had been studied in the Middle Ages and remained an important text in humanist schools, other historians, previously less read, now became more common. Livy, above all, to a lesser degree Sallust and, in Germany, Tacitus were read as examples of the exalted style suitable for describing the momentous feats of great men of the past. These authors also provided much information on the institutions of the Roman republic and the early empire. Studying history was part of linguistic training, but it also contributed to the student's moral and political education. The glorious and virtuous acts of heroes and heroines were held out as examples to be imitated, if not in one's own life, at least in one's writing. Celebrated figures of the past were used as literary *exempla* in Latin works about notable contemporaries, whose character and actions were compared to those of their ancient precursors. Caesar, the mainstay of nineteenth-century classical education, had different stylistic aspirations from Roman historians in the grand manner; in addition, he wrote few stories from which a moral could be drawn and did not offer much information on the political institutions of the Roman state; consequently, he was less frequently read in schools.[25]

Poets had been the most important element in the more advanced level of the medieval education, and they remained fundamental in humanist schools: Virgil, mainly the *Eclogues* and *Georgics*, but also the *Aeneid*; Horace's *Odes*; the epics of Statius; Lucan's *Bellum civile*; Juvenal's *Satires*; Ovid's *Metamorphoses* and *Tristia*; and the tragedies of Seneca. Like their prose counterparts, they were read mainly for their linguistic features. Grammar books contained rules for composing in the classical metres, since poetry was regarded as a skill which could be learned – more difficult than, but in essence no different from, other types of literary production. In 1526 the German humanist and religious reformer Philipp Melanchthon wrote that anyone unable to write poetry was not entitled to hold an opinion in learned matters, nor indeed could such a person be said to be a competent writer of prose.[26] The vast quantity of poems produced by humanists for specific occasions – political events, marriages, births, deaths, the publication of new books – demonstrates that poetry was viewed as a practical accomplishment rather than an inspired art.[27]

It must be stressed that not all humanist schools had a reading programme as extensive as this. Historians were read at the best schools only. In good but small schools students would not get much beyond Cicero's letters, Terence and Virgil. Some schools – even among those which sought to teach humanist Latin – retained a very conservative curriculum. For example, the 1508 statutes for St Paul's School, drawn up by John Colet and highly praised by Erasmus, described a syllabus that, with a few exceptions, any late medieval schoolmaster would have recognized.[28]

Reproducing the style of ancient authors was the chief aim of teaching written Latin in schools. Exercises consisted in writing prose or poetry which emulated a particular author's manner of expression. Melanchthon's belief that good prose writing depended on knowing how to compose poetry reflects what in the course of the fifteenth century had become one of the distinguishing aspects of humanist Latin: a concern for linguistic decorum. Whereas much medieval prose writing had contained poetic words, this was shunned in humanist Latin; and it was only by acquiring familiarity with the poetic vocabulary that one could avoid using it in a prose context. A poem should not include informal phrases found in Cicero's letters, while a letter should contain neither the high-flown prose of the historians nor the distinctive phraseology of the poets. Classical authors were to be imitated, but with discrimination.

The stylistic ideal of imitation required that the Latin language be purified of medieval words and phrases, since – as we have seen – classical usage was the criterion of correctness. It was obvious, however, that ancient authors wrote very differently from one another. Until the end of the sixteenth century, Seneca was not usually recommended as a model, nor was Sallust and even less Tacitus. Among the poets, few would have thought that Catullus or Martial were suitable to be imitated. There was a need to define a linguistic canon; and in the fifteenth and early sixteenth centuries the most radical solution to this problem was that proposed by the Ciceronians, who contended that only words found in Cicero were acceptable. This, in fact, posed insurmountable problems, and the movement always had more adherents in theory than in practice. It was opposed by many fifteenth-century humanists, among them Lorenzo Valla, who argued that new words were demanded by the contemporary social situation, which was very different from that which had existed in Cicero's day.[29] Moreover, arguments against Ciceronianism could be found in writings by Cicero himself, who had been quite happy to coin new words, particularly in the field of philosophy, when he felt they were needed.

The Church was an institution that had grown up in the post-classical period, and consequently numerous non-classical words were used to describe its structures, functions and functionaries. Many words had been borrowed from Greek; others were created in the Middle Ages, on the basis of classical words but not in accordance with classical morphology. Ciceronians sought to replace such terms with truly Latin words, that is, words found in Cicero. This involved using pagan terminology in Christian contexts: nuns were described as vestal virgins, priests as *flamines*, churches as temples. Erasmus, following Valla – as he so often did in both linguistic and religious matters – ridiculed this movement in his *Ciceronianus* ('The Ciceronian', 1528), which, with typically Erasmian irony, he wrote in the form of a Ciceronian dialogue, employing highly polished Latin. Erasmus saw Ciceronianism, which had found particular favour in papal Rome,[30] as an expression of the excessive worldliness and paganism of the papacy. Recognizing, but rejecting, the ideological link between the Church and ancient Rome, he had one of his characters say: 'Rome is not Rome. Nothing remains but ruins and debris, the scars and remnants of ancient calamities.'[31]

Ciceronianism disappeared from Roman circles shortly thereafter, not so much because of the blows dealt it by Erasmus as because of the new intellectual and religious climate associated with the Counter-Reformation.

Stronger links to the Church Fathers were demanded, which resulted in the stylistic and linguistic norms of patristic literature becoming dominant in the Rome of the late sixteenth century. But despite the criticisms levelled at it, the cult of Cicero continued as a force outside Rome. Soon France, with its new claims to cultural and political supremacy, became a centre of Ciceronianism.

Ciceronianism required the rejection of vocabulary which over a period of centuries had been adapted to fit every aspect of daily life, ranging from words for household implements to titles of public positions, institutions and functions. Such sweeping changes were very difficult to achieve. As we know from contemporary societies where linguistic reform has been attempted, much less radical reforms create problems for cultural and literary continuity. So, for instance, when Bishop Richard Foxe drew up statutes for Corpus Christi at Oxford in 1517, he wrote a general preface in humanist Latin; but he had to issue a warning that *barbara uocabula* ('barbarous words') were unavoidable for describing the workings of the college.[32]

The consequences were even more drastic for those academic disciplines which had developed a refined technical vocabulary during the late Middle Ages. In particular, the non-classical terminology used in logic and metaphysics came under attack. Valla's critique of late medieval logic had grave implications for all philosophical disciplines – indeed, for everything taught at university. Valla's attitudes were echoed in Martin Luther's rejection of metaphysics in the early 1520s. Precise technical terms were denounced as meaningless and as serving only to disguise the simple truth of faith. In this area neither the polemics of the humanists nor those of their Protestant followers were entirely successful. Philosophical discourse at universities continued to depend on medieval terminology.

Nevertheless, the general acceptance of humanist Latin as the norm had a profound impact on many university disciplines. Students who were used to reading humanist Latin and had been taught to judge works on their stylistic merit sometimes found it difficult to muster a profound interest in texts which were far from elegant, no matter how intellectually challenging they might be. In 1530 a small, easy textbook of natural philosophy by Giorgio Valla was edited by Heinrich Sybold, a professor of medicine at Strasbourg and also a publisher. Sybold wrote a preface in which he expressed the wish that the book would entice students back to the study of philosophy. He hoped Giorgio Valla's elegant Latin might arouse an interest among students whose apathetic attitude towards philosophy was due to their pedantic concern with style. Their disregard for philosophy, he asserted, had dire consequences for all university subjects.[33]

A danger inherent in the humanists' passionate interest in presentation and style was a disdain for factual knowledge. Teaching students to collect phrases and commonplaces from the works they read was an essential part of their training in imitation. Expressions they had excerpted were to be reused on suitable occasions, thus allowing ignorance of a topic to be disguised behind a skilful display of conventional utterances. Melanchthon, in his elementary rhetoric textbook, pointed to one of the problems brought about by the success of humanist educators when he warned against the attitude that compiling a list of sentences from classical poets and orators was equivalent to true knowledge. While he maintained that the use of commonplaces was necessary for both thought and expression, he insisted that a commonplace could not be understood without careful study of the discipline to which it belonged.[34]

Two trends played a role in limiting the undoubted success of humanist Latin. In the first place, the attitude of Christian writers to their elegant pagan counterparts has always been ambivalent. Should one read them in order to learn their skills of persuasion, which could then be directed against them? Or did one thereby run the risk of moral and religious contamination, and should one therefore reject them totally? This theme, articulated by the Church Fathers, remained a topic of discussion for centuries. Lorenzo Valla, like others before and after him, had rejected scholastic terminology partly because it was based on pagan philosophy and because its complexity served to obscure the divine simplicity of Christian faith.[35] But Valla's insistence on the need to imitate the style of pagan authors exposed him and other humanists to similar criticisms. Ciceronianism in particular was open to the charge that a return to paganism was its hidden agenda. Some feared that ancient pagan authors posed a threat to Christian society. Wimpfeling, despite his enthusiasm for improving the Latin taught at German schools, prescribed a curriculum which was almost entirely made up of late fifteenth-century writers. He was particularly anxious that the poems of Baptista Mantuanus should replace the works of Virgil, whose *Eclogues*, if properly understood, could not but ignite the most deplorable sexual desires in adolescent students. In the midst of humanist Florence, the Dominican Girolamo Savonarola, attempted to institute an anti-classical Christian programme, which would entail prohibiting the reading of ancient pagan authors;[36] this was closely related to his moral crusade against gambling, carnival songs and all forms of materialism – symbolized by the bonfire of vanities. The sixteenth century saw writers and teachers whose aim was to eliminate classical works from their schools. Sebastian Castellio composed a book of colloquies to replace Terence in the curriculum, for, as a pagan, he was as dangerous to the soul as he was delightful to the ear.[37] Martin Bucer, a radical Reformer, perceived that humanist Latin was a political instrument, an expression of the Roman Catholic claim to a unity between their church and ancient Latin culture. He therefore wished to abolish Latin entirely from his school and to teach instead Greek and Hebrew, the two languages of Scripture.[38] More moderate reformers, such as Luther, Melanchthon and Calvin, insisted on the importance of a classical curriculum in Protestant schools. But the paganizing tendencies of Ciceronianism were as firmly rejected by the reformers as they were by the leading lights of the Counter-Reformation.

Melanchthon, the major figure in the creation of a Lutheran school system in northern Europe, was wholeheartedly behind the stylistic ideals of humanist Latin. A pupil of his, Olaus Theophilus, headmaster of the cathedral school in Copenhagen 1565–75, listed the reasons for teaching Latin: 'Why is the teaching of Latin composition necessary? Without it God cannot be known. Without it we are mired in damnation. Through Latin composition we weaken – no, overthrow – the empire of the devil. It is necessary for the salvation of our souls.'[39] But although Melanchthon's curriculum was centred on Latin, its goals were fundamentally different from those of the early Italian humanist educators. Guarino and others had taught pupils from the very highest levels of society, while lesser Italian humanist schools had prepared their students for a university education most often in medicine or law. By contrast, schools inspired by Melanchthon's educational programme were designed first and foremost for pupils destined to study theology and become vicars. In this they continued a late medieval, northern European tradition of providing education geared to the needs of future theologians.

Like Luther, Melanchthon insisted on central control of the educational system and a uniform curriculum, which was regarded as necessary on account of the bitter religious controversies. The Roman Catholic Church achieved an even greater degree of uniformity through the Jesuit schools, which began to spread throughout Europe from the middle of the sixteenth century. Jesuit educators put together an overall plan, called the 'Ratio studiorum', designed to act as an educational blueprint for all their schools.[40] As in the Protestant schools with which they competed, the Jesuit curriculum was centred on the Latin language and its use. The dependence of Jesuit schools on aims defined by humanists some 200 years earlier is reflected in the names chosen to designate the various classes: after grammatical instruction, students progressed from *humanitas* to *rhetorica*.

With greater institutionalization the concept of humanist education changed. The uniform syllabuses adopted in sixteenth-century schools whether Protestant or Jesuit, encouraged tremendous growth in the production and use of manuals, often in separate editions for different levels of educational achievement. Although educators of both the Reformation and the Counter-Reformation endorsed the stylistic ideals of humanist Latin, the didactic trend of early humanist teachers was reversed: schools used ever more textbooks, and classical authors were read ever later in the curriculum.

NOTES

1 Enea Silvio Piccolomini, *De Europa*, in his *Opera* (Basel, 1551), p. 454.

2 See E. Garin, ed., *Prosatori latini del Quattrocento* (Milan, 1952), pp. 594–601, at 596.

3 M. Tavoni, *Latino, grammatica, volgare: storia di una questione umanistica* (Padua, 1984), pp. 117–69, especially 156–7. Valla's views on the colloquial Latin of ancient Rome were similar to those of Leonardo Bruni: see chapter 2 above, pp. 39, 41.

4 For Santritter's letter, dated 31 October 1492, to Augustinus Moravus from Olomouc, who had studied at Padua, see King Alfonso X, *Tabulae astronomicae* (Venice, 1492), sig. A3^{r-v}.

5 See his letter, dated 1495, in Jakob Wimpfeling, *Briefwechsel*, ed. O. Herding and D. Mertens, 2 vols. (Munich, 1990), I, pp. 239–40 (Letter 54).

6 Jakob Wimpfeling, *Isidoneus Germanicus de erudienda iuventute* (Strasbourg, c. 1500), f. 7^r.

7 Nicholas Orme, *Education and Society in Medieval and Renaissance England* (London, 1989), pp. 123–51, at 147 (section 77: MS London, British Library, Royal 12 B xx, f. 48^r).

8 *Exercitium puerorum grammaticale per dietas distributum* (Hagenau, 1491), sigs. a1^v–2^r.

9 See, e.g., the complaint of Aldus Manutius, in the preface to his *Rudimenta grammatices Latinae linguae* (Venice, 1501), that he had been forced as a boy to study grammar by means of Alexander's 'inept poem': *Aldo Manuzio editore*, ed. G. Orlandi, 2 vols. (Milan, 1975), I, pp. 39–40, at 40.

10 Franciscus Niger, *Grammatica* (Venice, 1480), sigs. dd1^v–4^v ('Peroratio').

11 See the letter of dedication to Francis I of France in Francesco Priscianese, *Della lingua romana* (Venice, 1540), ff. ii^r–iiii^v.

12 Erasmus, *Opera omnia* (Amsterdam, 1969–), I.2, pp. 111–51, at 114–15 (*De ratione studii*, ed. J.-C. Margolin); see also the English translation in Erasmus, *Collected Works* (Toronto, 1974–), XXIV: *Literary and Educational Writings* 2, pp. 661–91 (*On the Method of Study*, trans. B. McGregor).

13 Lorenzo Valla, *Repastinatio dialectice et philosophie*, ed. G. Zippel (Padua, 1982). On this work, see chapter 5 below, pp. 85–6.

14 Most importantly, the *Elegantiolae* by Agostino Dati, which was first published in Ferrara in 1471 and went through at least another 112 editions in the fifteenth century.

15 See the metrical colophon of *Compendium octo partium orationis* (Basel, c. 1485).

16 Wimpfeling, *Isidoneus Germanicus*, f. 7^{r-v}.

17 See Johannes Cochlaeus's prefatory letter to his *Grammatica* (Strasbourg, 1515), f. 1^v, referring to the grammar of Gianfrancesco Boccardo (Pylades Bucccardus), which he describes as 'composed in heavy-handed verses clouded over by a baffling commentary'.

18 Giovanni Sulpizio, *De arte grammatica [opusculum]* (Perugia, c. 1475), f. 31^v.

19 Hermannus Torrentinus, *Commentaria in primam partem Doctrinalis* (Cologne, 1508), f. 85^{r-v}.

20 Erasmus first published the *Proverbs* in *Opuscula aliquot* (Louvain, 1514); for the dedicatory letter, in which he assigns them to Publilius Syrus, author of the *Mimes*, instead of Seneca, see Erasmus, *Collected Works*, III: *Letters 298 to 445, 1514 to 1516*, trans. R. A. B. Mynors and D. F. S. Thomson, pp. 2–4 (Letter 298). Only the first half (up to the first few sentences beginning with the letter 'N') are now attributed to Publilius Syrus; the remaining sentences are by one or more unknown later Christian writers.

21 Giovanni Sulpizio, *Il carme giovanile: De moribus puerorum in mensa servandis*, ed. M. Martini (Sora, 1980).

22 Erasmus, *The Colloquies*, trans C. R. Thompson (Chicago, 1965).

23 See, e.g., Erasmus's advice on how to teach a comedy by Terence: Erasmus, *Collected Works*, XXIV, pp. 682–3 (*On the Method of Study*).

24 See, e.g., Erasmus's disparaging comments on Seneca's style in the preface to his 1529 edition of his works and also his denunciation of the Seneca-St Paul correspondence as a forgery: Erasmus, *Opus epistolarum*, ed. P. S. Allen, H. M. Allen and H. W. Garrod, 12 vols. (Oxford, 1906–58), VIII, pp. 25–41 (Letters 2,091–2).

25 In general, see E. B. Fryde, *Humanism and Renaissance Historiography* (London, 1983).

26 See his 1526 letter to Jacobus Micyllus in Philipp Melanchthon, *Opera quae supersunt omnia*, ed. G. G. Bretschneider and H. E. Bindseil, 28 vols. (Halle etc., 1834–60), I, cols. 782–4 (Letter 364).

27 See, e.g., F. J. Nichols, ed. and trans., *An Anthology of Neo-Latin Poetry* (New Haven, 1979); A. Perosa and J. Sparrow, eds., *Renaissance Latin Verse: An Anthology* (London, 1979).

28 For the statutes, see J. H. Lupton, *A Life of John Colet* ..., second edition (London, 1909; reprinted Hamden, CN, 1961), pp. 271–84; see also J. B. Gleason, *John Colet* (Berkeley, 1989), ch. 9.

29 I. Scott, *Controversies over the Imitation of Cicero* ... (New York, 1910), pp. 10–14.

30 J. F. D'Amico, *Renaissance Humanism in Papal Rome: Humanists and Churchmen on the Eve of the Reformation* (Baltimore, 1983), pp. 123–34.

31 Erasmus, *Opera omnia*, I.2, pp. 599–710, at 694 (*Ciceronianus*, ed. P. Mesnard); see also the English translation in Erasmus, *Collected Works*, XXVIII: *The Ciceronian*, trans. B. I. Knott.

32 See J. McConica, 'The rise of the undergraduate college', in *The History of the University of Oxford* (Oxford, 1984–), III: *The Collegiate University*, ed. J. McConica, pp. 1–68, at 18.

33 Giorgio Valla, *De physicis quaestionibus* (Strasbourg, [1530]), sig. A1^v.

34 Melanchthon, *Opera*, XIII, cols. 412–506, at 452 (*Elementa rhetorices*).

5 See, e.g., Lorenzo Valla, 'In praise of Saint Thomas Aquinas', in L. A. Kennedy, ed., *Renaissance Philosophy: New Translations* (The Hague, 1973), pp. 17–27.

6 Girolamo Savonarola, *Apologeticus de ratione poeticae artis* (Pescia, 1492).

7 Sebastian Castellio, *Dialogorum sacrorum ad linguam simul et mores puerorum formandos libri iiii* (Antwerp, 1552).

8 E.-W. Kohls, *Die Schule bei Martin Bucer in ihrem Verhältnis zu Kirche und Obrigkeit* (Heidelberg, 1963), pp. 69–73.

9 Olaus Theophilus, *Paraenesis seu praeceptiones sapientes et utiles de vitae ac studiorum honesta formatione* ... (Copenhagen, 1573), cited in K. Jensen, *Latinskolens dannelse* (Copenhagen, 1982), p. 13.

0 A. P. Farrell, *The Jesuit 'Ratio studiorum' of 1599* (Washington DC, 1970).

5
Humanist rhetoric and dialectic

PETER MACK

In 1576 the Cambridge University praelector in rhetoric, Gabriel Harvey began his spring series of lectures with an oration which he later published under the title of *Ciceronianus*. In this speech, he announced his conversion from the superficial Ciceronianism of those who express themselves only in the words and phrases of their master to the more profound Ciceronianism of those who understood the reasoning and expression of his speeches. He advised his audience:

> Pay attention not only to the brilliant greenery of words, but more to the ripe fruit of meaning and reasoning ... Remember that Homer [*Iliad* I.201] described words as *pteroenta*, that is, winged, because they easily fly away unless they are kept in balance by the weight of the subject-matter. Unite dialectic and knowledge with rhetoric. Keep your tongue in step with your mind. Learn from Erasmus to combine an abundance (*copia*) of words with an abundance of matter; learn from Ramus to embrace a philosophy which has been allied to eloquence; learn from Homer's Phoenix to be doers of deeds as well as writers of words.[1]

Harvey planned to devote his lectures to a rhetorical and dialectical analysis of Cicero's oration *Post reditum in Senatu*. The distinctive humanist contribution to rhetorical education was the use of dialectic and rhetoric together to read classical texts.[2] The precepts of rhetoric and dialectic would inform the reader's observation of the practice of Cicero and Virgil reading Cicero and Virgil would in turn enrich one's understanding of how to use both words and arguments. The classical authors would also provide a rich store of material for use in new compositions.

Central features of humanism also contributed to humanist rhetoric. New manuscripts were found, notably the complete texts of Quintilian's *Institutio oratoria* (1416) and Cicero's *De oratore* (1421), together with texts of several previously unknown orations of Cicero (ten of them discovered by Poggio Bracciolini in 1415 and 1417). But although fifteenth- and sixteenth-century writers made considerable use of Quintilian, the basic text for teaching rhetoric remained the *Rhetorica ad Herennium*, even after its traditional ascription to Cicero was disproved in 1491. The development of Greek studies led to new translations of Aristotle's *Rhetoric* and to adaptations of the second-century AD Greek rhetorician Hermogenes by the Byzantine émigré George of Trebizond (Trapezuntius) and by Jean Sturm, who reformed education at Strasbourg. But neither had much effect on the manuals which were the mainstay of rhetoric teaching. By contrast, the Latin adaptation of the *Progymnasmata*, composition exercises of the third-century AD Greek rhetorician Aphthonius, became one of the most successful schoolbooks of the sixteenth century. There were no significant textual discoveries in dialectic, and the publication of the Greek commentaries on Aristotle's *Organon* had more effect on sixteenth-century Italian Aristotelian philosophers than on the teaching of dialectic. The humanist preoccupation with improving Latin style resulted in the composition of dialectic manuals in classical Latin and the abandonment in some quarters of the more technical aspects of medieval logic. Very few humanists applied the idea of a 'return to the sources' to the Greek text of Aristotle's dialectic. What distinguishes humanist from medieval approaches to rhetoric and dialectic is that the two subjects were made to work together in the study of classical texts.

Rhetoric and dialectic, like other curriculum subjects, have undergone many changes since their emergence in the fifth and fourth century BC respectively. Both subjects aim to teach people how to persuade others. Dialectic concentrates on argument, which for Aristotelians is exemplified in the syllogism.[3] Rhetoric teaches a variety of means of persuasion, including self-presentation, manipulation of the audience, emotional appeals and the use of figures of speech, as well as arguments. Dialectic originated from the disputation (a debate conducted by question and answer, as in Plato's dialogues), rhetoric from the political or courtroom oration; but both came to be applied to other types of writing. Over their long history, rhetoric and dialectic have collaborated and competed, with both laying claim to certain areas of teaching, notably the discovery and formulation of arguments.[4]

In the later Middle Ages dialectic was the most important subject in the university arts course because it regulated the chief methods of teaching and examination: the lecture, the commentary, the *quaestio* and the disputation. Dialectic also became a specialized research subject in its own right, exploring difficult areas of the text of Aristotle's *Organon*, such as the nature of universals (*Categories*), the relationship between words, concepts and things (*De interpretatione*) and the ambiguities arising from the use of particular words or sentences (*Sophistical Refutations*). Although scholars continued to compose logical and linguistic commentaries on rhetoric textbooks, much of medieval rhetoric teaching focused on the practical art of letter-writing (*ars dictaminis*). Teachers of *dictamen* were among the earliest humanists, and letter-writing remained an important aspect of rhetoric. New letter-writing manuals were composed throughout the fifteenth and sixteenth centuries in the attempt to spread the idea of Ciceronian Latinity.[5]

Several hundred authors contributed more or less voluminously to the range of subjects denoted by rhetoric and dialectic in the fifteenth and sixteenth centuries. The present state of our knowledge does not permit us to organize them all into schools and periods. Instead, I shall summarize the contributions of seven influential authors as a sample of the humanist approach to these fields.

Antonio Loschi served in the chancery of Milan between 1391 and 1406 and was later a papal secretary. Around 1392 he composed his *Inquisitio super XI orationes Ciceronis* ('Examination of Eleven Speeches of Cicero'), which analyses a selection of Cicero's speeches in the light of classical rhetoric. In the preface he opens the Renaissance debate on the value of rules for composition by explaining that natural talent, practice and teaching are needed in order to attain eloquence. For Loschi, the orator must be a good man, with a wide knowledge of all aspects of philosophy, who understands the correct method of speaking. His analyses fall into six sections: (1) *argumentum*, the circumstances of the case and the purpose of the speech; (2) *genus causae*, the type of speech: judicial, deliberative or demonstrative; (3) *constitutio causae*, the main issue on which the case turns (2 and 3 relate to the aspect of rhetoric known as status theory); (4) *dispositio orationis*, the order of the sections of the speech; (5) *partes orationis*, in which he explains where each section of the speech begins and ends, and shows the purpose of each, giving examples of the arguments employed in each and showing how each section reflects rhetorical theory; (6) *elocutio*, labelling examples of the tropes and figures.[6] At times Loschi offers summaries of particular aspects of rhetoric before analysing what Cicero wrote; this helps bring theory and practice together. Although he gives a good deal of attention to particular arguments, he does not attempt to uncover the argumentative structure of a complete oration. Loschi's detailed and impressive analyses are considerably superior to the commentaries on five of Cicero's orations produced by Asconius Pedianus in the first century AD and rediscovered by Poggio in 1416.

George of Trebizond was a native of Crete, a Greek speaker, who came to Italy in 1416. He taught Latin in Vicenza, Venice, Florence and Rome, and was a papal scriptor from 1441. His *Rhetoricorum libri V* ('Five Books on Rhetoric'), completed in Venice in 1433–4, is the only large-scale original rhetoric book written in fifteenth-century Italy; most Italian humanists were content with the classical texts. In this work George attempted a synthesis of the Latin and Greek rhetorical traditions. To the basic structure of the *Rhetorica ad Herennium* he added: numerous examples from Cicero; Hermogenes' extensive discussion of status theory and his doctrine of style; the topics of the medieval logician Peter of Spain; and sections on refutation from Aristotle's *Sophistical Refutations* and the *Insoluble Objections* of Maximus the Philosopher, a Byzantine logician. It is an immense work and one which did not enjoy much direct influence, but it embodies George's lifelong commitment to making Greek learning available in the west, his interest in dialectic and his admiration for Cicero. George also composed a preliminary work on dialectic, the *Isagoge dialectica* ('Introduction to Dialectic', *c.* 1440), which summarizes Aristotle's teaching (without any medieval accretions) in a Latin acceptable to humanists. Although it was not much cited in the fifteenth century, this conservative manual was immensely successful in northern Europe in the sixteenth century. At about the same time George also produced a commentary on Cicero's speech *Pro Ligario* (1440), which was sometimes printed along with the commentaries of Loschi, those of his imitator Sicco Polenton and the ancient ones of Asconius Pedianus.[7]

The philologist Lorenzo Valla was among the most original intellects of the fifteenth century.[8] From early in his career Quintilian was his hero, the Aristotelian university establishment the target of his brilliant polemics. His *Repastinatio dialectice et philosophie* ('Reworking of Dialectic and Philosophy') was conceived in Pavia in the early 1430s, completed – like his other major works – in the years when he served Alfonso the Magnanimous on his campaigns to capture Naples (1434–41) and revised for the rest of his life (the second version *c.* 1444, and the third in 1457). It is a devastating (if sometimes philosophically naïve) attack on Aristotelian metaphysics. For Valla, rhetoric was the most important of the three arts of language, invaluable in persuading people to do what was right, but difficult to learn and only to be mastered by the most gifted. By comparison dialectic was simple, quick to learn and useful to everyone.[9] Valla attempted to simplify Aristotelian dialectic by subjecting it to the rules and usage of classical Latin. He employed grammatical analysis to disallow such philosophical words as *ens*, *essentia* and *quiditas*, replacing them with the simple classical word *res*.[10] He reduced Aristotle's ten categories to three: substance, quality and action; and he rewrote Aristotle's account of the proposition so that it conformed to the classical Latin vocabulary of quantity and negation.[11]

Valla was opposed to the formalism of Aristotle's approach to argument. For him arguments were discovered through the topics;[12] they were then expressed in various forms (of which the syllogism was merely one). The strength of an argument derived not from the form in which it was expressed but from the strength of the connection established through the topics and from the writer's skill in choosing his words. Valla saw logic as a linguistic skill, and he attempted to solve difficulties in argument (like those discussed by Aristotle in *Sophistical Refutations*) by evoking the context in which a sentence must have been uttered.[13] The *Repastinatio* is exciting and impressive, ambitious in its aim of refounding philosophy, but in the end dependent on Aristotle and without much influence. By contrast, Valla's *Elegantiae linguae Latinae* (1441–9), in which he discussed the history and usage of numerous words in order to restore the rich distinctions of classical Latin was much read and greatly valued in the late fifteenth and sixteenth centuries.

The Frisian humanist Rudolph Agricola studied Latin and Greek for ten years in Italy (1470–9).[14] His *De inventione dialectica* ('On Dialectical Invention') (completed in 1479, first printed in 1515) insisted on the unity of the three arts of language:

> All language has as its object that someone should make someone else share in his thoughts. Therefore, it is apparent that there should be three things in every speech: the speaker, the hearer and the subject-matter. Consequently, three points should be observed when speaking: that what the speaker intends should be understood; that the person addressed should listen avidly; and that what is said should be plausible and should be believed. Grammar, which deals with the method of speaking correctly and clearly, teaches us how to achieve the first goal. The second is taught by rhetoric, which provides us with linguistic embellishment and elegance of language, along with all the baits for capturing ears. Dialectic will lay claim to what remains, that is, to speak convincingly on whatever matter is included in a speech.[15]

Agricola matches the arts of the *trivium* (grammar, dialectic and rhetoric) to the defining characteristics of language. He assigns the key role of discovering and organizing subject-matter to dialectic. Later he suggests that dialectical invention is prior both to judgement (the part of dialectic concerned with the forms of argumentation) and to rhetoric, which he treats as synonymous with style.[16] Dialectic teaches the thinking part of language use. But this is not a straightforward exaltation of dialectic, for Agricola's version of dialectic is an original synthesis of material from both dialectic and rhetoric. Although the book is centred on the topics and includes discussion of the proposition and the forms of argumentation, these

lements from traditional dialectic are balanced by parts of the rhetoric
yllabus such as status theory, exposition, the handling of emotions and
disposition.

While Valla had recognized the importance of the topics but had
borrowed Quintilian's version of them, Agricola begins with a new and
extensive treatment of the topics. He explains why the topics are effective,
how they can be used by a speaker and how the list of topics is
constructed.[17] Within each topic he provides explanations, subdivisions and
examples, which help the reader explore the nature and the argumentative
usefulness of the relation involved in each topic.

Much of the rest of the work is devoted to the use of the topics. In Book II
Agricola explains how a writer must analyse the initial brief in order to
discover what kind of a question it is (which provides clues about the type of
answer required), what subsidiary questions are implied within it and which
of these will determine the outcome.[18] Once the decisive question has been
uncovered, topical invention must be applied to each of its elements in order
to generate arguments for the composition in hand. The method of topical
invention is set out carefully, with worked examples.[19] Agricola distinguishes
two basic types of discourse: exposition, in which matters or events are set
out, as if to an audience which follows willingly; and argumentation, in
which each point is argued for and the audience is compelled to assent.[20] He
describes the methods employed in each, how the two types are related and
how one may be converted into the other. In this section Agricola also
investigates (with examples from Virgil and Cicero) different methods of
achieving persuasion and a variety of ways of using arguments.

In Book III he provides an account of emotional persuasion, drawing on
Aristotle's *Rhetoric* and showing how the topics can be used to generate
effective material.[21] Agricola's account of emotion is noticeably more
thorough and systematic than those found in the rhetoric manuals, which
generally treat the subject only briefly in discussing the peroration and some
of the figures. His account of disposition also improves on the rhetoric
textbooks because, instead of taking the structure of the four-part oration
as given, he shows that many different arrangements are possible. A writer
must determine the organization of a work in the light of his subject and
aim, as well as the likely response of his audience.[22]

Agricola often uses literary examples to show how argumentative effects
are achieved, how different types of writing are organized and even how
comparisons work. He also proposes a technique of dialectical reading
which uncovers the argumentative structures that underpin an oration or a
poem. He gives an example of such a reading in his dialectical and rhetorical
commentary on Cicero's oration *Pro lege Manilia*.[23]

De inventione dialectica is an original and instructive work which create a new synthesis of elements from the *trivium*. It was printed forty-four time in the sixteenth century (with a further thirty-two editions of epitomes);[2] but it makes considerable demands on the reader, and it does not fit easil into the traditional division of the syllabus. Some of Agricola's ideas wer embodied in the educational reforms and the textbooks of Erasmus, Philip Melanchthon and Peter Ramus.

Desiderius Erasmus was the most famous humanist of the early sixteent century, the friend of princes and bishops, the author of textbooks an teachers' manuals, the editor of St Jerome and the New Testament.[25] In *D ratione studii* ('On the Method of Study', 1511) he suggests reading materia and study methods for grammar schools. He describes a procedure fo applying rhetorical analysis to other types of literary text, paying attentio to genre, characters, place and action.[26] Some of Erasmus's textbooks aim at improving style. In the *Adagia* ('Adages', 1500, with many additions i later editions) he comments on the use of classical proverbs; in th *Parabolae* ('Parallels', 1514) he collects together similes taken from Gree and Latin authors.[27] Erasmus also contributed to the humanist productio of practical rhetorics, with *De conscribendis epistolis* ('On the Writing o Letters', 1498 and 1522), the most successful of many sixteenth-century letter-writing manuals,[28] and his half-finished preaching manual, *Eccle siastes* ('The Preacher', 1535). But his most influential textbook was *D duplici copia verborum ac rerum* ('Foundations of the Abundant Style' 1512), which went through at least 150 editions in the sixteenth century. *D copia* explains that an abundant and varied style can be achieved by tw methods: thickening the verbal texture and adding to the subject-matter Book I focuses on ways of varying vocabulary and introducing stylisti embellishments. Book II looks to argumentative strategies and to the topic of person and thing to provide additional material.[29] In one way, then, a Gabriel Harvey suggested, *De copia* contributed to the bringing together o rhetoric and dialectic. But *De copia* provided stylistic supercharging afte the main outline of a work had been devised, so it would be truer to say tha it added the methods of dialectic to the resources of style. (The idea o exchanges between stylistic and argumentative devices is also found i Agricola and Melanchthon.) Apart from his praise of Agricola, Erasmu tended to be hostile to dialectic, regarding grammar and rhetoric as th subjects which humanism ought to promote.

Philipp Melanchthon, famous as the 'teacher of Germany', was one o Luther's closest associates, the author of the Augsburg Confession (1530 and of numerous Protestant-humanist educational reforms. He becam professor of Greek at Wittenberg in 1518. His first lecture course o rhetoric, published as *De rhetorica libri tres* ('Three Books on Rhetoric', 1519) contains so much dialectic, and insists so emphatically on its importance that the next year he felt compelled to produce a separate dialectic book, *Compendiaria dialectices ratio* ('A Short Course in Dialectic', 1520), followed by a companion rhetoric, *Institutiones rhetoricae* ('Rhetorical Instruction', 1521). From then on Melanchthon's accounts of both subjects develop together, for as he said: 'rhetoric and dialectic have a common purpose ... the discourse of dialectic is suited to teaching, the language of rhetoric to moving an audience'.[30] His manuals tend to be quite conservative in content, emphasizing the topics in the humanist manner, but including a good deal of scholastic logic as well. Melanchthon himself taught rhetoric and dialectic alongside classical and biblical texts, showing that the precepts of the arts of language were observed in practice in the texts. His published biblical commentaries apply the methods of rhetoric and dialectic to the elucidation of the Scriptures.

Peter Ramus built his academic career on scandalous attacks on the academic gods of his time: Aristotle, Cicero and Quintilian. Like Melanchthon, he understood that new textbooks could not make an impression without academic politics and educational reform. He too composed paired textbooks of rhetoric and dialectic, revising them in tandem.[31] He acknowledged that Sturm's teaching of *De inventione dialectica* in Paris around 1530 and Agricola's emphasis on the relationship between dialectic and good literature were the springboards for his own reforms.[32] For Ramus, invention (the topics) and method (the proposition, the syllogism and overall disposition) belonged to dialectic; style and delivery to rhetoric. This reflects Agricola's view, but Ramus's treatment of the material is simpler and more formal. His treatises operate by definition and division (and hence can be represented in the famous tree-diagrams).[33] He includes only what is undoubtedly true and what belongs to the subject, moving gradually from the most general element (the definition of the subject) to the most particular (examples of particular topics or figures of speech). Ramus's simplification made possible rapid understanding of the structure of a subject, but it could seem reductive. He taught literary texts alongside his manuals and published analyses of many classical works – though these too could seem insensitive since he had to wrench all texts into the only two structures he recognized: the method (from general to particular) and the prudent approach (from particular to general). Ramus's manuals were immensely influential, particularly in Protestant countries after his murder in the St Bartholomew's Day Massacre (1572).

Different as they are, these seven authors share certain preoccupations. Although the nature and relative importance of the two subjects was open to debate, most humanist authors conceived of rhetoric and dialectic together, seeing them as an education in the use of language; and most of them used the principles of rhetoric and dialectic to analyse classical texts. Dialectic remained primarily Aristotelian. Northern humanists produced new textbooks covering the entire subject, written to classical standards of Latinity and rejecting scholastic additions to the discipline. They emphasized dialectical invention of arguments through the topics. The two strongest critics of Aristotle, Valla and Ramus, differed considerably in the doctrines they attacked. In rhetoric, humanists generally retained the classical textbooks, especially the *Rhetorica ad Herennium* and Quintilian's *Institutio oratoria*, though Cyprian Soarez's *De arte rhetorica libri tres* ('Three Books on the Art of Rhetoric', 1557) became very influential as the standard rhetoric manual of the Jesuits. New manuals written by Northern humanists dealt mainly with subjects on the fringes of rhetoric: amplification, proverbs and imitation, for example. Relatively little attention was paid in such manuals to emotional persuasion.

Turning now from the textbooks, many of them aimed at university students, to a consideration of classroom practice, we can see how the humanist approach to dialectic in particular affected attitudes to reading and writing.

Commonplace books were widely used in sixteenth- and seventeenth-century classrooms. The main purpose of the commonplace book was to enable students to store away phrases or ideas from their reading for re-use in their own compositions. Students would enter a series of headings, such as justice, virtue and courage, at the top of the pages of an exercise book. When they came across a memorable passage in a book, they would enter it under the appropriate heading. In due course the book became a personal, subject-organized dictionary of quotations. But the effect of this training may also have influenced habits of reading, because the compiler of a commonplace book had always to be asking: under what heading might I enter this phrase and to which subject is this sentence logically related? It is possible that his habit of mental filing actually enabled a Renaissance reader to attend to a romance or a play on two levels simultaneously: following the story and also noting the development of a debate between the points of view expressed by the various characters on fortune, valour or wealth.[34]

The *Progymnasmata* (usually studied in the Renaissance classroom in the Latin adaptation by Agricola and Reinhard Lorich of Aphthonius' Greek text of the third century AD) are fourteen short exercises in composition, including the fable, tale, proverb, characterization and description. In each case Aphthonius provides an explanation of the function and types of each form, and one or more examples. For instance, a *chreia* consists of a piece of advice attributed to an author; praise of the author; paraphrase of the advice; elaboration of the advice from the topics of cause, contrary and analogy; an example illustrating the advice; a testimony of its importance taken from another author; and an epilogue. Ancient orators saw the *progymnasmata* as exercises leading up to the composition of an oration. Renaissance students may have found them useful in themselves. It is easy to see how descriptions, characterizations and arguments could be inserted into reports, romances and poems.[35]

Not all Renaissance grammar schools included in their syllabus a complete textbook of rhetoric, but they all used letter-writing manuals, handbooks of tropes and figures, and dictionaries of proverbs and comparisons. It is hard for us to imagine schoolboys working through the long lists of tropes, but something of the kind must have happened. Learning the figures of speech and their names may have encouraged students to overuse them; but it may also have made them more sensitive to the manner of their use, since labelling makes identification, discussion and comparison much easier. In the same way, studying handbooks of proverbs and that doubtful lore about animals and plants which a modern critic has called 'unnatural natural history' may have enabled students to compare and criticize the uses to which such stylistic devices were put.[36]

Reading the examples of 200 ways of saying 'your letter pleased me greatly' from Erasmus's *De copia* may well have encouraged a tendency towards dense and repetitive writing.[37] But it may also have helped students understand that in using any given expression they were choosing among alternatives, since there were 199 other inflections that could be given to the same material. It must also have encouraged students to rewrite their sentences and paragraphs, and shown them how rewriting could bring out different aims and emphases.

Some Renaissance schoolbooks embraced the fashion for imitation. Agricola outlined a method for varying each aspect of an admired text in turn until eventually one attempts to reproduce the manner of the original while discussing an entirely different subject.[38] John Brinsley set his students to work on Cicero's letters, first summarizing them, but later attempting to reply to Cicero in his own style. Brinsley also set out a step by step method for producing Ciceronian word order.[39] At its best, particularly where more than one model was involved, such imitation may have elucidated the many aspects which combine to produce an author's manner and may have challenged students to improve their command of Latin. At worst, it may have encouraged the restrictions on vocabulary and expression which are mocked in Erasmus's *Ciceronianus* ('The Ciceronian', 1528).[40]

Much of this is speculative. An exercise of imagination is involved in considering the possible effects of particular textbooks and classroom practices. But without it (combined with careful study of the evidence which survives) we cannot hope to understand the impact of humanist schooling.

The whole purpose of the humanist educational programme was to create readers and writers. In spite of difficulties in interpreting the evidence, it is essential to consider the effect of humanist literary education on the practice of reading and writing.

Many Renaissance readers wrote in their books (some teachers advised their pupils to mark figures of speech and unusual phrases);[41] some left notes on their reading; some even wrote up their notes as analyses of texts. The example below is taken from the notebook of Henry Addyter, a student at Christ's College, Cambridge (1588–93).

The exposition of the xixth psalme

In this psalme partly	he teacheth		By the creatures unto the 7v	the Church and Ethnicks
		1. Adjoynts	Perfect, sure v7	
			Pure, right v8	
		8	Cleare, perpetual	
			Trew, righteous v9	
		2. Effects	Converteth the soule	
		4	Giveth wisdom to the simple 7	
			Rejoyceth the hart	
By the law which he commendeth by			Lighteneth the eyes	8
		3. Comparisons	for pleasure, sweeter than	
		2	honey or the honeysuckle	
			for profitt, finess compared	
			to Gold	10
		4. Experiens	for that he knew the law to	
			make him circumspecte v11	
		5. the end	of keeping it which is a	
			greate reward	
he prayeth	to take away his Synnes and these are eyther			secret presumptuous

<pre>
              to accept him, both in his   words
                                                  thoughts

In teaching he eyther   compareth the teachers
                                        or
                                        expoundeth the properties, effects
                                        end of the teacher

                                        the first is common as well to them
                                        which are not of the church as to
                    Subject   those which are of the Church
                                        the second is proper to the church
The   of Christ
comparison is
eyther in the   the first teacheth that ther is a God
                    Effects   the second that we have a good and
                                        merciful God

                                        the one maketh us inexcusable
                    End   the other (in Chryste) maketh us
                                        inexcusable to salvation.[42]
</pre>

In his analysis Addyter observes different types of structure working together. He first breaks the Psalm into teaching (verses 1–11) and asking (12–14); he then subdivides teaching into that which arises from the creation (1–6) and that which comes from the law, or the word of God (7–11). Within this latter category he notes the topics the Psalmist employs in his description of the law. So, for example, the complements in verses 7, 8 and 9 are drawn from the topic of adjuncts, while the adverbial phrases of verses 7 and 8 are effects. After these divisions Addyter draws the two parts of the Psalm's teaching together, noting the implicit comparison between creation and revelation, under the topics of subject, effects and purpose or end. His command of dialectical terminology enabled Addyter to analyse the connections and distinctions which give this Psalm its force and meaning.

Such examples of a worked out response to a text, seen as a logical whole, are rare in any period, and we should be wary of drawing conclusions from what may after all have been a classroom exercise. Other kinds of evidence for the persistence of rhetorical habits of thought are found in Renaissance writing. François Rabelais delighted in mocking the absurdities of medieval learning; but he also poked fun at the humanist learning he favoured, composing parodies of disputations, trials and orations. For example, in his praise of debtors Panurge imagines a world in which everyone lends money freely:

I am lost in this contemplation. Among humans peace, love, pleasure, loyalty, repose, banquets, feasting, joy, gladness, gold, silver, small change, chains, rings and suchlike property would pass from hand to hand. No lawsuits, no war, no argument, no usurer, no glutton, no miser, no refuser. By God, wouldn't this be the golden age of Saturn's rule? The true picture of Olympus, where all other virtues cease and Charity alone reigns, rules, dominates and triumphs? All would be good, all would be beautiful, all would be just. O happy world! O happy people of that world! O three and four times happy![43]

Panurge's prose bears the imprint of the abundant style, with the subjects and objects multiplied into lists, with four verbs to emphasize the force of Charity's rule, with the tripling of parallel phrases. The whole texture of the passage is exuberantly copious. Among the more obvious rhetorical figures employed are anaphora (beginning successive sentences with the same word), isocolon (a sequence of phrases equal in length) and apostrophe (initial 'O' as an exclamation). The last phrase shows off Rabelais's classical reading with its ironic repetition of Aeneas' cry in the midst of the storm (*Aeneid* I.91): 'O, three and four times happy', while the passage on the reign of Charity looks like an allusion to St Paul (I Corinthians 13). When Pantagruel responds to this speech he hails Panurge as 'bon topicqueur' ('good at using the topics'). But even if Panurge went on until Pentecost (as his skill in invention might allow), Pantagruel insists that he would not be persuaded.

Whereas the verbal fabric of sixteenth-century writing provides evidence about stylistic training, the dialectical processes underlying the composition usually remain hidden. Some writers, however, exploited their audience's understanding of rhetoric and dialectic for literary effect. In Sonnet 1 of his sequence *Astrophil and Stella*, Sir Philip Sidney tackles the rhetorical question of the relative contributions of art and inspiration to good writing. His opening quatrain describes a process of deduction, from one step to the next:

> Loving in truth, and faine in verse my love to show,
> That the deare She might take some pleasure of my paine:
> Pleasure might cause her reade, reading might make her know,
> Knowledge might pitie winne, and pitie grace obtaine.[44]

This is also an example of the rhetorical figure of climax and is cited as such in Abraham Fraunce's *Arcadian Rhetorike* (1588). Later in the sonnet Sidney speaks of invention. Other sonnets embody a logical structure (in Sonnet 5, lines 1, 5, 9 and 12 concede arguments against a proposition which line 14 nevertheless asserts) or depend on logical distinctions (as in

Sonnet 61 where Stella is required to distinguish between act and agent, and Astrophil calls on Doctor Cupid to oppose her 'Angel's sophistrie').

In *Arcadia*, Sidney presents a debate between Pyrocles and Musidorus which allows us to see how each takes account of his notion of the other in the way he presents arguments and responds to those put forward by his opponent. Sidney relates that Musidorus had planned a logical riposte to his friend's arguments:

> For having in the beginning of Pyrocles' speech which defended his solitariness framed in his minde a reply against it in the praise of honourable action (in showing that such a kind of contemplation is but a glorious title to idleness; that in action a man did not only better himself but benefit others; that the gods would not have delivered a soul into the body, which hath arms and legs (only instruments of doing) but that it were intended the mind should employ them; and that the mind should best know his own good or evil by practice; which knowledge was the only way to increase the one and correct the other; besides many other arguments which the plentifulness of the matter yielded to the sharpness of his wit), when he found Pyrocles leave that, and fall to such an affected praising of the place [i.e., Arcadia], he left it likewise, and joined therein with him because he found him in that humour utter most store of passion.[45]

Sidney provides an outline for a pointed and logical speech. But Musidorus changes his mind and decides to answer *ad hominem*, with a compliment which simultaneously concedes and opposes (your reasons make me value solitude, but your words make me long for your company); with a rebuttal, naming other places; and with an argument from his purpose (you are praising this country to show your skill in invention). The real object of this speech, however, is found, not in the argumentative structure, but on the verbal surface, when Musidorus trails the word 'lover', at the end of the speech, to see how Pyrocles will react to it. The latter responds by confessing his true reason for wanting to remain in Arcadia. This exchange shows Sidney using ideas about argument and self-presentation to expose his characters and to entertain his readers.

The essay was the most important new genre of the sixteenth century. It has been suggested that the school handbook of quotations was the formal basis of the essay, since the earliest of Montaigne's *Essais* are stories linked to quotations.[46] This structure also recalls the fable and other exercises from the *progymnasmata*. In the 1580 edition, the essay 'Our emotions get carried away beyond us' (I.3) consists of five stories which show how individuals' preoccupations with reputation, power, bravery and modesty continued beyond their deaths. Montaigne comments that these stories reflect a common human concern with what will happen after one's death. In the 1588 version he adds an introduction which generalizes and explains his theme, suggesting that looking to the future is an essential part of human nature. He also adds comments: on the way death affects people's attitude to princes; on the Greek tradition that whoever asked to bury their dead after a battle thereby conceded victory; and on people who are ostentatious or ostentatiously modest about their funerals. These additions are all topically related to an element already present in the essay but are not necessarily linked to its main theme. In the Bordeaux copy, which has many manuscript additions, from which Montaigne no doubt intended to produce a third edition, he includes new stories about death or funerals and comments on his earlier comments. For example, he now criticizes the human preoccupation with the future and remarks on his own attitudes to modesty and funerals.[47] The form, which Montaigne once claimed as the most notable thing about his essays,[48] is generated by the combination of story plus comment and by topical invention (in this case through contraries, differences, causes, similars and subject) applied to elements of earlier drafts.

'On practice' (II.6) is centred on an account of an occasion on which Montaigne was concussed after being knocked from his horse.[49] This essay contains five kinds of material. In the first place, there is the narrative describing his fall and recovery. Mixed in with this are his reflections on how he felt at each moment. The third element consists of interruptions to this narrative: comparisons with other experiences; discussion of the nature of death; his fear of being in agony and unable to express it; his idea that people are unconscious of what they are doing as they approach death; reflections on unwilled actions; and, most valuable, the conclusion to the story, when he describes recovering knowledge of what had happened while he was unconscious and the importance of it as a lesson to him. The fourth element is the introduction: reflections on the usefulness of practice and on whether one can practise dying, whether thinking of dying is helpful and, more generally, on the relation between imagination and experience. The fifth element is the conclusion to the essay, added in the Bordeaux copy, which arises from the earlier conclusion to the story; in it he defends the portrayal of himself effected by the publication of the essays. Here he emphasizes the unusualness and value of what he is doing. All the elements of this admirable essay can be considered as developing successively by interpolation through topical connections.

These examples show how some sixteenth-century authors and readers followed the classroom precepts of dialectical reading and stylish expression, and in addition exploited humanist ideas about the use of language for their own purposes. The humanist tradition of bringing together rhetoric, dialectic and grammar helped create the conditions in which the linguistic inventiveness of sixteenth-century writers could flourish.

NOTES

1 Gabriel Harvey, *Ciceronianus*, ed. H. S. Wilson (Lincoln, 1945), p. 82. For the speech of Phoenix, see *Iliad* IX.443.

2 This and many of the points made below are argued in more detail in P. Mack, *Renaissance Argument: Valla and Agricola in the Traditions of Rhetoric and Dialectic* (Leiden, 1993).

3 A syllogism is a three-part argument, in which if the first two statements, or premises, are true, then the third statement, or conclusion, must also be true. Aristotle examined all possible combinations of three variables in three statements to determine which patterns were valid. An example of a syllogism would be: Socrates is a man; all men are mortal; therefore, Socrates is mortal.

4 On classical and medieval rhetoric and dialectic: Pseudo-Cicero, *Rhetorica ad Herennium*, ed. and trans. H. Caplan (London, 1954); William of Sherwood, *Introduction to Logic*, ed. and trans. N. Kretzmann (Minneapolis, 1966); G. Kennedy, *The Art of Persuasion in Greece* (Princeton, 1963); N. Kretzmann, A. Kenny and J. Pinborg, eds., *The Cambridge History of Later Medieval Philosophy* (Cambridge, 1982).

5 On medieval developments, see Kretzmann, Kenny and Pinborg, eds., *Cambridge History*; P. O. Kristeller, *Renaissance Thought and Its Sources* (New York), 1979), pp. 85–105; J. Monfasani, 'Humanism and rhetoric', in A. Rabil, ed., *Renaissance Humanism: Foundations, Forms and Legacy*, 3 vols. (Philadelphia, 1988), III, pp. 171–235, at 175, 192–4, 198–200.

6 Asconius Pedianus, *In Orationes M. Tullii Ciceronis ...*, comment. Antonio Loschi (Strasbourg, 1520), pp. 154–7.

7 George of Trebizond, *Rhetoricorum libri V* (Venice, 1523) and his *De re dialectica* (Cologne, 1539; reprinted Frankfurt, 1966), pp. 261–88; *Collectanea Trapezuntiana*, ed. J. Monfasani (Binghamton, 1984). See also J. Monfasani, *George of Trebizond: A Biography and a Study of his Rhetoric and Logic* (Leiden, 1976); and C. J. Classen, 'The rhetorical works of George of Trebizond and their debt to Cicero', *Journal of the Warburg and Courtauld Institutes*, 56 (1993), 75–84.

8 Lorenzo Valla, *Repastinatio dialectice et philosophie*, ed. G. Zippel (Padua, 1982) and his *Opera omnia* (Basel, 1540; reprinted, with a second volume edited by E. Garin, Turin, 1962); see also O. Besomi and M. Regoliosi, eds., *Lorenzo Valla e l'umanesimo italiano* (Padua, 1986).

9 Valla, *Repastinatio*, pp. 175–7.

10 Valla, *Repastinatio*, pp. 11–21; see also pp. 30–6.

11 Valla, *Repastinatio*, pp. 190–213, 363–6.

12 The topics are a list of headings (such as genus, species, cause, effect, adjunct, similars) which can be applied to any subject in order to generate material for discussion. For an account of their use see Mack, *Renaissance Argument*, pp. 130–42. See also Cicero, *Topica*; Rudolph Agricola, *De inventione dialectica* (Cologne, 1539; reprinted Nieuwkoop, 1967), pp. 6–177; and N. J. Green-Pedersen, *The Tradition of the Topics in the Middle Ages* (Munich, 1984).

13 Valla, *Repastinatio*, pp. 244, 304–6, 328–34.

14 Agricola, *De inventione dialectica*; see also the edition of this work by L. Mundt

(Tübingen, 1992); and F. Akkerman and A. J. Vanderjagt, eds., *Rodolphus Agricola Phrisius (1444–1485)* (Leiden, 1988).

15 Agricola, *De inventione dialectica*, p. 192; cf. Quintilian, *Institutio oratoria* III.8.15.

16 Agricola, *De inventione dialectica*, pp. 8, 180–2, 268, 316.

17 Agricola, *De inventione dialectica*, pp. 6–9, 22–5.

18 Agricola, *De inventione dialectica*, pp. 240–52.

19 Agricola, *De inventione dialectica*, pp. 362–72.

20 Agricola, *De inventione dialectica*, pp. 2, 258–60.

21 Agricola, *De inventione dialectica*, pp. 378–91.

22 Agricola, *De inventione dialectica*, pp. 412–50.

23 Agricola, *De inventione dialectica*, pp. 353–62, 461–71.

24 G. C. Huisman, *Rudolph Agricola: A Bibliography* (Nieuwkoop, 1985).

25 C. Augustijn, *Erasmus: His Life, Works, and Influence* (Toronto, 1991); J. Chomarat, *Grammaire et rhétorique chez Erasme*, 2 vols. (Paris, 1981).

26 For an English translation, see Erasmus, *Collected Works* (Toronto, 1974–), XXIV: *Literary and Educational Writings 2*, pp. 661–91, at 687–9 (*On the Method of Study*, trans. B. McGregor).

27 Erasmus, *Collected Works*, XXIII: *Literary and Educational Writings 1*, pp. 123–277 (*Parallels*, trans. R. A. B. Mynors); XXXI–XXXIV: *Adages*, trans. M. M. Phillips and R. A. B. Mynors.

28 Erasmus, *Collected Works*, XXV: *Literary and Educational Writings 3*, pp. 1–254 (*On the Writing of Letters*, trans. C. Fantazzi).

29 Erasmus, *Collected Works*, XXIV, pp. 279–659 (*Copia: Foundations of the Abundant Style*, trans. B. I. Knott).

30 Philipp Melanchthon, 'Epistolarum … liber secundus', in his *Opera quae supersunt omnia*, ed. G. G. Bretschneider and H. E. Bindseil, 28 vols. (Halle, 1834–60), I, cols. 64–5; this standard edition of his works does not include all stages of the rhetoric and dialectic textbooks. See also W. Maurer, *Der junge Melanchthon*, 2 vols. (Göttingen, 1967–9); and K. Meerhoff, 'The significance of Melanchthon's rhetoric', in P. Mack, ed., *Renaissance Rhetoric* (London, 1994), pp. 46–62.

31 Peter Ramus, *The Logike*, trans. R. M'Kilwein (London, 1574; reprinted Menston, 1966) is an accessible English version. On the sequence of Ramus's writings, see N. Bruyère, *Méthode et dialectique dans l'oeuvre de La Ramée* (Paris, 1984); K. Meerhoff, *Rhétorique et poétique au XVIe siècle en France* (Leiden, 1986), a work to which I am indebted throughout this paper; and P. Sharratt, 'Peter Ramus and the reform of the university', in P. Sharratt, ed., *French Renaissance Studies 1540–1570* (Edinburgh, 1976), pp. 4–20.

32 Peter Ramus, *Scholae in liberales artes* (Basel, 1569; reprinted Hildesheim, 1970), f. 2ᵛ.

33 Examples of these diagrams can be found in C. Vasoli, *La dialettica e la retorica dell'umanesimo* (Milan, 1968), an invaluable introduction to the whole subject; Bruyère, *Méthode*; and Mack, *Renaissance Argument*.

34 See Rudolph Agricola, *Lucubrationes* (Cologne, 1539; reprinted Nieuwkoop, 1967), pp. 198–9. For Milton's commonplace book, see John Milton, *The Works*, ed. F. A. Patterson, 18 vols. (New York, 1931–8), XVIII: *The Uncollected Writings*, ed. T. O. Mabbott and J. M. French.

35 See D. L. Clark, 'The rise and fall of *progymnasmata* ...' and R. Nadeau, 'The *Progymnasmata* of Aphthonius in translation', *Speech Monographs*, 19 (1952), 259–85.

36 J. R. Henderson, 'Erasmus on the art of letter-writing', in J. J. Murphy, ed., *Renaissance Eloquence* (Berkeley, 1983), pp. 331–55; L. A. Sonnino, *A Handbook to Sixteenth-Century Rhetoric* (London, 1968); W. J. Ong, 'Commonplace rhapsody', in R. R. Bolgar, ed., *Classical Influences on European Culture AD 1500–1700* (Cambridge, 1976), pp. 91–126.

37 Erasmus, *Collected Works*, XXIV, pp. 348–54.

38 Agricola, *De inventione dialectica*, pp. 453–4.

39 John Brinsley, *Ludus literarius*, ed. E. T. Campagnac (Liverpool, 1917), pp. 159–69; Ascham has a good discussion of imitation in his *Scholemaster*: see Roger Ascham, *English Works*, ed. W. A. Wright (Cambridge, 1904), pp. 264–77.

40 M. Baxandall, *Giotto and the Orators: Humanist Observers of Painting in Italy and the Discovery of Pictorial Composition 1350–1450* (Oxford, 1988), pp. 8–31; G. W. Pigman III, 'Versions of imitation in the Renaissance', *Renaissance Quarterly*, 33 (1980), 1–32.

41 Brinsley, *Ludus literarius*, pp. 46, 141, 203.

42 MS London, British Library, Harleian 3230, f. 4^v.

43 François Rabelais, *Oeuvres complètes*, 2 vols. (Paris, 1962), I, p. 421 (III.2–4). See also T. Cave, *The Cornucopian Text* (Oxford, 1979).

44 Sir Philip Sidney, *The Poems*, ed. W. A. Ringler (Oxford, 1962), p. 165.

45 Sir Philip Sidney, *The Old Arcadia*, ed. J. Robertson (Oxford, 1973), pp. 13–24, at 16.

46 D. Frame, 'Considerations on the genesis of Montaigne's *Essays*', in I. D. McFarlane and I. Maclean, eds., *Montaigne: Essays in Memory of Richard Sayce* (Oxford, 1982), pp. 1–12.

47 Michel de Montaigne, *Essais*, 3 vols. (Paris, 1969), I, pp. 47–53; for an English translation, see Montaigne, *The Complete Essays*, trans. M. A. Screech (London, 1991), pp. 11–18.

48 Montaigne, *Essais*, II, p. 78; *Essays*, p. 458.

49 Montaigne, *Essais*, II, pp. 41–51; *Essays*, pp. 416–27.

6

Humanists and the Bible

ALASTAIR HAMILTON

Humanists were brought up with the same Christian beliefs as scholastics. Many of them received a scholastic training and became members of the clergy, either regular or secular. True, humanists had a different attitude towards non-Christian sources. Yet for both humanists and scholastics the Bible remained a fundamental text. We may thus wonder why it took so long before the Scriptures were submitted to a scholarly and philological treatment and why the somewhat misleading term Christian humanism is applied only to the late fifteenth and early sixteenth century.

The problem was, in fact, formulated at an early stage by Petrarch. He himself seems to have realized the importance of the Scriptures only relatively late in life, when he was over forty. For what he described as this 'damnable lateness', he felt he should apologize. He had, he said, been led back to the Bible by reading the Church Fathers, particularly his own favourite, Augustine, who appears as a character in one of his dialogues,[1] but also by Ambrose, Gregory, Lactantius and, of course, Jerome, the saint to whom the accepted Latin translation of the Bible, the Vulgate, was attributed. What made the Church Fathers so attractive to Petrarch and later humanists was that they reconciled classical and Christian views of human life and morals, and that they presented them in an elegant style. Rather than use a Father such as Augustine as the source of a theological system in the way that scholastics were accustomed to do, humanists saw him as a model of rhetorical skill, a Christian counterpart to Cicero. Petrarch regarded Augustine as a master of self-analysis and followed him in his itinerary from worldly concerns and classical texts to a state of spiritual enlightenment and repose in God.

When he did at last tackle the Scriptures, Petrarch, like all humanists who followed him, approached the Bible as a work of literature, an example of inspired poetry. It was not to be treated as the scholastics tended to do when they applied an Aristotelian scheme of interpretation, the results of which then served to support their own theological elaborations. It should receive, rather, the same scholarly treatment as other works of literature. Yet for a lover of letters and an advocate of stylistic purity such as Petrarch, the Bible presented a problem: the style was far from elegant. This had been admitted by Jerome, who, in his version, had made every effort to be faithful to the original. Certainly for humanists, the precedent set by Jerome carried weight.[2] But they still asked questions. Was it perhaps necessary to express matters of such sanctity in a somewhat coarse style? The image of the Sileni of Alcibiades – boxes with a monstrous exterior containing some precious scent within – would later symbolize the paradox, and Petrarch could say that, despite their rough appearance, 'nothing is sweeter than the marrow [of the Scriptures], nothing smoother, nothing more healthful'.[3]

Petrarch, and after him Coluccio Salutati, admired the Scriptures, consulted them thoroughly, but never approached them philologically. To do so required knowledge of the languages in which the Bible was written: Greek for the New Testament; Hebrew and Aramaic for the Old. It was only after the study of Greek had been reintroduced into Italy that humanist biblical scholarship truly got under way. Even when it did, however, we can discern a development close to Petrarch's: among the first texts to be translated from Greek were the Church Fathers, and they were followed by the Scriptures themselves. Profiting from the introduction of Greek studies in Italy at the end of the fourteenth century, a humanist such as Leonardo Bruni might translate a single text by one of the Fathers.[4] The first to translate and edit them systematically, however, was Ambrogio Traversari, a Camaldolensian monk (he became general of the order in 1431) from the monastery of Santa Maria degli Angeli in Florence, who worked on patristic texts between 1415 and his death in 1439.

Traversari's principal motive, which was applauded by many of his fellow humanists, was to recover for the west the ancient Greek Christian tradition, which had been all but completely abandoned in the thirteenth century. Under the impact of humanism the Fathers, both Greek and Latin, had begun to be appreciated, moreover, not only as masters of rhetoric but also as the suppliers of an exegesis essential for understanding the Scriptures. Traversari even derived from their writings arguments for a much needed reform of the Church, as well as precepts which he thought might bring about the reunion of the Greek and Roman Churches at the Council of Florence in 1439. He translated from the Greek works by Basil, John Chrysostom, Athanasius, Gregory Nazianzen and Pseudo-Dionysius the Areopagite. Rejecting the standard medieval technique of providing a word for word translation, he followed the new humanist method of conveying both the sense and the style of the original in an acceptable form of Latin. At the same time he edited some of the Latin Fathers – Lactantius,

Tertullian, Jerome – emending Latin readings transmitted in the medieval manuscript tradition and restoring Greek words and phrases which medieval copyists had omitted.[5]

To pass from the Church Fathers to the Bible was a logical step since the first work that had to be dealt with was the Vulgate attributed to Jerome. The text had been prepared partly in Rome and partly in Palestine in the last decades of the fourth century and the first twenty years of the fifth. Disseminated in the west in a vast number of manuscripts, often differing substantially from one another, the Vulgate gradually came to be accepted by the Roman Church. The version that was ultimately standardized was edited to a large extent by the English scholar Alcuin in the eighth century. Adopted in France, it grew to be known as the 'Paris text', and from the early thirteenth century onwards, when it obtained a wide circulation, it became the foundation of dogmatic authority.[6]

When approaching the Scriptures, humanists had to face problems of increasing sophistication. The first question was one that had troubled biblical scholars even since the Vulgate reached the west: how reliable was the translation? How close was it to the Greek and Hebrew originals? Only at a comparatively late stage, when the text critical tradition of the humanists had been developed, was this followed by the question of the reliability of the available Greek and Hebrew manuscripts. To what extent did *they* reflect an original which had long since disappeared? Another question which arose was: how close was the accepted text of the Vulgate to the translation actually produced in the late fourth and early fifth century? So many different copyists over so many centuries must have introduced errors: how could these be removed? And this in turn was succeeded by another problem: how much of the translation which circulated under Jerome's name was by Jerome himself? In how many cases had he either revised, or simply adopted, existing translations?

To begin with, the first of these questions seemed the most urgent. Although Traversari started to learn Hebrew in order to answer it, it was a pupil of his who truly immersed himself in the study of the ancient languages. Giannozzo Manetti was a layman. He served Florence as an ambassador, worked as an apostolic secretary to Pope Nicholas V in Rome and acted as a member of the royal council of King Alfonso of Naples. He owed his knowledge of Greek to Traversari and then turned to Hebrew.

From a practical point of view, the study of Hebrew was easier than that of Greek. Thanks to the presence of Jewish communities, the knowledge of Hebrew (and Aramaic) had never disappeared in France, Spain and Italy in the way that Greek had done (except for some native speakers in southern Italy), and instruction had nearly always been available for the asking. The

Frenchman Nicholas of Lyra, who prepared a commentary on the Bible which was to become highly popular, the *Postillae perpetuae in universam Sacram Scripturam* (1322–31), was perhaps the greatest scholastic commentator of the late Middle Ages. He was ignorant of Greek but knew Hebrew well enough to make extensive use of the late Hebrew commentaries on the Old Testament and to compare the Vulgate with the Hebrew original. Some medieval schools actively encouraged the study of Hebrew, and the suspicion attached to association with members of the Jewish communities was by no means insuperable at a time when acquaintance with their language was believed to be useful for missionaries planning to convert them.[7]

Manetti too stated his desire to convert the Jews he encountered to Christianity. One of his converts was a young scholar he took as his tutor and who lived in his house. With another Jewish scholar, probably Immanuel ben Abraham of San Miniato, Manetti started to read through the Old Testament in 1442. At the same time he assembled a collection of Hebrew manuscripts, which were later to form the nucleus of the Hebrew collection in the Vatican Library and which included an Old Testament with commentaries by the great medieval rabbis David Kimhi, Abraham ibn Ezra, Rashi and Gersonides. Although he had begun to study Hebrew in Florence in 1435, Manetti did not embark on the translation of the Bible until he was in Naples between 1455 and 1458. He completed the New Testament, but of the Old finished translating only the Psalms. In justifying his undertaking, he talked of criticisms of Jerome made by both Jews and Christians, and presented his translation as a defence of the Church Father. In fact, however, his ambition, like that of nearly all his successors, was to improve on the Vulgate.

In spite of his fundamental loyalty to Jerome, Manetti marks an important phase in the process which led to severe criticism of the Vulgate. One of his objectives was to enable the reader to compare different versions of the text. In the copy of the Psalter he presented to the king of Naples, he provided his own translation of the Hebrew beside two translations attributed to Jerome, one directly from the Hebrew and the other from the Septuagint (the Greek translation of the Old Testament made in the third and second centuries BC). In his *Apologeticus* (1455–6) Manetti displays a strong interest in the textual history of the Scriptures, which foreshadows later developments, and discusses the differences between the Hebrew Bible and the Septuagint (preferred by the Roman Church). He also demonstrated his knowledge of the Hebrew tradition and sources in claiming, against Jerome, that the Psalter was divided into more than one book.[8] As a translator of the New Testament, Manetti, much in the tradition of Traversari, was a flexible stylist, by no means averse to rhetorical variety. In contrast, as we shall see, to Lorenzo Valla, he did not believe that the same word in Greek should necessarily always be translated by the same Latin word, but varied his translation according to the context. Although he never justified his approach or provided any form of critical apparatus to explain his divergences from the standard Latin translation, his intention of improving the style of the Vulgate is evident throughout.[9]

A striking feature of biblical scholarship in the fifteenth century is the absence of any collaboration between humanists engaged on the same task. This is particularly true in the case of Manetti and his colleague Lorenzo Valla. A follower of Leonardo Bruni, Valla was slightly younger than Manetti and had had a curiously similar career. He too worked in Naples from 1435 to 1448; and he spent the period from 1453 to 1457 as a papal secretary in Rome, at the very time when Manetti was employed in the same capacity.[10] Yet although the two men must have had almost daily dealings with one another between 1453 and 1455, there is no evidence that either was aware of what the other was doing.

Unlike Manetti, Valla did not actually retranslate the New Testament. He produced a series of notes on it, the first version of which seems to have been composed between 1435 and 1448 (when he was in Naples) and the second between 1453 and 1457 (when he was in Rome).[11] Valla was already a proven philologist when he came to the New Testament, arguably the best of his day. He had demonstrated that the Donation of Constantine the document in which Emperor Constantine was supposed to have conferred absolute primacy on Pope Sylvester I, early in the fourth century, was actually a medieval forgery.[12] He had also translated and edited a number of ancient Greek works, emending the received text according to philological criteria striking for their modernity. The treatment to which he submitted the New Testament was in fact slightly different, for – despite making a few observations on it – he was not primarily concerned with improving the Greek text. On the basis of various Greek manuscripts which had been discovered in Rome and in the vicinity of Milan but which have not been identified to anyone's satisfaction, he tried, as Manetti had done, to improve the extant version of the Vulgate.

In many respects Valla was astonishingly perceptive. He seems to have been the first scholar to believe that Jerome had not actually translated the Vulgate New Testament but had issued an already existing translation under his own name, only slightly revising certain parts. More important still, he corrected numerous words and passages in the Vulgate by comparing them to the Greek, aware, as he said, that some had been corrupted by negligent copyists, that others had been mistranslated in the first place and that still others had been deliberately altered to suit the dogmatic purpose of the moment. He was concerned too with improving the quality of the Latin style; but, in contrast to Manetti, he was opposed to rhetorical amelioration such as the use of different Latin words to translate the same Greek one.

Although some of Valla's alterations to the Vulgate were later to have grave dogmatic consequences – the most significant is his passage on faith and grace – he tended to avoid any interpretative comments.[13] His true importance lies in his insistence on the knowledge of Greek and the need to compare existing translations with the Greek text, his emphasis on grammatical precision and his use of non-Christian texts contemporary to the New Testament in order to attest usage. He was severely critical of all earlier theologians, including Augustine, who had ignored the Greek. Where Valla can be criticized – and where his methods were to be improved upon by later scholars – was in his choice of Greek manuscripts. These were by no means reliable, and Valla's treatment of them was uncritical.[14]

Despite the approval accorded to his methods by his employer, the humanist pope, Nicholas V, Valla was attacked fiercely in his lifetime. As in the case of Manetti, however, the manuscripts of his work seem to have had little circulation and no influence on his contemporaries. Only later was he more fortunate than Manetti. Valla's reputation was to be salvaged many years after his death by Desiderius Erasmus, who came across a manuscript of his notes on the New Testament in 1504 in a convent near Louvain and published them the following year. He himself elaborated on Valla's methods in the most influential work on the New Testament to appear in the early sixteenth century. But to this we will return after examining the parallel development of Old Testament studies.

In contrast to New Testament scholarship the study of the Old Testament was less connected with the hunt for manuscripts which might contribute to a more faithful rendering of the original. The reason for this is that, in the Renaissance, early manuscripts of the Hebrew text of the Old Testament were so rare as to be virtually inaccessible to European scholars. Later manuscripts, on the other hand, had been standardized by the Jewish grammarians known as the Massoretes, who, between the sixth and tenth centuries AD, provided the Hebrew text with vowel points. The problem which faced Renaissance scholars was one of understanding and interpretation far more than one of discovering codices. This meant the ability to read the targums, the Aramaic paraphrases of the Old Testament in circulation by the third century AD, and to understand the commentaries of far later rabbis writing between the twelfth and thirteenth centuries, especially those by Rashi, Abraham ibn Ezra and David Kimhi. The task of the Hebrew scholar was facilitated by the invention of printing in the middle of the fifteenth century and its application, at a relatively early stage, to Hebrew texts.[15] The centre of Hebrew typography was Italy, and in 1488, in the town of Soncino near Mantua, a fine edition was printed of the Massoretic text of the Old Testament.[16]

In comparison with this swift advance, largely the work of the Jewish communities, the knowledge of Hebrew among Christian scholars lagged behind. The man usually regarded as the pioneer of what is now known as Christian Hebraism, Giovanni Pico della Mirandola, was in fact very far from sharing the philological objectives of Manetti or Valla. Although he did comment on certain parts of the Bible, especially on Genesis and the Psalms, and although he occasionally cast a philological eye at the Hebrew, Greek and Latin texts, his deeper aim was to examine the Jewish Cabbalah, the medieval texts supposed to contain the more hidden doctrines of the Old Testament,[17] and to demonstrate the compatibility of Jewish and Christian revelation. Like Manetti, Pico learnt his Hebrew from Jews and Jewish converts to Christianity. His first encounter with Hebrew philosophy was at the University of Padua in the early 1480s, where he studied under the Jewish Averroist Elijah del Medigo. His true study of Hebrew, however, actually started later in the decade under the tuition of the convert Flavius Mithridates.[18]

The numerous observations on the Cabbalah scattered throughout Pico's writings, above all the idea that it could be reconciled with Christianity, lie at the beginning of the movement now called Christian Cabbalism. Pico was followed by the German Johannes Reuchlin, himself an outstanding Greek scholar, who was again primarily interested in the Cabbalah, but who assisted future students of Hebrew by publishing a grammar and dictionary in 1506. He was the first Christian to do so. The opposition which his commitment to Hebrew studies, and to the cause of the Jews, encountered illustrates the degree of prejudice which still had to be overcome. But it was thanks to Reuchlin that Christian Hebraism spread beyond the Italian borders and, owing to an ever wider group of practitioners, starting with Sebastian Münster in Basel, improved in the course of the sixteenth century.[19]

How deep Pico's – or indeed Reuchlin's – knowledge of Hebrew went is still open to doubt. It certainly fell far short of that of converted Jews. The first great product of biblical scholarship to be attributed to a combination of the new philological methods of the Renaissance and the knowledge of Hebrew came from another country which, like Italy, could call on the services of Jews converted to Christianity: Spain. The University of Alcalá was founded by the archbishop of Toledo and primate of Spain, Cardinal

Francisco Jiménez de Cisneros, late in the first decade of the sixteenth century. There the cardinal assembled the scholars who were to achieve the publication of a polyglot Bible, known as the Complutensian Polyglot after the Latin name of Alcalá de Henares (*Complutum*). Texts and translations of the Old Testament and the New, in the ancient languages, were to be presented beside versions in Latin. The six volumes of the work were printed between 1514 and 1517 but were only actually published in 1522. The Old Testament consisted of the Massoretic text of the Hebrew and the Greek Septuagint (with interlinear Latin translations) surrounding the Latin Vulgate. At the foot of the pages of the first volume, the targum of the Pentateuch (the first five books of the Old Testament) was given, also with a Latin translation. The New Testament was printed in Greek and in the Latin Vulgate version. The Old Testament, based on a variety of manuscripts including at least two of the Septuagint lent by the Vatican, was prepared mainly by three *conversos* or converted Jews: Pablo Coronel, Alfonso de Toledo and Alfonso de Zamora. The interlinear Latin translation of the Septuagint seems to have been the work of Juan de Vergara, also of *converso* descent, and of an Old Christian, Diego López de Zúñiga, later known for his attacks on Erasmus. The New Testament was edited by Demetrius Ducas, who was from Crete but had settled in Italy before coming to Alcalá, by Zúñiga and by the greatest scholar of all, Elio Antonio de Nebrija.[20]

Nebrija had studied at the universities of Salamanca and Bologna, and had lectured in Salamanca and Seville. In his two most important surviving works on the New Testament, his *Apologia* (*c.* 1507) and his *Tertia quinquagena* (1516), probably composed in the very first years of the sixteenth century, he showed himself to be a scholar of a calibre comparable to Valla. Yet at this stage he may not even have known Valla's writings on the New Testament, despite his ten-year stay in Italy between 1460 and 1470. Like Valla, he tried to improve the existing Latin text of the New Testament by comparing it with the Greek, and he advised the same technique where the Old Testament was concerned. Some of the solutions he suggested were even bolder and more ingenious than those of Valla, while others were similar.

The enlightened view of Nebrija did not always prevail over those of his more conservative colleagues, with whom he ended by quarrelling. The Alcalá Bible, as it stands, can be regarded as a defence of the Vulgate. Yet the editors were clearly aware of some of the more sophisticated problems posed by the manuscript tradition of the Scriptures. They were more sensitive even than Valla to the manner in which errors had entered the Latin manuscripts of the Vulgate as a result of the assimilation in passages by careless scribes of words, phrases or even sentences from similar passages in other parts of the Scriptures. Although the manuscripts they used were not always of the best quality, moreover, the editors realized that Greek codices were as subject to corruption as Latin ones. In their eagerness to defend what they thought to be Jerome's version, however, they sometimes showed a remarkable lack of scruples in emending the Greek to suit the Latin. The most notorious example is the 'Johannine comma' in the first of the Epistles of St John (1 John 5:7). The passage runs: 'For there are three that bear record in heaven, the Father, the Word and the Holy Ghost: and these three are one.' This important testimony of the Trinity is lacking in most Greek manuscripts but is to be found in the Vulgate. The editors of the Complutensian Polyglot went so far as to translate the passage from Latin into Greek and added it to the Greek text.[21]

The mere existence of the Complutensian Polyglot, and the fact that, by contemporary standards, it was a magnificent work of typography, stimulated similar efforts. These continued for some 200 years, becoming increasingly elaborate. Scholar after scholar endeavoured to produce multilingual editions of the whole or parts of the Bible with the object of establishing a text better than that delivered by his predecessor. The editors also sought to add further languages. One of the first to be added to Latin, Greek, Hebrew and Aramaic was Syriac, the study of which was introduced into Rome in 1515 by delegates from the eastern churches. The attraction of Syriac, apart from its proximity to Aramaic, was that it was widely read and sometimes still spoken by the eastern Christian communities with which the Vatican was renewing its relations in the hope of uniting them with Rome. Thanks to the Maronite monk who first gave lessons in Rome,[22] the knowledge of Syriac gradually spread from Italy to northern Europe. Teseo Ambrogio from Pavia, the Maronite's first pupil, taught Syriac to the Bavarian Johann Albrecht Widmanstetter. The relevance of Syriac to biblical (and patristic) studies came to be fully appreciated. The Peschitta, the Syriac translation of the Old Testament made mainly in the second century AD, was, in several books, too heavily influenced by the Greek Septuagint to be of much value for critical purposes; but the versions of the New Testament were thought to reflect an earlier version than any to which Jerome had access. Widmanstetter thus made a major contribution to biblical scholarship when he published his edition of the Syriac New Testament in Vienna in 1555.

The study of Syriac was attended by that of Arabic. The first attempt to incorporate an Arabic version of the Scriptures in a polyglot Bible was a Psalter which appeared in Genoa in 1516. Spread across two pages were the Psalms in Hebrew, a literal Latin translation, the Vulgate and Greek

Septuagint texts, an Arabic version and the Aramaic targum with a Latin translation. The editor was Agostino Giustiniani, a Dominican with a high reputation for scholarship, who had been appointed bishop of Nebbio in Corsica in 1514. Three years later he was invited by the French king, Francis I, to teach Hebrew in Paris. His Psalter, which was dedicated to Pope Leo X, was intended as part of an entire polyglot Bible, but Giustiniani was deterred from his plan by its lack of commercial success. Although it was criticized by Erasmus, the Psalter stood out in the development of biblical studies by providing a literal Latin translation of the Hebrew beside the Vulgate. This initiative was to be followed by the more expert Hebraist Sanctes Pagnini some years later when, as we shall see, he gave an interlinear translation of the entire Old Testament.[23]

While the Spanish scholars were preparing the Complutensian Polyglot and Giustiniani was compiling his edition of the Psalms, Erasmus was engaged in what has frequently been described as a truly revolutionary undertaking, but which was in fact rather more conservative than many historians would have one believe. This was an edition of the New Testament with the Greek version alongside his revision of the Vulgate, accompanied by a set of *Annotationes*. Erasmus had developed a strong distaste for scholasticism as a result of his education in Deventer in Holland (where considerable emphasis was laid on humanist learning) and his unhappy experiences at the University of Paris, which he attended in 1495 after obtaining permission to leave the Augustinian monastery of Steyn. This distaste, added to a deep love for the classics and the Church Fathers, whom he had been free to read in the monastery, was strengthened by a journey to England in 1499 and his encounter with John Colet, the future dean of St Paul's, who encouraged him to turn to New Testament studies. Colet himself had been influenced by three years spent in Italy, where, apart from reading the Church Fathers, he had started to study Greek. He also entered into correspondence with Marsilio Ficino.[24]

Erasmus's most effective encomium of the New Testament in these years was his *Enchiridion militis Christiani* ('The Handbook of the Christian Soldier'), which he started to write in 1502 and which was first published in 1503. It was here that he formulated his 'philosophy of Christ' (*philosophia Christi*), according to which the basic (and simple) precepts of the Scriptures should be regarded as the only moral values man need observe.[25] At this stage he advocated an allegorical interpretation of the Bible – and, indeed, he never seems to have abandoned the need to go beyond what he called the literal sense. Yet it was above all to the understanding of the literal sense that he was to contribute.[26]

In 1500 Erasmus had begun to study Greek. Four years later, as we have seen, he discovered a manuscript of Valla's notes on the New Testament in a convent library. These he promptly published in Paris, thereby securing Valla's reputation as a biblical philologist. An eloquent advocate of the direct consultation of the Scriptures, Erasmus came to believe that one of the most effective means of reforming Christendom was to produce a vastly improved Latin version of the New Testament. For this purpose, when he was lecturing on Greek at Cambridge in 1511, he embarked on the collation of Greek manuscripts. He saw a number of codices when he was in England, one of which, a fifteenth-century manuscript known as the Leicester Codex, is still regarded as being of value since it is related to a third-century text used by Origen. He consulted at least eight others in Basel and elsewhere. Finally, he based his edition of the Greek text of the New Testament above all on manuscripts of the twelfth century. By modern standards these codices are considered inferior since they are of the Byzantine text type rather than the Egyptian variety which Jerome had used. At the time, however, they were venerated and widely judged to be closer to the original than the manuscripts Jerome had revised for the Vulgate.

Although Erasmus's systematic collation of various Greek manuscripts shows that he was aware of the problems involved in establishing a Greek text, his primary concern in his edition of the New Testament was not the Greek but the Latin text. His criteria for improving on the existing version are set down in the vast volume of *Annotationes*, the first edition of which was to appear in 1516 together with the New Testament, and to which he added over the years. Where the Greek itself was concerned, Erasmus listed the numerous variant readings he had encountered not only in the manuscripts he had consulted but also in the Church Fathers. He resorted to the works of the Greek Fathers Chrysostom and Theophylact in order to recover variants often lost in the manuscript tradition, as well as to find interpretations current in the early Church. He was the first scholar to do this. Like Valla, moreover, he drew on non-Christian sources contemporary with the New Testament in order to elucidate difficult terms and to document the usage of the time.[27]

In his treatment and choice of variants Erasmus was ready to indulge in daring – and often correct – suppositions based on his own experience, knowledge and sensibility. He was aware of the existence of intentional alterations in the Greek text brought about by scribes. These could be attributed to various motives: the desire to complete a quotation or to harmonize it with the Septuagint, to make better sense of an obscure text and, worst of all, to attune a passage to theological needs. In assessing the certitude of the variants, Erasmus was the first scholar to suggest the principle of the 'harder reading' (*lectio difficilior*), maintaining that scribes would instinctively seek to replace a difficult expression by a simpler one rather than vice versa and that this could lead to corruption. He was also perceptive on questions of authenticity, doubting Paul's authorship of the Epistle to the Hebrews and John the Evangelist's of Revelation (a book which he regarded as of dubious authority). Sharing Valla's doubts about Jerome's responsibility for the Vulgate New Testament, Erasmus did not hesitate to emend the Latin. In the first edition of 1516, he also boldly omitted the 'Johannine comma', although he restored it in the third edition. He proved his thoroughness by collating a considerable number of manuscripts of the Vulgate, some of high quality and great antiquity. In his own emendations he did indeed attach some importance to the elegance of the Latin, but he did not go as far as certain humanists in his insistence on a fine style. Nor was he as inflexible as Valla in his rules for translating. Like Manetti and Traversari, he emphasized, rather, the need to convey the original sense in another language.

Erasmus was far more audacious than his predecessors in his treatment of earlier commentators on the Bible. He drew heavily, as we saw, on the Church Fathers for his emendations; but although he demonstrated his admiration by editing so many of them – Jerome, Augustine, Cyprian, Hilary, Chrysostom, Irenaeus and Origen – he did not spare his criticism when he considered them wrong. Jerome, he conceded, was fallible. 'I admit', he wrote in an annotation to Matthew 26, 'that he was a man of great learning, equally great eloquence, and of incomparable saintliness, but I cannot deny that he was human.' He was even sharper about the idol of the early humanists, Augustine, in his annotations on the Gospel of St John: 'undeniably a saint and a man of integrity endowed with a keen mind, but immensely credulous and, moreover, lacking the equipment of languages'.[28]

Erasmus thus treated the Church Fathers with respect but with discernment. For Origen he had a predilection which he shared with Ficino and Pico della Mirandola; for Erasmus, however, Origen was more than the great Christian transmitter of Neoplatonism: he was an instructor on every level. 'I learn more of Christian philosophy from a single page of Origen', he wrote in 1518, 'than from ten of Augustine.' Many of the Fathers suited Erasmus's purpose of the moment. The fourth-century Hilary of Poitiers, who led the fight against the Arian heresy and 'who because of the sanctity of his life, because of his extraordinary learning and because of his admirable eloquence was the light of his age', allowed Erasmus to deplore theological controversies in 1523, at a time when he was under particularly heavy attack from his opponents.[29]

In the 1516 edition of his New Testament, entitled *Novum Instru-*

mentum, Erasmus printed the Greek text next to his emended version of th Vulgate. A second and improved edition appeared in 1519. Three mor came out in Erasmus's lifetime – in 1522, 1526 and 1535 – each containing further emendations. Published by Johannes Froben in Basel, Erasmus' edition immediately obtained great publicity and circulated far more widel than the Complutensian Polyglot (which only appeared in 1522). Th publication was greeted with shouts of praise and cries of indignation. T most members of the world of learning Erasmus was already either a her or a villain, because of his 'philosophy of Christ' expressed in the *Enchir idion* and elsewhere and because of his appeals for reform and his outburst of savage criticism of the clergy in nearly all his works, the *Encomiun moriae* ('Praise of Folly', 1511) and the *Colloquia* ('Colloquies', 1522–33 being perhaps the most celebrated.[30] The reactions to Erasmus's Nev Testament ranged from those dictated by prejudice, a blind belief in th sanctity of the Vulgate and a terror of any attack on established ecclesias tical institutions, to those which reflected a true philological training an knowledge of the Greek text, such as the ones by López de Zúñiga an Nebrija.[31]

The swift diffusion of Erasmus's New Testament together with the annota tions meant that no theologian could afford to overlook the new philolo gical methods. So what effect did these methods have on the exegesis of th Bible? To begin with it seemed that the new critics' concern with linguisti precision had little to do with the traditional forms of scriptural interpreta tion and that the two could continue to survive independently of on another. According to the standard medieval scheme, four meanings shoul be sought in the Scriptures: literal or historical; allegorical or figurative tropological or moral; and anagogical or eschatological. Only the first o these needed to be affected by the new approach, and the philologists, as w saw in the case of Valla, at first made no attempt to invade the territory o the others. Nevertheless, the traditional division, with which Erasmu expressed his impatience, was gradually abandoned. What remained wa the literal sense, which might indeed depend on the progress of biblica scholarship, and a generally spiritual or moral sense. Erasmus and certai of his contemporaries, such as the French theologian Jacques Lefèvr d'Etaples,[32] sought to combine them; and to do so became increasingl common under the impact of the Reformation.

The attacks on Erasmus grew more violent and more dangerous in th course of the 1520s. This signalled a change which, however much it to owed to humanism, was going to challenge the humanist approach to th Bible. After Luther's final break with Rome in 1521, positions among hi ollowers polarized, and it was this that would jeopardize the objectivity which had inspired biblical scholars of the fifteenth century. The Protestant camp that developed included many humanists, admirers of Erasmus such as Johannes Oecolampadius, Philipp Melanchthon, Conradus Pellicanus and others. They carried on the task of editing the Church Fathers according to the philological criteria established by Traversari and Valla. Moreover, Théodore de Bèze (Beza), Calvin's successor in Geneva, drew up a series of annotations to the New Testament in the middle of the century, the object of which was to improve on, and ultimately to replace, those of Erasmus. The emphasis of the Protestants on the Bible as the word of God meant that the reading of the Scriptures was encouraged on every level of society and that the more learned Reformers, from Luther onwards, studied, and sometimes taught, the text in the original, offering instruction in Greek and Hebrew. The Vulgate was discredited and was replaced by new translations such as the German version by Luther. What was abandoned in this process was the doctrinal impartiality with which Valla and Erasmus had treated the Bible. Even in Bèze's annotations we see that special weight was given to the dogmatic consequences of the new translations. Valla's observations on faith and grace, for example, now obtained prominence because they suited Protestant doctrine. By the end of the sixteenth century, the Bible was read by Protestants not as an ancient work of literature to be studied in its historical context, but as a work addressed to contemporary readers to further the dogmatic purposes of the time and to support Protestant theological systems.[33]

The Catholic Church reacted even more sharply. On a popular level, the reading of the entire Bible was discouraged and sometimes even prohibited, especially in the vernacular. The Vulgate was hallowed as the only acceptable version. On an academic level, the Catholics too produced fine scholars, students of Greek and Hebrew, conversant with the rabbinic tradition. It was after all in Italy that the Flemish printer Daniel Bomberg, assisted by a converted Jew and with the full approval of Pope Leo X, printed for the first time in 1517 the rabbinic Bible, the Hebrew Old Testament accompanied by the targums and the rabbinic commentaries. Eight years later he produced a second improved edition.

One of the most distinguished practitioners of Hebrew was the Italian Dominican Sanctes Pagnini, who was at one time prefect of the Vatican Library as well as lecturer in Hebrew. With the backing of three popes (Leo X, Adrian VI and Clement VII) Pagnini provided a new translation of the Old and New Testaments, which he published in 1528. This version differed radically from the Vulgate and owed much to the commentaries of the rabbis when it came to translating obscure Hebrew words. For students of

Hebrew he also produced a grammar and a dictionary. Working in the years immediately after the Reformation, Pagnini could still avail himself of the tolerant climate that preceded it and concentrate on the study of the biblical tongues.[34] But this was not to last, as can be seen in the case of another Italian Hebraist towards the end of the century. The Jesuit Cardinal Roberto Bellarmino also taught Hebrew and published a good Hebrew grammar; he too was well acquainted with the rabbinic tradition; but rather than devote himself entirely to Semitic studies, he expended his talents above all on composing polemical writings directed against the Protestants.

Despite the polarization which became particularly evident during and after the Council of Trent, which was held from 1545 to 1563 and which defined orthodox Catholic doctrine against Protestantism, biblical studies did make some progress. This occurred above all in areas where changes of official faith and a consequently flexible confessional climate allowed certain tolerance. One of the last great products of humanism in the sixteenth century, the Biblia Regia or Royal Polyglot, was produced in Antwerp between 1569 and 1573. Although it was under the crown of Spain, Antwerp was sufficiently remote for a considerable liberty to be observed, and the plan to print the Bible was anyhow sponsored by the Spanish king, Philip II. Antwerp, moreover, had been Protestant shortly before. A town of merchants, it benefited from the continual contact between different confessional denominations. The printer of the Bible, Christophe Plantin, typographer royal, was a Catholic of notable adaptability in his beliefs, and the scholars assembled, the greatest in their field, could by no standards be considered orthodox.

In its final form the Antwerp Polyglot was a tribute to the foremost effort made in the domain of scriptural studies in the sixteenth century. In the Old Testament volumes, the Hebrew appears with the Vulgate, a literal Latin version of the Greek Septuagint and the Greek original, and the targum with a Latin translation. A separate volume gives the entire Hebrew text of the Old Testament once more, but with Pagnini's literal translation, slightly revised, printed between the lines. The New Testament is in two volumes: in the first the Greek appears beside the Syriac version and the Latin Vulgate; in the second the Greek is given with an interlinear Latin translation.

The Hebrew of the Old Testament was taken mainly from the Complutensian Polyglot with slight revisions based on the second edition of the rabbinic Bible. The targums of the Pentateuch also came from the Complutensian Bible, and the others from the second rabbinic Bible. The Greek texts were taken from the Complutensian Polyglot with variant readings from the third edition of the Greek text printed in Paris in 1550 and repared by Robert Estienne. This, the first edition of which had appeared 1 1546 and the second in 1549, was largely based on Erasmus's edition of he Greek text. The Syriac version was based on the New Testament published by Widmanstetter in Vienna in 1555.

Plantin and the chief editor of the Bible, the Spanish scholar Benito Arias Montano, had some difficulty in obtaining papal approval of the work: the use of Pagnini's translation (which was no longer in favour), the questionable orthodoxy of many of the editors, the implicit criticisms of the Vulgate - all inspired the papacy with scepticism. And even after approval had been gained, the work remained the object of suspicion in the Catholic world. One of the more illustrious editors, Andreas Masius, who had worked on he Syriac text and had himself learnt Syriac with Widmanstetter, got into still more trouble for pursuing the text critical tradition of the humanists. In his commentary on the Book of Joshua, he cast grave doubt on the Mosaic authorship of the Pentateuch, and his work was consequently placed on the index.[35]

The Antwerp Polyglot was accompanied by a large critical apparatus in which the Bible was treated as a work of literature in its historical context rather than as a source of dogma. This was where the future of high biblical studies lay. The great contributions of the following century, the *Annotationes* (1642) of the Dutch scholar Hugo Grotius, a Protestant, and the *Histoire critique du Vieux Testament* (1678) by the Frenchman Richard Simon, a Catholic, do the same thing. They seek to reconstruct the circumstances in which the Bible was composed on the basis of contemporary documentation, Christian, Jewish and pagan. In this they were deliberately following in the tracks of Valla and Erasmus; but even in the seventeenth century these works remain isolated monuments of scholarship in a field dominated by exegetes whose primary purpose was dogmatic.[36]

NOTES

My thanks are due to Professor H. J. de Jonge for his help and comments on a first draft of this article.

1   Petrarch, *Secretum*, trans. D. A. Carozza and H. J. Shey (New York, 1989).
2   See E. F. Rice, jr., *Saint Jerome in the Renaissance* (Baltimore, 1985), ch. 7.
3   Petrarch, *De otio religioso*, ed. G. Rotondi (Vatican City, 1958), p. 103. See also C. Trinkaus, *In Our Image and Likeness: Humanity and Divinity in Italian Humanist Thought*, 2 vols. (London, 1970), II, pp. 563–71. For the 'Sileni Alcibiadis', see M. M. Phillips, *The 'Adages' of Erasmus: A Study with Translations* (Cambridge, 1964), pp. 269–96.
4   In the first years of the fifteenth century Bruni translated a work by St Basil on the study of Greek literature.

5   C. H. Stinger, *Humanism and the Church Fathers: Ambrogio Traversari (1386–1439) and Christian Antiquity in the Italian Renaissance* (Albany, 1977), pp. 51–60, 84–166. See also G. C. Garfagnini, ed., *Ambrogio Traversari nel V centenario della nascita* (Florence, 1988).

6   See R. Loewe, 'The medieval history of the Latin Vulgate', in *The Cambridge History of the Bible*, 3 vols. (Cambridge, 1963–70), II, pp. 102–54.

7   B. Smalley, *The Study of the Bible in the Middle Ages*, third edition (Oxford, 1984).

8   Giannozzo Manetti, *Apologeticus*, ed. A. De Petris (Rome, 1981), pp. 20–2. On Manetti's career, see J. H. Bentley, *Politics and Culture in Renaissance Naples* (Princeton, 1987), pp. 122–7.

9   Trinkaus, *In Our Image*, II, pp. 573–601.

10 P. O. Kristeller, 'Valla', in his *Eight Philosophers of the Italian Renaissance* (Stanford, 1964), pp. 19–36.

11 Lorenzo Valla, *Collatio Novi Testamenti*, ed. A. Perosa (Florence, 1970); for the second version, known as the *Adnotationes*, see Valla, *Opera omnia* (Turin, 1962), pp. 801–95. See also C. Celenza, 'Renaissance humanism and the New Testament: Lorenzo Valla's annotations to the Vulgate', *The Journal of Medieval and Renaissance Studies*, 24 (1994), 33–52.

12 Lorenzo Valla, *The Treatise on the Donation of Constantine*, trans. C. B. Coleman (New Haven, 1922).

13 Valla's strongly held and often controversial views on theological issues were expressed instead in his treatises and dialogues; see C. Trinkaus, 'Italian humanism and scholastic theology', in A. Rabil, ed., *Renaissance Humanism: Foundations, Forms, and Legacy*, 3 vols. (Philadelphia, 1988), III, pp. 327–48 at 335–44; S. I. Camporeale, *Lorenzo Valla: umanesimo e teologia* (Florence, 1972); and M. Fois, *Il pensiero cristiano di Lorenzo Valla* (Rome, 1969).

14 J. H. Bentley, *Humanists and Holy Writ: New Testament Scholarship in the Renaissance* (Princeton, 1983), pp. 32–69.

15 About 140 extant books were printed in Hebrew in the fifteenth century, as compared to no more than 60 in Greek.

16 See S. Talmon, 'The Old Testament text', in *Cambridge History of the Bible*, I, pp. 159–70, and B. Hall, 'Biblical scholarship: editions and commentaries' *ibid.*, III, pp. 48–54.

17 G. Scholem, *Kabbalah* (Jerusalem, 1974); M. Idel, *Kabbalah: New Perspectives* (New Haven, 1988).

18 C. Wirszubski, *Pico della Mirandola's Encounter with Jewish Mysticism* (Cambridge MA, 1989), pp. 3–9, 53–65. On Elijah del Medigo, see D. Ruderman 'The Italian Renaissance and Jewish thought' in Rabil, ed., *Renaissance Humanism*, I, pp. 382–433, at 385–7. For Pico's cabbalistic interpretation of the opening verses of Genesis see his *Heptaplus*, in Giovanni Pico della Mirandola, *On the Dignity of Man ...*, trans. C. G. Wallis, P. J. W. Miller and D. Carmichael (Indianapolis, 1964), pp. 67–174.

19 F. Secret, *Les Kabbalistes chrétiens de la Renaissance*, revised edition (Milan 1985); J. Friedman, *The Most Ancient Testimony: Sixteenth-Century Christian Hebraica in the Age of Renaissance Nostalgia* (Athens OH, 1983).

20 See P. G. Bietenholz and T. B. Deutscher, eds., *Contemporaries of Erasmus: A Biographical Register of the Renaissance and Reformation*, 3 vols. (Toronto,

1985–7), II, pp. 348–9 (López de Zúñiga); and III, pp. 9–10 (Nebrija), 384–7 (Vergara). On Ducas, see N. G. Wilson, *From Byzantium to Italy: Greek Studies in the Italian Renaissance* (London, 1992), p. 146.

21 Bentley, *Humanists and Holy Writ*, pp. 70–111.

22 The Maronites were a Christian community of Syrian origin; they had been in formal communion with the Roman Catholic Church since 1182.

23 Bietenholz and Deutscher, eds., *Contemporaries of Erasmus*, II, pp. 102–3.

24 J. B. Gleason, *John Colet* (Berkeley, 1989); J. B. Trapp, *Erasmus, Colet and More: The Early Tudor Humanists and their Books* (London, 1991).

25 Erasmus, *Collected Works* (Toronto, 1974–   ), LXVI: *Spiritualia*, pp. 1–127 (*Enchiridion*, trans. C. Fantazzi).

26 C. Augustijn, *Erasmus: His Life, Works, and Influence* (Toronto, 1992), pp. 21–118; J. McConica, *Erasmus* (Oxford, 1991). For the theological dimension of Erasmus's biblical studies see E. Rummel, *Erasmus' Annotations on the New Testament: From Philologist to Theologian* (Toronto, 1986) and M. Hoffmann, *Rhetoric and Theology: The Hermeneutic of Erasmus* (Toronto, 1994).

27 H. J. de Jonge, '*Novum Testamentum a nobis versum*: the essence of Erasmus's edition of the New Testament', *Journal of Theological Studies*, new series, 35 (1984), 394–413; Bentley, *Humanists and Holy Writ*, pp. 112–93.

28 Rummel, *Erasmus' Annotations on the New Testament*, pp. 58–9. See also Rice, *St Jerome*, ch. 5.

29 Erasmus, *Collected Works*, VI: *The Correspondence: Letters 842 to 992*, trans. R. A. B. Mynors and D. F. S. Thomson, p. 35 (Letter 844); IX: *The Correspondence: Letters 1252 to 1355*, trans. R. A. B. Mynors, p. 261 (Letter 1334).

30 Erasmus, *Collected Works*, XXVII: *Literary and Educational Writings 5*, pp. 77–153 (*Praise of Folly*, trans. B. Radice); Erasmus, *The Colloquies*, trans. C. R. Thompson (Chicago, 1965).

31 See Erasmus's reply to López de Zúñiga: *Apologia respondens ad ea quae Iacobus Lopis Stunica taxaverat in prima duntaxat Novi Testamenti aeditione*, ed. H. J. de Jonge, in Erasmus, *Opera omnia* (Amsterdam, 1969–   ), IX.2. On Nebrija, see C. Gilly, 'Una obra desconocida de Nebrija contra Erasmo y Reuchlin', in M. Revuelta Sañudo and C. Morón Arroyo, eds., *El Erasmismo en España* (Santander, 1986), pp. 195–218.

32 See E. F. Rice, jr., 'The humanist idea of Christian antiquity: Lefèvre d'Etaples and his circle', in W. L. Gundersheimer, ed., *French Humanism* (London, 1969), pp. 163–80.

33 Bentley, *Humanists and Holy Writ*. pp. 194–219.

34 G. Lloyd Jones, *The Discovery of Hebrew in Tudor England: A Third Language* (Manchester, 1983), pp. 40–4.

35 Hall, 'Biblical scholarship', pp. 54–6, 73–5, 92.

36 H. J. de Jonge, 'Hugo Grotius: exégète du Nouveau Testament', in *The World of Hugo Grotius (1583–1645)* (Amsterdam, 1984), pp. 97–115.

7
Humanism and the origins
of modern political thought

JAMES HANKINS

Before the beginning of the sixteenth century, the humanist movement produced no political thinkers who could be ranked with figures like Plato or Thomas Hobbes. This is not surprising. Unlike modern political scientists or medieval scholastic philosophers, Renaissance humanists were not occupied with political theory as such. Professionally, humanists acted as teachers, diplomats, political propagandists, courtiers and bureaucrats. The writings they produced on politics were not cast in the form of *summae* or professional monographs intended for specialized audiences. Rather, they fell into the ancient tradition of moral-rhetorical literature aiming at the reform of individuals and society. Their models were Cicero and Seneca, not Aristotle or Thomas Aquinas; their virtues stylistic elegance, urbanity and learning, not subtlety. Such writings were intended for a general audience of liberally educated readers, which under Renaissance conditions meant mostly wealthy merchants, professionals and aristocrats. But 'political reflection need not be systematic analysis, and rarely is', as Sir Moses Finley has remarked. Though the humanists of the fourteenth and fifteenth centuries produced no great work of political philosophy, they did change fundamentally the intellectual world within which political thought would henceforward have to live. Their importance lay in producing not a system of thought, but a climate of thought. It is difficult to describe and assess this new climate of thought since the humanists themselves were hardly aware of it and might not themselves have approved of it had they been fully conscious of all its implications. The radical nature of the changes wrought by humanism becomes apparent only at the beginning of the sixteenth century. At that moment, in the space of a single decade, Europe produced two political thinkers of the highest rank – Niccolò Machiavelli and Thomas More – in whose writings were first revealed the characteristic dilemmas and tensions of modern political thought. Neither one of these thinkers had a simple relationship to the humanist movement. But neither one is imaginable apart from it.

It is sometimes said that reformers fall into two classes: those who believe in reforming the individual through the reform of institutions, and those who believe in reforming institutions by reforming individuals. The Italian humanists of the fourteenth and fifteenth centuries fall, by and large, into the latter class. The primary moral interest of humanists in these centuries lay in improving the level of prudence and wisdom among members of the ruling classes. It is easy to see why this should be the case. Humanists began to take part seriously in political life only in the late fourteenth century. Like our own, it was a post-ideological period. The great ideological battle of the Middle Ages, between papacy (supported by the Guelfs) and Empire (supported by the Ghibellines), had come to a close in the early fourteenth century. After the time of Dante the Empire ceased to have any real hold on Italian loyalties; political Guelfism was dead by the end of the fourteenth century. The Great Schism in the Church (1375–1415) had brought the pope and the ecclesiastical hierarchy into discredit. The great medieval movements for evangelical reform, apostolic poverty and popular government had become marginalized. Politically, the Renaissance was an age of tyrants and oligarchs, rulers with often questionable titles to legitimacy. In the general wreck of ideologies and political legitimacy, it was natural that humanists of the late fourteenth and early fifteenth centuries should turn their reforming energies to the individual. As the great humanist educator Guarino of Verona wrote:

> For he who is to take a leading part in the commonwealth, once provided with justice, goodness, prudence and modesty, can share the fruit [of his virtues] with all, and their utility commonly spreads to everyone. Philosophical studies do not have the same utility when undertaken by private individuals ... With good reason, then, did antiquity extol those who educated leaders, since in this way they reformed the mores and customs of the many by means of a single person: as, for example, Anaxagoras taught Pericles, Plato Dion, Pythagoras the Italian princes, Athenodorus Cato, Panaetius Scipio, Apollonius Cicero and Caesar; and, even in this age, Manuel Chrysoloras, a great man and a great philosopher, educated many men.[1]

A stress on individual rather than institutional reform may of course be read as a strategy of political conservativism, and it would not be unfair to describe humanist intellectuals as defenders of the status quo. Unlike modern intellectuals, who are almost by definition alienated from political authority, most humanists were dependent on the Church, secular princes or other members of the ruling class for their livelihood. Under such conditions, it was not prudent to advance a broad critique of the existing order. Most humanist writings on politics therefore took the form of moral admonition to rulers or panegyrics of the *patria* and its leaders. On the few occasions when analysis was called for, the tone was usually one of cool detachment and pragmatism, rather than fiery ideological commitment. In general, while humanists were frequently called upon to act as propagandists, they were not ideologues in the modern sense, that is, intellectuals committed to a single political ideology to the exclusion of all others. Humanist assessments of political systems were almost always in terms of better and worse, not good and evil. Following Aristotle, they accepted the existence of different constitutional forms as givens of nature. Political failures such as defeat in battle, civil strife or manifest injustice they tended to explain as the effects of vice; rarely if ever did they challenge the legitimacy of the three recognized 'good' constitutions – monarchy, aristocracy and the mixed polity – as such. Most of their political advice could as easily have been addressed to republican magistrates as to princes, and in some cases actually was. For example, the treatise *De principe* ('On the Prince'), written by Bartolomeo Sacchi (called Platina), was dedicated to King Ferdinand of Aragon in 1470; four years later it was slightly altered, given the title *De optimo cive* ('On the Citizen'), and dedicated to Lorenzo de' Medici. So, too, Francesco Patrizi of Siena, having composed a treatise in nine books *De institutione reipublicae* ('On Republican Education'), turned round immediately and composed another treatise of equal length and much the same content entitled *De regno et regis institutione* ('On the Kingdom and the Education of Kings', 1470s). In the former work, republics were praised as having the best constitutions; in the latter, kingdoms. Patrizi excused himself for the inconsistency by arguing the best state of a commonwealth depends on the virtue and wisdom of its rulers, not on its constitutional form.[2] If the humanists had any common political prejudice, it was against purely popular regimes. As civil servants who owed their political influence to specialized forms of knowledge, they were naturally suspicious of populism and naturally favourable to élitism, to guidance of the ignorant many by the wise few.

The lack of ideological commitment, the startling ability to change sides politically, typical of humanists from Petrarch and Coluccio Salutati to Machiavelli, is apt to seem hypocritical to modern eyes, and much ink has been spilt by modern scholars in the vain attempt to find some underlying consistency in the humanists' behaviour. What are we to make of republican humanists such as Leonardo Bruni and Salutati who were able to remain in office through violent changes of regime? Or Pier Candido Decembrio, who became secretary to the short-lived Milanese republic of 1448–50 after a quarter century in the service of the Visconti 'tyrant'? Or Giovanni Mario Filelfo, who wrote an epic poem in four books celebrating the Great Turk's conquest of Constantinople – an act surely unthinkable in the age of the great crusades? But their actions are more readily understandable if we consider the training and professional responsibilities of humanists and keep in mind the prevailing political climate.

All humanists had extensive training in rhetoric and delighted in their ability to argue both sides of a question. If reproached with levity on this score, they might admit (following Cicero) the ultimate duty of the orator to uphold moral virtue, but political consistency and ideological loyalty did not come into their definition of morality. The mental outlook and habits of expression fostered by rhetorical training permeated the culture. Renaissance Italians were not burdened with the cult of sincerity so typical of modern democratic societies; for them, sincerity was a trope like any other. It was more important that speech be appropriate, elegant and effective than that it be strictly true. The rules of decorum in fact called for the *celatio* (concealment) or *suppressio* of the truth, even the *suggestio* of the false, in the appropriate rhetorical situation.

The keen enjoyment of rhetorical virtuosity could lead to some arresting flights of insincerity. Such, for example, was the exchange of letters between Filippo Maria Visconti, the Duke of Milan, and the Florentine humanist Poggio Bracciolini in 1438. A truce had just been signed between the two states, and as a gesture of good will Visconti – or rather his humanist secretary Pier Candido Decembrio – wrote to the famous Florentine man of letters publicly denouncing some defamatory statements that had been made about the Florentines. This letter was a virtual panegyric of Florence: she was praised for her beauty, her freedom, for the brilliant culture and antique virtue of her citizens, for her martial valour, her well-known desire for peace, her defence of Italian liberty against Milanese aggression ('this one city by a kind of right has championed the liberty of the nations'), for 'never having desired to wreck the Empire by injury to its allies'. Nearly all the themes of this letter were taken directly from Florentine political propaganda, especially the *Laudatio Florentinae urbis* ('Panegyric of the City of Florence', 1403/4) written by the Florentine chancellor and humanist Leonardo Bruni. Nearly all had been fiercely contested by the same Pier Candido Decembrio during the previous war, especially in his *De laudibus Mediolanensium urbis panegyricus* ('Panegyric in Praise of the City of the Milanese', 1436). In this and other works of Milanese propaganda, Florence had been sharply criticized for her violence and her internal divisions, her reliance on mercenaries, her pretensions to cultural leadership, as well as for attempting to expand her empire under the cloak of defending Italian liberties. Her unprovoked attack in 1429 on her fellow-republic and former ally, Lucca, initiating an unsuccessful war of conquest, had provided a field-day for the Milanese propaganda machine; and when the Holy Roman Emperor took up residence in Lucca in 1431, Decembrio had been able to charge the Florentines with aiming at the ruin of the Empire. The reader of Visconti's letter to Poggio was thus expected to enjoy the rhetorical virtuosity and rich irony with which Decembrio had reversed his field. Poggio, of course, replied in kind. For half a century Filippo Maria and his father Giangaleazzo had been reviled by Florentine propaganda as the foulest of tyrants; now Poggio praised Giangaleazzo as a 'most excellent and praiseworthy prince', while Filippo Maria was described as 'the light and ornament of our age, in whom the ancient virtue and uprightness of the Italians shines forth anew'. This about a prince who slept with lighted candles, trained birds and relays of bodyguards lest he be murdered in his sleep by his subjects.[3]

While as propagandists the humanists could play rhetorical games such as these, as high level civil servants they were well acquainted with power politics and hard-headed political analysis. Councils of state charged with the conduct of foreign policy had to be concerned both with *riputatione*, the public image of the polity, and with its *utile*, its concrete economic and military interests. Often, the two were recognized to be in conflict. Humanist chancellors were responsible for composing the secret diplomatic correspondence sent to the state's *oratores*, or ambassadors (often themselves humanists), wherein the hidden aims and policies of the regime were set out, together with instructions for how those policies were to be publicly presented. Humanists also composed *missive*, or the foreign correspondence of the regime, which like the modern press conference aimed to place the publicly visible actions of the regime in the best possible light. Since they were spokesmen for, rather than formulators of, policy, no one thought of holding them morally responsible for the actions taken by their regimes; for their part, the humanists' attitude was that of permanent under-secretaries, loyal to the system rather than the regime, carrying out to the best of their ability the changing policies of successive political masters.

The habits of mind thus bred may be imagined: a certain moral flexibility, a certain hostility to theory, a well-developed ability to separate the normative from the descriptive, a settled belief that actual political behaviour follows interests rather than ideals. A striking example of how such 'realistic' attitudes might affect political thought is found in *Historia tripartita* ('An Enquiry in Three Parts', 1440), a set of dialogues by the papal secretary Poggio Bracciolini. One of the interlocutors is assailing the dignity of the law and the legal profession. After arguing that actual human laws bear no relation to natural law but vary with respect to times and cultures, the interlocutor continues:

Only the little people and lower orders of a city are controlled by your laws ... the more powerful civic leaders transgress their power. Anacharsis justly compared the laws to a spider's web, which captures the weak but is broken by the strong ... We observe, indeed, that commonwealths come to the height of empire through violence, and kingdoms are acquired not by law, but by strength and force, which are inimical to law ... What shall I say of the Roman commonwealth? Did it not grow by despoiling and devastating the whole world and slaughtering men – all of which are prohibited by the laws ... One may take the same view of the Athenians, whose power spread far and wide ... [They] would not have offered a home for literary study had they not enlarged their commonwealth. Philosophy, eloquence and the other civilized arts they discovered and cultivated would not have emerged ... For all famous and memorable deeds spring from injustice and unlawful violence, in contempt of the laws. To come down to our own times, have not the dukes of Lombardy, the Venetians and Florentines and many [others] thriven by desiring and seizing what belongs to others? ... Am I to believe that, when the Florentine people or the Venetians declare war, they call in the lawyers and declare war in accordance with their advice? Are they not rather motivated by utility and [the desire to] enlarge their commonwealth? Away then with these laws and rights of yours, which are an impediment to imperial expansion, the conquest of kingdoms and the enlargement of commonwealths, and are obeyed only by private persons and little folk who need their protection against the powerful! ... Grave, prudent and sober men do not need the laws; they declare a law of right living for themselves, being trained by nature and study to virtue and good behaviour. The powerful spit upon and trample the laws, as things suited to weak, mercenary, working-class, acquisitive, base and poverty-stricken folk, who are better ruled by violence and fear of punishment than by laws.[4]

The same empirical and utilitarian habits of mind are often visible, too, in humanist historical writings. Medieval historians tended to interpret events in moral and providential terms, regarding success and failure as divine rewards for virtue or divine punishments for sin. Humanist historians, by contrast, rigorously secularized the interpretation of historical processes, seeing events as the result of the virtues, aims and resources of human actors, or as outcomes dictated by the specific characteristics of a given political culture. Republican humanists, for instance, regularly argued that rule by the many tends to promote policies of peace. Cardinal Bessarion, in his *Oratio ad principes Italiae de periculis imminentibus* ('Oration to the Leaders of Italy regarding the Imminent Perils', 1471), offered a brilliant analysis of the logic of totalitarian expansionism, showing how the constitution of Ottoman society and government would inevitably compel the Turks to attack their neighbours. And while it is true that humanists believed history to be 'philosophy teaching by examples' – a source of positive role-models, as a modern person might say – it was also a school of prudence. Developing prudence meant understanding the real causes of events, not merely the apparent ones. This could lead, in historical works like Bruni's *Rerum suo tempore gestarum commentarius* ('Commentary on the Events of His Time', 1440/1) to a rudimentary awareness that the games of power politics operated according to rules distinct from the rules of morality.

The moral realism typical of humanist intellectuals helps explain the very different reception given to Plato's *Republic* and Aristotle's *Politics* in the fifteenth century. The *Politics* had been translated by William of Moerbeke in the thirteenth century, and was translated anew by Leonardo Bruni in 1436/7. The *Republic* was translated four times in the fifteenth century: by the Milanese humanist Uberto Decembrio (1402), by his son Pier Candido Decembrio (1439), by Antonio Cassarino in Genoa (*c.* 1447) and by Marsilio Ficino in Florence (1466/9). But though the *Republic* was more frequently translated than the *Politics*, the latter was by far the more popular text. While all 4 versions of the Latin *Republic* together survive in but 36 manuscripts and 2 incunables, Bruni's translation alone of the *Politics* survives in 208 manuscripts and 14 incunables. The *Politics* was read as a straightforward empirical approach to the actual behaviour of different kinds of polities, while its theoretical connections to Aristotle's naturalistic ethics and teleology were generally ignored. It was regarded as an invaluable store of political prudence and was widely used by humanist educators in Italian universities. The *Republic*, on the other hand, was never, as far as is known, publicly lectured upon and was even regarded with a certain suspicion. It was not simply that the outlandish social doctrines of Book V – communism, free love, female equality, abortion, euthanasia – were incompatible with traditional Christian morality. Plato's whole theoretical approach was held to be useless and impractical. Even humanists who defended Plato, such as the Decembrios, Bessarion and Ficino, admitted that the 'celestial polity' described in the *Republic*, while it might have some value as an ideal for saints or unfallen men, could certainly not be regarded as a blueprint for human society in its present state. It was simply too shocking, too experimental; it lacked the unreflective, sententious iteration of established bourgeois values that the humanists confused with wisdom. Bruni dismissed the *Republic* as inexplicably bizarre and useless, belonging to the same class as the writings of the despised scholastics, with their 'useless' preoccupation with natural science, metaphysics and other theoretical nonsense.[5]

Humanist political reflection, then, tended to be conservative, realistic, non-ideological and to stress education and individual moral reform. But though humanists fought shy of advocating the reform of political institutions, they could often be bold critics of prevailing social and cultural values. Such criticism, of course, could have important implications for political thought.

The roots of humanist social criticism are generally to be found in their worship of classical antiquity – the distinguishing mark of all Renaissance humanists. To be sure, the majority of late ancient and medieval Christian writers, from the age of Constantine forward, had approved certain parts of ancient pagan culture and had defended their incorporation into Christian civilization. But the rise of the humanist movement marked a general reorientation of Christian culture with respect to its classical past. It was the very definition of a humanist – of a *literatus* who practised 'good arts' to use contemporary terms – to advocate the restoration of classical cultural values. In his view, the failings of modern Christendom could mostly be traced to the loss of the classical heritage: the wisdom, virtue, military power and practical knowledge of ancient Italy. But to celebrate the past was inevitably to criticize the present. The effort to revivify the classical heritage inevitably brought these (mostly) urban, lay intellectuals into conflict with established guardians of culture and with the monastic and scholastic traditions of learning they represented. This is not to say that humanists were hostile to Christianity as such; this they would have denied heatedly; yet they were certainly hostile to many of the cultural values of medieval Christendom.

The condemnation of pride and vainglory, for example, had been a basic part of Christian teaching since its beginnings, but humanists correctly saw that reviving ancient traditions of public virtue would be impossible without also reviving the ancient prizes of fame and glory. So the rewards of virtue were transposed from the next life to this one. While the internal struggle between Christian humility and the desire for worldly glory had caused Petrarch considerable anguish, as can be seen in his *Secretum* ('Secret', 1340s or 50s), by the fifteenth century most humanists displayed no qualms about encouraging princes, popes and citizens to attain glory.

Fifteenth-century humanists also challenged traditional Christian ideas about marriage. St Paul had regarded marriage as a concession to those who could not control their lust. Late ancient monastic writers had developed an elaborate social hierarchy privileging sexual purity and the contemplative life; St Jerome had famously declared that the only real value of marriage was to procreate virgins for God. Humanist writers gave voice to more secular values. Matteo Palmieri in his *Vita civile* ('Civil Life', 1435/8) wrote: 'It is a useful thing to give birth to children: it increases the population and gives citizens to the fatherland. When they are carefully fitted for right living, they are useful outside the city and inside, in its wars and in peace, for the welfare and preservation of all.'[6] Marriage is the basis of the family, and families are the building blocks of the state. Husband and wife are a team designed by nature to guarantee the well-being of society. The husband's role is to acquire and the wife's to preserve; the wealth thus created benefits family, friends and the state. In defending wealth the humanists were implicitly criticizing the old Christian tradition of apostolic poverty, which since the thirteenth century had found an institutional voice in the Franciscan Order. Of course, there was an equally old tradition of interpreting poverty in a 'spiritual' sense, and medieval theologians had developed a body of casuistry defining an area of lawful mercantile transactions. But the attitude of many humanists was much more positive. Many humanists praised the acquisition of wealth as useful to individuals and to the state. The desire for wealth was universal and natural; the quest for it made one (as Poggio wrote), 'brave, prudent, industrious, sober, temperate, large-minded and wise in counsel'. Without wealth, it was impossible to display the virtues of liberality and magnificence. The poor were a threat to the welfare of the state; the rich rendered it beautiful, prosperous and powerful. It was money which gave strength and vitality to the commonwealth and enabled it to defend itself against enemies. In an age of mercenary armies, cities without rich citizens would soon lose their liberty. Monks and friars, on the other hand, contributed nothing to the common good: 'Please don't bring up the wild wastes of those hypocrites and strolling scoundrels who, posing as religious persons so as to catch their victuals without labour and sweat, preach poverty and contempt of the world to others (a very profitable line of business). Cities are founded on our labours, not by these lazy scarecrows', wrote Poggio in disgust.[7]

The praise of wealth was part of a larger revaluation of the active life of the citizen. Here fifteenth-century humanists were at odds not only with their medieval predecessors, but also with the dominant philosophical tradition of pagan antiquity. The Epicureans and Stoics, Plato and Aristotle, all held out little hope that those engaged in the public life of the Greek states could do so without compromising the highest philosophical and ethical standards. The life of the truly wise man was by definition one which renounced politics. Christianity reinforced this prejudice by making the contemplative life of monks the highest of vocations for Christians. But some humanists of the fifteenth century, drawing mostly on Roman sources, especially Cicero, called into question the traditional hierarchy of active and contemplative life. While generally not questioning the worth of contemplation in preparing the soul for the afterlife, humanists (and not only so-called 'civic' or republican humanists) established the political community as an alternative font of value. From the perspective of the community, as

Francesco Patrizi of Siena argued in his treatise *De regno*, the active life was much the more useful; it allowed greater scope for the practice of the virtues; while the goods coming from the contemplative life extended only to oneself. Beatitude (here, clearly, Christian salvation) was perhaps even easier to achieve in the active life than in the contemplative.[8]

Still more radical was Lorenzo Valla, who tried to break down entirely the distinction between active and contemplative lives in the interests of a kind of spiritual egalitarianism. Even humanists who preserved the distinction tended to extend the scope of the active life vastly beyond what their philosophical sources would warrant. While Aristotle confined the active life to those actually exercising political power or military command, humanists included in the active life rich businessmen, minor office-holders, bureaucrats, citizen-soldiers, courtiers, teachers and men of letters. Some theoretical consistency was thus sacrificed (Aristotle would probably have described such persons as following the pleasurable life); but the gain to humanists, in being able to preach virtue more profitably to a far wider audience, was considerable.

Humanists of the fifteenth century thus articulated an entirely new, lay view of Christian society that fused traditional Christian values with the civic values of the ancient pagan world. While they offered no direct challenge to the ecclesiastical polity of the Church and evaded issues of church and state, much of what they said had the effect of undermining the political claims of the late medieval Church. Often hiding behind the personae of interlocutors in their dialogues, humanists called into question the ideological bases of clericalism, hierarchy, monasticism and the subordination of political to religious ends. Sometimes humanist criticism of contemporary Christianity presented itself as a movement of reform, an attempt to return to the supposedly purer Christianity of the ancient world; sometimes it appears that preserving clerical orthodoxies was of less concern to humanist intellectuals than recovering the glories of classical civilization. In any case, it is clear that, at least in some matters, lay Christians were beginning to mount a serious intellectual resistance to the tutelage of their clerical superiors.

The emergence of a new humanist vision of Christian society had one other effect that is significant for the history of political thought. Humanist cultural criticism presented its audience with a choice between a powerful, united and highly civilized Golden Age in ancient Italy and a weak, corrupt and divided contemporary world. When preening themselves on their own achievements or flattering a prince, humanists praised the triumph of classical values over 'medieval' or 'Gothic' rudeness. In both cases, the mere existence of alternatives itself undermined the chief support of any traditional society: its inability to recognize the value and the possibility of other ways of doing things. The humanists' 'culture war' turned that inability into possibility, even actuality. Their intimate knowledge of another culture, their habit of comparing that culture with their own age, their realism and their habit of arguing both sides of a question led in the end to an incipient form of cultural relativism. This is perhaps most obvious in the writings of the late humanist writer Michel de Montaigne, but signs of it can already be found in Petrarch. A major lesson of cultural relativism, of course, is that what one is in the habit of thinking of as a given of nature may in fact be a product of culture. And what belongs to culture, not nature, is within human power to change. Applied to the sphere of high culture, the will to reject tradition and embrace change can lead to a Renaissance; applied to the political sphere, it can lead to a Utopia.

Medieval Italy produced two major traditions of constitutional thought, one that defended monarchy as the best form of government and another that saw in popular power the best guarantee against tyranny. Both these traditions were drawing consciously on ancient Roman authorities already in the twelfth century. Both traditions were continued and elaborated in the Renaissance. The most important innovation in the monarchical tradition during the Renaissance was the tendency among some humanists in the service of signorial regimes to break down the distinction between monarchy and tyranny. The revival of Greek studies in the fifteenth century provided new ideological resources encouraging this tendency. The translation of ancient Greek writings on tyranny, such as Isocrates' *To Nicocles*, Xenophon's *Hiero* and the *Letters* of Pseudo-Phalaris – all immensely popular texts – only reinforced the characteristic moral realism of the humanists. While the fourteenth-century jurist Bartolus of Sassoferrato had established usurpation and active injustice as the two criteria for identifying tyrants, Renaissance humanists had more pragmatic ways of assessing the worth of a prince. Some, like Pier Candido Decembrio, argued that, all power being originally illegitimate, what counted was its virtuous exercise. Sometimes, as in Francesco Griffolini's preface to his translation of the *Letters* of Pseudo-Phalaris, it was even argued that tyrants were much like other men; that some of their acts were just, others unjust; and that one should weigh the virtues and defects of the whole man rather than trying to fit him into artificial, *a priori* categories of 'good' or 'bad' prince, king or tyrant.

In modern histories of political thought humanist writings on republicanism have predictably attracted much more attention than their reflections on monarchy and tyranny. Yet the common term 'Renaissance republicanism' is to some extent a misnomer, since the republican tradition in Italy begins in the twelfth century and lasts until the end of the eighteenth. Expressions of republican ideology first appear in the mid twelfth century and are found continuously in the tradition until the fall of the Venetian republic to Napoleon in 1798. The chief turning points in the history of republican thought in Italy come with the recovery of Aristotle's *Politics* in the late thirteenth century and with the writings of Machiavelli at the beginning of the sixteenth. In comparison with these major influences, the humanist contribution to republican ideology before Machiavelli is a modest one. It did not significantly alter the terms of the medieval debate about republicanism; nor was it so original in other ways that one may usefully speak of a distinct tradition of Renaissance republicanism.[9]

Nevertheless, humanist republicanism does present some special features of interest. While the earliest humanists of the late thirteenth century had embraced a populist form of republicanism, the Florentine and Venetian humanists who revived the republican tradition in the late fourteenth century, yielding to current political realities, reinterpreted it in oligarchic terms. These humanists also adapted to contemporary conditions by learning to celebrate the glories of empire. In the later fourteenth century, Rome, Venice, Florence and Milan had begun to gobble up neighbouring cities and to incorporate them into territorial states; republican humanists, drawing upon the imperial ideology of republican Rome, learned to praise these achievements as the defence of liberty against tyranny. Later humanists, moreover, had a much wider and more sophisticated grasp of classical history and moral philosophy than the rhetoricians and scholastics who had been the spokesmen for republicanism in the Middle Ages, and they were able to put this knowledge to good use in enriching the concept of republican life, upholding the value and dignity of the active life, the *vivere civile*, against detractors. Finally, Leonardo Bruni and other Florentine humanists of the early fifteenth century, following the classical historians Sallust and Tacitus, developed a republican interpretation of history which associated the flourishing of arts and letters with periods of political freedom, while linking the decline of civilization with monarchy. They were the first Whig historians.

The writings of Leonardo Bruni provide a good example of how the populist folklore of the medieval commune was quietly reinterpreted as an oligarchic ideology. But like the regime whose interests they reflected, their oligarchic tendencies are often hidden under a cloak of populist rhetoric. Florentine political language and values had been forged in the period of the so-called *popolo secondo*, medieval Florence's second period of popular rule, which during the 1280s and 90s had drawn up the anti-aristocratic

Ordinances of Justice and had created the basic republican institutions by which Florence was technically ruled until 1494. After the 1290s, the popular character of the regime had been progressively eroded by a group of old, wealthy and powerful families who exercised power in a covert fashion while preserving the forms and language of the popular commune. Bruni's writings, too, while often seeming to celebrate Florence's traditions of freedom and popular participation in government, can objectively (as Marxists used to say) be seen as subtly reinterpreting those traditions in oligarchic terms. Read superficially, Bruni seems to favour a broadly based political class; but read more closely, with due attention to the rhetorical conventions he uses, it can be seen that Bruni in fact prefers rule by a narrow (though virtuous) oligarchy.[10]

Bruni's attitude to the Florentine empire can also be seen as a faithful reflection of the values of the oligarchy. The imperial expansion of Florence in Tuscany in the period from 1382 to 1440 was defended by the leadership as necessary to Florence's security requirements in its ongoing war with the 'tyrant' of Milan. In fact, it solidified the power of the oligarchy in many ways: by giving it the prestige of conquest; by creating enormous new opportunities for patronage in the subject towns; by relieving the fiscal pressure on Florence itself; by providing new markets for Florentine goods. Bruni, far from feeling shame that a free republic had put down the liberties of other cities, positively revelled in its triumphs. He became the Rudyard Kipling of the Florentine empire. In his *Laudatio Florentinae urbis* he had come close to articulating a jingoistic view of the Florentines as naturally superior to other peoples. He continued this line in the *Historiarum Florentini populi libri XII* ('History of the Florentine People in Twelve Books', 1416–44). The chief purpose, indeed, of Bruni's *Historia* was to celebrate the growth of Florence's empire. He endorsed the view of the oligarchy that the empire was an instrument of liberty, guaranteeing the safety of Florence and its subject towns from Milanese aggression (a view, needless to say, not always shared by the subject towns). But he also praised expansionism as desirable for its own sake. In a speech attributed to Pino della Tosa at the end of Book VI, Bruni argued that military conquest encouraged the growth of civic virtue and devotion to the common good. Yet when the imperial adventure turned sour in the 1430s after the failed war against the Republic of Lucca, Bruni blamed the failure on the rashness of the people, who had pushed the 'wise and prudent men', that is, the oligarchs, into action against their better judgement.[11] This verdict, too, was less than frank in allotting responsibility.

Bruni, then, was no populist, but a faithful servant of both the Albizzi oligarchy and the Medici party, and his writings largely reflect their outlook. This does not mean, however, that Bruni secretly thought Florence's liberty and republican institutions nothing but a sham. Though capable, in bulls written for the Roman pontiff, of defending the principle of papal monarchy, and though he might, in letters to princes, extol the wisdom and felicity of their rule, he may well have thought that Florence's way of life was significantly more free than that of contemporary signorial regimes. Certainly, he preferred for himself to live under a republican regime. The main reason for this preference was doubtless his conviction that arts and letters flourished best under republican government. In holding this view, Bruni was flying in the face of the fourteenth-century humanist tradition. Petrarch and other humanists of his time tended to associate literary study with the contemplative life and had argued that the contemplative life was most compatible with autocratic government. Bruni challenged this view by relocating arts and letters within the circle of the active life, seeing the life of letters and creative activity as a way of serving the city. Thus, the arts of civilization naturally flourished most under republican regimes, which placed the highest value on the active life of the citizen. Eventually, in his history of Florence Bruni worked out an entire theory of historical development which identified the highest moments of human culture with its moments of greatest political freedom: Periclean Athens, late republican Rome and the modern Florentine republic.

After the Medici coup of 1434 the fiction that Florence enjoyed popular rule became more difficult to maintain. Though some humanists like Platina continued to assert that Florence was a free popular republic under Medici leadership, there was an increasing tendency in the later Laurentian period to reinterpret or even reject Florence's traditional republican folklore. It is sometimes said that this tendency was encouraged by the revival of Platonism during the later fifteenth century in the Florentine circle of Marsilio Ficino. Some scholars have gone so far as to suggest that the revival of Plato was a conscious strategy of Medici patronage: that the Medici used Platonism as an ideological tool to justify their regime and render docile their citizens. The argument runs that Platonism, more clearly than Aristotelianism, preferred rule by philosopher-kings to democracy and encouraged a revival of the contemplative life which undercut the values of the republican *vivere civile*.

This argument is not totally false. It is true to say that the revival of Platonism, and especially of Plato's *Laws*, provided intellectual resources to some Medici partisans for the repudiation of Florence's republican tradition. But the argument needs strong qualification.

First, the revival of Plato in Renaissance Florence had begun with

Leonardo Bruni, not Marsilio Ficino. And even in the supposed heyday of 'civic humanism' in the early fifteenth century, there were many humanists, such as Ambrogio Traversari, Poggio, Niccolò Niccoli and Giannozzo Manetti, who did not embrace Bruni's attempt to relocate literary and philosophical studies within the sphere of the active life and to establish its equality with the contemplative life. Secondly, Plato was by no means the only philosopher to be invoked in favour of early Medicean government; Johannes Argyropulos used Aristotle's *Politics* to the same effect; Aurelio Brandolini found in Thomas Aquinas's *De regno* a rich source of monarchical arguments; Bartolomeo Scala and others adduced Stoic and Augustinian authorities. There is no reliable evidence that any of the early Medici favoured Platonism over other philosophical schools. Furthermore, Plato's writings could be, and were, used by Florentine humanists like Bruni to defend republican government and the active life. George of Trebizond used Plato's *Laws* to celebrate the aristocratic mixed constitution of the Venetians, and Francesco Patrizi's *De regno* used Plato and Socrates as authorities for the superiority of the active to the contemplative life. A number of writers (including Marsilio Ficino) used Plato's image of the cave in Book VII of the *Republic* to argue that philosophers had a duty to participate in political life. The statement in the pseudo-Platonic *Letter* IX (358A), that 'each of us is born not for ourselves alone, but also for our family, our friends and our country' became, indeed, a commonplace in the humanist defence of the active life. So it would be incorrect to say that the revival of Platonism in some way caused the shift from a republican to a monarchical ideology in Medicean Florence. Rather, it may be said that the emergence of the Medicean principate provided an opportunity for a particular interpretation of Plato's political thought to achieve expression. But it was far from being the only interpretation of Plato available in the fifteenth century.

The repudiation by the Mediceans of Florence's republican tradition did, however, produce what is arguably the most searching piece of constitutional analysis by any humanist before Machiavelli. This was Aurelio Brandolini's *De comparatione reipublicae et regni* ('A Comparison of Republics and Kingdoms', *c.* 1490), a work with almost no circulation – it survives in two manuscripts – and which is practically unknown to modern scholarship.[12] It was written by a Florentine exile at the court of King Matthias Corvinus of Hungary and dedicated to Lorenzo de' Medici. In form it is a Socratic dialogue modelled on the early works of Plato (the only true Socratic dialogue of the Renaissance known to the present writer); in content it is a devastating critique of the ideological assumptions of Florentine republicanism, placed in the mouth of Matthias Corvinus himself. Corvinus's interlocutor, a Florentine merchant named Dominicus

Junius, attempts to argue that republics are freer, that they are more just and equal, that they have a more splendid cultural life, that they are better governed, more stable and less subject to corruption. Corvinus destroys these arguments one by one. Interestingly, the analysis of liberty is conducted entirely in terms of 'negative' liberty, the ability to do as one pleases, rather than 'positive' liberty, the freedom to rule oneself. That self-government might be valuable in itself as necessary to the dignity or happiness of the individual seems a notion beyond the horizon of the interlocutors.[13] Also noteworthy is the empirical and even cynical tone of the debate: Corvinus points out the corruption of the electoral system; the way office-holders are controlled by the rich through debt and influence-peddling; the practical limits on free speech; the tendency of the judicial system to serve the interests of the rich; how the absence of economic equality turns any other form of equality into a sham; how arrogance and peculation are bred by Florence's imperial attitude to her subject towns; the way Florentine foreign policy is corrupted by economic interests; the impossibility of anyone serving the common good given the innate psychological characteristics of human beings. The dialogue shows better than any other text the bankruptcy of traditional Florentine republicanism in the generation before Savonarola and Machiavelli.

The end of the fifteenth century in Europe saw the beginnings of the military revolution and the emergence of the modern state, two developments which set off long crises in European society, government and political thought. At a geopolitical level, the Ottoman Turks had finally recovered from the long succession crisis following the death of Mehmed II in 1481 and were renewing their assault on eastern Europe and the Mediterranean; many western commentators, observing the political divisions and the lack of credible religious leadership in the west, believed the final extinction of Christendom had now become a real possibility. The European crisis was particularly acute in northern and central Italy, an area which lost its dominant position in the European economy soon after 1500 and for the first time since the mid thirteenth century came under the control of non-Italian powers. The disastrous decades around 1500 shattered the cultural self-confidence of some Italians, particularly in Florence, and led to some serious questioning of their cultural traditions. The naïve claim of the humanists that political reform could be effected through moral uplift among the political classes came to be regarded with scepticism. Humanists had had control of Italian education for a century before 1494. But where were Italy's great leaders, her patriot soldiers, her wise statesmen, when Charles VIII had marched the length of Italy in a few months virtually unopposed?

In the realm of political thought the crisis went still deeper. The assumptions of the entire western political tradition from Plato onwards were called into question by a generation of radical thinkers, of whom the greatest and most radical was Niccolò Machiavelli.

That Machiavelli was himself a humanist, in the most concrete professional sense, can no longer be denied.[14] His relation to the previous tradition of humanist thought, however, is more complex. Certainly, he inherited that flexibility of political loyalties characteristic of humanists in general; what he wanted was power, and he did not much care whether he enjoyed it under a princely or a republican regime. Like the humanists, he believed that encouraging virtue among the ruling classes was the most effective means of reform. He was interested more in changing political culture than political institutions. He believed that the study of classical antiquity held lessons for the modern world and that the Roman empire had a special exemplary status as the most successful polity in world history. He was certainly realistic in his political analysis; he eschewed teleology in historical explanation; and he was a frank critic of contemporary Christianity.

There, however, the resemblance ends. Machiavelli wrote treatises to curry favour both with the Medici and with their republican opponents, but when writing as a republican, he was far more populist in his outlook than his humanist predecessors. This was because the regime he served before 1512 and the regime he aspired to serve in the later 1520s both aimed at wide participation; the regime that ruled Florence between 1494 and 1512, indeed, enjoyed the widest extent of popular participation of any government in Florentine history since the time of the Ciompi revolt of 1378.[15] Whatever might be said about his own commitment to republicanism, Machiavelli was the first Renaissance humanist to defend popular government in his published writings.

Secondly, Machiavelli's critique of Christianity is far more radical than anything in the humanist tradition.[16] Previous humanists, aware of the conflict between pagan and Christian values, try either (like Valla) to recast current Christianity in light of pagan values; or (like Ficino) to minimize the differences between high pagan and Christian theology; or (like Bruni) to make a sharp distinction between political and religious values, assigning to each its proper sphere. Machiavelli makes no attempt to hide the fact that Christian morality is inconsistent with the morality needed to create a successful polity along the lines of the Roman republic. He boldly subordinates religion to the interests of civil society. His instrumental view of religion, surely incompatible with religious belief, has no parallel in earlier western political thought.

Machiavelli also breaks with humanist tradition in the way he uses classical authorities. Earlier humanists had advocated a gestural or external imitation of the ancients: the reproduction of speech, actions, artifacts and virtues. Machiavelli rejects this kind of imitation altogether as superficial. What he wants to know from the past, and especially from the Roman past, are the secrets of power and success. To do this he needs to get beyond the pieties of ancient and modern moralists, past the naïve belief that the ancients were somehow made of better human stuff than the moderns. One had to study the actions of the ancients (as well as the moderns) to discover, not their moral beliefs, but how they had actually behaved, and why this behaviour had failed or proved successful. One could then derive certain rules of conduct which would limit the role of fortune and increase the chances of success. By following these rules one would acquire, not the four cardinal virtues of traditional morality, but *virtù* in Machiavelli's special sense of the word: strength, prowess, ability, power.

In *Il principe* ('The Prince', 1513) especially, but also in his *Discorsi sopra la prima deca di Tito Livio* ('Discourses on the First Decade of Livy', 1513/19), Machiavelli stresses that the rules for successful behaviour in politics are unrelated to the rules of behaviour inculcated by traditional morality. It is here that Machiavelli challenges a set of assumptions fundamental to western political thought and unquestioned by any earlier humanists. From the time of Plato philosophers had agreed that there was an unbreakable connection between nature, happiness and virtue. Nature, it was held, wanted human beings to be happy; she was designed in such a way as to produce happiness for those who followed the rules of correct behaviour. The rules of correct behaviour, the laws of nature for mankind, were the virtues and were discoverable by reason. The exercise of the virtues led to happiness. An analogous system governed political life. States were natural institutions. If they were to be happy, their rulers had to act with virtue. The whole art of politics consisted in producing and conserving virtue in those who ruled the polity. Even Augustine, though he transposed the rewards of virtue to the next life, did not deny the ultimate connection between creation (both eternal and temporal), goodness and happiness. The part of nature we experience in this life, subject to time and change, might be defective in the sense of not rewarding virtue with happiness; but virtue aided by grace would ultimately enjoy beatitude when the soul escaped from temporal to eternal creation.

It is precisely this connection between nature, happiness and traditional virtue that Machiavelli denies. His reason for doing so is stated bluntly in the famous fifteenth chapter of *Il principe*:

Because there is so much difference between how men live and how they ought to live, the ruler who forsakes what is usually done for what ought to be done invites ruin, not self-preservation. For a man who wants to take a vow of goodness in all things must come to ruin among so many who are not good. Therefore a prince who wishes to remain in power must necessarily acquire the ability to do evil, using it or not using it as necessity requires.[17]

Machiavelli's point, no doubt a bitter lesson of the *calamità d'Italia* in his time, is that survival is a precondition of all other goods and that there can be no happiness in slavery. Since survival sometimes requires behaviour at variance with traditional morality, one must be prepared to abandon that morality if one is to maintain the minimal condition for happiness, political freedom. Machiavelli thus flatly denies the central conviction of Cicero's *De officiis* and of all earlier humanist moral thought, that there can be no conflict between the moral and the useful, between the *honestum* and the *utile*.

It has been argued by Isaiah Berlin that what Machiavelli is actually doing is reviving a 'pagan' morality to oppose to the Christian morality of his time and that his originality consists in his recognizing the incommensurability of these two moral systems.[18] But this cannot be the case. There are no ancient moralists – with the exception, perhaps, of Gorgias and Thrasymachus – who would condone the kind of behaviour Machiavelli calls for in his two famous political treatises. The wicked no doubt prospered in the ancient as in the modern world, but there was no pagan code of morality that sanctioned vice in the interests of political power. Equally mistaken is the contention of Benedetto Croce and his many followers that Machiavelli divorced politics from morality. What Machiavelli has in fact done, in effect, is to recognize the moral heteronomy of ends and means: that not all good ends can be secured by good means, that not all good means issue in good ends. In so doing he has left behind the unified eudaemonistic and teleological ethics of older western thought and has embraced the dilemmas of modern ethics, where *being* good and *doing* good are often seen to be in conflict. On the one hand, a 'consequentialist' ethics where the goodness of ends must be allowed to trump the goodness of means; on the other, a 'deontological' ethics where the goodness of an act is dependent on its being free from the interests (in the Kantian sense) of the actor: this is the new ethical world that Machiavelli began to explore in the second decade of the sixteenth century.

Machiavelli is sometimes called the father of political science, and it can now be seen why this is so. He argues that political life is subject to a different kind of moral calculus, one in which an actor must be held responsible for the results even of 'good' acts. The prince who allows disorders to arise because he shrinks from cruelty is responsible for the evils resulting from his 'goodness'. What this consequentialist ethic presupposes, however, is that we can predict accurately the full results of our actions in any given set of circumstances. Without a reasonable certainty about the consequences of our acts (as G. E. Moore pointed out), no moral principles can be derived; unless we know our cruelty will suppress disorders, there can be no possible justification for it. The claim, then, that a consequentialist ethics can be valid is tantamount to a claim that we have a scientific knowledge of human behaviour, taking 'scientific' in the sense of being able to predict behaviour according to known laws of human nature. This kind of knowledge-claim is one that Machiavelli makes over and over again in *Il principe* and the *Discorsi* (whence he was criticized by Guicciardini for putting things 'too absolutely'). Again and again he says that if rulers act in a given way, certain results must necessarily follow. He assumes (1) that human nature is uniform in time and space, (2) that human beings act nearly always from selfish motives and (3) that they act rationally. Applying these principles to particular circumstances, rigorously ignoring issues of right and wrong, will enable the experienced observer to predict the behaviour of political actors and hence to make the correct decisions so as to avoid undesirable outcomes. The structure of consequentialist ethics (and Machiavellian political science) thus requires the observer to make a rigid distinction between fact and value, between the descriptive and the normative. This distinction, too, is one of the characteristic marks of modern moral and scientific reasoning, distinguishing it from the teleological reasoning of the pre-modern west, in which value may be derived from fact and fact from value.[19]

There has never been any doubt that Thomas More should be classed as a Renaissance humanist: his professional employments, cultural style and the range of problems he addresses all clearly identify him as such. Yet More's relationship to earlier humanist political thought is even more complex and troubled than Machiavelli's. He agrees with earlier humanists that justice should be the fundamental aim of commonwealths; he upholds the centrality of virtue, the positive worth of the active life and the value of humanist education. At the same time, his attitude to the moral realism typical of Italian humanism is ambivalent at best. He is no social conservative: his denunciations of nobles and landowners and his glorification of the working poor have no parallels among his predecessors. Nor can one doubt his commitment to at least some political principles, for he sacrificed his life in protest against Henry VIII's moves to place the ecclesiastical polity of England under royal control. He had a far greater respect for traditional

Christian morality and for clerical orthodoxies than most Italian humanists: he could not agree, for example, that the pursuit of private wealth and military glory was beneficial to the commonwealth. Indeed, his most famous work, the *Utopia* (1516), has been described as 'by far the most radical critique of humanism written by a humanist'.[20]

Utopia begins by stating a dilemma which is also a clear challenge to earlier humanist thinking. The dominant tradition of humanism in the fifteenth century had believed true philosophy to be form of prudence – a practical wisdom to be studied by political leaders (or their advisers) in the interests of increasing their virtue. Plato's famous dictum from the *Republic* V (473C–E), that states would not be happy until philosophers ruled or rulers became philosophers, was quoted endlessly by humanists in support of this position; in the Italian context it was often little more than a veiled request for patronage. For More and his generation of English humanists, however, Plato's dictum had become a paradox. For them, a philosopher at court was like a cow in the parlour: his presence could only be a matter for laughter followed by speedy ejection. It was a mark of the true philosopher (as Plato had said) to speak his mind fearlessly in the presence of tyrants, tell the truth and accept no gifts from princes. But the dynamics of court life called for lying, flattery and dissimulation, for advertising one's standing by accepting gifts and honours, for telling the prince what he wanted to hear instead of what he needed to hear. The problem was, in effect, structural and cultural: it was not that the prince was necessarily a bad man, but rather that the social and cultural pressures on him to behave in particular ways were too strong to be overcome. The character of More in the dialogue, to be sure, calls for the man of good will to do his duty by advising the prince, using 'a more urbane form of philosophy'; but it is clear that he has no great hope of improving the situation thereby and feels that he has even in some way betrayed the highest kind of philosophy, represented by the character of Raphael Hythloday.

Book I concludes that the 'more urbane philosophy' of the Italian humanists (and perhaps also of Erasmus) has little hope of improving social and political life. The 'idealistic' More tells his 'realistic' predecessors that they have been too naïve in judging the atmosphere of courts. In Book II the argument is generalized. More in effect asks: what would have to change in society for it to embrace the values that we, as humanists and as Christians, believe in? What would it take for society to reward people according to their merit and their contribution to the common good, not according to their wealth and ancestry? Clearly, educating princes and oligarchs in the classics is not going to do the job. If we analyse the defects of human society, they can all be traced to money and pride. Through the mouth of

Hythloday, More suggests that the only way to rid European society of these evils would be to effect a radical social revolution, abolishing social rank and private property. Only thus can Christendom achieve the *optimus status rei publicae*, the best constitution of the commonwealth. Only thus can the conflict between active and contemplative lives be resolved: for only in Utopia can a philosopher speak his mind without fear and serve the common good without injury to his soul.

The central problem of interpreting *Utopia*, is deciding 'how far More intends us to admire the portrait of Utopian society sketched by Hythloday in Book II'.[21] The problem is doubly complex, for if Utopia is clearly a philosopher's republic, *Utopia* is, in part at least, a satire on contemporary Christendom. One approach to the problem is to see how philosophers' republics were regarded in the Renaissance. Here it can be said unequivocally that, in the case of Plato's *Republic* at least, all Renaissance interpreters were agreed in regarding it as a *divinus status rei publicae*: a polity for unfallen or sanctified men, meant as a ideal form to aid in the discovery of correct political principles, but not as a blueprint for actual societies of sinful men.[22] As the name 'Utopia' ('No-Place') implies, More, too, did not mean his commonwealth to serve as a practical model for contemporary European societies. It exposed the ineffectiveness of contemporary political nostrums and perhaps provided a few suggestions about how modern societies might be improved, but it could never be fully implemented in practice. This reading is reinforced by the framing irony of the whole work. For Hythloday, like the philosopher in Book VII of the *Republic*, is after all doing his duty to the rest of mankind (notwithstanding his protestations to the contrary) by leaving the sunlight of Utopia, returning to the darkened cave of contemporary Christendom and sharing his vision of true statecraft with two budding statesmen. Yet More the character (and, I would argue, More the author) at the end cannot accept Utopia as a model for Europe in any but a few inessential respects – exactly the reaction Hythloday (and Plato) predicted from the unphilosophical.

In the end, More glosses Plato's famous paradox with one of his own. His message is that states cannot reach their best condition until rulers become good men; but rulers cannot become good men until states are in their best condition. For More, this was a tragic message, no less tragic for the wit and imagination with which it was expressed. All attempts at political reform ultimately involve the reformer in a vicious circle. The humanist ideal of reform through education will not work because it fails to address the root causes of Christendom's disorders. Only radical reform will work, but modern Europe is too committed to private property and social hierarchy for such reform to have any hope of success. It may be thought that More here was only restating an Augustinian view of the post-lapsarian polity as necessarily corrupt. But there is an important, indeed crucial, difference between Augustine's necessity and More's. Augustine's necessity was metaphysical at root: there is no possibility of an *optimus status rei publicae* in the world of the senses, time and change – in the *saeculum* – since that world is nothing but an inferior reflection of the eternal and immutable world that is our true home. Nature herself forbids any real, permanent progress. More's necessity, by contrast, is human and mutable. An optimal constitution may be impossible in the world as we know it; the weight of tradition and human perversity may seem to us crushing; but we can without absurdity imagine a world where it is possible. The only obstacles to achieving progress are human obstacles. Though More probably thought those obstacles insuperable – he was, himself, no Utopian – he nevertheless founded a tradition of political reflection that took human institutions as the work of custom and history rather than of nature, and therefore plastic to the hand of human beings. In our own time we can never forget that political Utopianism has been responsible for the worst horrors in human history; but we should also remember that it is responsible for much of the genuine progress our civilization has made since the sixteenth century. It was Thomas More, no less than Niccolò Machiavelli, who helped mankind achieve that consciousness of its own power which is the curse and the blessing of the modern world.

NOTES

1 Letter of Guarino to Gian Nicola Salerno (1418), in E. Garin, ed., *Il pensiero pedagogico dell'umanesimo* (Florence, 1958), p. 328.

2 Francesco Patrizi, *De regno et regis institutione* (Paris, 1511), pp. vii–viii [I.1]; strikingly similar sentiments are expressed by Francesco Filelfo in a letter to Leonello d'Este; see his *Epistularum familiarium libri XXXVII* (Venice, 1502), f. 44^r.

3 Poggio Bracciolini, *Opera omnia*, ed. R. Fubini, 4 vols. (Turin, 1964–9), I, pp. 333–9.

4 Poggio, *Opera*, I, pp. 32–63, at 48–9 (*Historia tripartita*).

5 J. Hankins, *Plato in the Italian Renaissance*, 2 vols. (Leiden, 1990), especially vol. I, pp. 63–6.

6 Matteo Palmieri, *Vita civile*, ed. G. Belloni (Florence, 1982), p. 161.

7 Poggio, *Opera*, I, pp. 1–31, at 13 (*De avaritia*); for an English version of this work, see B. G. Kohl and R. G. Witt, eds., *The Earthly Republic: Italian Humanists on Government and Society* (Manchester, 1978), pp. 241–89.

8 Patrizi, *De regno*, p. cclvii (VI.5).

9 J. M. Blythe, *Ideal Government and the Mixed Constitution in the Middle Ages* (Princeton, 1992).

10 J. Hankins, 'The "Baron thesis" after forty years, and some recent studies of Leonardo Bruni', *Journal of the History of Ideas*, 56 (1995) 309–38.

11 Leonardo Bruni, *Difesa contro i reprehensori del popolo di Firenze nella impresa di Lucca*, ed. P. Guerra (Lucca, 1864).

12 I consulted Brandolini's *De comparatione reipublicae et regni* in MS Florence, Biblioteca Mediceo-Laurenziana, Plut. 77, 11.

13 On this characteristic of Renaissance republicanism, see Q. Skinner, 'The republican ideal of political liberty', in G. Bock, Q. Skinner and M. Viroli, eds., *Machiavelli and Republicanism* (Cambridge, 1990), pp. 293–309.

14 R. Black, 'Machiavelli, servant of the Florentine republic', in Bock, Skinner and Viroli, eds., *Machiavelli and Republicanism*, pp. 73–8.

15 N. Rubinstein 'Machiavelli and Florentine republican experience', in Bock, Skinner and Viroli, eds., *Machiavelli and Republicanism*, pp. 3–16.

16 Though not, perhaps, in private discussions among humanists. See Brandolini's *De comparatione*, f. 12^r, where 'Corvinus' remarks: 'nor are there lacking those who accuse the Christian religion, and say that we have been rendered fearful and ignoble by it' (a view the Corvinus persona rejects).

17 Niccolò Machiavelli, *Il Principe e Discorsi sopra la prima deca di Tito Livio*, ed. S. Bertelli (Milan, 1960), p. 65.

18 I. Berlin, 'The originality of Machiavelli', in M. Gilmore, ed., *Studies on Machiavelli* (Florence, 1972), pp. 147–206.

19 See A. MacIntyre, *After Virtue*, second edition (Notre Dame IN, 1984).

20 Q. Skinner, *The Foundations of Modern Political Thought*, 2 vols. (Cambridge, 1978), I, p. 256. My discussion here is indebted to this work and to Skinner's article, 'Sir Thomas More's *Utopia* and the language of Renaissance humanism', in A. Pagden, ed., *The Languages of Political Theory in Early Modern Europe* (Cambridge, 1987), pp. 123–57. The standard edition is in Thomas More, *The Complete Works* (New Haven, 1963–), IV: *Utopia*, ed. E. Surtz and J. H. Hexter.

21 Skinner, 'More's *Utopia*', p. 141.

22 Hankins, *Plato*, I, pp. 142–3, 227–32, 339–40.

8

Philologists and philosophers

JILL KRAYE

In the Renaissance the discipline of philosophy was based on ancient systems of thought: Aristotelianism predominantly, and to a lesser extent Platonism, Stoicism, Epicureanism and Scepticism. This continued to be the case well into the seventeenth century. As specialists in the study of classical antiquity, humanists were therefore able to make an important contribution to philosophy in this period: rediscovering ancient philosophical texts that had been lost or neglected for centuries and supplying editions, translations and commentaries both for these works and for other classical texts which had been part of the philosophical curriculum since the Middle Ages.

Though philosophers and humanists shared an interest in the same texts, their methods of approaching this material differed radically. Humanists believed that philosophical discourse, like all forms of learned communication, should be composed in a Latin style modelled on the best classical authors. The stress they laid on clarity, persuasiveness and, above all, eloquence was a deliberate challenge to the scholastics, who monopolized university teaching of philosophy and who wrote in a technical, jargon-laden language, incomprehensible to non-philosophers. More importantly, humanists studied philosophical works in the same manner that they dealt with literary or historical texts, that is, as philologists. As the name itself indicates, philologists were devotees (*philoi*) of the study of words (*logoi*): they drew on their expert knowledge of the language, culture and history of Greece and Rome to determine the precise meaning of an ancient author's words in a specific context. Philosophers, on the other hand, prided themselves on their devotion to the search for fundamental truths and timeless wisdom (*sophia*). For scholastic philosophers, this meant studying the treatises of Aristotle by means of logic and other analytical tools, seeking not so much to elucidate his words as to understand his arguments and to resolve complex problems, many of them deriving from the Middle Ages and only tangentially related to what Aristotle himself had written.

Such differences in approach meant that the interaction between philologists and philosophers was often difficult, and at times acrimonious. Nevertheless, as we shall see, humanists played a significant role in the development of Renaissance philosophy, and their influence continued to be felt in the seventeenth century, when what we now think of as modern philosophy began to take shape. The humanists' involvement in philosophy had an impact on them as well. In its early phases, humanism had focused on literary, rhetorical, grammatical and historical works. But, from the mid fifteenth century onwards, the intellectual horizons of humanists gradually began to widen, and increasingly they extended and sharpened their philological skills by applying them to the entire range of texts produced in antiquity, including all branches of philosophy.

Virtually the complete corpus of Aristotle's writings had been available in Latin since the end of the thirteenth century. While the medieval translations adequately served the purposes of philosophers, they did not suit the refined tastes of humanists, who complained that they were too literal (degenerating on occasion into mere transliteration from the Greek), that they were disfigured by numerous inaccuracies and that they were written in a Latin style which fell far short of the standards of classical antiquity. To remedy the situation, humanists made new translations that were less obscure and more elegant than their medieval counterparts. Frequently, however, the humanists' fondness for elegant variation led them to be inconsistent in their translation of technical terms; in addition, they abandoned the standardized vocabulary which scholastics had developed over the centuries, a specialized language which philosophers needed in order to maintain the continuity between their own arguments and those which had been formulated in the Middle Ages. Many professional philosophers therefore preferred to stick with the medieval translations: William of Moerbeke's version of *De anima* (*c.* 1268), for instance, continued to be used in university courses and in published commentaries (sometimes in conjunction with one of the new and more readable humanist versions) until the second half of the sixteenth century.[1] It also has to be said that for all the humanists' abuse of their medieval predecessors, many of their own versions were little more than cosmetic revisions of the older translations: errors were corrected and the Latin polished, but the underlying structure remained intact.[2]

From about 1450, a group of émigré scholars from the Byzantine Empire made important advances in the translation of Aristotle. Not only was their native knowledge of Greek superior to that of Italian humanists, they also had wider interests, including within their ambit all Aristotle's works, not just his treatises on moral philosophy, which had previously been the centre of humanist interest. Johannes Argyropulos, who taught at

Florence and Rome, translated *De anima*, *De caelo*, the *Physics*, the *Metaphysics* and a good portion of the *Organon*, as well as the *Nicoma chean Ethics*.[3] A more successful version of the *Metaphysics* (as late as the nineteenth century, it was still the standard Latin translation) was produced by Cardinal Bessarion, a Byzantine monk who rose to the highest levels of the Catholic Church and was a key player in the fifteenth-century revival of Platonism.[4] The translations of the *Historia animalium* and the pseudo Aristotelian *Problems* made by Bessarion's protégé, Theodore Gaza, won widespread (though not universal) praise: 'Aristotle', it was said, 'now appears speaking good Latin.'[5] Gaza also brought an impressive degree of philological acumen to his work as a translator: he recognized that Books VII and IX of the *Historia animalium* were transposed in the manuscrip tradition and regarded Book X as spurious – both judgements are accepted to this day.[6]

Gaza's disciple, the Venetian patrician Ermolao Barbaro, carried on the tradition of uniting eloquent Latin translations with careful, philological attention to the Greek text, the two hallmarks of humanist Aristotelianism.[7] He also added a third dimension to this programme, which was to be of considerable significance for Renaissance philosophy. Barbaro's 1481 Latin version of Themistius' *Paraphrases* (fourth century AD) was the first humanist translation of an ancient Greek commentary on Aristotle. Though a handful of these commentaries had been translated in the Middle Ages, they remained largely unknown.[8] Humanists believed that the Greek commentators, belonging themselves to the ancient world (though some, in fact, were Byzantines), had much greater insight into Aristotle's thought than the Latin scholastics or the influential Arabic commentator, Averroes.[9] It therefore became part of their agenda to make these texts accessible and to promote them as replacements for the medieval commentary tradition Barbaro combined this goal with his desire to demonstrate that even the more scientific and technical disciplines within philosophy, such as those treated by Themistius, could be expressed in elegant, classical Latin.[10] The Themistius translation was, in fact, part of his campaign to reform Aristotelianism: first, by grounding it in philological knowledge of the Greek text of Aristotle and his ancient commentators; and second, by retranslating the entire corpus into a Latin characterized by lucidity, precision and refinement – a practical demonstration of his belief in the union between philosophical wisdom and rhetorical eloquence.[11]

In the dedication of his translation of Themistius' commentary on the *Physics* to the humanistically inclined physician, Antonio De Ferrariis (Il Galateo), Barbaro made clear his strong disapproval of professional philo sophers, who regarded themselves as the only competent interpreters of

Aristotle's thought and looked with contempt on those who, like himself, studied philosophy from a humanist perspective. For Barbaro, on the other hand, to approach philosophy without a secure knowledge of ancient languages and culture, as contemporary Aristotelians did, was to pervert and corrupt it.[12] In thanking his friend for dedicating this important philosophical work to him, Galateo set out his own commitment to the ancient Greek commentators,[13] as well as his enthusiastic support for Barbaro's assault on the philistine character of university Aristotelianism. He too despised the convoluted and captious sophistry of the scholastics and rejected their belief that literary style was irrelevant to philosophy: would Aristotle have written the *Rhetoric* and *Poetics* if he had thought these disciplines were useless to the philosopher? But Galateo, unlike Barbaro, also perceived the dangers in going too far in the opposite direction. While philosophical discourse should not be so unpolished and unrefined that it gives offence to readers, equally it should not be deformed by an excess of rhetorical ornamentation. Nor should philosophy be reduced to mere philology, in the new-fangled manner of pedantic grammarians such as Lorenzo Valla.[14] Focusing on purely linguistic issues, these humanists continually complained that 'this word is not good Latin' or 'that one is obscure'; philosophy, however, was concerned not with words but with uncovering the secrets of nature.

A few years later Barbaro himself provided a textbook example of the narrowly philological approach to philosophy disparaged by Galateo. In a letter to another of his friends, Giovanni Pico della Mirandola, Barbaro dismissed medieval scholastics such as Thomas Aquinas and Albertus Magnus, not on account of their philosophical acumen, which he conceded was of a high order, but because of their unsophisticated and inelegant Latin. Pico, who had devoted many years to studying these philosophers, took the same line as Galateo: what mattered in philosophy was not words but reason, not style but substance. He had nothing but contempt for 'those grammaticasters' who preened themselves on every etymological discovery and regarded philosophers with aversion and disdain. And while eloquence was fine in its place – in letters to scholarly friends, for instance, as he brilliantly demonstrated in this very reply to Barbaro, or in speeches such as his famous *Oration on the Dignity of Man*[15] – it was not essential in works of philosophy written to demonstrate, rather than embellish, the truth. There, instead, what was required was unadorned accuracy, free from the distortions imposed by rhetorical gimmickry.[16] In 1489, when a young Aristotelian philosopher sent him a treatise dealing with the nature of sound, which began with an apology for his imperfect Latin, Pico replied:

There is no need to makes excuses to me about the fact that your style is not terribly learned. If a philosopher is eloquent, I am pleased; if he is not, I do not mind.[17] The philosopher has one duty and aim: to unlock the truth. Whether he does so with a wooden or a golden key is of no concern to me; and it is certainly preferable to unlock it with a wooden key than lock it with a golden one.[18]

The views of Pico's sparring partner, Barbaro, quickly bore fruit in hi native Venice. In 1495 the Venetian humanist Girolamo Donato, a clos associate of Barbaro, published a Latin translation of Alexander of Aphro disias' De anima (c. AD 200); this work was to exert a powerful influenc on the Tractatus de immortalitate animae ('Treatise on the Immortality c the Soul', 1516) of Pietro Pomponazzi, who drew on the ancient Gree commentator in order to demonstrate that Aristotle did not support th Christian position on the soul, thereby igniting a controversy which woul transform the Renaissance discussion of philosophical psychology.[1] Between 1495 and 1498 Aldus Manutius published in Venice the firs edition of Aristotle's works in Greek. And in 1497, Niccolò Leonic Tomeo, a Venetian of Greek ancestry, began to lecture on the Greek text c Aristotle at the nearby University of Padua, the stronghold of scholasti Aristotelianism. Leonico managed the difficult feat of putting Barbaro" humanist reform programme into action without losing his credibility as philosopher. He did so by studying the philological aspects of Aristotle" text without neglecting philosophical questions; by translating some of th more scientific works, such as the Parva naturalia (1523) and the pseudo Aristotelian Mechanics (1525), into a Latin which combined classica correctness with terminological precision; and by drawing heavily on th Greek commentators, but using them in conjunction with Thomas Aquina and other medieval interpreters.[20]

Barbaro's legacy still remained strong in Venice in the mid sixteent century, when Agostino Valier, the future cardinal and bishop of Verona taught philosophy at the Rialto school. A fervent admirer of both Barbar and Donato, Valier carried forward their new brand of Aristotelianism b studying the Greek text of Aristotle and giving prominence to the Gree commentators.[21] He stressed, in particular, the necessity of combinin wisdom with eloquence, as had been done by Plato, Aristotle and all th best philosophers. Though Valier maintained that the pursuit of stylisti elegance could be carried too far, he thought that those who were unable t produce good Latin should refrain from writing, or at least from publishing books of any sort. In fact, he believed that most books (including his own did not deserve to be published and noted pointedly that the wisest men – Socrates, Pythagoras and Christ – had written nothing at all.[22]

Among the more important contributions of humanists to Renaissance Aristotelianism was, as we have seen, their commitment to the Greek commentators on Aristotle.[23] Another way in which they influenced Peripatetic philosophy was their attempt to remove from the canon works that had been falsely attributed to Aristotle. As with the Greek commentators, here too Barbaro helped to show the way. In the *Corollarium* to his translation of the *Materia medica* (first century AD) of Dioscorides, he suggested that the treatise *De plantis* had been falsely ascribed to Aristotle: the appearance of Arabic plant names in the text showed that it had been translated into Greek from an Arabic work.[24] Barbaro was not alone in believing that *De plantis* was spurious – it was deliberately omitted from the Greek Aldine Aristotle and replaced by the botanical works of Aristotle's successor Theophrastus; but it was not until 1556 that a detailed attack on the treatise was published. Julius Caesar Scaliger, an Italo-French humanist who specialized in Aristotelian studies, used both philological and philosophical arguments to show that the work had originally been written in Arabic, then translated into Latin and, finally, rendered from Latin into Greek in the late Middle Ages. As an Aristotelian scholar (he had translated and commented on the *Historia animalium*), Scaliger was able to demonstrate how far *De plantis* differed from the method and doctrine found in the philosopher's other works. As a humanist, he employed his knowledge of ancient languages and history to point out both the Latin vestiges which remained in the Greek text and the anachronistic statements which signalled its inauthenticity – the mention, for example, of agricultural practices in Rome (821^b7–8), which even a child would recognize could not have come from Aristotle, information about Roman matters being very thin on the ground in fourth-century Greece.[25] The Dutch humanist Daniel Heinsius, a student of Scaliger's son Joseph, produced an equally impressive demonstration of the inauthenticity of *De mundo*, based on a vast amount of linguistic, literary, historical and philosophical evidence.[26] Such efforts did not radically change the shape of the Aristotelian corpus, especially since treatises with extant Greek texts, such as *De plantis* and *De mundo*, even though no longer believed to be genuine, continued (and still continue) to be printed in editions of Aristotle. Nevertheless, the valuable information turned up by these humanist endeavours became available to philosophers and helped to make them more discriminating when dealing with Aristotelian works.

Philosophers did not, of course, take kindly to the invasion of their territory by humanists, and many battles were fought before an accommodation of sorts was reached. The fact that most humanists were prepared, like Barbaro, to dismiss any philosophical treatise which was not eloquently written provoked anger and frustration among those philosophers who, like Pico, continued to value the inelegant but profound works produced by medieval thinkers. Ludovicus de Valentia, in the preface to his 1492 edition of Thomas Aquinas's commentary on the *Politics*, complained that contemporary rhetoricians 'take too much delight in verbal cleverness and embellishment; content to know what the words mean, they forget to inquire diligently into the natures and properties which the words express. The result is that they condemn works which lack polish, even though they contain the truth.'[27] A few years later, when the scholastic philosopher Lorenzo Maioli sent his treatise on dialectic to Aldus Manutius, the humanist publisher initially refused to print it, for while it contained worthwhile material, it fell below his required standard of literary quality. Maioli insisted, however, that Aldus should not regard with contempt the transmission of unadorned wisdom. Echoing Pico, he argued that philosophical works were not in need of artful presentation: their aim was to deliver unvarnished truth, not sparkle.[28]

Other aspects of the humanists' philological method of studying philosophy also met with resistance from traditional philosophers. When in 1492 Angelo Poliziano, the most learned classical scholar of his day, began to lecture at the University of Florence, not on Latin or Greek literature, as he had in the past, but on the *Prior Analytics*, one of the most difficult texts of Aristotelian logic, members of the philosophical faculty resorted to ridicule: 'Here he is, Poliziano, the jester, suddenly playing the philosopher.'[29] But Poliziano, whose interest in Aristotelian philosophy had been stimulated by his great friend Pico,[30] made no such claims: 'Even though I lecture publicly on Aristotle, I do not do so as a philosopher.'[31] In his inaugural lecture, full of verbal artistry and recondite classical erudition, he announced to his opponents (referred to as *lamiae*, or blood-sucking vampires) that as a philologist (*grammaticus*), an all-purpose expert on ancient texts, he was entitled to interpret any type of work – poetical, historical, rhetorical, medical, legal or philosophical.[32]

In his analysis of Aristotelian logic, Poliziano laid great emphasis on the views of the Greek commentators; like his friend Barbaro, he believed that they offered a sounder interpretation of Aristotle than the medieval commentators, for whom he felt typical humanist disdain: 'on account of their ignorance of both Greek and Latin, they polluted the purity of Aristotle's works with their vile and dreadful hair-splitting to such an extent that sometimes it made me laugh and at other times made me angry'.[33]

During the course of the sixteenth century, the humanist prejudice against the seemingly impenetrable complexities of scholastic logic led to its gradual decline: university philosophy textbooks began to focus solely on Aristotle and his ancient commentators, leaving aside the additions and innovations to his system made during the late Middle Ages. While this humanist approach brought the benefit of an improved understanding of Aristotelian logic, it also meant that the technical advances made by scholastic logicians were ignored, to be recovered only in the present century.[34]

The increasing tendency in the sixteenth century to replace Averroes's commentaries on Aristotle by the ancient Greek ones provoked a rearguard action. In 1550–2 an ambitious multi-volume Latin edition of Averroes commentaries, printed together with the works of Aristotle, was brought out in Venice by the publisher Tommaso Giunta. One of his aims was to counterbalance the extreme Hellenism of the humanists: 'so addicted are they to the Greeks that they proclaim the writings of the Arabs to be no better than dregs and useless trash'. This backlash, though forceful, was short-lived: few editions of Averroes were printed after 1575.[35]

Some aspects of scholastic Aristotelianism did manage to survive into the seventeenth century. For the most part, however, these were combined in a somewhat uneasy synthesis with a humanist approach to Aristotle. The Jesuit Tarquinio Galluzzi, for instance, in his massive commentary on the *Nicomachean Ethics* (1632–45), made liberal use of scholastic commentaries, especially those of Thomas Aquinas, and preserved the traditional *quaestio* format; yet he also included the Greek text as well as a Latin translation, paid careful attention to philological issues and took account of the Greek commentators.[36] Despite such attempts to clothe the scholastic Aristotle at least partially in humanist dress, those seventeenth-century philosophers who believed that Aristotelianism could provide a foundation for the new mechanical philosophy insisted on removing from it every trace of scholasticism. G. W. Leibniz, one of the founders of modern philosophy, through his support for this movement to recover the ancient Aristotle, divested of scholastic accretions, can be seen as a participant in the final stages of the humanist programme for the reform of Aristotelianism.[37]

Unlike Aristotelianism, the other sects of classical philosophy were not central to the entrenched interests of professional philosophers and made few inroads into the universities. Humanists, therefore, were free to apply their philological methods to the study of Platonic, Stoic, Epicurean and Sceptical texts without opposition from university-based philosophers.

In the case of Platonism, it was a combination of humanist linguistic skill and philosophical acumen, in the person of Marsilio Ficino, which proved fundamental to its revival in the Renaissance. Although Ficino received a traditional Aristotelian education at university, he was as much at odds with the scholastic philosophers of his day as his humanist contemporaries:

'they are not lovers of wisdom (*philosophi*) but lovers of ostentatious display (*philopompi*), who in their arrogance claim to have mastered Aristotle's thought, although they have only rarely and briefly listened to him – not even in Greek but stammering in a foreign tongue'.[38] His own philosophical inclination was towards Plato rather than Aristotle, primarily because, as a priest, he considered Platonism to be more compatible with Christianity. It was Ficino who put Platonism on the philosophical map of the Renaissance, first and foremost by providing Latin versions of all the dialogues (first published in 1484), most of which were unknown to western European scholars, as well as translating a large amount of Neoplatonic literature from late antiquity, which provided the intellectual framework for his Christianized interpretation of Plato.[39] A philosopher as well as a philologist, Ficino avoided many of the pitfalls of humanist translators of philosophical texts: his versions were accurate but without stylistic flourishes; he captured the precise meaning of technical expressions in the Greek and did not shy away from medieval terminology when it conveyed the sense more clearly than a classical construction.[40]

The Platonic studies of Ficino, which included commentaries and original treatises as well as translations,[41] soon attracted the attention of philosophers, even those solidly within the scholastic Aristotelian tradition. Yet, for university philosophers, the works of Plato and the Neoplatonists remained a point of reference against which Peripatetic positions could be defined rather than texts to be examined in their own right.[42]

Ficino had a more dramatic impact on humanism, particularly its literary side. Cristoforo Landino, a former teacher of Ficino but in philosophical matters his disciple, employed the tenets of Platonism and Neoplatonism which he had absorbed from Ficino as hermeneutic tools to uncover hidden levels of meaning in Books I–VI of Virgil's *Aeneid*. In Landino's interpretation, Aeneas' travels are revealed as an allegory for the soul's upward journey from mindless devotion to pleasure (Troy), through political activity (Carthage) to contemplation of the divine (Italy), the ultimate goal of human existence; the final six books of the poem, in which Aeneas fights bloody wars against the native Italians, are conveniently left out by Landino.[43]

Much of the literary influence of Ficinian Platonism was channelled through the vernacular tradition. Here the humanist preoccupation with classical antiquity was given wider dissemination through the more accessible medium of Italian, French and other European languages. Take the case of Ficino's Latin commentary on the *Symposium* (1469). He himself translated it into the vernacular, but it was also transformed by one of his followers, Girolamo Benivieni, into a densely allusive, not to say obscure,

Italian *canzone*. This poem was in turn commented upon, in the vernacular, by Pico (1486), who intended to rival Ficino's interpretation of the dialogue. The central theme of the *Symposium*, Platonic love, as Christianized and purified by Ficino – Plato's homosexual characters are converted into chaste male friends, united by their shared devotion to God – was later taken up by the humanist Pietro Bembo in his elegant Italian dialogue *Gli Asolani* ('The Lovers of Asolo', 1505) and by Baldesar Castiglione in the fourth book of his *Il libro del cortegiano* ('The Book of the Courtier', 1528). In both these works – and in the stream of imitations they inspired throughout Europe – the doctrine was further removed from its original Platonic context by giving it an entirely heterosexual orientation.[44]

Platonism as a philosophical system, rather than as a source of literary themes and motifs, was promoted in the mid seventeenth century by a group of Cambridge clergymen and professors. The Cambridge Platonists approached the works of Plato and his Neoplatonic followers primarily as philosophers and theologians, rather than as philologists. But at least one member of the group, Ralph Cudworth, brought to his writings a humanist style of erudition. In his *True Intellectual System of the Universe* (1678) abundant quotations from Greek, Latin and Hebrew texts were used as ammunition against contemporary materialism and atheism. While ancient authority still carried considerable weight with Cudworth and his fellow Platonists, it proved ineffective against the principal target of his polemic, Thomas Hobbes, who believed that arguments were validated not by citing classical philosophers but by applying the deductive procedures of the geometrical method. Turning his back on Plato and Aristotle, Hobbes looked to Euclid.[45]

The humanists' interest in the Greek commentators on Aristotle helped to provide a deeper understanding not only of Peripatetic philosophy but also of Stoicism. Poliziano, in preparing his 1479 Latin translation of the *Enchiridion* by the ex-slave turned Stoic philosopher, Epictetus, made use of an interpretation of the text by the sixth-century Aristotelian commentator Simplicius. As Poliziano explained in the dedication of the translation to his patron Lorenzo de' Medici, the two Greek manuscripts at his disposal were corrupt and full of lacunae. By examining the passages of Epictetus quoted in Simplicius' commentary, Poliziano was able to fill in the gaps and correct the text – a superb example of humanist philological technique. In addition, Poliziano gleaned information about the life of Epictetus from Simplicius' prologue, which he used to place the author and his work in their historical context – another characteristic feature of humanist philology.[46] Finally, when the austerity of Epictetus' philosophy – his belief, for instance, that the death of one's wife or child should be met with Stoic resignation rather than grief – was criticized, Poliziano employed Simplicius' Platonic interpretation of the treatise (he believed that it was based on Plato's *First Alcibiades*) as part of his defence of the *Enchiridion*.[47]

Another Greek commentator on Aristotle, Alexander of Aphrodisias, wrote a treatise on fate, in which he attacked Stoic determinism. The Latin translation of this work by Girolamo Bagolini, published in 1516, became an important source of knowledge about Stoic doctrines on this subject and was used extensively by the Aristotelian Pomponazzi in his *De fato* ('On Fate'), a treatise which he dared not publish in his lifetime, having already provoked a huge controversy with his work on the immortality of the soul, also inspired by Alexander of Aphrodisias.[48]

Humanists attempted to remove spurious texts from the body of works attributed to Stoic philosophers, just as they did with the Aristotelian corpus. Their most notable achievement in this line was to prove, by linguistic and historical arguments, that the correspondence between Seneca and St Paul was a forgery, thus discrediting the widely believed medieval legend that Seneca had been a secret convert to Christianity.[49] Employing similar methods, the Flemish humanist Justus Lipsius sorted out the longstanding confusion between Seneca, the philosopher and playwright, and his father, also named Seneca, who wrote rhetorical declamations. Lipsius's edition of Seneca (1605) was a monument of humanist scholarship, as were the two works he published the previous year, in which he reconstructed the history of the Stoa, along with its ethical and natural philosophy, by gathering together and analysing all the relevant ancient texts. Lipsius's involvement with Stoicism began with his philological interest in Seneca; but he soon came to believe that the philosophy contained in Seneca's works was directly relevant to his own times: the Stoic recommendation of a rational, emotion-free response to external events was the ideal solution for those caught up in the turbulence of the late sixteenth-century political and religious wars. His attractive presentation of Stoic ethics, particularly in *De constantia* ('On Steadfastness', 1574), in which areas of conflict with Christianity were reduced to the minimum, caught the imagination of the European public and led to a popular revival of Stoicism in the seventeenth century.[50]

Stoic ideas had considerable currency until the 1660s, some even finding their way into the new philosophical systems of Descartes and Spinoza: both sought to submit the emotions to the strict control of the intellect, and both endorsed the view that external matters were irrelevant to the achievement of the supreme good.[51] Both, however, had turned their backs on classical authorities and were committed to a radical refoundation of philosophy on purely rational grounds; consequently, neither drew attention to his debt to Stoicism nor to the humanists who had brought this ancient school of thought back to life.

Although a good deal of information about Epicureanism was available to medieval scholars in the works of Cicero and Seneca, the two most important primary sources became available only in the Renaissance, in both cases due to the efforts of humanists. The first of these, *De rerum natura*, is a long scientific poem by Lucretius, a Roman follower of Epicurus. It had been lost for centuries when Poggio Bracciolini discovered a manuscript of it in 1417, while attending the Council of Constance. Though quickly recognized as a masterpiece of Latin literature, the poem received relatively little scholarly attention on account of the prominence it gave to Epicurean doctrines such as the mortality of the soul and the denial of divine providence, which clearly ran counter to Christianity. It was not until 1511 that a full-scale commentary was published, the work of the Bolognese humanist Giovan Battista Pio. Over fifty years passed before the next commentary appeared: written by the French scholar Denys Lambin, it included a text which was to remain standard until the nineteenth century, supported by prolix notes. These dealt almost exclusively with philological and literary matters, providing manuscript readings, conjectural emendations and parallel passages from a wide range of Greek and Latin literature. As far as possible Lambin side-stepped the philosophical implications of the poem, announcing in the preface that he regarded Lucretius' Epicurean ideas as 'fanciful, absurd and opposed to Christianity'.[52]

The second newly available source was Diogenes Laertius' *Lives of the Philosophers* (c. AD 300), the tenth book of which contains three letters of Epicurus and a list of his principal doctrines, as well as a sympathetic account of the philosopher's life and thought. In 1433 Ambrogio Traversari, a humanist monk who combined scholarly activity with his position as general of the Camaldulensian Order, completed his Latin translation of the *Lives*, dedicated to Cosimo de' Medici. Traversari's version circulated widely in manuscript and reached print in 1472; his not entirely satisfactory text was improved by later editors and continued to be published throughout the sixteenth century,[53] enabling scholars to read Epicurus' own words, instead of relying on the predominantly hostile and often ill-informed accounts of his philosophy written by ancient, patristic and medieval authors.

The prejudice against Epicurus was, however, so deeply rooted that the accessibility of his own writings and those of Lucretius, made possible by humanists, did little to improve his standing. His unacceptable doctrine that pleasure was the highest good, on top of his glaring conflicts with Christian dogma, ensured the continued unpopularity of his philosophy. Epicureanism did not in fact achieve respectability until the middle of the seventeenth century, when its cause was taken up by a French priest who combined philosophical training with a mastery of humanist methods. Pierre Gassendi began his career in the 1620s as a philosophy professor; but his attacks on Aristotelianism, which still dominated the universities, led to his withdrawal to a parish in the south of France, where he pursued his anti-Peripatetic crusade as a private scholar. Instead of assailing Aristotle, however, he attempted to construct an alternative philosophy, one which was better suited to the mechanistic science being worked out by Galileo, Descartes and Hobbes. Although keenly interested in these new approaches, Gassendi retained a strong humanist belief that they needed to be grounded in a classical philosophical system. And the system which was most appropriate, in his view, was Epicureanism, with its atomist physics and empirical epistemology. Just as Lipsius had used humanist techniques to reconstruct ancient Stoicism, so Gassendi began to produce a comprehensive account of Epicureanism by writing a full-scale philological commentary on Book X of Diogenes Laertius: he established an accurate Greek text, provided a new and more reliable Latin translation and wrote erudite annotations, filled with references to Lucretius and to whatever further evidence, however scrappy, he was able to uncover by scouring the whole of Greek and Latin literature. He also wrote a life of Epicurus, showing him to have been a virtuous, almost puritanical, figure, the innocent victim of mud-slinging by his Stoic rivals.[54]

Not content with this philological approach, Gassendi went on to develop a version of Epicureanism which, like Lipsian Stoicism, was adapted to the needs of his contemporaries. This entailed drastically modifying a number of doctrines in order to remove the religious and moral objections which had severely damaged the reputation of Epicurus and his philosophy. In physics, Gassendi replaced the infinite, eternal and self-moving atoms of Epicurus and Lucretius with a finite number of atoms, created and set in motion by God; in ethics, he interpreted the Epicurean pleasure principle as part of a divine providential plan for the survival of mankind.[55] In the second half of the seventeenth century, thanks to Gassendi's campaign, it became possible to exploit the scientific potential of Epicurean atomism without incurring the change of atheism and to live by Epicurean ethics without being accused of immoral hedonism.[56]

The reception of Scepticism in the Renaissance followed the same basic pattern that we have seen in relation to Stoicism and Epicureanism: the initial humanist rediscovery and restoration of classical texts led, in the course of the late sixteenth and early seventeenth centuries, to a revival of the ancient philosophical system. The most important texts in this case were the *Outlines of Pyrrhonism* and *Adversus mathematicos* by the Greek physician Sextus Empiricus.[57] He presented a form of Scepticism associated with the much earlier thinker Pyrrho of Elis, who had argued that since it was impossible to penetrate beyond appearances to the nature of things, one should suspend one's judgement about any matter where there was conflicting evidence – including the issue of whether one should suspend one's judgement.

Humanists were responsible for bringing manuscripts of Sextus' works to the west from Byzantium, but their interest in these texts was not philosophical; instead, they treated them as repositories of information about the classical world: Poliziano, for instance, copied out extracts from a Greek manuscript of Sextus, organizing them into a sort of encyclopedia of ancient learning.[58] The first to exploit the philosophical content of Sextus' works was Pico's nephew, Gianfrancesco, in his *Examen vanitatis doctrinae gentium* ('An Examination of the Futility of Pagan Learning', 1520). A follower of Savonarola, he employed Sceptical arguments taken from Sextus in order to demonstrate the unreliability of all human knowledge, and in particular Aristotelian philosophy, compared with the absolute certainty of the divinely revealed Bible.[59]

No Latin version of Sextus was printed until 1562, when the French humanist and printer Henri Estienne published his translation of the *Outlines of Pyrrhonism*. A Latin edition of *Adversus mathematicos*, by Gentian Hervet, came out seven years later. Now that the principles of Greek Scepticism were more widely available, they began to be taken up by influential writers such as Michel de Montaigne, who in his *Essais* (1580–8) borrowed weapons from Sextus' arsenal to attack both the religious and philosophical dogmatism of his time.[60]

As it had done for Gianfrancesco Pico, so ancient Scepticism also offered seventeenth-century anti-Aristotelians, such as Gassendi, an effective means of subverting Peripatetic philosophy by showing that its supposedly irrefutable doctrines were in reality open to doubt. Moreover, he and many of his like-minded contemporaries were prepared to accept, at least partially, the Sceptical view that absolute certainty was unattainable and therefore to make only modest and limited claims for their scientific conclusions.[61] Others, however, were deeply troubled by the challenge which Scepticism presented to all systems of thought by undermining their epistemological foundations.[62] It was the determination to meet this challenge by finding a sure method of attaining certain knowledge which led Descartes to the principle of *cogito ergo sum* ('I think therefore I am'),[63] a crucial step in the fundamental reorientation of philosophy towards deductive rationalism and away from reliance on the authority of the classical past. It is not without irony that the humanist recovery of ancient Scepticism acted as one of the important catalysts for this intellectual revolution – a revolution which not only gave birth to modern philosophy but also turned philology into an obsolete tool of philosophical inquiry.

NOTES

1 F. E. Cranz, 'The Renaissance reading of *De anima*', in *Platon et Aristote à la Renaissance: XVIe Colloque international de Tours* (Paris, 1976), pp. 359–73.

2 For a typical example of a humanist polemic against a medieval translator, see Leonardo Bruni's 'Preface to the appearance of a new translation of Aristotle's *Ethics* (1416)', in *The Humanism of Leonardo Bruni: Selected Texts*, trans. G. Griffiths, J. Hankins and D. Thompson (Binghamton, 1987), pp. 213–17. See also E. Garin, 'Le traduzioni umanistiche di Aristotele nel secolo XV', *Atti e memorie dell'Accademia fiorentina di scienze morali 'La Colombaria'*, 16 (1947–50), 55–104.

3 A. Field, *The Origins of the Platonic Academy of Florence* (Princeton, 1988), ch. 5; N. G. Wilson, *From Byzantium to Italy: Greek Studies in the Italian Renaissance* (London, 1992), pp. 86–90.

4 L. Mohler, *Kardinal Bessarion als Theologe, Humanist und Staatsmann*, 3 vols. (Paderborn, 1923–42); J. Hankins, *Plato in the Italian Renaissance*, 2 vols. (Leiden, 1990), I, pp. 217–63.

5 Aristotle, *Problemata*, trans. Theodore Gaza (Rome, 1475), sig. a2^r (preface by Nicolaus Gupalatinus). Gaza's disgruntled Byzantine rival, George of Trebizond, who believed that scientific works should be translated literally, accused him of producing not a version but a 'perversion' of the *Problemata*: the text is printed in Mohler, *Bessarion*, III, pp. 277–342. Angelo Poliziano sided with George and believed that Gaza's translations were overrated: see *Miscellanea* I.95 in A. Poliziano, *Opera ... omnia* (Basel, 1553), pp. 301–3.

6 J. Monfasani, 'Pseudo-Dionysius the Areopagite in mid-Quattrocento Rome', in J. Hankins, J. Monfasani and F. Purnell, Jr., eds., *Supplementum Festivum: Studies in Honor of Paul Oskar Kristeller* (Binghamton, 1987), pp. 189–219, at 207–8.

7 For his admiration of Gaza, see E. Barbaro, *Epistolae, orationes et carmina*, ed. V. Branca, 2 vols. (Florence, 1943), I, p. 9: 'He alone seemed to me to rival the ancients, this man whom I worshipped and set up as a model.'

8 Only the collection of ancient and Byzantine commentaries on the *Nicomachean Ethics*, translated into Latin in the thirteenth century by Robert Grosseteste, gained widespread currency. For other medieval Latin versions of the ancient Greek commentators: B. Dod, 'Aristoteles Latinus', in N. Kretzmann, A. Kenny and J. Pinborg, eds., *The Cambridge History of Later Medieval Philosophy* (Cambridge, 1982), pp. 45–79, at 74–8.

9 See, e.g., Barbaro, *Epistolae*, I, p. 92: 'if you compare [Averroes's] writings with

those of the Greek [commentators], you will find that, word for word, they are stolen from Alexander [of Aphrodisias], Themistius and Simplicius'.

10 Barbaro, *Epistolae*, I, p. 23: 'It has been denied that natural philosophy can be written in good Latin; I have easily refuted this claim in my edition of Themistius.' For Barbaro's commitment to teaching the entire range of Aristotelian philosophy: *ibid.*, II, p. 38.

11 Barbaro, *Epistolae*, I, p. 92; only his version of the *Rhetoric* survives. In one of the dedicatory letters to his translation of Themistius (*ibid.*, I, p. 17), he criticizes contemporary Aristotelians for knowing neither Latin nor Greek and maintains that 'those who separate philosophy from eloquence are thought to be commonplace, insignificant and wooden philosophers'. See also V. Branca, 'Ermolao Barbaro and late Quattrocento Venetian humanism', in J. R. Hale, ed., *Renaissance Venice* (London, 1973), pp. 218–43.

12 Barbaro, *Epistolae*, I, pp. 10–11.

13 He says that he has been working for almost seven years (longer than it takes for an elephant to give birth) on Latin translations of Alexander of Aphrodisias' commentary on the *Meteorology*, along with his *De fato* and *Problemata* – none of which he ever completed; see Antonio De Ferrariis Galateo, *Epistole*, ed. A. Altamura (Lecce, 1959), pp. 85–96, at 88; and also F. Savino, *Un curioso poligrafo del Quattrocento, Antonio De Ferrariis (Galateo)* (Bari, 1941).

14 See L. Valla, *Repastinatio dialectice et philosophie*, ed. G. Zippel (Padua, 1982); P. Mack, *Renaissance Argument: Valla and Agricola in the Traditions of Rhetoric and Dialectic* (Leiden, 1993); and P. O. Kristeller, *Eight Philosophers of the Italian Renaissance* (Stanford, 1964), ch. 2.

15 E. Cassirer, P. O. Kristeller and J. H. Randall, Jr., trans., *The Renaissance Philosophy of Man* (Chicago, 1948), pp. 223–54.

16 Q. Breen, 'Giovanni Pico della Mirandola on the conflict of philosophy and rhetoric', *Journal of the History of Ideas*, 13 (1952), 384–412, at 392–4. See also B. Vickers, *In Defence of Rhetoric* (Oxford, 1988), pp. 184–96.

17 Cf. Cicero, *De finibus* I.5.15.

18 For Pico's response to Galgano da Siena's *Quaestio de genere soni*, see A. Verde, *Lo studio fiorentino 1473–1503: ricerche e documenti* (Florence, 1973–), IV.2, p. 988.

19 E. Kessler, 'The intellective soul', in C. B. Schmitt, Q. Skinner and E. Kessler, eds., *Cambridge History of Renaissance Philosophy* (Cambridge, 1988), pp. 485–534, especially 500–7. For Poliziano's praise of Donato as 'authoritative, learned and cultivated', see his *Opera*, p. 301.

20 See D. J. Geanakoplos, *Constantinople and the West* (Madison WI, 1989), ch. 5; and D. De Bellis, 'Niccolò Leonico Tomeo interprete di Aristotele naturalista', *Physis*, 17 (1975), 71–93. Leonico was a correspondent of Poliziano: see Poliziano, *Opera*, pp. 20–2.

21 A. Valier, *De recta philosophandi ratione libri duo* (Verona, 1577), especially f. 58[r]. See also A. L. Puliafito, 'Filosofia aristotelica e modi dell'apprendimento: un intervento di Agostino Valier su "Qua ratione versandum sit in Aristotele"', *Rinascimento*, 30 (1990), 153–72.

22 True to his convictions, Valier did not publish *De cautione adhibenda in edendis libris*, which was printed posthumously in Padua in 1719; see especially

pp. 10–11, 14, 43 and 47. See also G. Santinello, *Tradizione e dissenso nella filosofia veneta fra Rinascimento e modernità* (Padua, 1991), pp. 140–53.

23 See C. B. Schmitt, 'Philoponus' commentary on Aristotle's *Physics* in the sixteenth century', in R. Sorabji, ed., *Philoponus and the Rejection of Aristotelian Science* (London, 1987), pp. 210–30; E. P. Mahoney, 'The Greek commentators Themistius and Simplicius – and their influence on Renaissance Aristotelianism', in D. J. O'Meara, ed., *Neoplatonism and Christian Thought* (Norfolk VA, 1982), pp. 169–77, 264–2; and J. Kraye, 'Alexander of Aphrodisias, Gianfrancesco Beati and the problem of *Metaphysics a*', in J. Monfasani and R. Musto, eds., *Renaissance Society and Culture: Essays in Honor of Eugene F. Rice, Jr.* (New York, 1991), pp. 137–60.

24 Ermolao Barbaro, *Corollarii libri quinque* (Venice, 1516), f. 6^r.

25 J. C. Scaliger, *In libros duos, qui inscribuntur De plantis* (Paris, 1556), especially ff. 15^v and 128^r. See also K. Jensen, *Rhetorical Philosophy and Philosophical Grammar: Julius Caesar Scaliger's Theory of Language* (Munich, 1990), especially pp. 38–45. Scholars now believe that the origin of the treatise was a lost Greek work, attributed to a first-century BC author: Nicolaus Damascenus, *De plantis: Five Translations*, ed. H. J. Drossaart-Lulofs and E. L. J. Poortman (Amsterdam, 1989).

26 Daniel Heinsius, *Dissertatio de autore libelli De mundo*, in his *Orationes aliquot* (Leiden, 1609), pp. 68–88. See also J. Kraye, 'Daniel Heinsius and the author of *De mundo*', in A. C. Dionisotti, A. Grafton and J. Kraye, eds., *The Uses of Greek and Latin: Historical Essays* (London, 1988), pp. 171–97.

27 Thomas Aquinas, *Commentarii in libros octo Politicorum Aristotelis*, ed. Ludovicus de Valentia (Rome, 1492), sig. a2^r.

28 Lorenzo Maioli, *Epiphyllides in dialectica* (Venice, 1497), sigs. a2^r–3^r.

29 A. Poliziano, *Lamia: Praelectio in Priora Aristotelis analytica*, ed. A. Wesseling (Leiden, 1986), p. 4. See also Wilson, *From Byzantium to Italy*, ch. 12.

30 See Poliziano, *Opera*, p. 310. See also Pico's dedication of his *De ente et uno* to Poliziano, in G. Pico della Mirandola, *De hominis dignitate ...*, ed. E. Garin (Florence, 1942), pp. 386–7, and Poliziano's letter of thanks: *Opera*, p. 167.

31 Poliziano, *Opera*, p. 179.

32 Poliziano, *Lamia*, pp. 16–18.

33 See his 'Praelectio de dialectica' (1490–1) in Poliziano, *Opera*, pp. 528–30, at 529. See also V. Branca, *Poliziano e l'umanesimo della parola* (Turin, 1983), pp. 13–19.

34 A. Broadie, 'Philosophy in Renaissance Scotland: loss and gain', in J. MacQueen, ed., *Humanism in Renaissance Scotland* (Edinburgh, 1990), pp. 75–96.

35 Aristotle and Averroes, *Omnia quae extant opera*, 11 vols. (Venice, 1550–2), I, f. 2^v. See also C. B. Schmitt, 'Renaissance Averroism studied through the Venetian editions of Aristotle-Averroes', in *Averroismo in Italia* (Rome, 1979), pp. 121–42.

36 C. H. Lohr, *Latin Aristotle Commentaries* (Florence, 1988–), II, p. 161.

37 C. Mercer, 'The seventeenth-century debate between the moderns and the Aristotelians: Leibniz and the *philosophia reformata*', in I. Marchlewitz and A. Heinekamp, eds., *Leibniz' Auseinandersetzung mit Vorgängern und Zeitgenossen* (Stuttgart, 1990), pp. 18–29.

38 Marsilio Ficino, *Lettere*, ed. S. Gentile (Florence, 1990–), I, p. 176.

39 Hankins, *Plato*, I, pp. 267–359; Wilson, *From Byzantium to Italy*, pp. 90–100.

40 See the comparison of his technique with that of Poliziano in A. Wolters, 'Poliziano as a translator of Plotinus', *Renaissance Quarterly*, 40 (1987), 452–64.

41 He wrote full-scale commentaries on the *Philebus, Phaedrus, Sophist, Republic, Timaeus, Parmenides* and *Symposium*, and also on the *Enneads* of Plotinus; his most important independent philosophical work is the *Theologia platonica de immortalitate animorum* (1474).

42 E. P. Mahoney, 'Marsilio Ficino's influence on Nicoletto Vernia, Agostino Nifo and Marcantonio Zimara', in G. C. Garfagnini, ed., *Marsilio Ficino e il ritorno di Platone: studi e documenti*, 2 vols. (Florence, 1986), II, pp. 509–31; on Francesco Patrizi, one of the very few sixteenth-century philosophers to be a committed Platonist and to lecture on Plato at university level, see M. Muccillo, 'Marsilio Ficino e Francesco Patrizi da Cherso', *ibid.*, pp. 615–79.

43 C. Landino, *Disputationes Camaldulenses*, ed. P. Lohe (Florence, 1980), Books III and IV. See also C. Kallendorf, 'Cristoforo Landino's *Aeneid* and the humanist critical tradition', *Renaissance Quarterly*, 36 (1983), 519–46.

44 J. Kraye, 'The transformation of Platonic love in the Italian Renaissance', in A. Baldwin and S. Hutton, eds., *Platonism and the English Imagination* (Cambridge, 1994), pp. 76–85.

45 See the 'epistle dedicatory' to his *Philosophical Rudiments*, in Thomas Hobbes, *English Works*, ed. William Molesworth, 11 vols. (London, 1839–45), II, pp. iv–xi; and also his *Leviathan* (London, 1651), pp. 4, 15, 20–1.

46 Poliziano, *Opera*, pp. 393–4. See also R. P. Oliver, 'Politian's translation of the "Enchiridion"', *Transactions of the American Philological Society*, 89 (1958), 185–217.

47 Poliziano, *Opera*, pp. 405–9.

48 M. Pine, *Pietro Pomponazzi: Radical Philosopher of the Renaissance* (Padua, 1986), ch. 4.

49 L. Bocciolini Palagi, *Il carteggio apocrifo di Seneca e San Paolo* (Florence, 1978), especially pp. 22–34.

50 M. Morford, *Stoics and Neostoics: Rubens and the Circle of Lipsius* (Princeton, 1991), ch. 5.

51 T. Sorell, 'Morals and modernity in Descartes', in T. Sorell, ed., *The Rise of Modern Philosophy: The Tension between the New and Traditional Philosophies from Machiavelli to Leibniz* (Oxford, 1993), pp. 273–88; and S. James, 'Spinoza the Stoic', *ibid.*, pp. 289–316.

52 Lucretius, *De rerum natura*, ed. D. Lambin (Paris, 1563–4), sig. a3ᵛ. See also the article on Lucretius in *Catalogus translationum et commentariorum*, ed. P. O. Kristeller and F. E. Cranz (Washington DC, 1960–), II, pp. 356–65.

53 M. Gigante, 'Ambrogio Traversari interprete di Diogene Laerzio', in G. C. Garfagnini, ed., *Ambrogio Traversari nel VI centenario della nascita* (Florence, 1988), pp. 367–459.

54 Pierre Gassendi, *Animadversiones in decimum librum Diogenis Laertii* (Lyons, 1649) and *De vita et moribus Epicuri* (Lyons, 1647); see also L. Joy, *Gassendi the Atomist* (Cambridge, 1987), especially ch. 4.

55 See his *Syntagma philosophicum*, in Pierre Gassendi, *Opera omnia*, 6 vols. (Lyons, 1658), I–II. See also B. Brundell, *Pierre Gassendi: From Aristotelianism*

to a New Natural Philosophy (Dordrecht, 1987), ch. 3; and L. T. Sarasohn, 'The ethical and political philosophy of Pierre Gassendi', *Journal of the History of Philosophy*, 20 (1982), 239–60.

56 H. Jones, *The Epicurean Tradition* (London, 1989), chs. 7 and 8.

57 Other relevant ancient works were Cicero's *Academica* and the biography of Pyrrho in Diogenes Laertius' *Lives*. Traversari, in his Latin translation of the latter work, coined the term 'Scepticism'.

58 L. Cesarini Martinelli, 'Sesto Empirico e una dispersa enciclopedia delle arti e delle scienze di Angelo Poliziano', *Rinascimento*, 20 (1980), 327–58.

59 C. B. Schmitt, *Gianfrancesco Pico della Mirandola (1469–1533) and his Critique of Aristotle* (The Hague, 1967).

60 See especially 'An apology for Raymond Sebond' in Michel de Montaigne, *The Complete Essays*, trans. M. A. Screech (London, 1993), pp. 489–683. See also C. B. Schmitt, 'The rediscovery of ancient skepticism in modern times', in M. Burnyeat, ed., *The Skeptical Tradition* (Berkeley, 1983), pp. 225–51; L. Floridi, 'The diffusion of Sextus Empiricus's works in the Renaissance', *Journal of the History of Ideas*, 56 (1995), 63–85; and R. H. Popkin, *The History of Scepticism from Erasmus to Spinoza* (Berkeley, 1979), chs. 2–3.

61 See Book I of Gassendi's *Exercitationes paradoxicae adversus Aristoteleos* (1624); and also Brundell, *Gassendi*, ch. 1; Popkin, *History of Scepticism*, ch. 7.

62 For the attempts of some early modern Aristotelians to counter the challenge of Pyrrhonian Scepticism, see D. Krook, *John Sergeant and his Circle: A Study of Three Seventeenth-Century English Aristotelians* (Leiden, 1993).

63 R. H. Popkin, 'Scepticism and modernity', in Sorell, ed., *Rise of Modern Philosophy*, pp. 15–32.

9
Artists and humanists

CHARLES HOPE and ELIZABETH McGRATH

Two phenomena are always seen as central to the Renaissance, particularly in Italy: one is the new interest in classical Latin and Greek associated with humanism; the other the dramatic change that occurred in the visual arts, characterized by Giorgio Vasari in his *Vite* ('Lives', 1550 and 1568) as a process of rebirth and development to a level unsurpassed even by the ancients. Historians have often supposed that the two were closely related, yet it is not immediately obvious why this should be so. Humanism, after all, was an intellectual movement whose origins lie in the fourteenth century; it was principally concerned with texts which few if any artists would have read, not least because they did not possess adequate knowledge of Latin. By contrast, the revival of the arts began in the late thirteenth century; and Renaissance writers tended to parallel it not so much with humanism as with the birth of vernacular literature, especially given that Cimabue and Giotto were both mentioned in Dante's *Divina commedia* and Simone Martini featured in two famous sonnets of Petrarch.[1] Nor is there much reason to suppose that the preoccupations of humanists would have had direct bearing on the normal activity of artists: the production of paintings and sculptures on religious themes and the design of traditional types of building, such as churches and palaces.

There are four main ways in which the two groups might have interacted. The ideals of humanists could have influenced artists, by encouraging them to emulate the achievements of their ancient predecessors. Equally, artists could have influenced humanists, by opening their eyes to the aesthetic and historical significance of ancient art and architecture. Again, humanists might have changed the ways in which contemporary art was discussed and criticized by educated people. Finally, there is the issue of direct humanist involvement in the production of works of art, particularly in the employment of learned subject-matter.

The principal concerns of early humanists were the recovery of ancient texts and the re-creation of an authentic Latin style. Neither of these has an analogy in early Renaissance art. There was no sustained effort to recover masterpieces of classical art before the end of the fifteenth century; and it was only then that artists began to see in ancient art a distinct and uniquely admirable style. In the case of architecture, the development of a language based on antique models involved the codification of the architectural orders, rather than the more or less accurate borrowing of individual motifs. The first architect who came close to specific imitation of the antique was Leon Battista Alberti, in his façade of the Tempio Malatestiano in Rimini (c. 1454; figure 9.1), which is closely dependent on a Roman arch nearby; but even he did not copy the ancient capitals. Yet Alberti was supposedly not the first to study ancient architecture. According to Antonio Manetti, writing around 1480, Filippo Brunelleschi had spent many years in Rome at the beginning of the century, doing exactly this.[2] None the less, he did not quote from a single ancient structure in his own work. He may have used his knowledge of Roman building techniques to devise his solution for the construction of the dome of Florence cathedral – the greatest engineering achievement of the fifteenth century – but the result does not look like any ancient building, nor was it necessarily meant to.

It is not until the first decade of the sixteenth century, in the work of Donato Bramante, especially in his Tempietto in Rome, that one can talk of a precise scholarly imitation of ancient buildings. It is only around 1500 too that architects begin to make carefully measured drawings of antique remains. Before that time, emulation of the antique often amounted to little more than a rejection of Gothic. But even the idea that pointed arches were alien and somehow incorrect seems to have been slow to take root and cannot readily be correlated with the spread of humanism. In Venice, for example, Gothic and round arches were used even on the same buildings until late in the fifteenth century.

In the field of classical sculpture the notion that the Romans had developed a specific style also emerges in the sixteenth century. The first writer explicitly to assert that the best ancient sculpture possessed coherent stylistic principles shared by Italian artists of his own day was the Portuguese Francisco de Hollanda, writing in 1548 and reflecting ideas acquired in Italy a decade earlier.[3] At about the same time Vasari claimed that the discovery of a small number of outstanding ancient statues, including the Laocoön and the Apollo Belvedere, opened the eyes of Italian painters and sculptors to the possibilities of idealization in art;[4] and this seems fundamentally true. One of the first artists to model his own style on this canon of excellence was Raphael, whose work changed radically after his arrival in Rome in 1508. The care with which he studied ancient remains and the critical intelligence which he brought to bear on them is

Figure 9.1   Tempio Malatestiano, Rimini; designed by Leon Battista Alberti.

documented by a famous letter on the antiquities of Rome, in which he emphasized that all classical architects had followed consistent rules, but pointed out that the reliefs on the Arch of Constantine taken from buildings dating from the time of the early emperors were much more skilfully executed than those made under Constantine himself.[5]

Raphael, of course, was not the first to borrow from ancient sculpture. Italian artists had long exploited sarcophagi for drapery, nudes and figures in movement. But none of his predecessors had the ability or inclination to select the best models, to deduce general principles from them and to apply these in their own work in a systematic way. In the fifteenth century Roman art was used by painters and sculptors mainly as a source of decorative motifs; indeed, the term *all'antica* seems first to have been applied in the context of art to a type of decoration and in particular to rectangular frames for altarpieces, adorned with capitals, pilasters and grotesques.[6] This idiom retained its popularity until the end of the century, not least in printed books such as the *Hypnerotomachia Poliphili* (1499), which created a highly romanticized image of ancient civilization popular not just in Italy but throughout Europe.[7] Still more influential were Andrea Mantegna's *Triumphs of Caesar* (1486–c. 1506), engraved at an early date, which presented an unprecedentedly coherent, if inaccurate, picture of ancient Rome.[8] But it is significant that Mantegna's style was not discernibly influenced by his visit to Rome in 1488–90. Given that he was personally associated with humanists, notably Felice Feliciano, it is striking that he was no more interested than any of his contemporaries in the rigorous imitation of ancient artistic exemplars.

By the time of Bramante and Raphael the humanist enterprise had been under way for well over a century. There is no reason to doubt that the belief that ancient civilization possessed unique value had gradually encouraged artists to take classical art as a model of excellence. This process must have been assisted by social contact, as happened in the case of Mantegna and also of Lorenzo Ghiberti, who was a friend of Niccolò Niccoli; but before 1500 there is surprisingly little evidence of other relationships of this kind and virtually nothing to suggest that artists and humanists regarded themselves as in any sense sharing common goals. Still, this is something that artists and academics have seldom felt in any time or place.

Most humanists seem to have taken no more interest in the art of antiquity or that of their own time than artists did in humanism. Throughout the fifteenth century ancient monuments served them mainly as a convenient source of inscriptions, the one type of Roman writing to have survived, though Poggio, inspired by the example of Cicero, acquired at least three pieces of sculpture – heads of Juno, Minerva and a horned Bacchus – for his study (*gymnasiolum*).[9] A few scholars, notably Flavio Biondo, also tried to identify extant buildings, while Manuel Chrysoloras recognized that reliefs provided a vivid record of Roman costume and customs.[10] Yet the collections formed by scholars were largely confined to inscriptions, on occasion supplemented by coins and even portrait busts. It was only in the next century that the value of Chrysoloras's insight was generally recognized, as scholars came to see in archaeological remains key evidence for the study of ancient civilization. In this procedure artists played an indispensable role, documenting the new discoveries in drawings and prints. After 1600, this development led to an unparalleled degree of collaboration between antiquarians and artists, in the association of Nicolas-Claude Fabri de Peiresc with Peter Paul Rubens, and Cassiano dal Pozzo with Nicolas Poussin.

Already in the second half of the fifteenth century the antiquarian interests of humanists seem to have influenced some of their major patrons, such as the Medici. But by 1500 wealthy members of the upper classes had begun to turn their attention to the acquisition of more substantial examples of ancient art. This phenomenon was paralleled by a growing appreciation of the art of their own day. Paradoxically, the achievements of Renaissance painters and sculptors, rather than the preoccupations of humanists, were instrumental in establishing a canon of taste in which ancient art came to occupy the supreme place. It is no coincidence that artists themselves seem to have been pioneers in this type of collecting – Ghiberti and Mantegna both possessed notable works of antique sculpture – and it was to artists that collectors inevitably turned for expertise.

In accounts of Renaissance art the name of Leon Battista Alberti is always given pride of place. He had antiquarian interests; he designed a number of major buildings (figure 9.1), although all of them were constructed by other people; he is said to have worked as a painter and sculptor; and he was the author of the first modern treatises on painting, sculpture and architecture. Large claims are made for the influence of these texts on the artists themselves, as well as on their more educated clients. As a man with humanist training who also had direct experience of the visual arts, Alberti has thus always been seen as the figure who linked both worlds.

Attractive though these claims may be, they are difficult to substantiate. Alberti's *De statua*, in particular, a short and opaque treatise on the specific problem of producing large statues in separate sections – an issue of scant concern to contemporary sculptors – seems scarcely to have been read. His treatise on painting, *De pictura* (1435), is usually considered far more significant.[11] In particular, the fact that in 1436 he himself produced an Italian translation which he dedicated to Brunelleschi has been regarded as indicative of its direct influence on practising artists. But the circulation of the Italian version seems to have been very slight. Only one manuscript from the fifteenth century is known, and only one person seems to refer to the book before 1500, the Florentine architect and sculptor Filarete.[12]

Whether any practising artist would have found *De pictura* helpful is open to question. It is couched in the form of a treatise, but with conscious classicism follows the model of Quintilian's *Institutio oratoria*, with its tripartite division of *ars-opus-artifex* (art, work, artist); and the fact that it was composed in Latin seems to exclude the idea that Alberti's purpose was didactic.[13] Rather, he wished to demonstrate his humanist credentials by writing a work on painting of a type for which there was no extant ancient precedent and by doing so in a good classical style. Accordingly, the text refers exclusively to ancient painters, with the single exception of Giotto, and is scarcely concerned with religious subject-matter.

Although the true character of the book is widely recognized – and Alberti was entirely explicit about it in his preface – it is often supposed that the account of perspective in the first section must have had some impact on artistic practice. In the Latin text Alberti certainly claimed to have invented the technique which he describes, but we cannot say whether this was true. It is probably significant, however, that in the Italian version this claim is omitted. Whatever the truth of the matter, he was not the inventor of perspective as such, nor did he particularly want to communicate his ideas to artists; otherwise he would surely have provided diagrams, at least in the Italian version. *De pictura*, indeed, is the only major non-illustrated European discussion of perspective. In Florence of the mid-1430s, where the book was written, artists would certainly have found it easier to learn about the subject in one another's workshops.

Claims for Alberti's importance have also been made on the grounds that he introduced two fundamental concepts into the history of art – the notion that the highest type of painting was what he called a *historia* and the concept of composition. It is often supposed that Alberti himself coined the term *historia* and that by this he meant a particular type of representation of a historical subject, characterized by high seriousness and moral significance. This is certainly false. In Alberti's time – and for at least a century before – paintings were divided into two broad categories: images, that is to say non-narrative representations of people, and stories, or representations of events.[14] Typically such events were religious, since at this period artists were seldom required to represent scenes from mythology or even ancient history. In proclaiming that 'the great work of the painter is not a colossus but a *historia*', Alberti was merely asserting that narratives were more ✦ challenging than images – even the very largest images.[15] The term that he used had long been common currency in both Italian and Latin (as well as French), and there is no reason to suppose that his enthusiasm for narratives was in any way new. It may well have been a commonplace among artists.

Alberti divided the activity of the painter, whether in the production of images or stories, into three parts: circumscription, composition and reception of light. Circumscription is the process of tracing the outlines in a painting, and reception of light is concerned with colours and light and shade. He defines composition in painting as the procedure whereby the parts are composed together, whether surfaces or limbs or, in stories, bodies. The idea that the painter composes the individual elements to make up a figure was not new: Cennino Cennini, who wrote a strictly practical handbook on painting in Italian, used the word 'compose' in just this sense, and it retained this meaning throughout the Renaissance.[16] But Alberti was well aware that composition was a technical term from rhetoric, which referred to the creation of sentences out of their component parts – words and clauses. His extension of the term from individual figures to the combination of figures that made up a story may well be novel; and it is clear too that he was recommending a specific type of story, in which all the individual elements contributed to an overall effect achieved with a certain economy of means. As has often been noted, this seems to fit the kind of narrative painting practised in Florence by Masaccio.

Yet Alberti's division of circumscription and composition is difficult to reconcile with any credible idea of how artists might actually work. Moreover, his use of the term 'composition' is not equivalent to the modern one: like Cennini, Alberti saw it as a process, rather than the actual arrangement of forms within a painting; and his attempt to broaden its scope was not taken up. When in 1481 Cristoforo Landino, a humanist with an unusual sensitivity to the visual arts, included an assessment of several famous Florentine painters and sculptors in his edition of Dante, he described both Masaccio and Donatello as able 'composers' (*componitori*); but his comment that Donatello was also 'alert and with great vivacity both in the arrangement and placing of the figures' indicates that for him, as for Cennini, composition applied primarily to the design of individual figures, not to their arrangement.[17]

The most notable aspect of Alberti's treatise was not his advocacy of a particular style, but the fact that in concentrating on narrative and in giving pride of place to a term like composition, which was equally relevant to the production of written texts, he opened the way to the possibility of applying to painted narratives criteria drawn from literary criticism, such as decorum and variety. This was to be of the greatest importance, since classical rhetorical texts provided an abundance of models for the critical discussion of literature, but very few for the criticism of art. Yet Alberti's strategy here had ancient precedents. Horace, in a famous passage, had explicitly likened poets to painters (*Ars poetica* 361–5), and this comparison was known even to Cennini. Quintilian, too, had drawn a parallel between the *contrapposto* pose of Myron's Discobolus and the literary device of antithesis (*Institutio oratoria* II.13.8–11).

The first humanist writer to make explicit the parallel between painting and poetry was Bartolomeo Facio, who in 1456 included a few short biographies of artists in his *De viris illustribus* ('On Famous Men'); but in practice he scarcely made anything of it. His accounts consist of little more than a brief series of references to individual works, without any attempt to make stylistic distinctions between them.[18] Landino was much more ambitious. He aptly defined the specific characteristics of different artists, describing the work of Masaccio, for example, as 'puro sanzo ornato' ('plain and unadorned'), and that of Fra Angelico as 'ornato molto' ('very ornate'). Yet he evidently also drew on a tradition of vernacular criticism already established among artists themselves, singling out such qualities as the ability to create a powerful sense of relief, and the mastery of foreshortening and perspective. Still, Landino was an isolated figure. It was only after the publication of Alberti's *De pictura* in 1540 and an Italian translation in 1547 that works specifically devoted to the criticism of contemporary art began to appear, although already in the 1530s perceptive observations can be found, for example, in the letters of Pietro Aretino.[19] Like Landino, the sixteenth-century writers drew both on the conventions of literary criticism and on criteria evolved by the artists themselves.

Apart from Alberti, the only humanist to compose an independent text on the visual arts was Pomponius Gauricus, whose *De sculptura* (1503) was entirely derived from literary models. In general, early Renaissance humanists, like most of the writers of antiquity, had little occasion to discuss the art of their own day. Such comments as they made tended to be indebted, often in the most conventional way, to classical precedents and reflected the sense of superiority, or unease, with which educated writers regarded the activities of unlettered, though admittedly highly accomplished, craftsmen. Even in *De pictura*, Alberti avoided any direct engagement with the art of his time, and he did not take up the subject elsewhere in his writings. Most humanist praise of works of art was focused on the notions of verisimilitude and liveliness, and the remark which Angelo Decembrio credited to Leonello d'Este, that painters did not possess *ingenium*, inborn talent, but only *ars*, acquired skill, typified a widespread prejudice.[20] References to art usually occur in works devoted to other topics, and in general they were confined to the invocation of a few classical commonplaces: the story of Zeuxis creating an ideal figure from the best parts of five beautiful women; an allusion to birds being deceived by painted grapes; or a Horatian tag. This is also true of humanists in northern Europe. In a well-known passage written in 1528 in praise of the prints of Albrecht Dürer (cf. figures 9.3, 9.6), Erasmus struggled to apply terms borrowed from the Elder Pliny's account of the development of ancient painting – in which monochrome characterized the most primitive stage[21] – to the new medium which depended on the power of line.[22] Sometimes too, in imitation of Pliny, writers provided short biographies of modern artists; but even here no real attempt was made to characterize the achievements of specific painters and sculptors, except in some fragmentary passages composed by Paolo Giovio in the 1520s.[23] Humanism, in short, brought little that was distinctive to the appreciation of Renaissance art, and it had less impact on the development of informed discussion than the very different type of criticism that grew up within the culture of the studios.

Even that hackneyed notion of modern scholarship on art and humanism, the idea that the Renaissance saw the emergence of a particular way of describing works of art, the ekphrasis, is of questionable validity. Today this term is used almost indiscriminately for any description or literary✗ evocation of a painting or sculpture. But in antiquity the range of subjects of ekphrases was much wider, and writers who took works of art as their themes were generally quite unconcerned to define their particular qualities. Their purpose was not to describe a specific work of art but to bring the event depicted before the reader's eyes. Renaissance writers, by contrast, seem to have confined themselves to what was actually represented. This applies particularly to Vasari, who was probably not familiar with the term ekphrasis or the literary conventions that underlie it. He described what he saw or remembered having seen or simply what struck him as appropriate to the subject of the work in question.

The only fifteenth-century humanist text on architecture was Alberti's *De re aedificatoria*. Unlike his treatises on painting and sculpture, this book was of real historical importance. Completed in some form in 1452, it was similar to *De pictura* in being a pastiche of an ancient treatise; in this case, however, it was derived from an existing model, *De architectura* of Vitruvius, which Alberti rewrote with a clearer organization and in a more comprehensible style. But it remained very much a book addressed to a classically trained audience, rather than a guide to architectural practice. In this respect the vernacular treatise of the Florentine sculptor Filarete was far more useful. Thus Alberti talked of temples and basilicas, not of churches or palaces, and virtually all his examples were taken from antiquity. In contrast to *De pictura*, the architectural treatise circulated widely, particularly among sophisticated and wealthy patrons such as Lorenzo de' Medici, Federico da Montefeltro and Federico Gonzaga. Alberti, indeed, initiated the idea that an informed interest in architecture was a mark of culture – an idea whose influence was to persist for centuries throughout western Europe. His belief that antiquity provided the standard by which modern practice was to be judged had a more ready applicability there than in the field of painting, although, as we have seen, it was left to practising architects to codify the conventions of ancient architecture, doubtless with the sympathetic support of Alberti's wealthier readers. His book prepared the way for a development that gathered force towards the end of the century; and after 1500 the study of Vitruvius was dominated by collaboration between architects, notably Raphael and Andrea Palladio, and humanistically trained scholars such as Daniele Barbaro.

Besides architecture, the one area in which artists and humanists collaborated was iconography. It is here, in fact, that the association of humanism with the visual arts was closest and most durable. The involvement of humanists took many forms. On occasion they simply wrote inscriptions to accompany existing works of art; sometimes they advised patrons, and sometimes were consulted by the artists themselves; there are even instances of humanists commissioning art for their own pleasure or in the course of their professional activity. In a more general way, humanist ideals, and in particular the devotion to classical precedent, played a fundamental part in the gradual transformation of art from an almost exclusive involvement with the production of religious imagery into an activity embracing portraiture, secular history, classical mythology and allegory. Humanists themselves were seldom instrumental in initiating these developments, but they helped to create the climate in which such changes could come about and profoundly influenced their course.

Inscriptions were already applied to works of art in the fourteenth century, and humanists were involved in their composition at an early date. For example, probably before 1400 the Florentine Roberto Rossi composed a poem for an image of Hercules in the Palazzo Vecchio, and in 1439 Leonardo Bruni devised an inscription for Ghiberti's Shrine of St Zenobius.[24] Sometimes there might be disputes, as when Lorenzo Valla and Panormita produced rival inscriptions for the Virtues on the Arch of Alfonso of Aragon in Naples; on this occasion the king prudently decided to reject both contributions.[25] The practice of devising such inscriptions continued into the seventeenth century, its most notable exponent being Pope Urban VIII, who composed verses for several sculptures by Gianlorenzo Bernini. For epigrams about works of art, real or imaginary, there were obvious classical precedents, above all in the Greek and Latin Anthologies. From the early sixteenth century poems about pictures and sculptures were common, in both Latin and the vernacular, but they seldom attempted to evoke the style of the objects themselves. Although at first they were particularly associated with portraits, by the end of the century certain scholars regularly wrote verses to accompany prints with narrative subjects – and occasionally went on to publish these poems separately in their own anthologies.[26]

It was a small step to the devising of programmes of decoration in which the images and inscriptions were tailored to one another. A vernacular precedent is provided by the frescoes depicting the effects of good and bad government painted by Ambrogio Lorenzetti in the Palazzo Pubblico in Siena; here it is impossible to say whether the imagery illustrates the accompanying texts, or vice versa. The same applies to Domenico Ghirlandaio's six famous republicans in the Palazzo Vecchio (figure 9.2), with Camillus, for example, carrying a standard as Virgil describes (*Aeneid* VI.825).[27] Although it cannot be proved, it seems likely here that the same person composed the inscriptions and chose the exemplary figures to be depicted, all of whom allude by their attributes and gestures to the deeds which made them worthy of imitation in a republican context. In any decorative scheme involving a combination of subjects the presence of Latin inscriptions is almost always an indication of the participation of humanists – or at least of people with scholarly pretensions – in the invention of the iconography.

The use of historical *exempla* was a conventional feature of classical rhetoric but, rather surprisingly, does not seem to have been a standard genre of art in antiquity, as it became throughout Europe from the early Renaissance onwards. The precedent here was in stories of saints, which by definition provided models of exemplary conduct. It seems likely that humanists played a major part in promoting the representation of similarly didactic subjects from classical history, since this conformed so closely to their own concerns. Fortunately, there was a convenient ancient source in Valerius Maximus' *Factorum et dictorum memorabilium libri IX*, a moral compendium of history, in which episodes were categorized according to the particular virtues they illustrated. After 1500 a minor genre of humanist writing emerged, involving compilations along the same lines, which often incorporated Christian and other modern material.[28]

Among countless instances of decorative schemes involving exemplary subjects, a few can be attributed with some confidence to well-known humanists. The episodes illustrated by Hans Holbein the Younger in the Town Hall of Nuremberg, for example, may have been suggested by Beatus Rhenanus.[29] But in many cases the iconography could have been devised by anyone with a knowledge of Latin, given that books of *exempla* were readily available. Thus the themes painted by Domenico Beccafumi in the Sala del Concistoro of the Palazzo Pubblico of Siena around 1529 can all be found in the annotated edition of Valerius Maximus published at Venice in 1518.[30] Artists could on occasion find appropriate subjects for themselves in this way and might even be asked to provide ideas for others, as Rubens was in 1627 for pictures which were to be commissioned from French painters.[31]

Humanist involvement in iconographic schemes was not confined to exemplary themes and inscriptions. There was one other area, in particular,

Figure 9.2   Domenico Ghirlandaio, *Brutus, Scaevola and Camillus*. Sala dei Gigli, Palazzo Vecchio, Florence.

in which their expertise was sought: the devising of attributes for mythological figures and especially for personifications. The process by which the gods of pagan antiquity acquired generally recognized characteristics was a slow one, although their appearance was to some extent codified in a number of manuals of mythology dating from the mid sixteenth century onwards, of which Vincenzo Cartari's *Le imagini de i dei degli antichi* ('Images of the Pagan Gods', 1556) was the most widely used. Before this time patrons or artists requiring authentic representations of mythological characters had no choice but to seek the advice of a humanist; and thus around 1449 we find Guarino of Verona providing descriptions of Muses for a series of nine paintings for the study of Leonello d'Este, Duke of Ferrara.[32] Predictably, Guarino also composed verses to be placed under each Muse. Some fifty years later Willibald Pirckheimer seems to have given his friend Dürer an account of the figure of Nemesis from a poem by Angelo Poliziano – itself based on ancient texts; this inspired the winged woman with cup and bridle, indicating rewards and punishments, in the engraving of 1501–2 (figure 9.3).[33]

Humanists had a particular fondness for personifications, representations of abstract concepts such as virtues and vices. That these were normally female, in accordance with the gender of the relevant term in Latin, greatly added to their appeal. Moreover, they could be shown in conjunction with *exempla*, underlining the significance of the story. They could also serve as vivid summations of complex ideas, in the tradition of the famous figure of Philosophy which Boethius describes as having appeared to him in his *Consolation of Philosophy* (I.1): a woman of indeterminate stature with a torn dress, decorated with a ladder bearing the Greek letter *pi* at the bottom, for practice, and *theta* at the top, for theory. Throughout the Middle Ages personifications were familiar in didactic literature and art, but – except perhaps in manuscript illuminations – until about 1500 the range of concepts represented by artists was limited. After this time there was a new concern to justify and, increasingly, to standardize the attributes of these figures, often by appeal to classical precedent. In this, the knowledge possessed by humanists was at first essential.

On occasion they could point to a convenient ancient description, such as Ovid's famous characterization of Envy, a withered hag with foul breath and rotten teeth consuming snakes (*Metamorphoses* II.760–82). But there were also visual sources, notably the figures on the reverses of Roman coins, personifying qualities such as Liberality and Peace. This type of imagery became more popular after the publication of scholarly works on numismatics in the 1540s and 1550s.[34] Vincenzo Borghini was among the first to exploit such material, in his proposals for an elaborate scheme of

Figure 9.3 Albrecht Dürer, *Nemesis*, engraving of 1501–2.

decoration set up in the streets of Florence in 1565 for the reception of the Habsburg bride of the young Duke Francesco de' Medici.[35] This was an example, incidentally, of a humanist advising an artist, rather than his patron. Another source for attributes was the language of hieroglyphs, visual symbols supposedly invented by the ancient Egyptians to represent, among other things, concepts such as Piety and Strength. Following the discovery in 1419 of a Greek manuscript attributed to the Egyptian Horapollo which purported to provide a key to hieroglyphic writing, these enjoyed a vogue among humanists both north and south of the Alps.[36] An early instance of the appearance of the hieroglyphs in art was in the vast woodcut (192 different sheets) of the Triumphal Arch of Maximilian I (1517–18); here Dürer's crowning portrait of the emperor was incongruously set among several of these images to express the extent of his power. This 'Mystery of the Egyptian Hieroglyphs' was devised by Pirckheimer, who wisely produced a translation in Latin, while the court historian Joannes Stabius added one in German.[37]

The publication of Pierio Valeriano's monumental work, *Hieroglyphica* (1556), enriched the rather limited symbolic vocabulary of Horapollo with a mass of material from ancient literature, natural history and philosophy. Valeriano's book, for example, was the source of some of the imagery devised for the entry of Charles IX into Paris in 1571.[38] Eleven years earlier a group of Venetian humanists and scholars had used the same text for the attributes of twelve allegorical figures to be painted in the Ducal Palace.[39] But Valeriano's greatest influence on art was an indirect one. His book was the principal source for Cesare Ripa's *Iconologia* (1593), a dictionary of personifications and their attributes which was used extensively by artists throughout Europe for the next two centuries. Not that such figures were normally supposed to be self-explanatory. Ripa himself recommended that they should be accompanied by inscriptions, and even before his time this was common practice.

There was a long artistic tradition of combining personifications to form more complex allegories. A famous case was the picture of Calumny supposedly painted by Apelles and described by Lucian (*On Not Giving Credence to Calumny without Due Consideration* 2–4), which Alberti singled out in *De pictura* as an instance of notable invention.[40] In a characteristically humanist way, Alberti remarked that 'invention is such that even by itself and without pictorial representation it can give pleasure'. Perhaps this remark was prompted by his awareness of ancient texts which purported to describe works of art. He did not suggest that writers should themselves devise visual allegories of this kind; and there is little indication that humanists often did so.

Figure 9.4 Sandro Botticelli, *Primavera*. Uffizi, Florence.

The most celebrated example of an allegorical invention by a humanist, albeit a minor one, is the set of instructions devised in 1503 by a literary figure at the court of Mantua, Paride da Ceresara, for Perugino's *Combat of Love and Chastity*, one of a series of allegorical compositions commissioned by Isabella d'Este for her private room.[41] In this instance the invention was quite straightforward, indeed conventional, even though Paride demonstrated his scholarly prowess by including a detail – cupids riding on swans – taken from a late antique writer, Philostratus (*Imagines* I.9.3). It is largely on the strength of this episode, and of Alberti's suggestion that painters should associate with poets and orators who might help them with the inventions for their painted stories,[42] that scholars have supposed that humanists were regularly consulted on the subject-matter of Renaissance art, even providing artists with very detailed instructions. Leonardo Bruni, the chancellor of Florence, certainly did suggest a list of subjects for Ghiberti's second set of bronze doors for the Florentine Baptistery, the so-called Gates of Paradise.[43] Bruni's intervention is easily explained by the fact that Ghiberti's doors decorated one of the most prominent public buildings in the city, where the artist would hardly have expected to be given complete licence in the choice of theme. But it is significant that there was nothing specifically humanist or theologically sophisticated in Bruni's proposal, which was not followed in practice. As Ghiberti reports in his *Commentarii*, he himself adopted a different format for the doors.[44]

In any case, Bruni's intervention is no precedent for the kind of humanist involvement often assumed for, say, Botticelli's *Primavera* (figure 9.4). This has frequently been seen as a didactic, even philosophical, allegory, possibly embodying abstruse doctrines of Florentine Neoplatonism, rather than simply a depiction of Venus, goddess of love and spring, with various appropriate attendants. There is one detail in the picture which may well depend specifically on a classical text, namely the group on the right, which seems to correspond to a passage in Ovid's *Fasti* (V.195–222), in which Flora explains how she had once been a nymph named Chloris, but when ravished by the wind-god Zephyr had been transformed into the goddess of flowers. Botticelli himself could have found plenty of precedents in vernacular poetry for associating Zephyr and Flora with the advent of spring; but his depiction of the metamorphosis of Chloris might be an instance of a painter following Alberti's recommendation to seek the advice of poets and learned men. A few years later in Florence Poliziano supposedly suggested to the young Michelangelo the classical theme of the battle between Lapiths and Centaurs as a suitable subject for a marble relief; and already in 1479 a scholar at the court of Cardinal Francesco Gonzaga was consulted by his patron about specific details of this and other subjects from Ovid which were to be painted in his garden.[45] Neither of these instances, of course shows humanists devising original allegories for artists. This should no surprise us, given the generally patronizing attitude of most humanist towards the activity of artists and their own concern with expressing thei ideas through the medium of language. Again and again, when they wer asked to participate in devising schemes of public decoration, we find tha their real concern is with the inscriptions, to which the paintings merel provide accompanying illustrative material. It is significant too that th painted allegories so typical of Baroque decoration, involving the interactio of different personifications, seem to have been largely due to initiatives b artists, especially those with some literary pretensions. Even though th individual figures were often taken from the *Iconologia*, there is no indica tion that Ripa himself anticipated that his inventions would be used i combination in this way.

We can get closest to the attitudes of humanists towards art by seeing wha use they made of it in their own houses or in the books they wrote. Ancien libraries had been decorated with portraits of great authors and philoso phers; and some humanists certainly sought out and commissioned image of writers they admired, ancient and modern. Erasmus, for example displayed Dürer's engraving of Pirckheimer in his study at Basel;[46] and th two portraits he ordered in 1517 from Quentin Massys of himself an Pieter Gillis for their friend Thomas More are probably the most distin guished paintings ever executed for a humanist.[47] Marsilio Ficino owned picture of the Greek philosophers Democritus and Heraclitus, laughing an crying respectively over the sphere of the world. This work was presumabl inspired by a reference in the late antique writer Sidonius Apollinaris to pair of pictures of the weeping Heraclitus and the laughing Democritus i the *gymnasia* of the Athenian Areopagus (*Epistolae* IX.9.14);[48] Ficin displayed it in his own *gymnasium*, probably his classroom in Florence. Th novel subject had a certain impact, but there is no reason to suppose tha Ficino's painting was commissioned from any of the celebrated Florentin artists with whom modern scholars like to associate him.

One humanist study which survives is that of Michel de Montaigne. Hi library was decorated with maxims in Greek and Latin – a reflection of th humanist valuation of words above images, especially for the transmissior of ethical and philosophical ideas. It anticipates the advice of Gabriel Naud in his treatise on the decoration of libraries (1627) that pictures were waste of money in such contexts.[49] In the adjacent room, however Montaigne did have at least two paintings. One represented 'Cimon an Pero', the story of the young woman who suckled her father in prison, celebrated example of filial devotion; the other was Vulcan's discovery of Mars and Venus.[50] The explicitly lascivious content of the latter suggests that Montaigne recognized the erotic implications of the former. Evidently he did not entirely share the concern expressed by some humanists, especially Erasmus, about the potential moral dangers of art.

Instances of humanists commissioning or acquiring art for themselves are rare, whether for lack of interest, opportunity or resources. Justus Lipsius, however, ordered a painting of the Stoical deaths of Arria and Paetus from his friend Otto van Veen; it was to hang in his entrance hall, accompanied by verses on the subject by the ancient poet Martial (*Epigrammata* I.13).[51] In general, it is among the humanists of northern Europe that we find most interest in contemporary art and artists, usually combined with a preference for edifying subject-matter. On several occasions, for instance, Erasmus recommended the representation of exemplary themes such as the Continence of Scipio.[52] He certainly appreciated the power of art – hence his worry about its corrupting effect – and even granted that a visual image might occasionally express more than words. In his *Lingua* of 1525, he gave instances of 'wordless symbols' (*muta symbola*) being used to present a message vividly. One was the story of King Scilurus, who explained to his eighty quarrelsome sons that a bundle of arrows, the emblem of concord, could not be broken when it was kept bound together. The second was Lycurgus with two dogs, one an untrained thoroughbred and the other a well-trained mongrel, showing how the mongrel ignored a plate of food and went hunting as required, while the other disregarded his master's instructions. The third was Sertorius, a Roman general, demonstrating that a strong man cannot pull out the tail of an old horse all at once, while even a feeble old man can pull out the hairs of a young horse one by one.[53] These unusual subjects had already been illustrated on three painted glass roundels in the house of Erasmus's friend, Hieronymus Busleyden, in Mechlin.[54]

Many humanists were teachers, and some regarded images as useful visual aids. An ancient precedent was provided by the so-called *Tabula Cebetis*, an elaborately symbolic representation of human life described in a first-century AD work attributed to the Greek philosopher Cebes, supposedly set up in a temple by a wise man for the instruction of the young. Erasmus already recognized that this picture was essentially a fiction, a rhetorical device. But it provided a useful model, all the better for being in a clear and almost diagrammatic form.[55] These qualities are also evident in the one context for which we have good evidence of humanists giving very specific instructions to artists – for illustrations to their own works. Conrad Celtis planned the layout as well as specifying the texts for at least two elaborate woodcuts in his *Libri amorum* (1502). One of these (figures 9.5, 9.6), executed by Dürer,

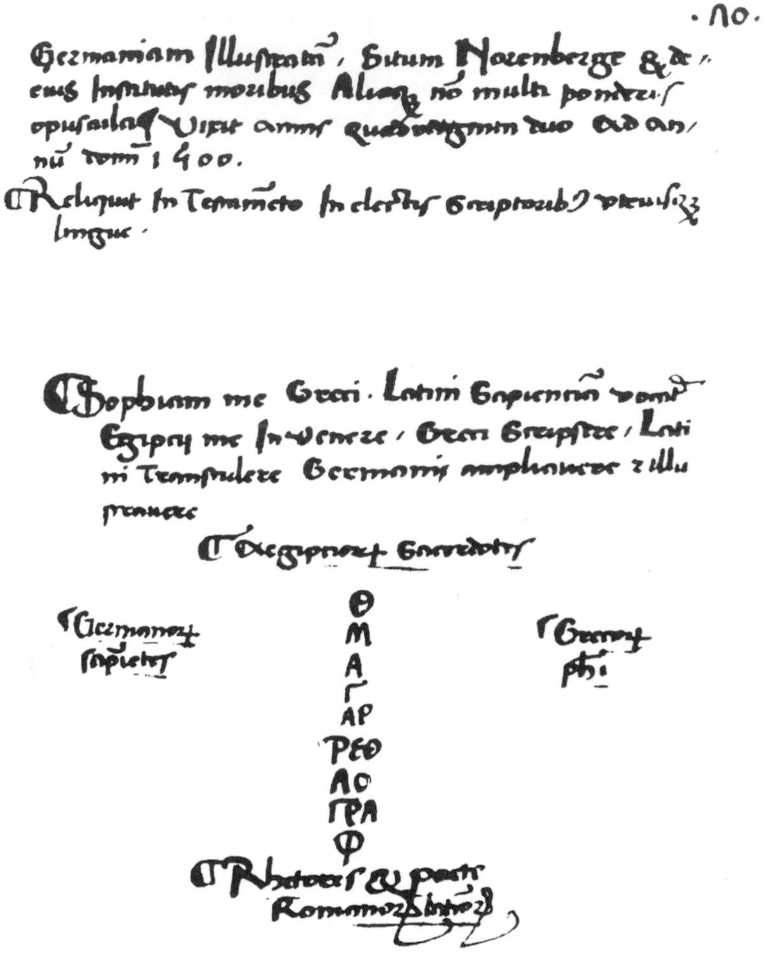

Germaniam Illustrarem, Situm Norembergae & c, eius Intrinsecus moribus Aliaq, no multa ponderis opusculaq Visui armis que... duo ...

CReliquit In Testamento In clerihis Scriptoribus...

CSophiam me Greci. Latini Sapientiam ...

CGermanorum Sapientes

CGreci phi.

Θ
M
A
Γ
AP
PEΘ
AO
ΓPA
Φ

Figure 9.5   Conrad Celtis (or Hartmann Schedel after Celtis), Scheme for a woodcut illustration to the *Libri amorum* (Nuremberg, 1502): MS Munich, Bayerische Staatsbibliothek, clm 434, f. 70ʳ.

Figure 9.6 Albrecht Dürer, *Philosophy*, from Celtis's *Libri amorum* (Nuremberg, 1502).

whose work Celtis celebrated in advance in an epigram, was an adaptation of Boethius' personification of Philosophy, with symbolic embellishments. For example, she is enthroned within a garland decorated with representatives of Egyptian, Greek, Latin and German wisdom, and the rungs on her ladder have become references to the seven liberal arts. (The substitution of a *phi* for Boethius' *pi* may imply a progression from philosophy to theology, rather than from practice to theory.)[56] Celtis also designed the scheme for Hans Burgkmair's print of a symbolic double-eagle, an allegory showing how the Emperor Maximilian fostered the whole body of human knowledge, religious and secular.[57]

The complexity of the symbolism here, as in the Triumphal Arch of Maximilian, is characteristic of German humanist imagery of the early sixteenth century. But the taste for visual symbols was shared by humanists elsewhere and in part explains the attraction that hieroglyphs held. Commenting on the image of the snake biting its tail, Ficino observed that this captures the whole notion of Time 'in one well-defined picture (*firma figura*)', all the more striking for its strangeness.[58] For similar reasons many humanists were drawn to the genre of *imprese*. These combinations of word and (non-human) image, intended to encapsulate the character or aspirations of a particular person, enjoyed immense popularity from the early sixteenth century, partly because the relationship between its 'body', the image, and its 'soul', the motto, was not meant to be immediately comprehensible. The terms used for the individual elements indicate the relative value that was accorded to them. Erasmus was particularly attached to the 'personal symbol' which he himself devised, inspired by the image on an ancient gem given to him in Italy. Its most effective formulation, on the reverse of the medal struck in 1519 by Quentin Massys (figure 9.7), showed the god Terminus, who once refused to give place to Jupiter, as a bust with windblown hair on a solid base, buffeted yet rooted to the spot, together with the motto *concedo nulli* ('I yield to none'). There was much speculation about the significance of the device in the scholar's lifetime; and the question is still debated. Some saw in it an expression of arrogance on the part of Erasmus, but whether the additional inscriptions in Latin and Greek included on Massys's medal were intended to modify or amplify the original meaning is unclear. At any rate, these inscriptions – *Mors ultima linea rerum* ('Death is the final boundary') and *hora telos makrou biou* ('Look to the end, even when life is long') – suggest that Terminus could be identified not with Erasmus himself but with Death, allowing for a sentiment compatible with Christian humility.[59]

Another combination of word and image that intrigued some humanists was the emblem. This consisted of three parts, rather than two: a motto; an

Figure 9.7   Medal of Erasmus by Quentin Massys (1519), with Terminus on the reverse.

image which could include figures, on occasion illustrating an exemplary story; and a poem providing moral instruction (figure 9.8). The genre originated with Andrea Alciati's *Emblemata* (1531) and throughout the sixteenth century provided humanists, especially in northern Europe, with a pretext for the display of wit. Indirectly Erasmus had a great influence on emblems, for his *Adagia* (first edition 1500), a rich compilation of ancient proverbial wisdom, supplied material and mottoes in abundance. He even suggested that the proverbs might make effective illustrations.[60] Emblem literature continued to be produced until the nineteenth century, but increasingly served for banal moralizing, particularly directed at children. Alciati, who evidently took the Greek Anthology as his model, at first does not seem to have thought that his book would need illustrations; this idea

Fortuna uirtutem superans.   **XL.**

Cæsareo poſtquàm ſuperatus nulite uidit
   Ciuili undantem ſanguine Pharſaliam:
Iamiam ſtricturus moribunda in pectora ferrum,
   Audaci hos Brutus protulit ore ſonos:
Infelix uirtus & ſolis prouida uerbis,
   Fortunam in rebus cur ſequeris dominam?

Figure 9.8   The suicide of Brutus, illustrating 'Virtue overwhelmed by Fortune', from Andrea
Alciati, *Emblemata* (Paris, 1542), p. 96.

came from the publisher.[61] Alciati's attitude was typical of the humanists. Most of them were committed to the belief that texts alone were the proper vehicle for the expression of ideas, even if these could on occasion be made more palatable and memorable by accompanying illustrations. They accepted the traditional Christian view that art should be didactic, and for this reason, for all their professional concern with ancient texts, they were less interested than the artists themselves in the revival of the subject-matter of ancient art, which was usually devoid of edifying content.

NOTES

1 On the rebirth of the arts, see W. K. Ferguson, *The Renaissance in Historical Thought* (Cambridge MA, 1948), pp. 1–28; E. Panofsky, *Renaissance and Renascences in Western Art* (Stockholm, 1960), pp. 1–41.

2 Antonio Manetti, *The Life of Brunelleschi*, ed. H. Saalman, trans. C. Enggass (University Park PN, 1970), pp. 50–5.

3 Francisco de Hollanda, *Da pintura antiga*, ed. J. de Vasconcellos (Oporto, 1918), especially pp. 91–5, 113–16.

4 Giorgio Vasari, *Le vite de' più eccellenti architetti, pittori, et scultori italiani* ... (1550), ed. L. Bellosi and A. Rossi (Turin, 1986), pp. 540–1.

5 V. Golzio, *Raffaello nei documenti* ... (Vatican City, 1936), p. 85.

6 See, e.g., Neri di Bicci, *Le ricordanze*, ed. B. Santi (Pisa, 1976), *passim*.

7 See Francesco Colonna, *Hypnerotomachia Poliphili*, ed. G. Pozzi and L. A. Ciapponi, 2 vols. (Padua, 1964).

8 See J. Martineau, ed., *Andrea Mantegna*, exhibition catalogue (London, 1992), pp. 349–92.

9 See P. Castelli, ed., *Un toscano del '400: Poggio Bracciolini 1380–1459* (Terranuova Bracciolini, 1980), pp. 109–15.

10 R. Weiss, *The Renaissance Discovery of Classical Antiquity*, second edition (Oxford, 1988), pp. 59–72; M. Baxandall, *Giotto and the Orators: Humanist Observers of Painting in Italy and the Discovery of Pictorial Composition 1350–1450* (Oxford, 1988), pp. 80–1.

11 Leon Battista Alberti, *On Painting and On Sculpture*, ed. and trans. C. Grayson (London, 1972).

12 Antonio Averlino detto il Filarete, *Trattato di architettura*, ed. A. M. Finoli and L. Grassi, 2 vols. (Milan, 1972), II, p. 646. Cristoforo Landino, who mentioned that Alberti had written on painting and sculpture, presumably knew of the Latin text: Cristoforo Landino, *Scritti critici e teorici*, ed. R. Cardini, 2 vols. (Rome, 1974), I, p. 117.

13 D. R. E. Wright, 'Alberti's *De pictura*: its literary structure and purpose', *Journal of the Warburg and Courtauld Institutes*, 47 (1984), 52–71.

14 See C. Hope, 'Aspects of criticism in art and literature in sixteenth-century Italy', *Word and Image*, 4 (1988), 1–10.

15 Alberti, *On Painting*, p. 73.

16 Hope, 'Aspects of criticism', 1–2.

17 Landino, *Scritti*, I, pp. 123–5.

18 Baxandall, *Giotto*, pp. 103–9.
19 Pietro Aretino, *Lettere sull'arte*, ed. F. Pertile, C. Cordié and E. Camesasca, 3 vols. (Milan, 1957–60).
20 Baxandall, *Giotto*, p. 16.
21 Pliny the Elder, *Natural History* XXXIII.154–7; XXXIV.5–93, 140–1; XXXV. 15–29, 50–149, 151–8; XXXVI.9–44.
22 Erasmus, *Collected Works* (Toronto, 1974–), XXVI: *Literary and Educational Writings* 2, pp. 347–475, at 398–9 (*The Right Way of Speaking Latin and Greek*, trans. M. Pope); for the Latin text see Erasmus, *Opera omnia* (Amsterdam, 1969–), I.4, pp. 1–103, at 40–1 (*De recta Latini Graecique sermonis pronuntiatione*, ed. M. Cytowska). See also E. Panofsky, 'Erasmus and the visual arts', *Journal of the Warburg and Courtauld Institutes*, 32 (1969), 200–27, at 223–7.
23 P. Barocchi, ed., *Scritti d'arte del Cinquecento*, 3 vols. (Milan, 1971–7), I, pp. 7–23.
24 M. M. Donato, 'Hercules and David in the early decoration of the Palazzo Vecchio: manuscript evidence', *Journal of the Warburg and Courtauld Institutes*, 54 (1991), 83–90; G. Poggi, *Il Duomo di Firenze* (Berlin, 1909; reprinted Florence, 1988), pp. 187–8, no. 931.
25 Baxandall, *Giotto*, pp. 111–13, 174–6.
26 I. M. Veldman, *Maarten van Heemskerck and Dutch Humanism in the Sixteenth Century* (Maarssen, 1977), pp. 103–8; E. McGrath, 'Rubens's "Susanna and the Elders" and moralizing inscriptions on prints', in H. Vekeman and J. Müller Hofstede, eds., *Wort und Bild in der niederländischen Kunst und Literatur des 16. und 17. Jahrhunderts* (Erftstadt, 1984), pp. 73–90.
27 See N. Rubinstein, 'Classical themes in the decoration of the Palazzo Vecchio in Florence', *Journal of the Warburg and Courtauld Institutes*, 50 (1987), 35–9, with references to previous literature.
28 These range from Baptista Fregoso, *Dicta factaque memorabilia* (Milan, 1509) to Justus Lipsius, *Monita et exempla politica* (Antwerp, 1601).
29 See J. Rowlands, *Holbein* (Oxford, 1985), pp. 220–1, figs. 159–82, with references to earlier literature.
30 R. Guerrini, *Studi su Valerio Massimo* (Pisa, 1981).
31 See Peter Paul Rubens, *The Letters*, trans. R. S. Magurn (Cambridge MA, 1955), pp. 187–91 (Letters 113 and 114).
32 A. Eörsi, 'Lo studiolo di Lionello d'Este e il programma di Guarino da Verona', *Acta historiae artium*, 21 (1975), 15–52.
33 See W. L. Strauss, ed., *The Intaglio Engravings of Albrecht Dürer* (New York, 1981), pp. 112–15, with references to earlier literature; also E. Panofsky, *Albrecht Dürer*, 2 vols. (Princeton, 1943), I, pp. 80–2.
34 See M. H. Crawford, C. R. Ligota and J. B. Trapp, eds., *Medals and Coins from Budé to Mommsen* (London, 1990).
35 R. Scorza, 'Vincenzo Borghini and *invenzione*: the Florentine Apparato of 1565', *Journal of the Warburg and Courtauld Institutes*, 44 (1981), 57–75.
36 R. Wittkower, *Allegory and the Migration of Symbols* (London, 1977), pp. 114–28.
37 Panofsky, *Dürer*, I, pp. 173–9; II, pls. 225–8.

38 V. E. Graham and W. McAllister Johnson, *The Paris Entries of Charles IX and Elisabeth of Austria, 1571* (Toronto, 1974), especially pp. 117–19.

39 See C. Hope, 'Veronese and the Venetian tradition of allegory', *Proceedings of the British Academy*, 71 (1985), 389–428, at 403–4.

40 See J. M. Massing, *Du texte à l'image: la Calomnie d'Apelle et son iconographie* (Strasbourg, 1990), especially pp. 77–92.

41 See D. S. Chambers, *Patrons and Artists in the Italian Renaissance* (London, 1970), pp. 133–43.

42 Alberti, *On Painting*, p. 95.

43 R. Krautheimer, *Lorenzo Ghiberti*, 2 vols. (Princeton, 1970), I, pp. 169–71; II, pp. 372–3.

44 Krautheimer, *Ghiberti*, I, p. 14.

45 A. Condivi, *Vita di Michelangiolo*, ed. A. Maraini (Florence, 1927), pp. 18–19; D. S. Chambers, *A Renaissance Cardinal and His Worldly Goods: The Will and Inventory of Francesco Gonzaga (1444–1483)* (London, 1992), pp. 87–8.

46 Panofsky, 'Erasmus', 218–19.

47 L. Campbell, M. M. Phillips, H. Schulte Herbrüggen and J. B. Trapp, 'Quentin Matsys, Desiderius Erasmus, Pieter Gillis and Thomas More', *Burlington Magazine*, 120 (1978), 716–24; L. Jardine, *Erasmus, Man of Letters* (Princeton, 1993), pp. 27–54.

48 See A. Blankert, 'Heraclitus en Democritus, in het bijzonder in de Nederlandse kunst van de 17de eeuw', *Nederlands Kunsthistorisch Jaarboek*, 18 (1967), 36–40, 85–6.

49 Gabriel Naudé, *Advis pour dresser une bibliothèque* (Leipzig, 1963), pp. 107–12.

50 See A. Masson, *Le Décor des bibliothèques du moyen âge à la Revolution* (Geneva, 1972), p. 80.

51 Justus Lipsius, *Epistolarum selectarum centuriae ad Belgas*, 3 vols. (Antwerp, 1605), III, pp. 101–3 (Letter 73, to Van Veen, giving an account of the subject; the picture itself is lost).

52 See, e.g., Erasmus, *Collected Works*, XXVII: *Literary and Educational Writings 5*, pp. 199–288, at 248 (*Education of a Christian Prince*, trans. N. M. Cheshire and M. J. Heath); for the Latin text, see Erasmus, *Opera* IV.1, pp. 95–219, at 177–8 (*Institutio principis Christiani*, ed. O. Herding).

53 Erasmus, *Collected Works*, XXIX: *Literary and Educational Writings 7*, pp. 249–412, at 289–90 (*The Tongue*, trans. E. Fantham); for the Latin text see Erasmus, *Opera* IV.1a: *Lingua*, ed. J. H. Waszink, p. 56.

54 J. Bruyn, *Over het voortleven der middeleeuwen* (Amsterdam, 1961).

55 R. Schleier, *Tabula Cebetis* (Berlin, 1973).

56 MS Munich, Bayerische Staatsbibliothek, clm 434, f. 70ʳ (which belonged to the humanist Hartmann Schedel). See K. A. Wirth, 'Von mittelalterlichen Bildern und Lehrfiguren im Dienste der Schule und des Unterrichts', in B. Moeller, H. Patze and K. Stackmann, eds., *Studien zum städtischen Bildungswesen des späten Mittelalters und der frühen Neuzeit* (Göttingen, 1983), pp. 339–43; figs. 40–1.

57 *Hans Burgkmair: Das graphische Werk*, exhibition catalogue (Stuttgart, 1973), no. 17, pl. 20.

58 Marsilio Ficino, *Opera omnia*, 2 vols. (Basel, 1576), II, p. 1768 (*In Plotinum epitomae* VIII.6).

59 See notably Panofsky, 'Erasmus', 214–20.

60 Erasmus, *Collected Works*, XXIV: *Literary and Educational Writings* 2, pp. 661–91, at 671–2 (*On the Method of Study*, trans. B. McGregor); for the Latin text, see Erasmus, *Opera*, I.2, pp. 79–151, at 119 (*De ratione studii*, ed. J. C. Margolin).

61 H. Miedema, 'The term "emblema" in Alciati', *Journal of the Warburg and Courtauld Institutes*, 31 (1968), 234–50.

10

Vernacular humanism in the sixteenth century

WARREN BOUTCHER

Cato in yeares learn't Greeke, for Romanes w[e]re
    To deale with Grecians, and in Greeke was writt
    Philosophie of nature, manners, witt:
    Which grace to him, good to his Rome might reare.

Owr English Cato then (who manie a yeare   5
Censorious maie in vertues Senate sitt)
It maie without disparagement befitt
    To knowe Italiane; since Italianes beare
Inteligence with moste, and writing showe
What Greece or Rome, ages, or places knewe: 10
They best inuent, or best inuented choose.
Which yow my lord maie more exactlie knowe
    (If knowledge more exact maie be in yow)
If yow sometimes this Dictionarie use.[1]

The scholar-diplomat John Florio, translator of Michel de Montaigne's
Essais into English (1603), copied this sonnet of his friend Matthew Gwinne
into a presentation-copy of his Italian-English dictionary (1598) destined for
the Lord Keeper of the Great Seal of England, Sir Thomas Egerton.[2] The
language used points to a late humanistic context. The central idea is still
the discovery and use of ancient wisdom, compared here to the gathering of
secrets by 'inteligence'. Humanist logic's classification of the two aspects of
all intellectual activity is prominent: the finding and storing, or *inventio*
('invention'), of philosophical matter; and the choice and deployment, or
iudicium ('judgement') of that matter in specific contexts – the whole
process amounting to the successful mediation of ancient wisdom (lines
8–11). The sonnet itself exemplifies this in so far as it compares Egerton to
Cato the Censor, who was known from the collections of famous *Lives* by
Plutarch and Cornelius Nepos and from Cicero's *De senectute* as the
Roman patrician who, even as he censored Greek culture, learned its

language, studied its literature and dealt with its embassies and representatives (lines 1–6).[3]

It is identifiably 'late', however, in at least two of its aspects. We are a long way here from Erasmus's 'philosophy of Christ', which synthesized the study of the Bible and of classical letters on a single literary path to moral and spiritual salvation. In its stead there is a more secular-sounding 'philosophie of nature, manners, witt'. Furthermore, Egerton is being urged to accept the idea that the dictionary and the vernacular Italian literature to which it is a guide amount to a useful conduit of the Graeco-Roman philosophical tradition. Tacitly dropped is the notion that direct, philological work on Greek and Latin texts is the only way to that tradition. All the emphasis is on finding and disposing the material which is most useful, as in the operation of an intelligence service, not on the link between classical literary language and good morals. Furthermore, the textual and topographical mediation of ancient wisdom through the vernacular (line 10, 'what ages, or places knewe') is conflated with the process which, in this sonnet, now openly becomes its principal justification: political, commercial and cultural dealings with foreign cultures informed by 'inteligence' (lines 1, 9). It is arguable that the ability to assist in the conduct of relations with foreign cultures had been one of the selling-points of humanistic study since Italian humanism first arrived in England in the fifteenth century.[4]

The lists of books which accompanied the two editions of the Italian-English dictionary give us some clues as to what a library of Italian books understood to be mediating classical wisdom might have looked like. In all the subject areas the norm is a balance between 'classical' (whether ancient or Italian fourteenth and fifteenth century) and modern, so that, for example, in the area of history and politics the lists contain Italian translations of classical works such as Bernardo Davanzati's Tacitus, Jacopo Nardi's Livy, M. A. Gandini's Xenophon, alongside works such as the *Ragion di stato* ('Reason of State') by the Tacitean, Machiavellian and Catholic Giovanni Botero.[5]

But the lists are, naturally, confined to Italian works. We know that Florio also taught, at the very least, French, and that at his death his library contained about 340 Italian, French and Spanish books. A look at other, comparable library lists, polyglot dictionaries, rhetoric and language manuals of the period helps situate Florio's work in an area of late humanistic activity which has largely escaped analysis due to the placement of disciplinary and sub-disciplinary boundaries. This is the ground between university Latin and the European vernaculars, between the world of academe and the world of diplomacy and commerce, a cultural environment which was not only interdisciplinary but interlinguistic in a particular and highly consistent fashion: people utilized a continuum of languages that most usually included Latin, French, Italian and Spanish – alongside, in the case of English humanists, English itself, and with other, less common inclusions such as Greek and German.[6]

In this environment, multilingual editions of the guides to the philosophy of manners and wit by Baldesar Castiglione, Stefano Guazzo and others probably doubled up as grammatical and rhetorical manuals. Drummond of Hawthornden, for example, possessed a copy of Giovanni della Casa's *Galateo* (Lyons, 1598) printed in parallel columns of Latin, Italian, French and Spanish for those 'who take pleasure not only in the Latin language, but also in the three vernaculars which derive from it'.[7] One English rhetoric manual explicitly designed for this purpose has survived: Abraham Fraunce's *The Arcadian Rhetorike: Or the Præcepts of Rhetorike made Plaine by Examples, Greeke, Latin, English, Italian, French, Spanish, Out of Homers Ilias, and Odissea, Virgils Æglogs, Georgikes, and Æneis, Sir Philip Sydneis Arcadia, Songs and Sonets, Torquato Tassoes Goffredo, Aminta, Torrismondo, Salust his Iudith, and Both his Semaines, Boscan and Garcilassoes Sonets and Æglogs* (1588). In this case, individual figures of elocution, voice and gesture are exemplified from texts across the linguistic and literary range under discussion.[8]

Most of the courtiers, aristocrats and gentlemen supporting humanists such as Florio, and by extension English participation in late humanistic polyglot culture, were involved in the world of politics, diplomacy and commerce. Historically, this participation – which we saw Matthew Gwinne seeking to encourage in his sonnet – finds its roots at the European court of Henry VIII and Thomas Cromwell, where Latin-and-vernacular humanism, closely tied to the active life and practical concerns, was first promoted in England.[9] In Europe as a whole, in terms both of printing and of international diplomacy, the 1530s and 1540s were the decades which first saw the rise of the major vernaculars as international rivals to Latin, as when, in 1536, Charles V spoke Spanish to Pope Paul III at Rome. In correspondence of the 1550s and 1560s held amongst the English State Papers, it is easy to see how close the relationship had already become between channels of international diplomacy, commercial exchange, international book distribution and polyglot humanistic culture and pedagogy – between international mediation and textual 'inteligence'.

The diplomat Sir William Pickering, for example, intermingles news of political and commercial dealings at the French court with news of books that he is procuring for his correspondent, Sir William Cecil. In December 1551 he informs Cecil that 'a New Testament in Greek; l'Horloge de

Princes;[10] le Discours de la Guerre de Laugnay, and notes to the Ethics of Aristotle in Italian' will be conveyed by a merchant courier. Three other books intended for Cecil – including a Euclid and a discourse of Machiavelli's – were subsequently 'so buggerly bound' that he burnt them.[11] A diplomatic letter of 31 March 1554 in which Dr Nicholas Wotton praises Dr Valentine Dale's handling of some commercial affairs reveals how a concern with the scholar-statesman's mastery of modern European languages and places and his effectiveness in gaining 'familiarity' with politicians had been grafted onto the traditional concern with the 'honesty' gleaned from Greek and Latin:

> The man is honest, and hath both the Greek and the Latin tongue well; his learning in law is competent; sober and discreet in his doings; he speaketh the French tongue well. Finally, he hath used himself so well in this Court that not only men of learning ... have him in honest estimation, and are glad to talk with him; but even the Constable himself ... hath ever been content to hear him, and divers times to talk familiarly of other matters besides with him. And I believe he will prove one of the meetest men you have at home to do the Queen's highness service abroad; whereunto he should yet be the apter, if he had been a year or two in Italy.[12]

The measure of humanistic success here is not textual elegance in Latin but 'familiar' vernacular talk on important and confidential matters with influential courtier-friends – crossing the cultural gap between 'learned men' and 'the Constable himself'. It is the story of the partial emergence of a promising young humanist diplomat onto the international court scene, but in a rather specific sense. Dale is demonstrating mastery of language and action in a new private space of 'affective' communication he has himself opened up but which is folded *within* public space; he has shown ability to reach and hold a 'select' private audience in the sight of the court public.[13] He has caught the French court's ear.

When diplomats from foreign and potentially hostile powers were known to have received the same form of polyglot humanistic cultural training, then these terms of praise were merely inverted. In 1560, during the height of the ultra-Catholic Guise family's rule in France and of English fears concerning French conspiracies in Scotland, Nicholas Throckmorton wrote to the Privy Council to warn them of the magically persuasive powers of the new French Ambassador to England, Michel de Seurre. Throckmorton warned against his 'disguisings and fawnings', describing him as an 'enchanter' who had been trained in 'Italy, Spain, Portugal, Almain [Germany], and all other places where experience is to be learned ... He speaks many tongues, and has by experience and judgement bridled his nature ... He is kept in store as a select vessel, to be employed in such a time as this is, to be a maker of dissembled friendship and a soon broken peace.'[14]

In 1569 doubts fell on the 'straightforwardness' of the proceedings of the Spanish ambassador Guerau de Spes and on the zeal with which he was preserving 'peace and amity' in the international relations between England and Spain. He was detained by the Privy Council, and one document redacted in Spanish, Latin and French reveals that the question of Spes's 'amity' revolved around a dispute concerning the textual interpretation of some remarks and some literary allusions (to a Spanish chivalric romance, *Amadís de Gaula*) he had been found to have made in intercepted and 'familiar' correspondence.[15]

High-level, pan-European diplomatic and commercial relationships were, then, transmitted in this mid-century period through the culture of eclectic, polyglot and pragmatic humanism. In terms of interest and demand the progenitors of this culture were the diplomats and advisers surrounding the monarch. One of the core trends in its development is the increased interest in multiple vernacular versions of classical literature and the greater intermingling of generically heterodox materials, including chivalric romance.[16] The books which circulated between these figures, which were collected in their libraries and which often played a role in the education of the young monarchs of the period, contained a large proportion of European vernacular material, often in the form of cribs, and grammatical and rhetorical aids.

Sir William Pickering, for example, provided modern language materials for the education of Edward VI, including a copy of a French grammar and a Spanish collection of classical commonplaces, Pedro Mexía's *Silva de varia lección* (1540). The young king most probably learned Spanish, French and Italian through Latin and Greek, and vice versa.[17] Pickering's own library, meanwhile, was eventually added to that of his kinsmen the Wottons. It was this Kentish land-owning family of humanists and diplomats that produced the great ambassador and courtier, Edward Wotton, prime mover of Florio's Montaigne. The Wottons' library, started by Edward's father Thomas in the 1540s and 1550s, abounded in Latin and French translations, along with Italian vernacular literature.[18] In the case, finally, of the lists of books kept by James VI of Scotland's tutor, the same story emerges: an education in which Latin classics and French vernacular versions interact, and in which there is also room for Italian and Spanish materials, including chivalric romances.[19]

The generation of scholar-courtiers and courtier-scholars which followed that of mid-century humanist statesmen such as William Cecil, Nicholas

Wotton, William Pickering and Valentine Dale, emulated their achievements and cultural pursuits. This is particularly clear in the now very well-documented case of the Cambridge University professor and would-be courtier, Gabriel Harvey, born some time in 1550–1 and thus of the generation of Philip Sidney, Edmund Spenser and Edward Wotton. His library, and the use to which he put its books in reading, were very much of the eclectic, pragmatic, Latin-and-vernacular variety with which we are now familiar.[20]

Furthermore, his annotations show him to have been particularly aware of the textual and linguistic canniness of the French, Italian and Spanish in communicating humanistic wisdom in their discourses, placing the French above the others and naming in particular two natives of Gascony, Montaigne and the poet Guillaume (de Salluste) Du Bartas.[21] He understood the principal application of these skills – which he referred to as French dexterity and Italian confidence – to be in ambassadorial and commercial dealings. Notes gathered in his copy of his Italian teacher's first book of Italian-English language dialogues, the *Firste Fruites* of 1578 (now in the Houghton Library, Harvard University), reveal why. They show that his admiration for the previous generation of scholar-statesmen, and particularly for Bishop Stephen Gardiner, whom he compared with Nicholas Wotton and Thomas Cromwell, lay in the way that their mastery of Latin and the modern languages served them in the conduct of diplomatic and political dealings.[22]

That this mastery ultimately derived from skill in the mediation of classical materials is clear when we read Harvey's note reporting how Sir Thomas Smith and Sir Nicholas Throckmorton relied on classical authors in the conduct of their embassies. It is also clear when we catch him and his friends reading Livy in the 1570s and 1580s in the light both of Sir Anthony Cope's English translation (1544) and of Machiavelli's Italian commentary on the first ten books (the *Discorsi* of 1513/19), with specific diplomatic and political ends in mind.[23] It is, indeed, these decades of the 70s and 80s which first see an infiltration of vernacular cribs into Oxbridge colleges on any appreciable scale. Thomas Martin of New College, Oxford, bequeathed to the college library on his death in 1584 copies of Livy in French, Italian and Spanish alongside a French Thucydides and Aristotle's *Politics* in French.[24]

Edward Wotton, born in 1548, likewise emulated his father's generation of scholar-statesmen. As awesomely plausible and well-trained as Michel de Seurre, he was educated on the Continent and learned French, Spanish and Italian before being employed in a glittering series of diplomatic missions. We are now perhaps in a position to understand the logic behind his commissioning a translation of 'one Chapter' of Montaigne's *Essais* from

John Florio. For the chapter in question was almost certainly I.25: 'Of the institution and education of children; to the Ladie Diana of Foix, Countesse of Gurson'.[25]

In this chapter, Montaigne adapts humanistic education for the aristocracy using the same criterion – usefulness – with which the French educational reformer Peter Ramus had secularized arts teaching for the middle classes. Ramus had found that the new mercantile class invested in literary education not only for the general 'culture' it offered to their aspiring offspring, but also for those skills in applied reasoning and discourse which they would need to argue a case in public, to write memorandums and to make medical reports. Montaigne is similarly utilitarian, but he disdains Ramist middle-class goals and elevates aristocratic ones: '[Learning] is much more readie and fierce to lend her furtherance and direction in the conduct of a warre, to attempt honorable actions, to command a people, to treat a peace with a prince of a forraine nation, than she is to forme an argument in Logick ... to canvase a case at the barre, or to prescribe a receit of pills.'[26]

As in the Ramist programme – which saw classical and French examples assembled side-by-side in textbooks – Latin and vernacular materials interact in the textual foundations of Montaigne's suggested course. In the chapter's central evocation of the pupil's lived experience of the philosophical path to virtue the crowning moment of moral judgement is a reworking of the classical mythology of choice – the judgements of Paris and Hercules – as a choice between two female characters ('Bradamant, or Angelica') from a modern vernacular text, Lodovico Ariosto's *Orlando furioso*.[27]

New in Montaigne's treatment, though, is the playing-down of textual exegesis and the strong emphasis on the cultural production of the 'natural' person: the idea is that the pupil is still 'inventing' and 'judging', knowing and disposing, but in the real landscape of nature rather than the textual landscape of 'places', just as the lesson will take place not in the schoolroom with textbooks but 'naturally' and in the course of ordinary life, without the pupil noticing. As such it is *res*, the matter, and its invention and judgement, which is fundamental, and not *verba*, the language – which might be Gascon, French or 'Bergamask' for all Montaigne cares, as long as the conception is good. The spiritual mystique of grammatical humanist training in Latin and Greek here evaporates.[28]

In another chapter Montaigne avers that just as a linguistically competent tourist who is without Italian can draw on the whole lexicon of the European family of languages to fashion 'accidentally' and 'naturally' an effective communication ('he should ... use such words as came first to his mouth, whether they were Latine, French, Spanish, or Gascoine ... adding the Italian terminations'), so any of his own 'humours' or natural 'customes' as portrayed in print 'will be found to have relation to some ancient humour' as expressed in classical literature. This will give his humours textual authority, but, paradoxically, Montaigne claims at the same time a natural integrity of his own: 'A new figure: An unpremeditated Philosopher and a casuall'.[29] The late humanism of Montaigne shares with early natural philosophy a non-pietistic justification of study as a form of intellectual husbandry in nature.[30]

This is why, much to the annoyance of Florio, he does not reveal (though modern editions do) the sources of the Greek, Latin, French and Italian texts with which his own is intertextually related, for he wants the reader's focus to be on his own natural and vernacular authority, his own mental husbandry, and not on the authority of his sources. But from our point of view the perceived purpose of the *Essais* must have been, in fact, to *create* the sense of a common European cultural language of 'customes' and 'humours' shared by Latin, French, Spanish, Gascon and Italian, by ancient and modern, and to *invest* that idiom with a moral authority borrowed neither from theology nor from the classical languages, but from nature itself – a new *lingua franca*. Pedagogues and intellectuals with a foot in the world of diplomacy and politics in late Elizabethan and early Jacobean England perceived the work to have succeeded in this respect and welcomed it as such. Diplomat Edward Wotton, language-teacher John Florio, Oxford scholar Matthew Gwinne and poet Samuel Daniel – they all saw Montaigne as the first writer in this difficult period successfully to offer a form of integrity to the new eclectic, pragmatic, Latin-and-vernacular style of humanist philosophy under discussion here.[31]

There was, then, a trans-national European literary market in such vernacular treatments of 'ancient humours' which post-dated the heyday (*c*. 1480–1530) of humanist Latin as the *lingua franca* of élite northern Europe, and in which Montaigne was, briefly, regarded as the most sophisticated dealer by gentlemen, aristocrats and their humanist advisers. For he was dealing with commonplaces which were not only familiar to contemporary English readers but which were also already being handled or 'judged' by them in related – though less ingenious and complex – ways. As Lady Politic Would-Be says in Ben Jonson's *Volpone*:

> All our English writers . . .
> Will deign to steal out of this author [G. Battista Guarini], mainly;
> Almost as much as from Montaignié:
> He has so modern, and facile a veine,
> Fitting the time, and catching the court-ear.[32]

Two examples. In the course of his defence of poetry, and of Ariosto's *Orlando furioso* in particular, Sir John Harington admits in the face of censure that: 'Cupido is crept even into the Heroicall Poemes' – largely, in the sixteenth century, the fault of the classical precedents set by Ovid's *Metamorphoses* and *Heroides*. But he goes on to cite passages in established, canonical works – Virgil's *Aeneid* and Chaucer's *Canterbury Tales* – where Cupid has so crept, but with decorum. Two of these are the 'entertainment' of Dido and Aeneas in *Aeneid* IV and, quoted verbatim in Latin, *Aeneid* VIII.387–90 and 404–6. In the latter passage, Venus enacts the erotic pathos of her declamatory plea to her husband Vulcan that he make armour for her son Aeneas with the *notus calor* ('familiar heat') of her body as it envelops his. Harington asks us to 'confesse this is plaine enough, and yet with modest words, and no obscenous phrase'.[33]

Exactly these selections from Book VIII of the *Aeneid* (with lines 391–2 added) are the very 'verses of Virgil' at the centre of Montaigne's magnificent chapter on language and sexuality, III.5: 'Upon some verses of Virgil'. The point here is neither merely to show that the verses in question are therefore commonplaces, nor that Harington was or was not directly 'influenced' by Montaigne. It is rather to indicate that the commonplaces which circulated in the trans-national Latin-and-vernacular literary market were more sophisticated in their use than a general form of currency like money, for they were intended for specific conceptual and emotional applications: they were known to affect the humanistically educated audience in certain familiar ways – *notus calor*. Individual vernacular writers in diverse European locations would draw or play on this familiarity with different twists on the same basic theme.

In Montaigne's usage, then, the commonplace verses still stand for what we might label a 'winning and pathetic expression of erotic, married love' (though Montaigne at first humorously judges it *too* erotic for marriage), which as a familiar and canonical poetic fragment acts to license the masculine freedom of expression ('poetic licence') achieved by the broader category of textual acts to which it belongs: heroic depictions of erotic experience and sentiment ('Cupido is crept even into the Heroicall Poemes'). But the Frenchman's usage is considerably more nuanced and complex. On one level the point of the whole chapter is Montaigne's bold winning of textual liberties; he aims at 'familiarities' with his readers which are imagined in one passage in specific spatial terms: 'it vexeth me, that my Essayes serve Ladies in liew of common ware and stuffe for their hall: this Chap[ter] wil preferre me to their cabinet: I love their society somewhat private; their publike familiarity wants favor and savor'.[34]

He is actually, like Harington, trying to persuade us that these liberties, though apparently obscene, are decorous. Partly by arguing that the consideration of temperance requires him to excite his imagination with literary erotica because his elderly body is *too* reformed, in the 'extreame of severity'.[35] Partly by deriving the template for a truly virile but familiar vernacular literary style from the language of the Virgilian commonplace and from Lucretius' account of the clandestine and adulterous sexual encounter between Venus and Mars (I.32–40), quoted later in the chapter. This affective but proper style is 'heroic' in that: '*contextus totus virilis est* ... *[t]he whole composition or text is manly* ... [t]his is not a soft quaint eloquence, and only without offence ... [but] filling and ravishing'; it is heroic but its matter is 'ordinary [e]motions', such as the love felt by a page. Montaigne's own winning style, in short.[36]

In fact, it becomes clear in the chapter and the *Essais* as a whole that the imagined winning of a place for his book in ladies' cabinets stands for the general, promiscuous contracting of 'friends' which Montaigne hopes his textual persona will achieve through its particular brand of 'heroic' but familiar eloquence: 'if there be any body, or any good company in the cuntry, in the citty, in *France*, or any where els, resident [or] travelling, that likes of my conceites, or whose humours are pleasing to me, they neede but hold up their hand, or whistle in their fiste, and I will store them with Essayes'. As Samuel Daniel says:

> this Prince Montaigne ...
> Hath more adventur'd of his owne estate
> Than ever man did of himselfe before.

Montaigne is heroically familiar in print.[37]

A second example. Reading his Livy the English humanist Gabriel Harvey picked out the story of the Roman ambassador Popillius' legation to the powerful king of Egypt, Antiochus. Popillius had peremptorily drawn a circle around the king with a staff and demanded he answer the Roman senate's letters, just handed him, before stepping out. Antiochus agreed to the senate's written commands, and Rome thereby regained Egypt. Harvey's notes stress the ambassadorial virtuosity of Popillius and find that Valentine Dale had successfully converted textual study of this episode and other texts into an effective ambassadorial action of his own. For Dale had heroically rebutted the Spanish Duke of Parma's threats to invade England with a contemptuous 'non-verbal noise', even in the midst of Parma's army. This bearding of Parma is presumably perceived by Harvey as an act of diplomacy which cleared the way, in some sense, for the subsequent military victory over the Armada.[38]

Reading the same episode, Montaigne builds a short chapter – II.24: 'Of the Roman greatnesse' – around it and makes what is again a related though disparate application. Behind Harvey's annotations on Livy's accounts of Roman legations lies a concern with the practical gains won by the affective style, both in the printed Livy and in practical, diplomatic action. This interest in the then newly exploitable and socially powerful humanistic medium of 'letter and affection', as Shakespeare's Iago resentfully calls it, was centred pedagogically in study of the 'familiar' – including the amorous – letter. This is Montaigne's emphasis when he reads the story of Popillius, for he starts the chapter with an extract from '*Ciceroes* familiar Epistles' in which it is made clear that Caesar, then a 'simple Roman Citizen', intends to prefer Marcus Furius to the throne of Gaul entirely on the basis of Cicero's epistolary commendation of the same. In Iago's words, again, 'preferment goes by letter and affection'.[39]

It is thus the exemplification of the power of 'letter and affection' which is the context for Montaigne's choice of the story of Popillius, in which 'the only impression of three written lines' regained a kingdom for Rome. This 'historical' episode is, like so many humanist-adopted mythological stories, the story of the heroic and opportunistic seizing of place and voice, and the affective exercise of command by 'presence'.[40]

Two general points are being made here. Firstly, we have seen how not only English but Italian, Spanish and French treatments of classical concepts, stories and texts were widely used in Renaissance England as a pedagogical and intellectual resource alongside Latin (and, more occasionally, Greek) 'originals'. Furthermore, the modes of mediation of these stories in disparate vernacular contexts were related and interdependent. Secondly, the late northern Renaissance persistently singles out effective/affective conduct – whether in person or in writing or in print – in the private-and-public spaces of court and household politics as the practical measure of humanistic success. It is a matter of how well you catch the court ear.

NOTES

1 Sotheby & Co., *Catalogue of Rare First Editions of English Literature of the 16th to the 20th Century*, 8–9 November 1965, lot 122 (with punctuation in the text of the sonnet emended from the facsimile in the catalogue). I am grateful to Peter Beal of Sotheby's for originally drawing my attention to this sonnet.

2 Matthew Gwinne and John Florio appear together as friends of 'the Nolan' in the second dialogue in Giordano Bruno's *Ash Wednesday Supper*, trans. E. A. Gosselin and L. S. Lerner (Hamden CN, 1977), pp. 109–32, especially 110–11 and 128 n. 6.

3 *The Cambridge Ancient History*, second edition, 8 vols. (Cambridge, 1982–9), VIII, pp. 451–63.

4 R. Weiss, *Humanism in England during the Fifteenth Century*, third edition (Oxford, 1967), pp. 75, 123.

5 C. Longworth Pineton, Comtesse Chambrun, *Giovanni Florio: un apôtre de la Renaissance en Angleterre à l'époque de Shakespeare* (Paris, 1921), pp. 210–16, 220.

6 Private library catalogues providing evidence for this include those of Monsieur Le Doux, a diplomatic agent and language teacher (MS London, Lambeth Palace Library, Bacon 655, ff. 185–6), and of Thomas Tresham (MS London, British Library, Additional 39830); see also R. H. MacDonald, ed., *The Library of Drummond of Hawthornden* (Edinburgh, 1971).

7 MacDonald, ed., *Library of Drummond*, p. 206 (no. 995).

8 Abraham Fraunce, *The Arcadian Rhetoric [1588]* (Menston, 1969).

9 See D. Starkey, ed., *Henry VIII: A European Court in England* (London, 1991); G. Elton, 'Humanism in England', in A. Goodman and A. Mackay, eds., *The Impact of Humanism on Western Europe* (London, 1990), pp. 259–78.

10 A French version of the Spaniard Antonio de Guevara's collection of medieval- and humanist-style commonplace counsels to princes.

11 W. B. Turnbull, ed., *Calendar of State Papers, Foreign Series, of the Reign of Edward VI, 1547–1553* (London, 1861), pp. 204–6.

12 W. B. Turnbull, ed., *Calendar of State Papers, Foreign Series, of the Reign of Mary, 1555–1558* (London, 1861), pp. 68–9.

13 I have in mind here a particular early modern understanding of the term 'affect' and its cognates (though the adjective is not used until the mid seventeenth century). These words convey the sense of an active process whereby (according to *Oxford English Dictionary*, sb. 3) a person or an author, exercising 'the craft of soules' (Shakespeare, *King Richard II*, I.iv.30, quoted from the 1623 First Folio) attracts 'affect': 'Feeling towards or in favour of; kind feeling, affection' from another. In early modern high culture this craft is particularly associated with private, intimate forms of one-to-one communication and with the composition of letters written in a consciously familiar style (see also n. 39 below).

14 J. Stevenson, ed., *Calendar of State Papers, Foreign Series, of the Reign of Elizabeth, 1559–1560* (London, 1865), p. 351.

15 M. A. S. Hume, ed., *Calendar of Letters and State Papers Relating to English Affairs, Preserved Principally in the Archives of Simancas*, 4 vols. (London, 1892–9), II: *Elizabeth 1568–1579*, pp. 105–6.

16 L. Hutson, 'Fortunate travelers: reading for the plot in sixteenth-century England', *Representations*, 41 (1993), 83–103, at 93.

17 T. W. Baldwin, *William Shakspere's Small Latine & Lesse Greeke*, 2 vols. (Urbana, 1944), I, pp. 215, 218.

18 T. A. Birrell, *English Monarchs and Their Books: From Henry VII to Charles II* (London, 1987), p. 14; G. Ungerer, *The Printing of Spanish Books in Elizabethan England* (London, 1965), p. 179; I. G. Philip, 'Sir William Pickering and his books', *The Book Collector*, 5 (1956), 231–8; W. E. Moss, *The English Grolier ...: Life, Lineage, and Library, and its History for Four Hundred Years, of Thomas Wotton, 1521–1587* (Worth, 1941–3 and Sonning-on-Thames, 1952); Sotheby & Co., *Catalogue of Valuable Printed Books, Illuminated Manuscripts and Autograph Letters: The Property of a Nobleman*, 8 April 1919.

19   G. F. Warner, 'The library of James VI', in *Miscellany of the Scottish History Society* (Edinburgh, 1893–), I, pp. xi–lxxv, especially xxx–xxxiii.

20   See V. F. Stern, *Gabriel Harvey: His Life, Marginalia and Library* (Oxford, 1979); C. Brown Bourland, 'Gabriel Harvey and the modern languages', *Huntington Library Quarterly*, 4 (1940–1), 85–106; and L. Jardine and A. T. Grafton, ' "Studied for action": how Gabriel Harvey read his Livy', *Past and Present*, 129 (1990), 30–78.

21   Brown Bourland, 'Gabriel Harvey', 103–4.

22   Stern, *Gabriel Harvey*, pp. 153–6 and the Houghton Library copy.

23   Jardine and Grafton, 'Gabriel Harvey', 40–4, 54, 57–8.

24   N. R. Ker, 'Oxford college libraries in the sixteenth century', *The Bodleian Library Record*, 6 (1959), 459–515, at 504–5. See also the library of Abraham Tillman (d. 1589/90) in E. S. Leedham-Green, *Books in Cambridge Inventories: Book-Lists from Vice-Chancellor's Court Probate Inventories in the Tudor and Stuart Periods*, 2 vols. (Cambridge, 1986), I, pp. 482–3.

25   Michel de Montaigne, *Essays*, trans. John Florio, 3 vols. (London, 1910), I, p. 3. Chapter I.25 in Florio's text is I.26 in all twentieth-century English and French editions. The textual evidence for the identification of the unnamed chapter involves various respects in which the text of I.25 as printed in 1603 singles itself out from all the other chapters as having been composed in early and special circumstances. Chapter I.25 is also the essay which is most prominent in seventeenth-century English receptions of Montaigne, as in the cases of James Cleland, Henry Slingsby and Samuel Hartlib. See my forthcoming book, *Montaigne's 'Essais' in Early Modern Europe* (Oxford University Press).

26   Montaigne, *Essays*, I, p. 154. On Ramus, see A. T. Grafton and L. Jardine, *From Humanism to the Humanities: Education and the Liberal Arts in Fifteenth- and Sixteenth-Century Europe* (London, 1986), pp. 161–200; and chapter 5 above, p. 89.

27   Montaigne, *Essays*, I, pp. 170–1.

28   Montaigne, *Essays*, I, pp. 155, 174–5, 180, 182.

29   Montaigne, *Essays*, II, p. 256. See T. Cave, *The Cornucopian Text: Problems of Writing in the French Renaissance* (Oxford, 1979), pp. 299–312 for a brilliant exploration of this paradox.

30   A. M. Patterson, *Pastoral and Ideology: Virgil to Valéry* (Oxford, 1988), pp. 133–7.

31   For a straightforward confirmation of this, see Samuel Daniel's dedicatory poem to the Florio translation in Montaigne, *Essays*, I, pp. 12–14.

32   Ben Jonson, *Volpone, or The Fox*, ed. R. B. Parker, The Revels Plays (Manchester, 1983), III.iv.87–92.

33   Lodovico Ariosto, *Orlando furioso in English Heroical Verse*, trans. Sir John Harington (London, 1591), 'A preface, or rather a briefe apologie of poetrie, and of the author and translator of this poem'.

34   Montaigne, *Essays*, III, pp. 70, 119.

35   Montaigne, *Essays*, III, p. 62.

36   Montaigne, *Essays*, III, pp. 100–2.

37   Montaigne, *Essays*, I, p. 13; III, p. 65.

38   Jardine and Grafton, 'Gabriel Harvey', 63–5.

39 William Shakespeare, *Othello*, ed. N. Sanders, The New Cambridge Shakespeare (Cambridge, 1984), I.i.36; Montaigne, *Essays*, II, p. 412. For the centrality of the Ciceronian familiar epistle to 'familiar' vernacular writing in seventeenth-century England, see A. M. Patterson, *Censorship and Interpretation: The Conditions of Writing and Reading in Early Modern England* (Madison WI, 1984), ch. 5.
40 Montaigne, *Essays*, II, pp. 412–13.

11

The new science and
the traditions of humanism

ANTHONY GRAFTON

Constantijn Huygens was one of the most virtuous of the seventeenth-century virtuosi who collected antiquities, devised scientific instruments and cultivated a taste for natural curiosities. He painted, wrote poetry in several languages and played the lute for the king of England. The most modern English thinkers and writers appealed to him: he translated John Donne into Dutch and copied out Francis Bacon's theories about progress. He loved the humanist art of Rubens, but recognized the young Rembrandt's supremacy as a history painter. His unfinished classic in Dutch, the *Dagwerck*, celebrated the discoveries of the new science, which he tried to connect with the domestic life of the Dutch Golden Age, the sunny world of scrubbed tile floors, tables covered by rich rugs and crystalline windows so memorably depicted by Vermeer.

Huygens came honestly by his wide range of skills and interests: he was raised to have them. His father had him taught to speak French by the direct method as a child and encouraged him to study science, music and painting. As a teenager he enrolled at Leiden, the most modern university of his day. There he attended not only courses in Latin on canonical texts but also courses in Dutch on modern mathematics and military engineering. Even the professors of classical humanities wrote Dutch poetry. Soon Huygens became a habitué less of universities than of courts, ambassadors' residences and scientific societies. He seems as prototypically modern a figure as Descartes; and like Descartes, he saw the story of his own progress as worth recording in a carefully constructed autobiography.[1]

At this point, however, the resemblance ends. Descartes described in the *Discours de la méthode* ('Discourse on Method', 1637) the formation of a revolutionary, one who had deliberately turned away from the humanist learning and scholastic philosophy of the colleges and built the world anew. Huygens, by contrast, described the formation of a moderate, one who combined humanist and scientific interests, classical and modern tastes without strain. He was as delighted to remember how he learned to write Latin verse as how he learned to use the microscope. He saw no opposition between his up-to-date and his traditional endeavours. And he wrote his memoirs in what he still considered the language of science and learning: not French or Dutch but Latin, and not plain Latin at that but an elaborate, formal prose studded with allusions and quotations. Even when Huygens wished to praise a quintessentially modern enterprise – like Hugo Grotius's treatise in the vernacular on the principles of Dutch law – he did so as a classicist, remarking that Dutch farmers would be most grateful to Grotius 'sua si bona norint' – 'if they knew their own good'. He rightly assumed that his contemporaries would recognize his quotation from Virgil's *Georgics* (II.458).

An active command of elegant Latin still mattered deeply in the Holland of the Golden Age. It gave those who possessed it an entrée to the international Republic of Letters. It expressed ideas and reported events with a precision that the vernacular lacked. And it proved perfectly adequate for dealing with the most modern concepts and inventions – at least if, like Huygens, the Latinist was willing to ransack texts and lexica for plausible ways of referring to 'military engineers' (*architectones castrenses*) and other non-classical beasts. Latin eloquence, the core skill and mental discipline of the Renaissance humanist, lived.

For a variety of reasons, until the last generation or so most historians of civilization, literature and art assumed that Renaissance humanism died as the sixteenth century wound to a close. On the one hand, the cutting edge of change in early modern literature did not seem to belong to the Latin language, whose elegances the humanists cultivated with so much pains-taking attention. By the sixteenth century, after all, Italian had become not only a literary language but a classical one in its own right. The young aristocrat had to read, speak and write it as well as Latin, and its canon of once smooth-hulled classics, from Dante, Petrarch and Boccaccio down to Ariosto and Tasso, had developed a thick new barnacling of literary and philological commentary. The French poets of the Pléiade, the tragic and comic playwrights of the London theatre and the young Dutch poets in the circle of the University of Leiden all showed in their turn, to widespread satisfaction, that one could imitate, emulate and satirize the ancients in their languages as well. Just as close imitation of Greek models had turned the primitive babble of early Rome into a language of high literature, so close imitation of Greek, Latin and Italian precedents could make any modern vernacular a vehicle fit for epic or lyric, history or tragedy. The easily imitated oxymorons and ekphrases of Petrarch's lyrics, for instance, found creative imitators in every European language. Latin was still needed, at least by professional intellectuals.[2] But the age of creative writing in classicizing modern Latin – the age that stretched from Petrarch to Erasmus and a little beyond – had presumably reached its natural end.

On the other hand, it also seemed reasonable to infer that the content of the humanist curriculum had become either elementary or sterile – or both – by the turn of the seventeenth century. True, the creators of the Scientific Revolution enjoyed in almost every case that fine classical education, based on a thorough study of Greek literature, which, according to Thomas Gaisford's famous remark, 'not only elevates above the vulgar herd, but leads not infrequently to positions of considerable emolument'.[3] But a standard genealogy of modern thought, one inherited from its seventeenth-century creators, suggested that the new philosophy that called everything into doubt grew in soil fertilized by the ashes of the humanist tradition. Montaigne, himself the beneficiary of an idiosyncratic but excellent humanist training, showed in his last essay (III.13: 'On experience') that the whole enterprise of trying to find guidance for modern behaviour in classical texts required readers to rip their supposed authorities out of time and context. Individual lives and situations, societies and religions differed so radically that one could not reasonably hope to make the past shed light on the present.[4] He also subjected the wasted time required by a normal humanist education to a searching critique, which reformer after reformer would paraphrase or quote.

Where Montaigne questioned and subverted, two of his faithful readers inserted dynamite and lit the fuse. Bacon treated Renaissance humanism, like scholasticism before it, as a fatal disease of learning. The humanists had failed to see that the world had changed, that modern voyages were more extended, modern empires more far-flung and modern technology more powerful than those of the ancients. They had confused the 'antiquity' of the Greeks and Romans – the fact that their texts had existed for a long time – with the authority that human beings gain as they age – an authority that can be invested only in people, who continue to learn as they age, not in books, which are impervious to experience (if not to damage). The philology of the humanists, with its obsessive citation and imitation of authorities, had been an intellectual distraction from the thinker's true mission of extending man's empire. The humanists had entirely failed to see how much they could have learned from the practical men of their own day, whose theories about the natural world rested on practical experience, not mere textual exegesis – and who lived their intellectual lives, with every appearance of satisfaction, in the vernacular.[5] Descartes, for his part, admitted that the historical learning he had acquired at the Jesuit college of La Flèche had a certain value: it had taught him that values and behaviour differed from place to place and age to age. But travel could have taught the same lesson, and probably in a fresher way. As for the study of past philosophers, it showed only that – as Montaigne had already seen – they disagreed with each other on so many central points that none of their systems could claim the status of offering certain knowledge.

Many other prophets of the new science joined the chorus of those who groaned at the thousands of hours they and others had lost scribbling halting verse in a dead language or hoping vainly to find solid knowledge in antiquated books. Galileo used his brilliant Italian to present the results of his investigations to a wide public. He made wicked fun of those who 'think', as he wrote to Johannes Kepler, 'that philosophy is a sort of book like the *Aeneid* and the *Odyssey*, and that truth is to be found not in the world or in nature but in the collation of texts (I use their terminology)'.[6] The members of the Oxford Experimental Philosophy Club and the Fellows of the Royal Society, the Paris Académie des Sciences and the Roman Accademia dei Lincei agreed that the results of experiments and voyages were most clearly and plainly presented in the vernacular. A host of proposers tried to make up for the one great problem that the downfall of Latin posed – the loss of an international language – by devising universal symbolic or hieroglyphic or pictorial languages, not to mention methods for learning all European vernaculars in a couple of weeks each.[7] Even Sir Isaac Newton, who used his fluent Latin as the appropriate dress for the great baroque world picture of the *Principia*, used English for the pullulating experimental details of his *Optics*. Even G. W. Leibniz, who corresponded in Latin with half of learned Europe, used French to develop his modern metaphysics. These examples – and many more could be cited – suggest that in the seventeenth century Latin humanism played the crowd-pleasing role of the star in a dramatic execution scene. Just when the humanists had rediscovered most of the ancient texts that would see the light before the second Renaissance of the papyrologists, captured the new medium of printing and established their position at the start of the educational food chain, the basic futility of their central disciplines was publicly exposed and denounced – and by the most authoritative voices of their day.

Many humanists, finally, admitted, if not that their studies were useless, at least that their age had run its course: 'the age of criticism and philosophy', said the classical scholar J. F. Gronovius in the 1650s, 'has passed, and one of philosophy and mathematics has taken its place'.[8] Even those who continued to insist on the possibility of and the need for historical knowledge generally accepted that the forms of argument and presentation needed updating. Thus Pierre-Daniel Huet tried to make his anti-Cartesian *Demonstratio evangelica* (1679), in which he revealed the biblical origin of the ancient myths, rigorous and convincing in a way that could meet the criticisms of the Cartesians, convinced as they were that all philology was a waste of time.[9] He also tried to make the vast echo-chamber of the accumulated humanist commentaries on classical texts coherent and accessible by editing a series of editions of the classics, in the first instance for the French dauphin, in which only the notes that remained of interest were reprinted, after being boiled down. If humanist scholarship was to survive, in short, it needed to adopt at least the protective colouring of philosophical rationalism. Richard Bentley, Master of Trinity College and master of textual criticism, insisted, in a famous phrase in his commentary on Horace, that 'ratio et res ipsa' ('reason and the case in point') mattered far more to him than the testimony of 100 old manuscripts. He also devoted a famous series of Boyle Lectures to arguing for the philosophical and theological advantages of Newton's cosmology – which, he clearly saw, was no revival of an ancient theory but a new creation with no ancient counterpart.[10] No wonder that most standard narratives of the intellectual history of early modern Europe insist on the transition 'from the humanists to men of science', or on the change from a principle of authority to one of free investigation. This modern periodization has ample period support.

In fact, however, humanism long survived the sniping of its critics and the depression of its advocates – and even contributed a surprising amount to some of the intellectual enterprises that eventually replaced it. During the last generation, intellectual historians have come to see more and more clearly that late sixteenth- and seventeenth-century announcements of the death of humanism were a considerable exaggeration. Characteristic humanist enterprises, both philological and philosophical, continued to be carried out, sometimes on a grand scale, throughout the age of the new science. If some of them showed evidence of wear, and their advocates signs of edginess, others revealed a clear capacity to serve modern needs.

Throughout the late sixteenth and early seventeenth centuries, the need for young men trained to work in government expanded. From the ever larger courts of late Elizabethan and early Stuart England to the little police states of the Holy Roman Empire, bureaucracies grew, paper circulated in larger quantities and monarchs demanded more and more detailed advice about political options and social policies.[11] The humanist curriculum continued – so most teachers and most government officials agreed – to provide the skills and qualities young men needed to carry out these vital tasks. Across Europe, educational theorists continued to argue with unmistakeable energy and conviction that the best formation for a young man lay in the close study of the same classical disciplines that Leonardo Bruni and Guarino of Verona had defined, following Cicero and Quintilian, as key skills for one who hoped to lead an active life. The young man who wished to serve his prince as a judge or an ambassador, so the influential Helmstedt scholar Arnold Clapmarius explained, must begin by attaining real mastery of Latin, even if he could already read the language and had only three years to spend on all the disciplines: 'you need to possess it in a polished and elegant form, unless you want to philosophize in the way of vulgar writers. I approve entirely of their intelligence, so long as they produce their ideas in an eloquent form. But they do the reverse, and instead of shedding light on their learning, they obscure it with their awkward brushwork.' Real mastery, in turn, meant not only a written command of the language, but oral fluency: 'It is my advice that you should always speak Latin with your roommate. If either forgets, let him pay a penalty.' Only those who had attained this level – which required systematic reading of the comedies of Plautus, to amass a store of colloquialisms – could hope to avoid the humiliation suffered by many Germans, who, since they normally spoke no Latin, found themselves crippled by nervousness when they had to do so, because they had to take such scrupulous care to avoid solecisms.[12]

Clapmarius's belief in the need to immerse oneself in Latin, to strain for active command of a dead language, was not unusual: G. J. Vossius, the influential teacher of rhetoric at the Amsterdam Academy, also wanted his students to begin their studies by mastering as pure a Latin as possible. Though he admitted that no ancient author had treated all subjects and found all the writers of Golden Latin prose acceptable models, he urged them to concentrate on systematic – though not slavish – imitation of Cicero, the greatest single master of Latin eloquence and the only master of the highest, periodic form of Latin prose.[13] The Jesuit colleges that began in the mid sixteenth century to offer such successful instruction that they won the children of many Protestant noble families for their curriculum (and for Catholicism), even in parts of the Holy Roman Empire and Poland that had threatened to adopt the new religion permanently, adopted similar ideals. Like the Protestant academies, they specialized in active mastery of Latin poetry and history, and imposed the speaking of Latin as a vital scholastic discipline. But their curriculum was no more strictly classical and rhetorical than that of the influential Protestant academies in Strasbourg and Altdorf or of the English public schools, all of which offered their pupils much the same mix of Latin grammar, rhetoric and prosody, spiced with historical examples and moral lessons.[14]

The curriculum that young men were advised to undertake in the late sixteenth and seventeenth centuries embraced many subjects. Grotius urged a prospective diplomat to devote himself not only to the literary arts, but also to logic, physics and even to parts of the scholastic theology of Thomas Aquinas. This demand perhaps reflected unusually – and unrealistically – high standards. Grotius had himself been a brilliant prodigy at Leiden, where he mastered textual criticism, under the tutelage of Joseph Scaliger, at the ripe age of twelve, and became one of the most original intellectuals of the time, the writer of massive treatises on Christian theology and international law. But Grotius stood in the main line of educational writing when he defined the small core of subjects that the young politician absolutely had to study. Vossius maintained that the future 'politicus' must master rhetoric above all: only with the help of this instrument of persuasion could he hope to win friends and influence people in private or to address them effectively in public. Grotius agreed absolutely: the young man should begin by studying Cicero's letters, which showed 'how to fit the general precepts to particular topics'. Then he must read Aristotle's *Rhetoric* in the light of his ethical and political works, which showed 'how streams of moral and political wisdom should be gently drawn down to form the craft of persuasion'. Study of the orations of Cicero and Demosthenes would provide worked examples of these more sophisticated precepts.[15] Clapmarius also recommended the study of rhetoric in this sophisticated form, sternly insisting that his young men must learn ethics and politics, as well as Latin, before they could venture to compose anything so demanding as an oration. Close study of moral philosophy and rhetoric, attentive reading of the central ancient texts, carried on in an orderly and systematic way, would make the young man virtuous and eloquent – a 'vir bonus dicendi peritus', just as Roman and Italian educational theorists had always said. These doctrines have the ring of familiarity: *mutatis mutandis*, Bruni or Erasmus could have advanced similar arguments for making the study of ancient literature and the classical discipline of rhetoric the core of an education for civil life. It is not surprising, then, that Bruni's *De studiis et litteris* (1424) and Erasmus's *De ratione studii* (1511) were reprinted, along with more up-to-date texts, in seventeenth-century collections on educational theory.[16]

The production of classicists naturally required close study of the classics. Like earlier humanists, those of the late sixteenth and early seventeenth centuries were certain that classical texts embodied ethical and prudential principles of eternal value. Grotius, for example, advised his mature students to study the tragedies of Euripides, the comedies of Terence and the *Satires* of Horace. The young, he admitted, would see in such works only 'the purity and brilliance of their language'. Older students, however, would appreciate these texts' more important quality – their provision of ethical lessons as valid now as they had been in antiquity: 'they will regard there, as in a mirror, the life and conduct of humanity'.[17] Caspar Barlaeus, a brilliant

Neo-Latin poet, agreed as he recommended that the young try to transform the best of Horace's *Odes* into their 'blood and marrow', finding in them not only the beautiful language that naturally appealed to boys but also incomparably sound doctrines on piety, morality and the disasters that ensue after civil war, which only mature men could hope to appreciate.

Most of the methods that teachers recommended were as traditional as these justifications for reading the classics. They had read their Montaigne as well as their Cicero and Quintilian, and emphasized the need to make the classical curriculum practicable for young men born to high political and military rather than a purely literary and philological life. Promising young men must not be overworked: they must – as Vittorino da Feltre had shown long before – be allowed time for physical exercise and other honest forms of leisure. More important still, they should not be 'dried out' and transformed into desiccated pedants. The teacher should not, for example expect the ordinary young scholar to commit long works in Latin prose – as opposed to verse, more easily remembered – to memory.[18] Often this meant that reading the classics had to become a collaborative enterprise: a young scholar by profession must help the young nobleman to gain access to the elements of classical culture. Like Guarino of Verona, who had advised his patron and star pupil Leonello d'Este to find a poor but able lad to help him compile systematic notebooks on his classical reading, Grotius advised his prospective diplomat not to study a logic text himself, but to have his 'study helper, who has more free time, read some outstanding expert on this art and remember to report to you anything worthy of note that he finds'. This *coadjutor*, not the young noble, should also undertake the tedious but necessary task of working through the ancient and modern commentators on Aristotle's *Ethics* and *Politics* and abridging their remarks for his pupil.[19] The tutor, who accompanied his young charge to school and university, went over lessons with him and took him on travels later on, was a familiar figure in noble families across Europe. So was the professional *anagnostes*, or reader, who read classical texts with the mature king or nobleman, explaining the continued relevance of classical precepts and examples for the modern active life and helping in the compilation of study aids. Sir Philip Sidney, for example, told his brother Robert in a famous letter on the study of history that that 'excellent man', Mr Henry Savile, could help him at this task – thereby giving a glimpse of the humble tasks which could occupy, in his earlier years, a man who later rose to be Provost of Eton College, the creator of a magnificent edition of the works of Chrysostom, a great book-collector and an original mathematician.[20] To this profession belonged Henry Cuffe, whose lessons on Aristotle's *Politics* were blamed by Essex for having brought him to rebel against Elizabeth; not to mention Thomas Hobbes, who carried out similar jobs for no less a patron than Francis Bacon.[21]

Reading had to be systematic as well as collaborative. The young man should learn as early as possible – so Barlaeus explained – to keep careful notes on what he read.

> Meanwhile, as they read, they should have notebooks at hand, in which they may copy out the more elegant phrases and sentences; or let them have some blank pages bound in at the end of the books they read, and on them they may note down the number of the page in question and the heading of some remarkable topic. Then, when need arises, they will be able to make reference to it.[22]

Meticulously kept notebooks on the graces of Latin style, in which classical ways for beginning and ending a sentence, making a transition or quoting an authority were organized by type, so Vossius explained, could produce real copiousness in Latin, preventing the student from revealing the poverty of his linguistic resources by repetition.[23] And equally meticulous notes on historical reading – as Jean Bodin taught in his influential *Methodus ad facilem historiarum cognitionem* ('Method for Readily Attaining Knowledge of History', 1566) – would provide the knowledge of peoples and customs, constitutions and laws that the jurisconsult or politician must have at his fingertips.[24] In every case, the categories into which the student divided the matter he collected were essential: only these would enable him to impose a logical order on the spiralling mass of details he would gather as he read any major classical text – not to mention enabling him to find them again when necessary. As Sidney told his brother:

> ... but that I wish herein is this, that when you read any such thing, you straight bring it to his head, not only of what art, but by your logical subdivisions, to the next member and parcel of the art. And so, as in a table, be it witty words, of which Tacitus is full, sentences, of which Livy, or similitudes, whereof Plutarch, straight to lay it up in the right place of his storehouse, as either military, or more especially defensive military, or more particularly defensive by fortification, and so lay it up. So likewise in politic matters ...[25]

The late humanist and his pupil – like the humanists of the fifteenth and early sixteenth century – trained themselves to read with their pens ever ready in their hands. Word-for-word paraphrases of set texts, entered by hand between the lines of specially printed school editions, made them readily accessible. So, even more, did the longer remarks that teachers dictated and that students recorded in the wide margins or on interleaved sheets of their texts. And all this material, endlessly sorted and copied, processed and reprocessed, moved inexorably from margins to notebook and back again into school compositions and formal treatises. When the natural philosopher John Jonston described the work that had gone into his *Thaumatographia naturalis* (1630), he claimed not to have explored the natural world but to have done an immense amount of reading and excerpting, drawing on both the ancient *Natural History* of the Elder Pliny – itself avowedly a work of compilation – and the great modern texts of Georgius Agricola and Girolamo Cardano.[26] In doing so he merely described more explicitly than usual a method of intellectual work adopted by generations of writers and readers – from the political thinkers Bodin and Lipsius to the great essayist Montaigne, who published not only his essays, laden with artful quotations, but also the formal summary judgements that he had entered, like a good pupil of his humanist masters, in his copies of ancient and modern historians. The literary methods of Guarino and Erasmus, in short, survived and flourished: the student, armed with a notebook and a set of *loci*, places or categories, in which to store material for rapid retrieval, set out as confidently in 1630 as his counterparts had one or two centuries before to break the classics up into bite-sized segments and organize them for aggressively confident reuse.

Naturally, this literary regime could easily reduce itself – in uncreative hands – to a sterile exercise in *bricolage*, the endless recycling of the same commonplaces to no creative effect. Even the ablest students spent a vast amount of time and energy on meticulous, almost verbatim adaptations of particular classical texts. Johannes Kepler, for example, while a student at Tübingen in the 1590s, spun a laboriously clever epithalamium for a law student out of the ancient *Laus Pisonis*: parts of his work, as was common, effectively amounted to a patchwork of lines from the original.[27] Textbooks often provided little more than lists of ways to perform a particular literary task – quoting an authority, for example – in a suitably classical way.[28] And even loyal believers in the value of classical learning complained bitterly of the length of time it took to be initiated into the mysteries of artistic Latin Jan Amos Comenius, for example, devised his celebrated *Orbis sensualium pictus* ('The Visible World', 1666), in which simple pictures directly expressed the meanings of the words that referred to them, not to replace but to abridge the rule-based teaching of the humanists.

If the framework of humanist pedagogy was astonishingly traditional however, its content was both contentious and protean. Controversies continued to rage about every element in the humanist curriculum. Marc-Antoine Muret and Justus Lipsius argued that the Latinist of the later sixteenth century should find his models not only in the oratory of the

Roman republic but also in the close-knit, sententious writing of Tacitus and Seneca. Lipsian Latin, in particular, became a fad in Protestant and Catholic Europe alike: but it also came under sharp attack. The great Calvinist scholar Joseph Scaliger was appalled by Lipsius's numerous abrupt phrases and minimal use of conjunctions: 'I do not know', he plaintively told the students who lodged with him, 'what sort of Latin this is.'[29] Scaliger set out systematically to extirpate trendy Tacitisms from the Latin written by students at Leiden – and thereby found himself in agreement, unexpectedly, with the Jesuit pedagogues he loathed, who insisted that Lipsius's 'Laconism' was not the right way to attain the stylistic qualities of wit and paradox that they thought students should strive for.[30]

Not only the niceties of style, but also the structure of the curriculum as a whole, came in for sharp debate. Reformers like the Protestant martyr Peter Ramus and his followers, who attained considerable influence in Cambridge as well as Paris, urged educational authorities and students to take up a new, pragmatic version of dialectic and rhetoric. The teacher should treat every literary text, including the poems of Horace and the Psalms of David, as a systematic argument, which could be reduced in principle to a series of logical statements. Regent masters in Paris collèges and Continental universities found this a splendid way to teach the skills of argumentation through the literary classics. They presumably considered it useful, as well as witty, to treat 'Dulce et decorum est pro patria mori' ('It is sweet and fitting to die for one's country'), Horace's often-quoted exhortation to spill one's gore in a patriotic way, as simply one move in an argumentative game.[31]

But the Ramists also ran into opposition in many quarters, in part from Aristotelians who detested Ramus's effort to alter the traditional structures of dialectic and rhetoric. Many humanists insisted that literary texts should be analysed in a literary way, that the teacher should pay more attention to metaphors and turns of speech than to structure and forms of argument. The pamphlet wars that blazed up wherever Ramus and his followers went illuminate their progress rather as exploding land-mines illuminate the progress of an army attacking entrenched positions: resistance almost every-where was vigorous. The survival of the ideal of eloquence, in short, did not remotely imply unanimity about its content. Indeed, the heat and extent of the debate are the best indicator of the vitality humanism retained – especially in those cases, as in France around 1600, when divisions about the nature and purpose of eloquence corresponded to a large extent with political and religious divides. When the Gallican lawyers of the Paris *parlement* and the Jesuits they briefly drove from Paris disagreed about the proper models of Latin prose, they also debated alternate political and social ideals of life. Not even the sharpest humanistic debates of the fifteenth century over the virtues of republics and monarchies reveal deeper divisions over principle than those that took place, still in Latin and still taking classical writers as their main figures, two centuries later.[32]

For all the range of argument that attended problems of style and substance, however, a single, visibly homogeneous model for the core of humanistic learning took shape in institutions as apparently different as the medieval colleges of the University of Paris and the new Protestant 'illustrious academies' that sprang up in Strasbourg, Altdorf and other cities that wanted the prestige and income that an institution of higher learning could bring, as well as a safe and reliable training for their sons. In most of these institutions – as opposed to new environments like the French court, where new models of vernacular eloquence flourished – the teaching of rhetoric centred, much as it had in the fifteenth century, on the analysis of works of Cicero. Within his canon, however, the emphasis shifted, moving from the orations which had fascinated the civic humanists of fifteenth-century Italy to the letters. Written rather than oral texts, apparently personal and informal rather than public and theatrical, these offered the student a vast range of models of prose rather than the highly formal one of Cicero's oratory. They also seemed more appropriate models for young men whose future tasks would involve far more document preparation than public speaking. Accordingly, students at early stages of their education, from Strasbourg to Rome, spent large amounts of time reading, translating and imitating Cicero's letters. Humanism modernized itself, responding to practical needs with pragmatic, sensible solutions.

One side of this modernization took the form of an increasing attention to material objects, both as found in nature and as reworked by man. This interest grew in part from classical texts. No text fascinated the humanists more, from the fifteenth century onwards, than Pliny's *Natural History*, and this great encyclopedic work, though itself mostly compiled from written sources, offered a wealth of information about the development of sculpture and the range of natural objects and species. Though Pliny remained the richest source of information about the arts in antiquity, Aristotle's works on animals and Theophrastus' on plants, translated into Latin in the mid fifteenth century, complemented it with further material, much of it derived from direct inspection of the natural world. Humanists collected gems, fragments of ancient sculpture and modern art objects, shells and fossils. Connoisseurship became almost as central a skill of the educated young man as Latin eloquence.[33]

By the middle of the sixteenth century, humanist households regularly contained not only a library but a collection, the contents of which were as painstakingly sorted and labelled as the contents of the owner's schoolbooks had been sorted and copied into notebooks: in 1543, for example, the historian and collector Count Wilhelm Werner von Zimmern showed Sebastian Münster, who visited him in his castle of Herrenzimmern bei Rottweil, 'an enormous treasury of texts, especially the historians, an almost infinite number of antiquities, golden and silver vessels shut away in a niche in the wall, a stock of simples adorned with varied confections'.[34] The Paduan antiquary Lorenzo Pignoria was one of relatively few Italian scholars of the period around 1600 to enjoy the whole-hearted respect of humanists throughout the Protestant north as well as patrons in his own region. He had not only a fine library, which included manuscripts of Dante and Boccaccio, humanist Latin poetry and a treatise on pumping machines, but also a museum stocked with coins, medals, shells, busts, papyri and a whole 'iconotheca', or collection of paintings of illustrious men – not to mention a graphic work by Dürer 'showing the image of a woman, of wonderful skill' – *Melencolia I*, perhaps?[35] His collection differed only in extent, not in character, from that of his older contemporary Joseph Scaliger, who doted on the headless bird of paradise he had been given by Dutch merchants in an uncharacteristic fit of generosity, used drawings he had made as a young man in Italy and southern France to introduce his students to the study of antiquities and found mummies and papyri rivetingly interesting. The better-endowed or better-supported colleges had museums of their own. The Jesuit Collegio Romano of the mid seventeenth century, for example, swarmed with the giant bones and wooden model obelisks collected or fabricated by its dominant intellectual figure, Athanasius Kircher. Not only the critics of traditional book-learning, in sum, took a serious interest in the material world. Humanists did so as well. They ventured, with varying success, to interpret relics of the ancient world, like the Egyptian cult object known as the *Mensa Isiaca* and the pagan temples of ancient Scandinavia, which were not explicitly described in preserved texts. And they compiled exhaustive studies of the development of the visual arts in antiquity, which made clear their belief that the educated young Latinist must be able to discuss the work of artists as well as that of writers, in detail and with a sophisticated conceptual apparatus. In this belief – if not often in their own abilities as draughtsmen and architects – the late humanists showed themselves the direct heirs of Leon Battista Alberti.[36]

No single discipline shows the interplay of tradition and innovation in late humanism more clearly than history. On the one hand, humanist teachers and historians around 1600 clearly saw themselves as the heirs of the Greek and Roman statesmen who had defined what history should be. They agreed, that is, that the historian should try to form readers for public life. To that end he should deal, above all, with political events of great importance. From these he should extract for especially precise treatment examples of good and evil, effective and ineffective conduct, which his readers would be able to imitate (or avoid) in their turn. The way of precepts, so the humanists endlessly repeated, was long and winding; but the way of examples was short and direct. *Exempla* not only revealed which principles worked and which did not, but impressed them on the malleable mind and memory of the young reader with a force no general presentation could attain – and gave him a stock of quotations and allusions which would serve him in good stead when he had to speak or write on public issues.[37]

These convictions, firmly based on Livy and Polybius, echoed from one end of the humanist Republic of Letters to the other. Philip Sidney expressed them with characteristic force in the letter to his brother Robert:

> In that kind you have principally to note the examples of virtue and vice, with their good or evil successes, the establishment or ruins of great estates, with the causes, the time, and circumstances of the laws then written of, the enterings and endings of wars, and therein, the stratagems against the enemy and the discipline upon the soldier; and thus much as a very historiographer. Besides this, the historian makes himself a discourser for profit, and an orator, yea a poet, sometimes for ornament.[38]

Sidney took his own advice: to prepare for his embassy to the court of the Holy Roman Emperor in 1577, he spent some time reading the first three books of Livy with the erudite Gabriel Harvey. Harvey later recalled that 'the courtier Philip Sidney and I had privately discussed these three books of Livy, scrutinizing them so far as we could from all points of view, applying a political analysis ... Our consideration was chiefly directed at the forms of states, the conditions of persons, and the qualities of actions.'[39] In doing so he showed himself, for all his renowned dash and spontaneity, as docile a follower of humanist tradition as the Nuremberg scholar Philip Camerarius, son of the famous Joachim, who liked to tell the students of the Altdorf Academy that 'when one considers the past and pays attention to the present, one can draw reasonable conclusions about the future. The present is a riddle, which time solves.'[40] In offering this advice, so everyone knew, Camerarius simply gave voice to the traditional beliefs of the Roman historians about the value of their craft. 'Historia magistra vitae' ('history, the teacher of life') – the age-old doctrine, expressed with matchless clarity by Cicero, that the texture of human life remained fundamentally the same through the centuries, so that examples from any good historian should serve for imitation by an intelligent later reader, lived on in the lecture courses about how to read the historians held by thinkers who diverged as radically as Agostino Mascardi, ex-Jesuit professor of eloquence at Genoa and Rome, and Degory Wheare, professor of history at Oxford.

Yet the study of ancient history was anything but static in the crucial years around 1600. In fact, it underwent a series of changes, as scholars and teachers made a deliberate effort to adjust their practices to fit the immediate needs of their pupils and patrons. Already at the beginning of the sixteenth century, Machiavelli and Guicciardini had called the traditional humanist justifications for studying history into question. Both had insisted that one should draw only pragmatic, not moral lessons from the ancient past. Machiavelli had implicitly questioned the ability of modern readers to follow even the former, since all individuals tended to follow one line of behaviour, even if it proved unproductive, and to misread their own situation as well. Guicciardini explicitly complained that even Machiavelli had gone wrong by concentrating so exclusively on the lessons of Roman history, since the modern world hardly resembled the one the ancient historians had described: 'How wrong it is', he complained, 'to cite the Romans at every turn.'[41]

Two generations later, humanists adapted as their own the fundamental points of what had been intended as a critique of their predecessors. Marc-Antoine Muret, whose lectures on classical texts at the Collegio Romano attracted as much attention as his influential earlier ones had in Paris, admitted that 'there are very few republics in our days'. From this, however, he drew a novel conclusion: not that one should cease to study Roman history, but rather that one should transfer one's interests from the lost republic, evoked with such nostalgic eloquence by Livy, to the early empire, analysed with such searching irony by Tacitus. In the empire, as in the modern world, he reasoned, most states were ruled by an individual: to that extent at least, he told his pupils in 1580, the 'state of affairs under the emperors comes closer to resembling our times than that which obtained when the people ruled. Though, thanks be to God', he went on with his characteristic irony, 'our age has no Tiberiuses, Caligulas, Neros, it is still useful to know how even under them there lived good and prudent men...' After all, he reflected, the art of dissimulation was essential to anyone living in a modern court: 'Princes often have many qualities which a good man cannot praise, but can conceal and pass over in silence. Those who do not know how to wink at these both endanger themselves and generally make the princes worse.'[42] Tacitus, in short, could teach the art of silence so essential to life in the court of a Philip II or the curia of a Gregory XIII. More generally, close attention to the context in which a given historian had written could overcome the objection that examples were too generalized to be instructive.

What Muret offered as the justification for lecturing on Tacitus became the programme for two generations of politically minded humanists. Justus Lipsius, the brilliant young Fleming who learned – and plagiarized – much from Muret during his early years in Rome, brought back with him to the Low Countries the notion that historical training must rest on 'similitudo temporum' – on the careful, analytical establishment of parallels between countries and periods. He made it the foundation of his brilliant courses on Roman history and antiquities, in which he explained exactly how one could and should revive the secrets of the Roman army in modern times. Lipsius's most brilliant pupil, Maurice of Nassau, Prince of Orange, put these lessons into practice as he created the disciplined, professional land army that kept the northern Netherlands free from Spain – even though his teacher had to explain to him, repeatedly, that he had in mind not a slavish revival of Rome's now obsolete military technology, but a systematic effort to drill soldiers to the same level of discipline and cohesion, in small units, that had made the Romans so formidable. Lectures and disputations on pragmatic politics, centring on Tacitus and emphasizing how hard it was to draw the marrow from the bones of his uniquely clipped style, made Leiden the largest and most fashionable university in northern Europe for the first half of the seventeenth century.[43] Even after Lipsius himself moved to Louvain and returned to the Catholic faith he had been born in, the tradition of politically engaged, contextually sensitive teaching of history that he founded was carried on by men like Daniel Heinsius, who deeply appreciated Tacitus' ability, comparable to that of Thucydides, to grasp and express the real secrets of state action. Throughout Europe, humanist historians could claim to be the reigning experts in a subject of immediate and obvious contemporary relevance. They had better access than anyone else to the *arcana imperii* of the ancient world, the secret rules by which – as Clapmarius explained in his most famous book – the Roman empire had really functioned.[44] It is not surprising, therefore, that Kepler, when called upon to offer precise political advice to erudite, touchy patrons like the Emperor Rudolf II, preferred to do so not as an 'astrologus' but as a 'politicus' – an experienced reader and interpreter of Tacitus and other classics of political history.[45]

Late humanist students of history, however, did not confine themselves to pragmatics, to meeting the charge of statesmen that their ways of reading were too innocent. In the first place, they also set out to make the study of the ancient historians methodical and systematic, in ways that Machiavelli and Guicciardini – and perhaps Muret as well – never anticipated. Alongside the study of historical texts flourished a second branch of humanist scholarship, equally classical in origin but often far more technical in character: antiquarianism, the systematic effort to reconstruct the institutions and mores, religions and rituals of the Greek and Roman world, which Alberti, Flavio Biondo and others had refounded in the fifteenth century. The antiquaries of the sixteenth century compiled enormous corpora, of ancient objects and inscriptions, which they organized not in chronological or geographical but in systematic order. Inscriptions were arranged, first in notebooks and then in printed editions, and carefully indexed, to illustrate not examples of good and evil conduct but permanent features of ancient societies: religion and ritual, family relations and parental affection, styles of patronage and forms of priestly brotherhood. Antiquities became essential to the study of ancient history, which they enlivened and enriched. Illustrations of objects could give a vivid, almost three-dimensional reality to what would otherwise have remained pale and unconvincing descriptions of gladiatorial combat or the making of encampments.[46]

The antiquarian enterprise became a standard support to historical research and teaching. Lipsius, for example, not only lectured on Tacitus at Leiden, but drew from Polybius' famous analysis in Book VI of his *Histories* and a wealth of complementary sources a coherent reconstruction of the Roman army, which he presented first to his Leiden students, as well as to his pupil Maurice of Nassau, and then to the readers of his *De militia Romana* (1596). The French jurist François Hotman urged his students to learn Roman antiquities by studying Cicero, whom he explicated to them with such success that a German baron who came to him in 1557 barely able to utter a word of Latin produced his own book on Roman families two years later.[47]

Though the marriage between history and antiquarianism proved hard at first to consummate, it was eventually more fertile than those who served as witnesses had expected. Traditionally, humanists saw the ancient historians as privileged witnesses to the history of Greece and Rome. They offered corrections for textual errors and even, occasionally, for factual ones, but made no effort to replace the narratives of Livy or Tacitus with new ones. But the antiquarian looked for kinds of information about the past that ancient historians had offered only in passing. The categories he used in compiling a collection of inscriptions, for example, were systematic rather than moral or pragmatic, and aimed at reconstructing the basic institutions of a past society rather than emulating the great deeds of its leaders.[48] Gradually, however, some Renaissance antiquaries came to see that this approach represented something of a challenge to the reigning one. Lipsius, for instance, urged the student to make himself notebooks for reading history, which he should divide into the same categories as he would have divided a notebook of inscriptions: everything that he read which bore on the beliefs or rituals, magistracies or priesthoods, military insignia or gladiatorial games of the Greeks or Romans should be entered under those heads. He also suggested that the student compile notes on fine examples. But this bow to tradition does not conceal the radicalism of his approach. In effect, Lipsius accepted that the ancient historians should not enjoy a more privileged status than other remains of the ancient world. All of them – literary texts and stone inscriptions alike – should be submitted to the same forms of analysis. All of them should be forced, that is, to yield an analysis of ancient history quite unlike that to be found in any ancient writer. For only thus, said Lipsius, anticipating the much later scholars who spoke of a 'hermeneutic circle', could one hope to understand texts that merely referred to, but did not explain in detail, the *mores* and institutions of the societies they described.[49]

Other humanists challenged the limits of traditional historical method at other points. The Roman antiquaries Carlo Sigonio and Onofrio Panvinio and northern polymaths like Scaliger and the well-named chronologer Joannes Temporarius agreed that one could not derive a full and accurate chronology of ancient history, a firm backbone of facts and dates, from any preserved source. They set out to use Roman monuments, the fragments of Greek and Jewish historians and the data of the new astronomy to rebuild this lost structure. And they succeeded not only in creating a new and fashionable discipline – one known for making bold hypotheses about history and myth, Egyptian dynasties and Jewish kingdoms – but also in calling into question the accuracy and authority of the traditional narratives of biblical and classical history.[50] In the hands of Scaliger and Temporarius, Romulus disappeared from world history, and Moses threatened to follow him.[51] Still others, like the influential satirist John Barclay, argued that the historian should concern himself not with technical details but with the larger question of identifying the 'genius', or spirit, which had inspired the writers and artists, politicians and generals of each distinct historical period – much as a different natural 'genius' should be identified and studied by the well-informed and intelligent traveller.[52] History, in other words, a pre-eminent discipline of the Latin-writing, learned citizens of the late humanist Republic of Letters, was alive, flourishing and even rife with sophisticated discussion. No wonder, then, that other disciplines flourished as well: that the Latin writers of a relatively backward country, England, produced substantial contributions to virtually every literary and scientific, philosophical and historical genre known in the time of Elizabeth I and James I.[53] Humanism lived.

NOTES

1 For this paragraph and what follows, see his autobiography, ed. J. A. Worp in *Bijdragen en mededeelingen van het historisch genootschap*, 18 (1897), 1–122; for a modern translation with excellent introduction and notes, see Constantijn Huygens, *Mijn jeugd*, ed. and trans. C. Heesakkers (Amsterdam, 1994).

2 See, e.g., L. Forster, *The Icy Fire* (Cambridge, 1969).

3 Quoted by R. Jenkyns, *The Victorians and Ancient Greece* (Oxford, 1980), p. 67.

4 Michel de Montaigne, *Essais*, ed. P. Villey (Paris, 1965), pp. 1,065–116; for an English translation, see Montaigne, *The Complete Essays*, trans. M. A. Screech (London, 1993), pp. 1,207–69.

5 See R. F. Jones, *The Triumph of the English Language* (Stanford, 1953; reprinted 1966).

6 Johannes Kepler, *Gesammelte Werke*, ed. W. von Dyck and M. Caspar (Munich, 1937–), XVI, p. 329.

7 H. Aarsleff, *From Locke to Saussure* (Minneapolis, 1982).

8 Quoted by F. F. Blok, *Nicolaas Heinsius in dienst van Christina van Zweden* (Delft, 1949), pp. 111–12.

9 C. Borghero, *La certezza e la storia: cartesianismo, pirronismo e conoscenza storica* (Milan, 1983), pp. 170–95.

10 L. Gossman, *Medievalism and the Ideologies of the Enlightenment* (Baltimore, 1968); S. Timpanaro, *La genesi del metodo del Lachmann*, second edition, reprinted with corrections and additions (Padua, 1985), ch. 1; J. M. Levine, *Humanism and History* (Ithaca NY, 1987).

11 See G. Oestreich, *Neostoicism and the Early Modern State*, ed. B. Oestreich and H. G. Koenigsberger (Cambridge, 1982); M. Stollcis, *Staat und Staatsräson in der frühen Neuzeit* (Frankfurt, 1990), pp. 197–231; P. S. Donaldson, *Machiavelli and Mystery of State* (Cambridge, 1988).

12 A. Clapmarius, 'Nobilis adolescentis triennium', in Hugo Grotius *et al.*, *Dissertationes de studiis instituendis* (Amsterdam, 1645), pp. 145–6.

13 G. J. Vossius, 'Dissertatio bipartita,' in Vossius *et al.*, *Dissertationes de studiis bene instituendis* (Utrecht, 1658), especially pp. 15–18.

14 For the fullest study of the late humanist curriculum see the analysis of the influential academy designed by Jean Sturm for Strasbourg in A. Schindling, *Humanistische Hochschule und freie Reichsstadt* (Wiesbaden, 1977).

15 Grotius, *Dissertationes*, pp. 4–5.

16 Erasmus's *De ratione studii* is reprinted in Grotius, *Dissertationes*, pp. 319–39, as is another early sixteenth-century treatise by Joachim Fortius Ringelberg, pp. 252–316 with an appendix on 317; Bruni's *De studiis et litteris* appears on pp. 414–31.

17 Grotius, *Dissertationes*, p. 4.

18 Caspar Barlaeus, 'Methodus studiorum', in Grotius, *Dissertationes*, p. 353.

19 Grotius, *Dissertationes*, pp. 2–3.

20 Philip Sidney to Robert Sidney, 18 October 1580, in S. A. Pears, ed., *The Correspondence of Sir Philip Sidney and Hubert Languet* (London, 1845), pp. 199, 201.

21 See, in general, L. Jardine and A. T. Grafton, '"Studied for action": how Gabriel Harvey read his Livy', *Past and Present*, 129 (1990), 30–78.

22 Barlaeus, 'Methodus', in Grotius, *Dissertationes*, p. 353.

23 Vossius, 'Dissertatio bipartita', p. 17.

24 Jean Bodin, *Methodus ad facilem historiarum cognitionem* (Paris, 1566) and reissued several times up to 1650; see also A. Blair, 'Restaging Jean Bodin', PhD thesis, Princeton University, 1988.

25 Pears, *Correspondence of Sidney and Languet*, p. 201.

26 John Jonston, *Thaumatographia universalis* (Amsterdam, 1665), epistola dedicatoria. See I. Maclean, 'The interpretation of natural signs: Cardano's *De subtilitate* versus Scaliger's *Exercitationes*', in B. Vickers, ed., *Occult and Scientific Mentalities in the Renaissance* (Cambridge, 1984), pp. 231–52; and, more fully, W. Schmidt-Biggemann, *Topica universalis* (Hamburg, 1983).

27 F. Seck, 'Keplers Hochzeitgedicht für Johannes Huldenreich (1590),' *Abhandlungen der Bayerischen Akademie der Wissenschaften*, mathematisch-naturwissenschaftliche Klasse, new series, 155 (1976).

28 See, e.g., H. Arning, *Medulla variarum earumque in orationibus usitatissimarum connexionum* (Altenburg, 1652), chs. 12–14.

29 *Secunda Scaligerana* (Cologne, 1667), pp. 140–3, at 141.

30 See M. Croll, *Style, Rhetoric and Rhythm: Essays*, ed. J. M. Patrick and R. O. Evans (Princeton, 1966); W. Kühlmann, *Gelehrtenrepublik und Fürstenstaat* (Tübingen, 1982).

31 A. T. Grafton, 'Teacher, text and pupil in the Renaissance class-room: a case study from a Parisian college', *History of Universities*, 1 (1980), 37–70.

32 See M. Fumaroli, *L'Age de l'éloquence* (Geneva, 1980).

33 See J. Tribby, 'Body/building: living the museum life in early modern Europe', *Rhetorica*, 10 (1992), 139–63; T. DaC. Kaufmann, *The Mastery of Nature* (Princeton, 1993); P. Findlen, *Possessing Nature* (Berkeley, 1994).

34 Sebastian Münster, *Briefe*, ed. and trans. K. H. Burmeister (Ingelheim am Rhein, 1964), p. 67.

35 See G. F. Tomasini, *De vita, bibliotheca et museo Laurentii Pignorii canonici Tarvisini dissertatio*, in Lorenzo Pignoria, *Magnae Deum matris Idaeae et Attidis initia* (Amsterdam, 1669).

36 See A. Ellenius, *De arte pingendi* (Uppsala, 1960). The most accessible product of these efforts is the new edition of the 1638 edition of Franciscus Junius's *De pictura veterum: The Painting of the Ancients*, ed. K. Aldrich, P. Fehl and R. Fehl, 2 vols. (Berkeley, 1991).

37 See, e.g., G. Nadel, 'Philosophy of history before historicism,' *History and Theory*, 3 (1964), 291–315; R. Koselleck, *Vergangene Zukunft* (Frankfurt, 1984).

38 Pears, *Correspondence of Sidney and Languet*, p. 200.

39 Jardine and Grafton, 'Gabriel Harvey', 36.

40 J. G. Schellhorn, *De vita, fatis ac meritis Philippi Camerarii ... commentarius* (Nuremberg, 1740), p. 120.

41 Francesco Guicciardini, *Maxims and Reflections of a Renaissance Statesman*, trans. M. Domandi (New York, 1965), C 110.

42 Marc-Antoine Muret, *Scripta selecta*, 2 vols. (Leipzig, 1887–8), I, p. 155.

43 See T. H. Lunsingh Scheurleer and G. H. M. Posthumus Meyjes, eds., *Leiden*

University in the Seventeenth Century: An Exchange of Learning (Leiden, 1975); Stolleis, *Staat und Staatsräson*, pp. 37–72; Kühlmann, *Gelehrtenrepublik*; and H. Wansink, *Politieke wetenschappen aan de Leidse Universiteit, 1575–±1650* (Utrecht, 1981).

44 A. Clapmarius, *De arcanis rerumpublicarum libri sex*, new edition (Amsterdam, 1644).

45 See B. Bauer, 'Die Rolle des Hofastrologen und Hofmathematicus als fürstlicher Berater', in A. Buck, ed., *Höfischer Humanismus* (Weinheim, 1989), pp. 93–117.

46 The best introduction to this development is still A. D. Momigliano, 'Ancient history and the antiquarian', *Journal of the Warburg and Courtauld Institutes*, 13 (1950), 285–315.

47 Schellhorn, *De vita Camerarii*, pp. 36–7.

48 See E. Mandowsky and C. Mitchell, *Pirro Ligorio's Roman Antiquities* (London, 1963).

49 Justus Lipsius, 'De ratione legendi historiam', in Grotius, *Dissertationes*, pp. 157–69. A nice example of this sort of note-taking is provided by Friedrich Lindenbruch's 'De servis, deque eorum conditionibus, poenis, ac manumissionibus commentarius' (MS Hamburg, Universitätsbibliothek, philol. 291), which includes ample notes on legal and literary texts, and instructions on which historians to trust (and to examine for further information). See in general E. Horváth, 'Friedrich Lindenbruch, Späthumanist und Handschriftsammler des 17. Jahrhunderts', dissertation, University of Hamburg, 1988, pp. 185–6: Lindenbruch seems to have taken these notes as a young student at the University of Leiden, which he attended in the mid-1590s, not long after Lipsius's departure.

50 D. C. Allen, *Mysteriously Meant* (Baltimore, 1970); A. T. Grafton, *Joseph Scaliger*, 2 vols. (Oxford, 1983–93), II.

51 H. J. Erasmus, *The Origins of Rome in Historiography from Petrarch to Perizonius* (Assen, 1962).

52 E. Hassinger, *Empirisch-rationaler Historismus*, second edition (Freiburg im Breisgau, 1994).

53 J. W. Binns, *Intellectual Culture in Elizabethan and Jacobean England: The Latin Writings of the Age* (Leeds, 1990).

12

Humanism and Italian literature

M. L. McLAUGHLIN

This chapter will examine the ways in which Italian literature was influenced by the humanist movement in the crucial period in which the *studia humanitatis* dominated the intellectual agenda in Italy, broadly speaking from the time of Petrarch to the age of Lorenzo de' Medici. The two centuries surveyed here embrace a period which begins with the embryonic 'medieval' humanism of Dante Alighieri and terminates in the early sixteenth century, when Italian humanists ceased to form part of the mainstream of creative literature in Italy and the *studia humanitatis* became institutionalized in the university system.

At the outset it is important to distinguish between the classical tradition in general and the humanist movement in particular. To consider every Italian work inspired by the legacy of antiquity in this classicizing age of Italian literature is beyond the scope of this chapter and this book. Instead, I shall focus on vernacular literature in Italy which was either written by humanists or informed by humanist values.

Although Dante is not usually regarded as a humanist, the *Divina commedia* (*c.* 1307–18) presents a number of features which indicate that to a certain extent the poem derives from a humanist matrix. In a sense Dante 'discovered' the *Aeneid*, in that he was the first to make Virgil talk again to his age after centuries of silence. As he himself was aware, he was the first Italian writer to read the Roman poet in both a political and intertextually creative way – the latter is alluded to in Dante's famous address to Virgil when he meets him in the first canto of the whole *Commedia*: 'You are the single author from whom I derived the fine style which has brought me such honour' (*Inferno* I.86–7). In terms of content, this first vernacular poem on an epic scale, in which Virgil even appears as a character, embraces an ambitious attempt to rewrite in Christian terms the sixth book of the *Aeneid*. The echoes of Virgil are prominent as early as *Inferno* III, notably in the description of Charon, though Dante tends to demonize and portray as a Christian devil Virgil's merely melancholy ferryman.[1] The references

224

continue throughout the poem, including the climactic moment of Virgil's departure on the summit of Mount Purgatory, when Dante on sighting Beatrice cites Dido's famous words about her love for Aeneas: 'I recognize the signs of the old flame of love' (*Aeneid* IV.23; *Purgatorio* XXX.48). There are also countless echoes of the other three Latin poets that constitute Dante's canon of epic poets: Ovid, Lucan (both appear briefly as characters in Limbo in *Inferno* IV, and Dante explicitly challenges and claims to outdo them in *Inferno* XXV.94–7) and Statius (who also appears as a substantial character, *Purgatorio* XXI–XXXIII). Dante's imitation of classical authors extends from broad borrowings of content to minute reworkings of brief phrases from the ancient poets. But these allusions, though clearly evincing respect for antiquity, nevertheless nurture a constant undercurrent of attempting to outdo or supersede in Christian terms the classic pagan texts.[2]

Underlying this at times minute intertextual practice is Dante's rather vague theory of literary imitation outlined, but not developed, in *De vulgari eloquentia* ('On Vernacular Eloquence', 1304–7) II.6.7. There Dante urges a generic imitation of classical authors as beneficial to the development of the best style in vernacular poetry. But while the four epic poets named (Virgil, Ovid, Lucan, Statius) are predictable, the four prose authors commended as models for improving poetic style constitute a curious list: Livy, Pliny, Frontinus, Orosius. There is no sensitivity here to major and minor authors: the four prose authors are merely names to balance the four poets; Dante certainly could never have read them in any depth, if at all, and unlike the poets mentioned, they make no impact whatsoever on his (or anyone else's) vernacular poetry. Dante's sensitivity to Latin literature is in this sense typical of his time: he is convinced of the prestige of the classical tradition and consequently of the need to imitate Latin authors, yet he can believe that the Latin of his contemporaries is identical to the language of classical antiquity;[3] and despite his sophisticated imitation of the epic poets in the *Commedia*, his general knowledge of the ancient world is defective in many areas.[4]

Dante's attitude to antiquity stressed continuity. His belief that Latin had remained unchanged is paralleled by his being allowed to join the 'bella scola' of classical poets in Limbo: there Homer, Virgil, Horace, Ovid and Lucan welcome him as a sixth member of an élite academy (*Inferno* IV). By contrast, Petrarch's more accurate knowledge of the past made him aware of the discontinuities between antiquity and the present, reflected in his sense of loss and exclusion from that golden age and in his stylistic awareness of the difference between classical and medieval Latin. The case of Horace provides a measure of Petrarch's more precise knowledge of antiquity: little more than a name to Dante ('Orazio satiro', *Inferno* IV.89), Horace will be rediscovered as a major lyric poet thanks to Petrarch. Another key divergence between Dante and Petrarch was the latter's official denigration of vernacular language and literature in the face of Latin's incomparable achievements. This theoretical primacy of the learned language over the *volgare* was reflected in Petrarch's own writings, which comprised many more works in Latin than in the vernacular (unlike Dante's more equal distribution between the two languages); this preponderance of Latin over Italian output became the norm for his humanist successors in Italy. One consequence was that the new Italian literature, which had started in so revolutionary a manner with Dante's ambitious epic *Commedia*, with Petrarch's own lyric collection, *Rerum vulgarium fragmenta* (*c.* 1342–70) and Boccaccio's *Decameron* (*c.* 1348–51), soon atrophied under Petrarch's Latin counter-revolution, and Italian intellectuals for a century after Petrarch's death channelled their efforts into perfecting Latin rather than Italian. In this so-called 'secolo senza poesia' ('century without poetry') humanists did write some works in the *volgare*, but the largest part of their output was in Latin.

Petrarch's theoretical diminution of the status of the *volgare* is, however, undercut by his own work in the vernacular, in particular his collection of lyrics, the *Rerum vulgarium fragmenta*. Despite the disparaging title ('Fragments in the Vernacular'), and his repeated claim that these were 'nugae' ('trifles') on which he worked as a youth, but which he abandoned on reaching maturity, we know from his autograph manuscript that he continued to work both on individual poems and on the order of the whole collection right up until the 1370s.[5] Indeed, at one early stage it seems that this collection of *rime* was to have been a lyric synthesis of Latin and romance poetic motifs on a par with Dante's epic fusion of the classical and vernacular traditions. In 1342 Petrarch intended that the opening poem of the collection should be 'Apollo, s'ancor vive il bel desio' ('Apollo, if the fine desire is still alive', *Rerum vulgarium fragmenta* XXXIV), a classicizing sonnet establishing at the outset the myth of Apollo and Daphne as one of the carrying structures of the whole collection.[6] At another stage the concluding poem was to have been 'Vago augelletto, che cantando vai' ('Wandering bird, singing on your way', CCCLIII), a sonnet with a rather Virgilian tone (like CCCXI, it echoes the simile in *Georgics* IV.511–19).[7] However, in harmony with Petrarch's myth of his own development from young poet to mature Christian philosopher, the whole collection was restructured to open with the penitential sonnet 'Voi ch'ascoltate in rime sparse il suono' ('You who listen to the sound [of my sighs] in scattered rhymes', I), and to close with the recantation of his love for Laura in the *canzone* to the Virgin (CCCLXVI). In Petrarch, then, as in Dante, the classical tradition is superseded by the Christian one.

Within this official Christian framework, however, many of the individual poems offer views onto a distinctly classical landscape. Recent studies have highlighted the importance of the classical subtexts and Petrarch's sense of chronological distance from antiquity.[8] In terms of the content of the whole collection, Petrarch acted like a Renaissance architect, supporting the flimsy vernacular edifice of the love lyric with the sturdy classical columns of two morally weightier themes: the passing of time and the vanity of earthly pleasures.

As for language and style, Petrarch is remarkably consistent in both Latin and Italian. Eschewing in both languages the two extremes of vulgar and scholastic/technical terminology, he cultivates a middle elegance in lexis, as well as a classical harmony and euphony in his famous balanced or antithetical lines, a practice which he imitated from Virgil and Horace.[9] By endowing vernacular love poetry with morally elevated themes like the passing of time, and by imitating ancient poetry in its attention to structure and formal properties, Petrarch projected the Italian lyric towards a new status of serious rivalry with classical verse.

One poem which illustrates his intertextual practice in both languages is 'Tutto 'l dí piango; e poi la notte, quando' ('All day I weep, and yet at night', *Rerum vulgarium fragmenta* CCXVI), which was rewritten by Petrarch in a way that excised unwitting vernacular echoes and deepened classical resonances.[10] The underlying strategy in such rewritings is to retain and even enhance allusions to classical *auctores*, but to eliminate traces of *volgare* texts. The imitative rationale behind the rewriting of this sonnet is explained in Petrarch's famous letter of 1359 to Boccaccio (*Familiares* XXI.15.12), where he stresses that he is particularly keen to avoid verbatim imitation especially in the vernacular ('in his maxime vulgaribus');[11] yet even an almost direct translation of a line from Virgil or Cicero does not offend him, presumably because by the very act of writing in the *volgare* he is faithful to his precept of using different words from the model.[12] What subtends Petrarch's imitative practice, unlike Dante's, is a more precise theory of literary imitation, which he derived largely from Seneca (*Epistulae* LXXXIV), Cicero (*De oratore* II.89–96) and Quintilian (*Institutio oratoria* X.2), and which he elaborated in a series of important letters.[13]

But although many individual poems reflect a classical/vernacular fusion, Petrarch's public pronouncements on the status of the two languages proved more influential and discouraged his successors from further experiments in this direction. In particular, the 1359 letter to Boccaccio mentioned above, in which he denied any imitation of Dante and distanced himself from his predecessor, effectively drove a wedge between the humanist and vernacular publics and proved extraordinarily effective in determining attitudes to Dante in particular and to literature in the *volgare* in general.[14]

The most spectacular illustration of its divisive influence was in its addressee, Giovanni Boccaccio. A great admirer of Dante in his youth, he had begun writing by imitating the ornate *dictamen* ('letter-writing technique') of Dante's Latin epistles and by translating Valerius Maximus and a decade of Livy into Italian.[15] But after encountering Petrarch in 1351 and discovering the classical sobriety of his Latin letters and his disdain for vernacular culture, Boccaccio erased his own name both from his early Dantesque epistles and from his *volgarizzamenti* (vernacular versions) of the Latin historians.[16] Petrarch's influential separation of the two cultures meant that it was no longer respectable for a humanist to write scholastic Latin or to translate from classical Latin into the *volgare*: Quattrocento humanists, such as Leonardo Bruni and Lorenzo Valla, would translate from Greek into Latin, but the Latin classics had to be read in the original.[17] One work in particular by Boccaccio epitomizes the radical nature of the Petrarchan revolution: his biography of Dante, the *Trattatello in laude di Dante* ('Short Tract in Praise of Dante').

The first version of the *Trattatello* was written between 1351 and 1355; the second one some time between 1361 and 1363. The main differences between the first (I) and second (II) versions were Boccaccio's suppression, in the second redaction, of all mention of Dante's *Epistole*, of the title of the *Monarchia* and of the number of Latin *Eclogues* Dante wrote.[18] It is now clear that it was Petrarch's 1359 letter to Boccaccio about Dante which was the most influential factor in the rewriting of the *Trattatello*, particularly in the implied criticism of Dante's Latin works in the second redaction.[19] In the light of Petrarch's segregation of the Latin and *volgare* public in the letter, Boccaccio was forced to moderate claims which had associated Dante too closely with humanist, Latin culture. In the first edition he had claimed that Dante had restored the Muses to Italy and had revived dead poetry (I.19), performing for the Italian vernacular what Homer and Virgil had done for Greek and Latin (I.84). In the later version such claims are omitted, largely because of Petrarch's categorical separation of the two cultures, aligning Dante's work with the vernacular audience of woolworkers and innkeepers, but putting himself alongside Homer and Virgil (*Familiares* XXI.15.22). In the second redaction Dante no longer appears as the reviver of poetry, presumably because Petrarch wished to claim that glory for himself, and because in the new humanist view of things this literary renaissance could now only be associated with work in Latin, not in the *volgare*. Even more indicative of the new anti-vernacular atmosphere is the modification of this passage: '[Dante] became extremely familiar with Virgil, Horace, Ovid, Statius and all the other famous poets: not only was he keen on knowing their works, but in his sublime poetry he managed also to imitate them' (I.22). In the second redaction this is reduced to 'he became extremely familiar with all [of the classical poets], and particularly with the more famous of them' (II.18). All mention of Dante's 'imitation' of classical authors is omitted because for a humanist like Petrarch, and therefore also now for Boccaccio, proper *imitatio* could only take place when writing in Latin.

Petrarch's official condemnations of vernacular literature caused Boccaccio to repent of his early enthusiasms for Dante's Latin letters, of his translations from Latin into the *volgare* and indeed of all his works in Italian (*Epistole* XXI). After 1351 Boccaccio, like Petrarch, turned from poetry to prose and from the *volgare* to Latin, devoting himself to erudite works in Latin prose: *De casibus virorum illustrium* ('The Fall of Illustrious Men'), *De mulieribus claris* ('On Famous Women'), *De montibus* ('On Mountains'), *Genealogie deorum gentilium* ('Genealogies of the Pagan Gods'). Even his late efforts at interpreting Dante's *Commedia* in public (1373–4) he regarded as a misguided 'prostitution of the Muses' which led to his being punished by 'Apollo' with a severe illness (*Rime* 122 5).[20] Boccaccio thus epitomizes the cultural schizophrenia induced in Italian intellectuals in the second half of the fourteenth century by Petrarch's radical separation of Latin and vernacular literature, a dichotomy which was not to be overcome until the final quarter of the fifteenth century.

The Italian Quattrocento opens, almost symbolically, with the perfectly classical edifice of Leonardo Bruni's *Dialogi ad Petrum Paulum Histrum* ('Dialogues dedicated to Pier Paolo Vergerio', 1401–6), an almost exact copy of a Ciceronian dialogue.[21] The content is secular, the Latin is impeccably Ciceronian and the structure recalls that of Cicero's own *De oratore*. Its dramatic date is Easter Sunday 1401, significantly a century and a year after the fictional date of Dante's *Commedia* (Easter 1300): if the fourteenth century had opened with a major work in vernacular verse, the fifteenth began with an equally revolutionary work in Latin prose. The shift from poetry to prose and from Italian to Latin are both direct consequences of the Petrarchan revolution – Petrarch's prose works in Latin outnumbered his poetic compositions, and the disappointment which greeted his Latin epic, *Africa*, when it eventually circulated among humanists at the end of the fourteenth century, discouraged others from attempting serious Latin poetry.

Bruni's attitude both to his classical and vernacular predecessors was extremely open and unprejudiced. The criticism of Dante, Petrarch and Boccaccio, which Niccoli articulates in *Dialogi* I, may be to an extent counterbalanced by the unconvincing palinode or recantation in Book II; but Bruni maintains his rigorous approach to the 'Three Crowns' of Florentine literature (Dante, Petrarch, Boccaccio) in his *Vite di Dante e di Petrarca* ('Lives of Dante and Petrarch', 1436).[22] His interest in the genre of biography stemmed from his enthusiasm for Plutarch, which had already resulted in his writing new, critical lives of Cicero (*c.* 1415) and Aristotle (*c.* 1429).[23]

Bruni was inspired to write the *Vite*, not only to dignify vernacular authors with Plutarchan parallel lives, but also because he found Boccaccio's *Trattatello* 'entirely full of love stories and sighs and burning tears'. Bruni's secular biography also eschewed Boccaccio's fondness for vernacular love lyric and the mystical, theological overtones of his discussion of poetic allegory. But although the biographies illustrate Bruni's enthusiasm for Dante and Petrarch, an important number of critical nuances remain. Unlike Salutati's hypothesis about a Latin *Divina commedia* which would have surpassed Homer and Virgil, Bruni openly admits that Dante chose to write his poem in the vernacular because he knew his Latin writings, notably his *Eclogues* and the *Monarchia*, were inferior to his work in the *volgare*. The latter work is written 'in an extremely inelegant fashion, without any stylistic refinement', and as in the *Dialogi*, Dante's Latin is associated with the hated medieval idiom ('in the scholastic style of the friars').[24]

Similarly, Bruni's famous praise of Petrarch as the pioneer of the humanist Renaissance also contains hints of criticism which are too often overlooked. For Boccaccio Petrarch had been the reviver of poetry, and for Salutati he had been the supreme Latinist; however, Bruni's tribute to Petrarch is not on account of his Latin works, which fall short of the present age of perfection ('yet his [Latin] style was not perfect'), but in the more general terms of pioneering scholarship, opening up the road of humanist studies, by discovering ancient works. Petrarch's Latin represented a limited Ciceronianism ('modelling his Latin, *within the limits of his knowledge and abilities*, on the most elegant and perfect eloquence [of Cicero]', my italics), clearly below 'the present perfection' achieved by Bruni and his generation. For Bruni, as for Flavio Biondo, a genuine return to Ciceronian Latin was possible only after the 1421 discovery at Lodi of the complete *Orator, De oratore* and *Brutus*.[25]

In 1435 there was an important debate among Italian humanists about what kind of Latin was spoken in antiquity. This has come down to us in the exchange between Bruni and Flavio Biondo, in which Bruni claimed that there was an equivalent of the *volgare* in ancient Rome, while Biondo rightly argued that the vernacular was born in the wake of the barbarian invasions of Italy.[26] The dispute itself can be seen as another consequence of the Lodi discovery, since Cicero's *Orator* and particularly the *Brutus* provide much important linguistic and literary information about the development of Latin rhetoric before Cicero. But if the cause of the debate lay in one Lodi manuscript, its effects were more wide-ranging. The polemic lies behind both Bruni's vernacular lives of Dante and Petrarch, in which he claims that there is a theoretical parity between Latin and Italian, and behind two other innovative works of the decade: *Della vita civile* ('On the Life of the Citizen', *c.* 1434) of Matteo Palmieri, and *I libri della famiglia* ('The Dialogues on the Family', *c.* 1433–41) by Leon Battista Alberti. These were revolutionary because in the wake of Bruni's *Dialogi* the moral dialogue had quickly established itself as the flagship genre of humanist Latin, whereas Palmieri's and Alberti's works were the first moral dialogues to be written in the Italian vernacular. Until the 1430s prose works in the *volgare* had been either city chronicles, religious tracts or *novelle*.

The ground-breaking nature of Palmieri's and Alberti's dialogues meant that both works had to be accompanied by explanatory proems. Palmieri's prologue articulates the humanist impasse in the 1430s: his subject is to provide guidance for citizens to lead the good civic life, but since the best precepts for 'bene vivere' ('living well') are in Latin, and the vernacular translations of the classics are so poor as to be unrecognizable, he initially turned to *volgare* texts.[27] But he found Dante's poetry obscure, Petrarch's verse too restricted in its treatment of moral matters, while Boccaccio's *Decameron* was replete with dissolute and lascivious matter. The limitations both of *volgarizzamenti* of classical texts and of the 'Three Florentine Crowns' inspired Palmieri to write his own work in the vernacular, and in order not to follow the idealizing tendencies of classical authors like Plato, he composed it in the form of a dialogue with speakers who really existed.

The proem also informs us of the structure of the work: Book I deals with the proper civic instruction of the young person from the moment of birth to maturity; Books II and III are entitled 'De honestate', the former dealing with three of the cardinal virtues (prudence, temperance and fortitude), and the latter with the last but most important virtue, justice; while Book IV, 'De utilitate', deals in its first half with the usefulness to the state of children, wealth and soldiers, and in the second half recounts a legendary vision, granted to Dante, of the rewards meted out to those who serve the state well.

Much of the first book is indebted to Quintilian, echoing key passages from the opening of the *Institutio oratoria* and stressing the superiority of active, civic virtues over the contemplative life. But the most important passage in the first book is Palmieri's discussion of cultural renaissance. He argues that these periods of excellence are rare because most men are either content with the inventions of their predecessors (Quintilian X.2.4), or are bent on merely making wealth out of the arts. But he acknowledges that he is living in one such rare period at present, when painting has been revived by Giotto, sculpture and architecture are enjoying a renewal, while litera-ture, particularly in Latin, has been reborn for the first time in 800 years, thanks especially to the brilliance of Leonardo Bruni. Like other humanists, he castigates the ignorance of his 'medieval' predecessors, above all in Latin, which is the source and medium of philosophy and other disciplines. By contrast, the present excellence in literature derives from this period of renaissance (Palmieri is the first vernacular author to use the verb *rinascere*) which he sees as a recurrent phenomenon, observable in antiquity as well:

> You will see from one day to the next the flourishing of the genius of your fellow citizens, since it is in the nature of things that forgotten arts should be reborn (*rinascere*) when necessity demands it. This is what happened in ancient Greece and Rome, where in one generation orators flourished, in another poets, in another jurists, philosophers, historians, sculptors, de-pending on whether this or that art was more necessary, more esteemed and therefore taught by the masters of that time.[28]

The most striking part of the work is the final section of Book IV, in which Palmieri recounts a fictitious vision beheld by Dante on the battlefield of Campaldino (1289), which is clearly intended to represent the vision that inspired the *Divina commedia*, but which is also patterned on Cicero's *Dream of Scipio*. In a passage bristling with echoes of the *Commedia* (especially *Inferno* X and *Purgatorio* V), Dante finds three days after the battle the body of his best comrade rising up before him on the field of combat. His friend tells Dante that in his semi-alive condition he found himself on the edge of the sphere of the moon, where Charlemagne showed him both the lower spheres and hell, as well as the higher ones and heaven, in which he saw 'the souls of all the citizens who governed their republics in a just manner'.[29] It is a brief vision of the afterlife, more closely modelled on Cicero than on Dante, including the Ciceronian phrase so much admired by Petrarch, 'the life you lead on earth is but a certain death'.[30] The main objective of this final sequence is to harness the vernacular outlook of Dante to the mainstream of classical thought, and also to secularize it, omitting the Christian framework of his poem, in order to stress, as Bruni does in his *Vita di Dante*, Dante's interest in the rewards pertaining to the good citizen.

Alberti, who possessed his own copy of the *Brutus* and the *Orator*, both discovered at Lodi in 1421,[31] explicitly alludes to the 1435 polemic in the famous proem to Book III of *Della famiglia*, siding with Biondo's thesis of the barbarian origin of the vernacular, but arguing in favour of the utility of writing in a language comprehensible to the majority. Book I articulates a number of key humanist concepts. The main interlocutor argues that the study of classical literature is both aesthetically pleasurable in itself and an ideal training for public life. In another crucial passage it is recommended that the best Latin authors to study are Cicero, Livy and Sallust, not medieval compilations such as the *Chartula* and the *Grecismus*. Where Alberti differs from his peers is in his appreciation of some other writers who are in style 'crudi e rozzi' ('crude and unrefined') but who should still be studied for their content, if not their language: 'The Latin language should be sought in those writers whose style was clear and in a state of perfection; from the other writers let us take the various scientific ideas which their works teach.' Alberti's interest in the content of these 'scientific' writers (Vitruvius, Cato, Varro) is characteristic of his own polymath personality and of his pluralist approach to style.[32]

Throughout *Della famiglia* there is an attempt to imitate the secular tone of ancient dialogue, and mentions of Christianity and modernity are kept to a minimum. In most places God is equated with nature: 'Nature, that is to say God, created man to be partly heavenly and divine, and partly to be the noblest and most beautiful of all mortal creatures';[33] and even when contemporary Christian practice is alluded to, it is camouflaged in pagan terms: 'tempio' ('temple') and 'sacrificio' ('sacrifice') are regularly used instead of 'chiesa' ('church') and 'messa' ('Mass').[34] Book III, the most widely read of the four books, in which the unlettered Giannozzo undercuts Lionardo's humanist rhetoric, was explicitly intended to be a modern, vernacular equivalent of Xenophon's *Oeconomicus*.[35]

Alberti's works in the *volgare*, whether moral dialogues or technical treatises on grammar or painting, consistently embrace the project of validating the vernacular as a medium on a par with Latin. The *Grammatichetta* (c. 1440), the first Italian grammar, now almost certainly attributed to Alberti, is modelled on the structure of Priscian's *Institutiones*,[36] and also stems from the 1435 dispute about the status of the vernacular. Though Alberti espouses Biondo's theory that the *volgare* derived from the barbarian invasions, he maintains that it too has a grammatical regularity like Latin. Also connected with Alberti's programme of enhancement of the vernacular was the *Certame Coronario* ('Poetic Contest for the Crown') of 1441.[37]

The *Certame* was a poetry competition promoted by Alberti, in which he solicited compositions on the classical theme of *amicitia* ('friendship'). But the contest ended in stalemate, with the panel of humanist judges refusing to award the silver laurel wreath to any of the vernacular entries. Alberti's own submission was a poem entitled 'De amicitia', consisting of sixteen lines of Italian written for the first time in classical hexameter verse, beginning: 'Tell me, you mortals, who have placed such a gleaming crown before us, what do you hope to achieve by looking at it?'[38] It was probably Alberti who penned the anonymous 'Protesta', in which he berated the humanists for not imitating antiquity by declining to encourage literary competitions of this sort. Certainly, the 'Protesta' shows a sensitivity to the diachronic development of both Latin and the vernacular, which is paralleled in the proem to *Della famiglia* Book III and which shows close reading of Quintilian: 'we shall complain if you, as it seems, demand from our age what the ancient Romans never demanded of theirs: before the Latin language became as refined as it subsequently was to become, they were content with their earliest poets just as they were, that is to say, clever perhaps but lacking in stylistic artistry (*ingegniosi, ma chom poca arte*)'.[39]

Underlying all of Alberti's works is the question of originality in the face of the classical tradition. It is discussed most famously in the prologue to *Della pittura* (1436), his vernacular version of *De pictura* ('On Painting'). Here he rejects the topos that nature is now too old to produce geniuses, since in Florence he has seen that Brunelleschi, Donatello, Ghiberti, Masaccio and Luca della Robbia are as talented as any of the artists of antiquity; indeed, they are superior in that in their own fields they had no ancient model to imitate and could produce 'arts and sciences never before seen or heard of'.[40] The topic of originality recurs in the *Profugiorum ab aerumna libri* ('Flight from Tribulation'), also known as *Della tranquillità dell'anima* ('On the Tranquillity of the Soul', 1441–2). At the start of Book III Alberti cites Terence's 'Nihil dictum quin prius dictum' ('Nothing is ever said that has not been said before', *Eunuchus* 41), but embroiders it with a characteristic metaphor. He draws a parallel between the man who invented mosaics from the fragments of material left over from the construction of the Temple of Ephesus and the contemporary writer who adorns his work with the precious remnants of the temple of classical culture. The only originality left to the modern writer lies in selecting a different variety of classical gems and in arranging them to suit the new context.[41]

Alberti thus confronted the classical tradition directly and in a series of enterprises attempted to bolster the status of the vernacular: writing serious Ciceronian dialogues and technical treatises in it, demonstrating its grammatical regularity and similarity to Latin in the *Grammatichetta*, and organizing the *Certame Coronario* in an attempt to emulate the poetry contests of antiquity which had proved so beneficial to the development of

Latin. However, nearly all his efforts remained original, even genial, ideas, which were doomed to end in stalemate. The Latinate style of his dialogues had no successors until the more natural Italian prose, a century later, of Baldesar Castiglione's dialogue *Il libro del cortegiano* ('The Book of the Courtier', 1528); his grammar made little impact until the 'questione della lingua' ('the Italian language controversy') erupted fully in the first decades of the sixteenth century; his vernacular hexameters had no immediate heirs and the *Certame* as a whole ended with no winners.

The more successful assimilation of the classical tradition into Italian poetry occurred in the writers of the generations after Alberti: Cristoforo Landino, Angelo Poliziano and Lorenzo de' Medici. As we turn to the second half of the century, it is important to bear in mind that it is characterized by a move back from prose to poetry in the vernacular, and by an enthusiasm for Platonic ideas which was inspired by the translation of all of Plato from Greek into Latin by Marsilio Ficino. In particular, Platonic notions of love blended harmoniously with many of the concepts of the vernacular love lyric tradition, thus enhancing its status.

Landino was the theorist of a vernacular literature resting solidly on the strengths of the classical tradition, a theory summed up in his phrase 'è necessario essere latino chi vuole essere buono toscano' ('whoever wants to write Tuscan well has to know Latin'),[42] and which found its practical counterpart in the works of Poliziano and Lorenzo. Landino's qualification of his motto with the caveat that phrases and ideas should be borrowed from classical writers without making the *volgare* unnatural ('non sforzando la natura') is both a parenthetical critique of the Latinate style of Palmieri and Alberti, and the clue to why the writers of the Laurentian age were more successful in their synthesis of classical and vernacular elements.

In both his Latin and Italian works Poliziano was concerned to avoid imitation of major models, cultivating instead 'minor' authors such as Quintilian and Statius (on whom he first lectured in 1480), rather than Cicero and Virgil. His critical judgements are reflected in his practice in both languages: as he never wrote a Latin dialogue, so in the *volgare* he avoided the major genres popularized by Petrarch, writing only four sonnets and two *canzoni*, and concentrating instead on the minor, popular forms: *canzoni a ballo* (dance or carnival ballads, consisting of a short stanza with refrain) and *rispetti* (brief eight-line love poems).[43] Even in these minor poems, though, one can observe many points in common with his Latin works. The poem about Echo (*Rispetti* XXXVI), for instance, is a conscious attempt to transfer to the vernacular lyric tradition the kind of learned, witty poem that the epigrammatic poet Gauradas had written in Greek, as Poliziano himself tells us in *Miscellanea* I.22.[44]

His most important vernacular work was the unfinished *Stanze per la giostra* ('Stanzas for the Joust', 1475–8).[45] Even had it been completed, it would never have been an epic on a grand scale, but would probably, given Poliziano's tastes in literature in general, have remained within the genre of the epyllion, or short epic. The title itself suggests a modest work, a number of stanzas not an epic 'Iulieid' about Giuliano, Lorenzo de' Medici's younger brother. The content, structure and style of the work confirm that it is to be classified as a brief, erudite poem in the middle rather than the grand style. The chief models and sources are Claudian and Statius, not Homer and Virgil. It is a poem not about military victories, but about a young man falling in love and winning a joust for his lady. Structurally, it exhibits one of the standard ingredients of the short epic: the ekphrasis describing a work of art and occupying a disproportionately large part of the narrative.[46]

In the *Stanze* Poliziano puts into practice that eclectic imitation of different models that he defends in his Latin works. Indeed, certain octaves recall the standard images of the anti-Ciceronians: the bee (I.25), the flowers (I.77), the choir (I.90), the mosaic (I.96). One stanza not only describes the bee moving from flower to flower, as he would later do in his prolusion to Statius and Quintilian, but is also a practical demonstration of this theoretical eclecticism:

> Zefiro già, di be' fioretti adorno,
> avea de' monti tolta ogni pruina;
> avea fatto al suo nido già ritorno
> la stanca rondinella peregrina;
> risonava la selva intorno intorno
> soavemente all'ora mattutina,
> e la ingegnosa pecchia al primo albore
> giva predando or uno or altro fiore.   (I.25)

(Zephyr, the springtime wind, bearing little flowers in his breath, had removed all hoarfrost from the mountains; the little swallow, weary from her wanderings, had already returned to her nest; all around, the woods rustled in the morning breeze, and in the first light of dawn the industrious little bee flew around stealing [honey] from a variety of flowers.)

The theme here is a traditional set-piece description of spring, but the phrasing reworks several lines from Petrarch, one from Dante and an echo of Virgil's first *Eclogue*.[47] The diminutives 'fioretti' ('little flowers'), 'rondinella' ('little swallow') and the unusual 'pecchia' ('little bee'), which actually derives from a rare Latin diminutive ('apicula'), are typical of Poliziano's vocabulary; while the bee moving from flower to flower symbolizes, in a self-referential way, the author's poetics, shown to best advantage in this very stanza.[48] But unlike Alberti's rather heavy-handed Latinate prose, in Poliziano we find polished Tuscan verse coupled with the most exquisite intertextual play and intricate strategies of self-reference.

The *Orfeo* (c. 1480) also embodies the constants of Poliziano's poetics. It is a work of considerable originality, a serious drama about a secular subject in the vernacular and perhaps also an imitation in the *volgare* of a Greek satyr-play;[49] it is a short work rather than a classical five-act drama; it is eclectic in metre, poetic register and language, including as it does an ode in Latin. The Orpheus myth, with sources in so many ancient texts, including the ekphrasis of the epyllion in Virgil's fourth *Georgic*, automatically allowed Poliziano to echo a variety of classical authors. Originality, eclecticism, brevity and erudition, the main components of Poliziano's literary credo, are to be found in the *Orfeo* as much as in the *Stanze*.

His works in both languages exhibit that 'docta varietas' ('learned eclecticism') that he defends against Paolo Cortesi's Ciceronianism in a famous exchange of letters (c. 1485);[50] and all his writings betray a penchant for eclecticism and minor models, as well as a connoisseur's delight in lexical rarities. There is certainly a shift in Poliziano's literary career from poetry to philosophy, from 'imitatio' to 'philologia', from the early imitations of classical models in the youthful Latin and Italian works of the 1470s, to the philological restoration of the actual texts of antiquity in the 1480s and 90s. But this shift is not so radical as it appears since for Poliziano humanist scholarship was integral to his own best poetry. His cult of eclecticism is the literary equivalent of his contemporary Botticelli's exploitation of different classical and vernacular sources in his two great secular works of the 1470s and 1480s, the 'Primavera' and the 'Birth of Venus'.[51]

Poliziano's patron, Lorenzo de' Medici, was not a scholar, but an important vernacular poet, who in his *Comento de' miei sonetti* ('Commentary on My Sonnets', 1475–91) harnessed some of the key humanist notions of the century to the defence of vernacular poetry. The *Comento* consists of forty-one sonnets linked by a prose commentary. Not only do the sonnets reveal Lorenzo's skill in grafting Neoplatonic motifs onto the vernacular tradition of love poetry, but in the opening pages his defence of the *volgare* is particularly indebted to the humanist debate about language. Thanks to his patronage of the philosopher Giovanni Pico della Mirandola, he knew something about Hebrew: he was aware that Greek was a richer language than Latin, and Latin than Hebrew;[52] and he was of the view that all three ancient languages – Hebrew, Greek and Latin – despite their hallowed status, were in origin vernaculars: 'but they were spoken or written more accurately, regularly or rationally by those who attained honour or prestige in those languages, than they were by the majority of the populace on the whole.'[53] By the end of the century, increasing humanist knowledge about the ancient languages is exploited in defence of the Italian vernacular.[54]

Apart from Poliziano's *Orfeo* with its lyrical shepherds, there were other manifestations of a renewed interest in pastoral in the last decades of the century. Bernardo Pulci's translation of Virgil's *Eclogues* was published in Florence in 1482 along with a number of other vernacular eclogues by Tuscan poets such as Francesco Arsochi and Girolamo Benivieni. This popular volume was probably the chief inspiration behind the most important pastoral work of the period, the *Arcadia* (1504) of Jacopo Sannazaro. Consisting of a framing prologue and epilogue, and a narrative of twelve prose chapters, each followed by an eclogue in a variety of metres (*terza rima, sestinas, canzoni*), *Arcadia* represents a felicitous synthesis of classical bucolic motifs and the troubled present of Sannazaro's Naples, caught between the powerful invading forces of France and Spain at the end of the century. Sannazaro is particularly skilled at fusing the nostalgia of Virgil's *Eclogues* with the traditions of vernacular love lyric and is proud of his role as the reviver of pastoral poetry: 'I was the first to reawaken the woods which had fallen asleep, and the first to show the shepherds how to sing the forgotten songs.'[55] Thanks to Sannazaro's initiative, pastoral remained popular in the sixteenth century and eventually gave rise to the successful new genre of pastoral drama in Torquato Tasso's *Aminta* (1573) and Battista Guarini's *Il pastor fido* (1590).

By far the most extraordinary vernacular text to emerge under the influence of humanism was the *Hypnerotomachia Poliphili*, attributed to Francesco Colonna and published by Aldus Manutius in 1499. A prose romance in two books, it narrates the dream of Poliphilo and the story of his love for Polia, firstly in an allegorical dream sequence in the twenty-four chapters of Book I, then in a shorter narrative in the fourteen chapters of the second book. Apart from the beautiful woodcuts that accompany the text, the work is astonishing for two other reasons: its profound antiquarian knowledge of ancient architecture and technical terms; and its bizarre style, clearly intended to be a *volgare* equivalent of the Apuleian Latin that was so fashionable in northern Italy at the end of the century.[56] Like Poliziano's *Stanze*, the work remains in descriptive rather than narrative mode: the many descriptions of woods, pyramids, obelisks, sculptures, triumphs and inscriptions allow not only for imitation of vernacular authors,[57] but in particular of the difficult, technical writers favoured by the anti-Ciceronian humanists in the Quattrocento: Plautus, Pliny, Apuleius, Vitruvius and his modern counterpart Alberti.[58] The rare lexis is embedded in Latinate syntax, with heavy adjectivization, use of gerunds and participles and a fondness for Greek terms, diminutives of nouns and compounds of verbs and adjectives.[59] But this exotic vernacular, like the eclectic Latin of the anti-Ciceronians at the end of the fifteenth century, was a singular, virtuoso achievement that left no heirs.

It seems appropriate to end the story of humanism's impact on Italian literature at its apogee, with the publication of the *Hypnerotomachia* in 1499. The first decades of the next century saw a return to Ciceronian classicism in both Latin and the vernacular, largely under the influence of Pietro Bembo. Although writers working in Italian still took inspiration from the literature of antiquity, Bembo was the only important vernacular author to make a career as a humanist. His *Gli Asolani* ('The Lovers of Asolo', 1505) expounded Platonic ideas of love, and in the *Prose della volgar lingua* ('Dialogues on the Vernacular Language', 1525) he took humanism's tripartite periodization of golden age, decadent and Renaissance Latinity, and rigidly applied it to the vernacular literature written in the fourteenth, fifteenth and sixteenth centuries respectively; hence his conclusion that as in Latin only Cicero and Virgil were acceptable models, so in the *volgare* Boccaccio and Petrarch were the sole writers one could imitate. But Bembo's other vernacular works owe little to the legacy of humanism. The major Italian authors of the sixteenth century, from Ariosto and Castiglione to Tasso and Guarini, continued to draw nourishment from the classical tradition, but none of them was a practising humanist, and none drew creative inspiration from scholarship in the way that Petrarch, Alberti and Poliziano had done.

The impact of the *studia humanitatis* on Italian Renaissance literature appears to be threefold. First, although humanism initially retarded the development of vernacular literature, diverting intellectual energy into the writing of Latin, it also in one sense emancipated the *volgare*. When Quattrocento humanists realized that Latin was not a supernatural monolith, but a language with a diachronic development, they accepted that the vernacular was not innately inferior, but rather a young language in need of development. Knowledge of Greek, and particularly awareness of the fact that, unlike Latin, it had possessed dialects as well as a literary *koine*, meant that Italian had a prestigious model in one of the ancient languages. Only when the vernacular was defended by humanists, such as Alberti and Landino, and not just by the unlettered champions of the 'Three Crowns', did intellectuals accept the *volgare* as a serious alternative to Latin.

Secondly, humanism enhanced the status of the vernacular in practical terms by introducing new genres, themes and stylistic sophistication. Although a genuine epic would not be written until Torquato Tasso's *Gerusalemme liberata* (1575), humanist enthusiasms promoted the introduction of the pastoral, the comedy and the satire into the vernacular. In prose, fifteenth-century humanism inaugurated at least two new genres: the moral dialogue and the biography, alongside the *novelle* and chronicles of the fourteenth century. In thematic terms, poets such as Petrarch and Poliziano could elegantly graft classical themes onto the more slender traditions of romance lyric, and even make poetry out of their own scholarship and study of the past – Petrarch's obsession with the passing of time; Poliziano's eclectic poetics of the fragment and his desire to recover the *disiecta membra* ('dispersed fragments') of the past; Lorenzo de' Medici's introduction of Neoplatonic themes into the vernacular lyric. Humanist writers of Italian not only incorporated some of the great themes of antiquity, but also elaborated a theory of intertextual allusion that was indebted to classical notions of *imitatio*.

Lastly, humanism can be said to have emancipated vernacular literature from its religious origins. Dante, Petrarch and Boccaccio had inscribed their classical echoes within an overarching Christian framework, but in the Quattrocento the secularization of Italian literature begins. Bruni's biographies, and Alberti's and Palmieri's dialogues, are entirely secular in tone, while at the other end of the century the important vernacular works of Poliziano, Sannazaro and Colonna are a joyful celebration of the mythical, pagan world of antiquity.

Without humanist influence Italian literature would certainly have developed along very different, but probably more limited, and certainly more religious, lines. With the input supplied by the leading humanist writers of the fourteenth and fifteenth centuries, the vernacular was at last able to achieve a theoretical parity with the classical languages, and Italian literature was able to expand the number of genres open to it, to increase the range of themes and to elaborate complex imitative strategies in a secular atmosphere which ushered in the golden age of the first half of the sixteenth century, the age of Machiavelli, Castiglione and Ariosto.

NOTES

1   The physical detail of Charon's white beard (*Aeneid* VI.299–300: 'masses of white, unkempt hair lay on his chin') is echoed once by Dante (*Inferno* III.83: 'an old man, with white, ancient hair'), then expanded into a more grotesque

image: 'his woolly cheeks' (*Inferno* III.98); similarly Virgil's detail about Charon's eyes (*Aeneid* VI.300: 'flames stood in his eyes') is alluded to once (*Inferno* III.99: 'around his eyes he had wheels of fire'), then expanded into something more diabolical: 'Charon the demon, with his eyes of burning coal' (*Inferno* III.109).

2 K. Brownlee, 'Dante and the classical poets', in R. Jacoff, ed., *The Cambridge Companion to Dante* (Cambridge, 1993), pp. 100–19. For intertextual allusions, see M. U. Sowell, ed., *Dante and Ovid: Essays in Intertextuality* (Binghamton, 1991); R. Jacoff and J. T. Schnapp, eds., *The Poetry of Allusion: Virgil and Ovid in Dante's 'Commedia'* (Stanford, 1991).

3 Dante, *Convivio* I.5.8: 'Consequently we can see in the ancient works of Latin tragedy and comedy, which are not subject to change, the same Latin language that we have nowadays; this does not happen with the vernacular, which alters according to the dictates of taste.'

4 On his knowledge of antiquity, see, apart from Brownlee, 'Dante and the classical poets', G. Padoan, *Il pio Enea, l'empio Ulisse: tradizione classica e intendimento medievale in Dante* (Ravenna, 1976), pp. 7–29.

5 MS Vatican City, Biblioteca Apostolica Vaticana, Vat. Lat. 3196.

6 P. Hainsworth, 'The myth of Daphne in the *Rerum vulgarium fragmenta*', *Italian Studies*, 34 (1979), 28–44, and his *Petrarch the Poet* (London, 1988), pp. 138–43.

7 E. H. Wilkins, *The Making of the 'Canzoniere' and Other Petrarchan Studies* (Rome, 1951); and more recently, M. Santagata, *I frammenti dell'anima: storia e racconto nel 'Canzoniere' di Petrarca* (Bologna, 1992).

8 For example: 'Erano i capei d'oro a l'aura sparsi' ('Her golden hair was spread out to the breeze', *Rerum vulgarium fragmenta* XC, inspired by *Aeneid* I.319–28); 'Or che'l ciel e la terra e 'l vento tace' ('Now that the heavens, the earth and the wind are silent', CLXIV, from a famous Virgilian description of nocturnal serenity contrasting with the lover's torment in *Aeneid* IV. 522–32); 'Almo sol, quella fronde ch'io sola amo' ('All-nourishing sun, that tree which I love above all others', CLXXXVIII, deriving from Horace, *Carmen saeculare* 9–12); and 'Quel rosignuol che sí soave piagne' ('That nightingale which laments so sweetly', CCCXI, modelled on a famous Virgilian simile in *Georgics* IV. 511–19). See T. M. Greene, *The Light in Troy: Imitation and Discovery in Renaissance Poetry* (New Haven, 1982), pp. 111–43.

9 On his language, see G. Contini, *Varianti e altra linguistica* (Turin, 1970), pp. 167–92. For the balanced lines, see D. Alonso, 'La poesia del Petrarca e il petrarchismo (mondo estetico della pluralità)', *Studi petrarcheschi*, 7 (1961), 73–120. Virgil's *Eclogues*, one of Petrarch's favourite texts, provide the most frequent classical models of such balances (e.g., *Eclogues* I.3, 33, 63, 79 etc.) These are also a feature of Horace's *Odes*, another of Petrarch's favourite classical texts, four of which he transcribed into his famous manuscript copy of Virgil (*Odes* II.3, 10, 16; IV.7): see U. Dotti, *Vita di Petrarca* (Rome, 1987), p. 7 n. 7.

10 The echoes of Dante in the first version ('da le fatiche loro' at the beginning of a line, as in *Inferno* II.3; 'Quanti dolci anni, lasso perdut'aggio! / Quanto desio ...' too similar to 'Oh lasso! / Quanti dolci pensier, quanto desio ...' of *Inferno* V.112–13) were removed. But Petrarch retained the Virgilian allusion in

'quando / prendon riposo i miseri mortali ...' (cf. *Aeneid* II.268–9: 'It was the hour when the first repose descends on weary men ...'), as well as adding the line 'di questa morte che si chiama vita' ('of that death which is called life'), a reworking of a Ciceronian phrase (cf. *De re publica* VI.14: 'Vestra ... quae dicitur vita mors est'. For a full discussion of the rewriting, see M. Fubini, *Studi sulla letteratura del Rinascimento* (Florence, 1947), pp. 1–12.

11 For an English translation of the letter, see Petrarch, *Letters on Familiar Matters: Rerum familiarium libri I–XXIV*, trans. A. S. Bernardo, 3 vols. (Albany, 1975–85), III, pp. 202–7.

12 Cf. Hainsworth's conclusion, in *Petrarch the Poet*, p. 85, on the echo of Ovid in CCLXIV.91–2: 'Citation ceased to be citation by the mere fact of translation ...'

13 In addition to *Familiares* XXI.15, see also I.8, XXII.2 and XXIII.19. Petrarch's own annotations on his manuscripts of *De oratore* and Quintilian are studied in P. De Nolhac, *Pétrarque et l'humanisme*, 2 vols. (Paris, 1907), II, pp. 83–94; P. Blanc, 'Pétrarque lecteur de Cicéron: les scolies pétrarquiennes du *De oratore* et de l'*Orator*', *Studi petrarcheschi*, 9 (1978), 109–66; and M. Accame Lanzillotta, 'Le postille del Petrarca a Quintiliano (Cod. Parigino lat. 7720)', *Quaderni petrarcheschi*, 5 (1988), 1–201.

14 G. Tanturli, 'Il disprezzo per Dante dal Petrarca al Bruni', *Rinascimento*, 25 (1985), 199–219.

15 For the text of Boccaccio's epistles, see Boccaccio, *Opere latine minori*, ed. A. Massèra (Bari, 1928). For the translations, see M. T. Casella, *Tra Boccaccio e Petrarca. I volgarizzamenti di Tito Livio e di Valerio Massimo* (Padua, 1982). Even if Boccaccio's authorship of the translation of Livy's Third Decade is disputed, most critics now concur that he translated the Fourth Decade: see G. Tanturli, 'Volgarizzamenti e ricostruzione dell'antico: i casi della terza e quarta Deca di Livio e di Valerio Massimo, la parte di Boccaccio (a proposito di attribuzione)', *Studi medievali*, ser. 3, 27 (1986), 811–88.

16 Giuseppe Billanovich, *Restauri boccacceschi* (Rome, 1945), pp. 49–78.

17 Giuseppe Billanovich, 'Tra Dante e Petrarca', *Italia medioevale e umanistica*, 8 (1965), 1–44, at 42–3; and C. Dionisotti, *Geografia e storia della letteratura italiana* (Turin, 1967), pp. 103–44, especially 115–17. A similar development is visible in the fact that in the 1340s Giovanni Villani could boast about his reading of Latin historians (Sallust, Livy, Valerius Maximus and Orosius) in the vernacular (*Cronica* VIII.36), but that his nephew Filippo Villani writing in the 1380s complained about his uncle's chronicles being written in the vernacular: see Giovanni Villani, *Cronica, con le continuazioni di Matteo e Filippo*, ed. G. Aquilecchia (Turin, 1979), p. 78; and Filippo Villani, *De origine civitatis Florentie et de eiusdem famosis civibus*, ed. G. C. Galletti (Florence, 1847), p. 40.

18 See P. G. Ricci's 'Introduzione' to his critical edition of the *Trattatello*, in G. Boccaccio, *Tutte le opere*, ed. V. Branca (Milan, 1964–), III, pp. 425–35, especially 431–5.

19 C. Paolazzi, *Dante e la 'Comedia' nel Trecento. Dall'Epistola a Cangrande all'età di Petrarca* (Milan, 1989), pp. 131–221.

20 See Boccaccio, *Tutte le opere*, V, pp. 95–6.

21 A Latin edition with facing Italian translation is in E. Garin, ed., *Prosatori latini*

del Quattrocento (Milan, 1952), pp. 44–99; for an English translation, see *The Humanism of Leonardo Bruni: Selected Texts*, trans. G. Griffiths, J. Hankins and D. Thomson (Binghamton, 1987), pp. 63–84.

22 Leonardo Bruni, *Humanistisch-philosophische Schriften*, ed. H. Baron (Leipzig, 1928), pp. 50–69; for an English translation see *Humanism of Bruni*, pp. 85–100.

23 Bruni, *Schriften*, pp. 41–9, 113–20; *Humanism of Bruni*, pp. 184–90, 283–92.

24 Bruni, *Schriften*, pp. 61–2; *Humanism of Bruni*, pp. 93–5.

25 On the Lodi discovery, see R. Sabbadini, *Le scoperte dei codici latini e greci ne' secoli XIV e XV*, ed. by E. Garin, 2 vols. (Florence, 1967), I, p. 100; see also chapter 2 above, pp. 29, 38–9. Biondo, in his *Italia illustrata* (Basel, 1531), p. 346, shared Bruni's estimate of Petrarch: 'yet [Petrarch] never attained that flowering of Ciceronian eloquence which we now see adorning the work of many in this century ... Even though he boasted of having discovered at Vercelli Cicero's Letters to Lentulus, he never saw except in a lacerated and mutilated form Cicero's three books *De oratore* and Quintilian's *Institutio oratoria*.'

26 For the texts and the whole question, see M. Tavoni, *Latino, grammatica, volgare: storia di una questione umanistica* (Padua, 1984). See also A. Mazzocco, *Linguistic Theories in Dante and the Humanists* (Leiden, 1993).

27 Matteo Palmieri, *Vita civile*, ed. G. Belloni (Florence, 1982), pp. 3–10.

28 Palmieri, *Vita civile*, p. 46.

29 Palmieri, *Vita civile*, p. 208.

30 Palmieri, *Vita civile*, p. 205. See also n. 10 above.

31 G. Mancini, *Vita di L. B. Alberti* (Rome, 1911); C. Grayson, 'Alberti, Leon Battista', in *Dizionario biografico degli italiani* (Rome, 1960–   ), I, pp. 702–9.

32 Leon Battista Alberti, *Opere volgari*, ed. C. Grayson, 3 vols. (Bari, 1960–73), I, pp. 70–1. For an English version of the work, see Alberti, *The Family in Renaissance Florence: A Translation of 'I libri della famiglia'*, trans. R. N. Watkins (Columbia SC, 1969). See also C. Grayson, '*Cartule e Grecismi* in Leon Battista Alberti', *Lingua nostra*, 13 (1952), 105–6; Giuseppe Billanovich, 'Leon Battista Alberti, il *Grecismus* e la *Chartula*', *Lingua nostra*, 15 (1954), 70–1.

33 Alberti, *Opere*, I, p. 133.

34 See, e.g., Alberti, *Opere*, I, pp. 158, 243.

35 Alberti, *Opere*, I, p. 156: 'You will hear [Giannozzo's] bare, simple style in which you can see that I wanted to find out how far I could imitate that most gentle and pleasing writer Xenophon.'

36 See Leon Battista Alberti, *La prima grammatica della lingua volgare: la grammatichetta vaticana, Cod. Vat. Reg. Lat. 1370*, ed. C. Grayson (Bologna, 1964), p. xxxix.

37 On the *Certame*, see A. Altamura, *Il Certame Coronario* (Naples, 1952); G. Gorni, 'Storia del Certame Coronario', *Rinascimento*, 12 (1972), 135–81.

38 Alberti, *Opere*, II, p. 45.

39 Cited from Gorni, 'Certame Coronario', 172. Cf. Quintilian X.1.40, where Cicero is said to have imitated even the earliest orators: 'Cicero himself admits that he was helped enormously also by those earliest authors, who were certainly clever but lacked rhetorical skill (*ingeniosis quidem, sed arte carentibus*).'

40 Alberti, *Opere*, III, pp. 7–107, at 7. For the topos of nature growing old, see

E. Gombrich, 'A classical topos in the introduction to Alberti's *Della Pittura*', *Journal of the Warburg and Courtauld Institutes*, 20 (1957), 173, who refers to Pliny, *Epistulae* VI.21. But the source is probably Columella, *De re rustica*, I Preface 1–2, especially as that preface contains another idea found in Alberti's prologue, the notion that there are no writers to imitate in writing on agriculture, as well as the phrase 'pingui Minerva' ('of dull intellect', Preface 33), used in the opening lines of *De pictura*.

41 Alberti, *Opere*, II, pp. 105–83, at 160–1.

42 Cristoforo Landino, *Scritti critici e teorici*, ed. R. Cardini, 2 vols. (Rome, 1974), I, p. 38.

43 See D. Delcorno Branca, 'Il laboratorio del Poliziano: per una lettura delle *Rime*', *Lettere italiane*, 39 (1987), 153–206, as well as her introduction to Angelo Poliziano, *Rime* (Venice, 1990), pp. 18, 25.

44 Angelo Poliziano, *Opera ... omnia* (Basel, 1553), p. 244.

45 Angelo Poliziano, *Stanze, Orfeo, Rime*, ed. S. Marconi (Milan, 1981), pp. 77-137; see also the English translation of the *Stanze* by D. Quint (Amherst, 1979). Although W. Welliver, 'The subject and purpose of Poliziano's *Stanze*', *Italica*, 48 (1971), 34–50, argues that the poem is complete as it stands, no other critic has followed him: cf. P. McNair, 'The bed of Venus: key to Poliziano's *Stanze*', *Italian Studies*, 25 (1970), 40–8; V. Branca, *Poliziano e l'umanesimo della parola* (Turin, 1983), pp. 44–54.

46 R. H. Terpening, 'Poliziano's treatment of a classical topos: *ekphrasis*, portal to the *Stanze*', *Italian Quarterly*, 17 (1973), 39–71, sees the description of the *intagli* in the doors of Venus' palace as the centrepiece of the poem.

47 Cf. Petrarch's 'Zefiro torna' (*Rerum vulgarium fragmenta* CCCX.1); 'la stanca vecchiarella pellegrina' (L.5); Dante's 'l'ora mattutina', also at the end of a line (*Purgatorio* I.115); and Virgil's 'resonare doces ... silvas' (*Eclogues* I.5). Another similar set-piece description is that of night (*Stanze* I.60), which echoes two lines of Dante (*Paradiso* XXIII.1, 3), one from Petrarch (*Rerum vulgarium fragmenta* CCCXI.1) and two from Ovid (*Metamorphoses* III.507, XI.592). Similarly, the portrayal of Polyphemus (*Stanze* I.116) blends both classical and vernacular sources: from Theocritus for subject, from Petrarch (*Rerum vulgarium fragmenta* L.19) for 'alpestre note' ('alpine notes') and from Dante (*Inferno* III.97) for 'lanose gote' ('woolly cheeks').

48 Similarly, the variety of flowers and the multicoloured grass in Venus' garden (I.77) can be interpreted as emblems of *varietas*. The birds singing in Venus' realm – 'e fra più voci un'armonia s'accoglie / di sí beate note e sí sublime ...' (I.90: 'and from the several different voices a harmony emerges of such blessed and sublime notes ...') – recall one of Seneca's images of eclectic imitation: 'Do you not see how a chorus consists of many individual voices, yet it is one sound which emerges?' (Seneca, *Epistulae* LXXXIV.8). The image of the mosaic (I.96) is associated with the eclectic style in Poliziano's important *Miscellanea* preface (*Opera*, p. 214), and the final couplet about adorning the floor with a variety of stones recalls Alberti's image of the mosaic (*Opere*, II, pp. 160–2), which also associates the mosaic image with literary eclecticism.

49 For the elements of the satyr-play evident in the *Orfeo*, see Section V of the introduction to Angelo Poliziano, *Orfeo*, ed. A. Tissoni Benvenuti (Padua, 1986).

50 See the edition in Garin, *Prosatori latini*, pp. 902–6.
51 See C. Dempsey, *The Portrayal of Love. Botticelli's 'Primavera' and Humanist Culture at the Time of Lorenzo the Magnificent* (Princeton, 1992), especially p. 36.
52 Lorenzo de' Medici, *Comento de' miei sonetti*, ed. T. Zanato (Florence, 1991), p. 144: 'Greek is adjudged more perfect than Latin, and Latin more than Hebrew, simply because one language expresses better than the other the concepts of the writer or speaker.'
53 Medici, *Comento*, p. 149.
54 For other classical and humanist ideas that underlie the *Comento*, see T. Zanato, *Saggio sul 'Comento' di Lorenzo de' Medici* (Florence, 1979), pp. 11–44.
55 J. Sannazaro, *Opere*, ed. E. Carrara (Turin, 1952), p. 219. For his synthesis of classical and vernacular traditions, see *Egloga* II, which reworks the competitions in Virgil, *Eclogues* III and VIII; and *Prosa* IV, which is modelled on Virgil, *Eclogue* VII: 'the two shepherds were handsome in body, and very young in age: Elpino looked after goats, Logisto tended the woolly sheep; both had hair more golden than mature ears of corn, both were from Arcadia and both were ready to sing and reply to the other's song'; cf. Virgil, *Eclogue* VII.3–5: 'Into the same place Thyrsis had driven his sheep, Corydon his goats with their udders distended with milk: both were in the flower of youth, both were from Arcadia, both were capable of singing and of responding to the other's song.'
56 On Apuleian Latin, see C. Dionisotti, *Gli umanisti e il volgare tra Quattro e Cinquecento* (Florence, 1968); E. Raimondi, *Codro e l'umanesimo a Bologna* (Bologna, 1950) and his *Politica e commedia: dal Beroaldo al Machiavelli* (Bologna, 1972); and J. F. D'Amico, 'The progress of Renaissance Latin prose: the case of Apuleianism', *Renaissance Quarterly*, 37 (1984), 351–92.
57 The opening sequence in the dark wood clearly recalls the beginning of Dante's *Inferno*, the later accounts of triumphs rework parts of Petrarch's *Trionfi*, while the many descriptions of nymphs are indebted to Boccaccio's *Ameto* (or *Commedia delle ninfe fiorentine*) and the source of much of Book II is the story of Nastagio degli Onesti (*Decameron* V.8).
58 For his borrowings from classical and vernacular authors, see M. T. Casella and G. Pozzi, *Francesco Colonna: biografia e opere*, 2 vols. (Padua, 1959), II, pp. 78–149.
59 One example must suffice, but almost any sentence in the work would illustrate the style; Francesco Colonna, *Hypnerotomachia Poliphili*, ed. G. Pozzi and L. A. Ciapponi, 2 vols. (Padua, 1980), I, p. 137: 'Et de soto la strophiola, compositamente uscivano gli pampinulati capegli, parte tremulabondi delle belle tempore umbregianti, tutte le parvissime aurechie non occultando, più belle che mai alla Mimoria fusseron dicate. D'indi poscia, el residuo del flavo capillamento, da drieto el micante collo explicato et dalle rotunde spalle dependuli ... ' It is worth noting that where Colonna here borrows just a few words ('capillamento', 'dependuli') from a famous description of hair in Apuleius (*Metamorphoses* II.9), Boccaccio's imitation of the passage reworks whole sentences of the sequence: see G. Boccaccio, *Decameron, Filocolo, Ameto, Fiammetta*, ed. E. Bianchi, C. Salinari and N. Sapegno (Milan, 1952), p. 932.

13
Humanism and English literature in the fifteenth and sixteenth centuries

CLARE CARROLL

Although humanism took root in the learned culture of fifteenth-century England, it was not until the next century that it bore fruit in vernacular literature. In the period between the Florentine humanist Poggio Bracciolini's visit to England (*c.* 1418–22) and Bishop William Waynflete's founding of Magdalen College School at Oxford (1480), English book collectors, diplomats and grammarians increased their knowledge of Italian classical learning. These cultural links with Italy fostered the creation of the humanist libraries and grammar schools which would educate the Tudor élite – among them the first great English humanist writer, Sir Thomas More, who, unlike many of his contemporaries, had no direct contact with Italy. As in Italy, humanism took root in England at a time when the education it promoted was suited to the needs of the governing classes: the monarch, members of the council, church officials and civil servants. It became necessary to write Latin *well*, with the humanist's attention to grammar and the elegantly subordinated syntax of the Ciceronian style, in order to carry on diplomatic and domestic matters of state. Since, however, this humanist programme was also appropriated and deployed to produce great literary works, it can be said to have been much more than a mere pragmatic tool to attain influence and power. Indeed, humanist-inspired works of literature even allowed for scepticism about the principles underlying the primary realm of power – the economy, politics, institutional religion – as well as criticism of the aims of humanism itself. The purpose of this chapter is to illustrate some of the ways in which humanism, with its new interest in classical texts and its new methods of interpreting them, came to have an appreciable influence on English literature in the era of the Tudor monarchs.

First, it is necessary to give a brief account of the fifteenth-century developments which led to the growth of a close relationship between humanism and literature in sixteenth-century England. The contrast between English learning of the fifteenth and the sixteenth centuries can be gauged by comparing the responses of two Continental humanists who travelled to England. Arriving around 1418, Poggio complained in a letter to his friend Niccolò Niccoli that his search for classical texts had proved fruitless: 'better give up hope of books from England for they care little for them here'.[1] Yet when Erasmus visited England for the first time in 1499, he came away with praise for the native humanists William Grocyn, Thomas Linacre and Thomas More: 'It is marvellous to see what an extensive and rich crop of ancient learning is springing up here in England.'[2] Although Poggio may have been somewhat unlucky in his choice of manuscript collections to search,[3] still there is a tale to be told between these two historical moments. What happened in fifteenth-century English intellectual life to account for these opposing views of England as cultural desert and fertile soil?

The works of three fifteenth- and early sixteenth-century authors, Sir Thomas Malory, John Lydgate and John Skelton, serve to illustrate how little influence humanism had on the literature of this period. First edited and published by William Caxton in 1485, Malory's *Morte Darthur* is medieval not only in subject-matter but also in style, which derived from its sources in the French prose Arthurian cycle and English alliterative poetry. Unlike the romance epics of Italian authors educated in the humanist tradition, such as Matteo Maria Boiardo's *Orlando innamorato* (Books I and II, 1483; Book III, 1495) and Lodovico Ariosto's *Orlando furioso* (1516), Malory's work lacks the ironic play between allusions to classical and medieval texts. Lydgate's *Fall of Princes* (c. 1431–9), which translates and expands Laurent de Premierfait's French version of Boccaccio's *De casibus illustrium virorum* ('The Fall of Illustrious Men'), seems closer to Italian humanism: the tragedies of Cato and Scipio, for example, stress their Roman virtues. Lydgate's poetic narratives, however, are thoroughly medieval, like those of Laurent and Boccaccio – and to a large extent those of *The Mirror for Magistrates* (1559), which was originally intended as a continuation of the *Fall of Princes*.[4] For Lydgate, the decline from happiness to misery is ultimately seen as a fall from grace and is explained in terms of a moral lesson. Some sixteenth-century tragedies, especially the earliest ones, are also of this type; the great tragedies of Marlowe and Shakespeare, however, share with their classical antecedents a tragic fall that is impelled by a heroic greatness which, because it is mysteriously mixed with human weakness and evil, is not easily moralized. Unlike Malory and Lydgate, Skelton was a humanist: he was crowned poet laureate, as Petrarch had been; and he translated into English Cicero's letters (*Tully's Familiars*) and Diodorus Siculus' *Historical Library* (from Poggio's Latin version).[5] Skelton's own poetry, however – from the allegorical dream vision of *The Bowge of Courte* (1499) to the typologically expressed moral and political criticism of *Speke, Parrot* (1521) – rings with the rhymes and rhythms of late medieval English, while his conceptual framework is that of the liturgy and the Scriptures.[6] One indication of how far Skelton's poetry was from the humanistic standards of the later sixteenth century is George Puttenham's dismissal of the poet laureate as 'a rude rayling rimer'.[7] Skelton's tutoring of the young Henry VIII probably had a greater impact on the development of humanist writing in England than his poems.

It was visits to and from Italy, donations of classical texts to university libraries, humanist instruction in Latin and Greek and, above all, the establishment of a new curriculum in the schools which contributed to the development of fifteenth-century humanist culture in England and paved the way for the emergence of sixteenth-century humanist literature. One of the first Italian humanists after Poggio to visit England was the papal collector Pietro del Monte. Like many other Italians and Englishmen who travelled between the two countries, del Monte's journey was made possible by his official church position: much of the cultural interaction between Italy and England took the form of embassies to and from Rome. Del Monte contributed to English humanist culture by spreading the reputation of his teacher Guarino of Verona and by giving advice to Humfrey, Duke of Gloucester, a major book collector and patron; he dedicated his Latin treatise on the virtues and vices (1438) – the first humanist work written in England – to Duke Humfrey and also encouraged him to support the Ferrarese humanist Tito Livio Frulovisi. Under Humfrey's patronage, Tito Livio wrote a life of the duke's dead brother, Henry V (*Vita Henrici Quinti*, c. 1437). This work later influenced Polydore Vergil, an Italian scholar living in England, whose *Anglica historia* (1534) would in turn make an impact on sixteenth-century English chronicles. Duke Humfrey is perhaps best known for the collection of books that he amassed and donated to Oxford: he owned Leonardo Bruni's Latin translations of some of Plutarch's *Lives* and of Aristotle's *Ethics* and *Politics*; Pier Candido Decembrio's Latin version of Plato's *Republic*, which was dedicated to him; and various works by Italian humanists from Petrarch to Coluccio Salutati.[8]

Of the Englishmen who travelled to Italy in the fifteenth century, several went to study in Ferrara with Guarino, where they practised their Latin style by writing letters and heard their teacher lecture on classical authors. The theologian William Grey, one of few Englishmen of his time to learn Greek, went to study with Guarino from 1456 to 1458 and later sent John Free there. Free translated *De laudibus calvitii* ('In Praise of Baldness') by the early Christian Neoplatonist Synesius from Greek into Latin and presented it to the aspiring humanist patron John Tiptoft, Earl of Worcester and for a time Lord Deputy of Ireland.[9] Another of Guarino's students was

Robert Flemmyng, author of *Lucubratiunculae Tiburtinae* (1477), the only important work of Neo-Latin poetry produced in England before 1500. Ludovico Carbone, in his funeral panegyric for Guarino, paid tribute to Flemmyng's learning and to the practical applications of a humanist education, claiming that it was the Englishman's excellence in the *studia humanitatis* that had won him his appointment as King's Proctor in Rome.[10]

The next important development in English humanism, the introduction of the study of Greek into England, links the fifteenth-century scholar George Neville with the first great humanist of the early Tudor period, William Grocyn. Neville, a contemporary of John Free at Balliol College and Chancellor of Oxford University (1453–72), appears to have known Greek. He was the patron of several Byzantine scribes working in England, two of whom, Johannes Serbopulos and Emmanuel of Constantinople, may have been Grocyn's first Greek teachers (he owned manuscripts written by both of them). Out of this context of Oxford humanism came Waynflete's establishment of Magdalen College School and the *Compendium totius grammaticae* (*c.* 1483) of John Anwykyll, a Magdalen schoolmaster whose textbook combined the humanist and medieval systems of Latin grammar.

A more thoroughly humanist educational programme (though with a conservative syllabus, heavily weighted towards Christian authors) emerged at St Paul's School, London, founded by John Colet.[11] Inspired by Erasmus's ideas on education, Colet collaborated with the school's first high master, William Lily, a former scholar of Magdalen, on the most influential grammar of the century, known as 'Lily's Grammar'.[12] The first part, the 'Accidence', was written in English for younger students and published as *An Introduction of the Eyght Partes of Speche* (1542): it combined Colet's *Aeditio* (1527), on the parts of Latin speech, and Lily's *Rudimenta* (*c.* 1516), on Latin syntax. A more advanced grammar in Latin for older students, the *Institutio compendiaria totius grammaticae* (1540), covered orthography, etymologies, syntax and prosody. The educational principles on which this widely used grammar was based can be traced back to Erasmus's *De ratione studii* (1511).[13] Erasmus prescribed the study of ancient Greek and Latin authors as models for literary imitation. The rules of Latin grammar and versification, the rhetorical figures (such as climax and distribution) and the topics or 'places' (such as cause and effect, like and contrary examples), the parts of compositions, ranging from the epistle to the oration – all were to be memorized and appropriated through the reading and imitation of Cicero, Sallust, Virgil and Terence. Cardinal Wolsey's statement in 1529 that 'Lily's Grammar' was prescribed for all students in English grammar schools attests to the widespread influence of its Erasmian-inspired pedagogy.[14]

The circle of Lily, Colet and Erasmus also included William Grocyn and Thomas Linacre, both of whom had studied Greek and Latin with Angelo Poliziano and Demetrius Chalcondyles in Florence; both, moreover, later taught Greek to Thomas More.[15] The humanistic accomplishments of Linacre, a graduate of the University of Padua in medicine, are represented by his Latin translations of Galen;[16] and those of Grocyn, a theologian, by his arguments – based on the historical and philological methods developed by Lorenzo Valla – that the Dionysius the Areopagite who is mentioned in the Bible (Acts 17:34) could not have been the author of the *Celestial and Ecclesiastical Hierarchies* (in reality a Christianized version of the philosophy of the fifth-century Neoplatonist Proclus).[17] Perhaps an even greater achievement was Grocyn's establishment of regular lectures on Greek at Oxford in the 1490s.

Although Thomas More was at Oxford during this period, it was a decade later, while he was living in London, that he received serious instruction in Greek. The first published result of these studies were the Latin translations which he and Erasmus made of the Greek comic author Lucian,[18] whose spirit of playful and mocking irony would later influence the most famous works of both men: Erasmus's *Encomium moriae* ('The Praise of Folly', 1511) and More's *Utopia* (1516).[19] Some of the earliest manuscripts of Lucian known in the west were brought from Constantinople to Italy by Guarino and Giovanni Aurispa; Latin translations of Lucian's works were printed from the 1470s onwards, while the Greek *editio princeps* appeared in 1496.[20] More may have first read Lucian in the Greek edition published in 1503 by the Venetian printer Aldus Manutius, to whom he would later pay tribute by having his Utopians learn the art of printing from Aldine editions of the classics.[21] More was the first Englishman to translate Lucian, and his versions were well received: they were published nine times during his life, more frequently than *Utopia*. The More–Erasmus translations of Lucian highlight a key feature of the transmission of classical works in the Renaissance: Greek texts, even after their recovery, were mainly known through Latin translations. That More's *Utopia* was translated into English by Ralph Robinson as late as 1551 further reminds us that, for the most part, sixteenth-century English humanist literature – not only scholarly but also fictional writing – belonged to the Latin culture of the Renaissance.

Lucian's *Tyrannicida*, one of the works which More translated, is a *declamatio*. The declamation was a regular part of classical rhetorical education, in which the speaker would have to argue some historical question persuasively (*suasoria*); impersonate a fictional character and make a fictional argument (*prosopopoeia*); or, as in the case of the *Tyrannicida*, represent a legal case (*controversia*). Both *Encomium moriae* and *Utopia* belong to the genre of *prosopopoeia*: Erasmus speaks through the persona of Folly, and More through that of the traveller Raphael Hythloday. More importantly, both works, like those of Lucian, combine moral criticism with satiric wit. Lucian, as More writes, 'everywhere reprimands and censures, with very honest and at the same time very entertaining wit, our human frailties'. At the end of Lucian's *Menippus*, for example, the souls in the underworld vote that the rich, 'who plunder and oppress and in every way humiliate the poor', should be reincarnated as 'donkeys ... bearing burdens and being driven by the poor'.[22] (It seems significant that More chose to translate this dialogue, given his harsh indictment of the rich in Book I of *Utopia*.)

Encomium moriae and *Utopia* both reflect their Lucianic inspiration by enlightening readers about the need for moral and political reform.[23] Erasmus satirizes the pomposity of those who believe themselves to be wise – from theologians to lawyers to authors like himself. More, in Book II of *Utopia*, criticizes the notion of human perfectibility without grace by portraying the moral contradictions of a society which allows slavery to coexist with communal sharing of wealth and which hires mercenaries while professing to hate war. More's satire does not even spare humanism. The notion that by living according to reason the Greek-reading, but non-Christian, Utopians had escaped original sin and created an ideal society was presented as an illusion.[24] As the Greek etymology of the title suggests, this good place (*eu topos*) exists no place (*ou topos*).

The treatment of tyranny in Lucian's *Tyrannicida* may have attracted More to translate it, since this theme was a major preoccupation of his, apparent in his short Latin poems (*Epigrammata*, 1518) and, above all, in his *History of Richard III* (c. 1514/18).[25] Like Tito Livio's *Vita Henrici Quinti* and Polydore Vergil's *Anglica historia*, More's *Richard III* is both biographical in form and influenced by the new humanist standards of history writing. But whereas Vergil's concern was to achieve a Ciceronian style and to make critical use of his sources, as recommended by Guarino, More's main aim was to employ classical history as a means of interpreting the present.[26] The humanist method of historical interpretation was explained by Erasmus as reading 'according to the standards of the time' (*pro ratione temporis*),[27] that is, understanding a text in its specific historical context. Paradoxically, it was only by recognizing the distinctiveness of the past and taking into account its differences from the present that the humanist historian could allow it to influence his interpretation of contemporary events. It is this conviction that the study of the past is relevant to the analysis of the present that Machiavelli sets out in the preface to his *Discorsi*

(1513/19).[28] Such an attitude helps to explain the relationship between More's *Richard III* and the classical historians he drew upon: they provided not source material but a medium and method of interpretation.

In More's *Richard III* the influence of the past on the present operates partly on the level of prose style. While the Italian humanists Tito Livio and Vergil wrote in Latin, More chose to write in both English and Latin (neither version was published until after his death: the English in 1557, the Latin in 1565). The English version shows the impact of More's study of classical Latin on his vernacular prose. The rhythms and dramatic effects of his style are well illustrated in his description of how Richard 'neuer hadde quiet in his minde' after ordering the murder of his young nephews:

> Where he went abrode, his eyen whirled about, his body priuily fenced, his hand euer on his dager, his countenance and maner like one alway ready to strike againe, he toke ill rest a nightes, lay long wakyng and musing, sore weried with care & watch, rather slumbred then slept, troubled wyth feareful dreames, sodainly sommetyme sterte vp, leape out of his bed & runne about the chamber, so was his restles herte continually tossed & tumbled w^t the tedious impression & stormy remembrance of his abominable dede.[29]

The swift movement of this sentence is achieved through various stylistic features borrowed from classical Latin: clear syntax, parallel construction ('wakyng and musyng', 'care & watch', 'leape out ... runne about', 'tossed and tumbled') and a measured rise and fall in the number of syllables in each successive verbal phrase, building towards a climax in the longest clause of all, which is subordinated to the rest of the sentence as cause to effect and which ends with the single syllable that convicts Richard of the crime. Here verbal rhythm, mimetic action and moral are fused together to create a powerful dramatic impression.

Classical history informs not only the diction and rhetoric of *Richard III* but also its philosophical outlook. More's acute understanding of the psychological and moral effects of tyranny upon a people was gained from his reading of Tacitus' *Annals*. The model for the biographical portrait of Richard III may have been Suetonius' salacious *Lives of the Caesars*, but it was Tacitus who knew how to tell the tale. More appropriated a great deal from Tacitus: the explanation of events from multiple perspectives; the ominous sense of the tyrant's influence on the narrative, even when he is not present; the connection between character and the course of events; the tragic inevitability of sudden deaths and disasters; and the pervasive atmosphere of moral decay.[30]

In *Richard III* More also gives literary expression to the irony and tragedy of history. If anything, his Richard seems more menacing than the

Tiberius of Tacitus and Suetonius because more intelligent. The success of Richard's deceptions at times springs from his arbitrary power (as when he requires the people to consent to his being made king); but in other instances it comes from his masterful manipulation of language (as when he argues that it was wicked of the queen to keep her son in sanctuary). Rather than endorsing the humanist belief in the reforming power of education, More's history underlines the deceptiveness and frightening power of rhetoric. Tyranny is not a condition easily amenable to change, but rather part of a fateful tragedy in which human beings conspire, as can be seen when More writes of the council's decision to make Richard protector of the boy king Edward V: 'were it destynye or were it foly'.[31] That More left *Richard III* unfinished – the Latin version ending with Richard's accession, the English with Bishop John Morton encouraging Buckingham's revolt – may have been the result of the tragic view of history that runs through the entire work.

It is' this tragic view, along with the portrayal of an energetic and clever villain, which Shakespeare took over from More in composing his own *Tragedy of Richard III*. Shakespeare may seem to us to be presenting a biased account of history, but this was *the* version of the story available to him, since More's text was incorporated into all the major chronicles of the Elizabethan era. The reasons why Shakespeare selected the story of Richard for his first tragedy and chose to represent it both as part of a historical cycle and as a tragedy in its own right have in some way to do with the character of Elizabethan humanist culture. The popularity of chronicles in this period is a reflection of the influence of humanist historiography, with its interest in the lives of great princes and its concern to base historical writing on a weighty theme. Shakespeare's use of the chronicles of Edward Halle and Raphael Holinshed to construct his history cycles – first *Henry VI, Parts 1–3* and *Richard III* (1590–3) and then *Richard II* to *Henry V* (1595–9) – for the popular theatre indicates the attraction of vernacular humanist history as a vehicle for the formation of national identity.[32] Even today, it is Shakespeare's account of the Plantagenet and Tudor monarchs that informs the public imagination.

Shakespeare was not the only Elizabethan dramatist to portray English history as tragedy. There are at least two other plays about Richard that demonstrate the appeal of this story in particular and of history plays in general: Thomas Legge's *Richardus Tertius*, never printed but performed at St John's College, Cambridge, in 1579/80; and the anonymous *True Tragedie*, printed in 1594, perhaps to benefit from the success of Shakespeare's play. Legge's drama is one of some 150 Latin plays written in England during the sixteenth and early seventeenth centuries. Though little known today, these university plays deserve further study, since, along with the tragedies of Seneca and the comedies of Plautus, they were a part of the dramatic culture of Tudor England, seen not only by visiting aristocrats but also by local students.[33] Though only the epilogue of Richard Edes's *Caesar infectus* ('The Murder of Caesar') survives, the title calls to mind Polonius's response, when questioned by Hamlet if he 'played once i' th'university': 'I did enact Julius Caesar. I was killed i' th' Capitol. Brutus killed me' (*Hamlet*, III.ii.97–103). Also part of this learned humanist dramatic culture were plays such as *Gorboduc* (1565) by Thomas Sackville and Thomas Norton, considered to be the first real tragedy in English. Like *Richard III*, it is based on a story from English history, in this case the twelfth-century *Historiae regum Britanniae* by Geoffrey of Monmouth.[34] In the late sixteenth century not only did history plays and tragedies influence one another, there was often no clear demarcation between them.[35]

Another important influence on Shakespeare's *Richard III* – as on other English plays of the time, by dramatists such as Christopher Marlowe, John Marston and John Webster – were the tragedies of Seneca. This is in large part due to the place accorded to Senecan tragedy in the humanist curriculum. The topic of tyranny seemed to draw playwrights to Seneca: the first Renaissance tragedy of Senecan inspiration, the early fourteenth-century *Ecerinis* of Albertino Mussato, is, in the manner of *Richard III*, an historical drama about a tyrant, the Paduan Ezzelino da Romano, whose character is perhaps modelled on Nero in the *Octavia* (a spurious work then believed to be by Seneca). Seneca's tragedies were read and imitated, in both Latin and English.[36] The translations collected together in *Seneca His Tenne Tragedies* by Thomas Newton in 1581 are a clear sign of English interest in Senecan drama. Many features of Elizabethan drama – the five-act structure, stichomythia (staccato verbal cross-fire in which one line picks up a word from the previous one and uses it in a different sense) and *sententiae* (or pithy maxims) – were taken over from Seneca,[37] as were the predilection for haunting ghosts, dreams and ominous curses. Even the iambic pentameter of blank verse may have emerged in part from the sound of the Senecan iambic.

The impact of Seneca on Shakespeare's *Richard III* is direct and profound. Clarence's dream (not indebted to chronicle history) derives some of its imagery from Seneca's *Hercules Furens* and *Hercules Oetaeus*, as well as from Thomas Kyd's *The Spanish Tragedy* (1592), itself heavily Senecan.[38] And the way in which the female characters – Margaret (whose presence violates the historical record), Elizabeth, the Duchess of York and

Lady Anne – relate to each other and to Richard has its origins in Seneca's *Troades*.[39] A deeper Senecan influence is seen in the portrayal of the divided self, terrified of its own guilt, which transforms Richard's sarcastic delight in his crimes to desperate self-loathing and self-disgust:

> What do I fear? Myself? There's none else by;
> Richard loves Richard, that is, I and I.
> Is there a murderer here? No. Yes, I am!
> Then fly. What, from myself? Great reason why,
> Lest I revenge? What, myself upon myself?
> Alack, I love myself. Wherefore? For any good
> That I myself have done unto myself?
> O no, alas, I rather hate myself
> For hateful deeds committed by myself . . .
> All several sins, all us'd in each degree,
> Throng to the bar, crying all 'Guilty! guilty!'
>
> (V.iii.183–91, 199–200)

These lines recall Seneca's Oedipus: 'I flee myself, I flee my sense of guilt for all crimes' (*Phoenissae* 216) and the description of Phaedra's tormented soul: 'filled with guilt and fearful of itself' (*Hippolytus* 163).[40] Towards the close the tragedy, as the ghosts cry out to Richard, 'despair and die', recalling Marlowe's 'Damned art thou Faustus, damned, despaire and die', the Christian notion of the unforgivable sin of despair combines with Senecan torment and fatalism: 'I shall despair.'[41]

The Tragedy of Richard III, like More's history, presents the politics of tyranny and the personality of the tyrant – characteristic humanist concerns, having roots in both the dramatic and the historiographic traditions – with moral and psychological insight. The portrayal of Richard combines the clever villainy of the Elizabethan stage 'Machiavel', the antics of 'Vice' from the medieval morality plays and the pathos of a Senecan tragic hero. What Shakespeare takes from the classical, humanist and popular traditions, as well as what he adds from his own imagination, makes the story more terrifying, more pitiable and more unsettling than it appears in his historical sources because he transforms all these elements into a unified dramatic whole.

This kind of imitation – which Seneca (*Epistulae* LXXXIV.3–8) likens both to the process whereby bees turn the juice they gather from the flowers into honey and to the digestion of food – has been called transformative, because the source is so fully reinterpreted and so well integrated into the end product that it is almost unrecognizable. In Bartolomeo Ricci's *De imitatione* (1541), discussed by Roger Ascham in *The Scholemaster* (1570), at least two other types of imitation are named: 'following' and 'emulating'.[42] Erasmus, using similar terms, explains the 'follower' as one who merely 'treads in someone else's footsteps and obeys rules', and the 'challenger', or 'emulator', as one who 'endeavours to speak even better if he can'.[43] While More's use of Tacitus and Shakespeare's of Seneca may be called transformations, many English sixteenth-century imitations would be more accurately described as followings. A number of works from this period, for instance, simply incorporate quotations from classical texts to serve as examples of wisdom or as *sententiae* designed to further the argument. It was for this purpose that collections such as Erasmus's *Adagia* (first published in 1500, followed by many enlarged editions) and William Baldwin's *A Treatise of Morall Phylosophie* (1547) were made.

Many translations and imitations, however, rose above mere following to create new metre and verse forms, which would be taken up by later generations of English poets. Among the most influential of these were the translations of Petrarch's lyric poems by Sir Thomas Wyatt and the English version of Virgil's *Aeneid* by Henry Howard, Earl of Surrey. The poetry of Wyatt and Surrey forms a major part of the inward-looking phase of English humanism, which, unlike the international humanism of More, who wrote in Latin for a learned European audience, concerned itself with translating classical and Italian Renaissance culture into the vernacular.[44] Although Wyatt and Surrey originally wrote for aristocratic readers, after their deaths their works were widely disseminated in the popular *Tottel's Miscellany* (first published in 1557, with nine further editions in the reign of Elizabeth). The preface of this collection exhorts 'the unlearned, by reding to learne to be more skilfull, and to purge that swinelike grossenesse', anticipating the complaint of Ascham, who wanted English verse to adopt the quantitative metrics of classical poetry, that 'to follow rather the Gothes in Ryming, than the Greekes in trew versifying, were euen to eate ackornes with swyne, when we may freely eate wheate bread [amongst] men'.[45] In his version of Books II and IV of the *Aeneid* (also published by Tottel in 1557), Surrey departed from the paths followed by previous translators, eschewing both the rhymed couplets and colloquial language of the Scots poet Gavin Douglas and the quantitative English verse, based on the Latin model, of the Dublin poet Richard Stanyhurst.[46] Instead he developed the unrhymed iambic pentameter of blank verse for Virgil's dactylic hexameter and found an English equivalent for the complexity and restrained sublimity of Virgil's Latin syntax and diction. He can therefore be credited with achieving 'a humanist ideal' and with creating a poetic form that would influence the dramatic verse of Marlowe and Shakespeare.[47]

The poetry in *Tottel's Miscellany*, however, is rhymed, with the metres edited to improve the scansion, a change which mars the more striking rhythms of stress in the originals. Some of the more interesting poems, such as Wyatt's 'The longe love that in my thought I harbor' and Surrey's 'Love that doth raine and live within my thought', are translations of Petrarch's *Rime sparse*, which alter the Italian sonnet rhyme scheme of two quatrains and two tercets to create a concluding couplet. The *Rime* constitute a fictionalized spiritual autobiography in verse, telling of the poet's contemplation of and struggle to transcend his earthly love for the beautiful and angelic Laura, the symbol of his eroticism, poetic creativity and spirituality. In addition to adapting Petrarch's metre and verse form to English, Wyatt transformed his lyrical autobiographical medium into a vehicle for the expression of a different personality – as tormented as Petrarch's persona but angrier and wittier – located in a different context: the sophisticated and perilous world of the Henrican court.

While Wyatt and Surrey were influenced by Petrarch and his Italian imitators, Sir Philip Sidney and Shakespeare took their inspiration from the anti-Petrarchism of Joachim Du Bellay. Humorous poems such as Shakespeare's 'My mistress' eyes are nothing like the sun' (Sonnet CXXX) and Sidney's 'Dumbe Swannes, not chatring Pies, do Lovers prove' (*Astrophil and Stella* LIV) mock and invert the stock Petrarchan descriptions of the beloved's spiritual and physical beauty and her effect upon the suffering lover. Shakespeare also parodies aspects of Petrarchism – the self-absorption of the lover and the catalogue of the beloved's beauties, or *blazon* – in such comedies as *Twelfth Night*.

Petrarch had already been parodied in another text, one which was important for the transmission of Italian humanist culture to England: Ariosto's *Orlando furioso*, in which the eponymous hero goes mad when his Petrarchan delusions about his beloved Angelica (whose name suggests the *donna angelicata* of lyric tradition) are shattered. The longest and most popular romance epic of the Renaissance, it was first translated into English in 1591 by Sir John Harington.[48] Even earlier, Spenser had imitated Ariosto in the first three books of *The Faerie Queene* (1590). One of Gabriel Harvey's letters (1579/80) to Spenser describes the poem as a self-professed attempt 'to emulate' or 'to overgo' Ariosto's work.[49] While taking many of his stories (that of Radigund and her Amazonian women, for instance) and characters (such as Britomart from Bradamante) from *Orlando furioso*, Spenser expressed the poem's action through allegory, harking back to a medieval tradition and responding to more recent allegorizations of Ariosto. Torquato Tasso's *Gerusalemme liberata* (1581) and Homer's *Odyssey* also provided Spenser with inspiration for stories such as the knight Guyon's journey into a world of seductive sexual temptation. Both indirectly and directly, Spenser appropriated material from the *Metamorphoses* and the *Aeneid*, so that Ovidian and Virgilian matrices, too, form part of the complex literary texture of *The Faerie Queene*.[50]

Spenser, in the 'Letter of the authors expounding his whole intention in the course of this work' (1589), addressed to Sir Walter Raleigh, his friend, patron and neighbour on the Munster plantation in Ireland, explains that his aim in *The Faerie Queene* is 'to fashion a gentleman or noble person in vertuous and gentle discipline' by creating heroes whom the reader can interpret as moral examples. But, well aware of Horace's famous statement that the poet must blend usefulness with delight (*Ars poetica* 343), Spenser is swift to add that his poem is 'coloured with an historicall fiction, the which the most part of men delight to read, rather for variety of matter, then for profite of the ensample'. Humanist ethics accompany humanist poetics in the 'Letter': Spenser expresses his intention to organize his portrayal of Arthur around 'the twelue priuate morall vertues, as Aristotle hath deuised'.[51] The poem itself, however, in large part presents these virtues in an English nationalist and Protestant mode which, while perhaps sharing the partisan character of More's anti-Lutheran polemics,[52] seems inimical to the European character of pre-Reformation humanism. For example, in Spenser's allegory, Redcrosse, the knight of 'Holyness', must defend Una, the Protestant faith, from 'Duessa', the whore of Babylon (the Catholic Church). In the second edition (1596), Artegall, the hero representing 'Justice' in Book V, allegorically figures Arthur, Lord Grey de Wilton, whose harsh colonialist policies Spenser praises in his *A View of the Present State of Ireland*, which circulated widely in manuscript from 1596 on, though it was not published until 1633.

Spenser's poem, with its Protestant moral vision, dramatized in narrative form philosophical problems such as the relation between nature and art (in the sensuous but artificial Bower of Bliss, II.xii) and the connection between art and virtue (in the masque of Cupid, III.xii) – issues which were also at the heart of a controversy in Elizabethan humanist poetics. The catalyst of this debate was Stephen Gosson's tract *The Schoole of Abuse* (1579). For Gosson, poetry and drama are morally disruptive of the entire society because they mislead and seduce their audiences into sinful actions; hence he argues that they should be banned from the commonwealth. Interestingly, Gosson does not appeal to the Scriptures but rather to Cicero and Plato; his attack on the literary arts is thus based on sources within the classical humanist tradition. He notes that while Cicero enjoyed poetry in his youth, 'in yeares, riper in iudgement' he accounted poets 'fathers of lyes,

Pipes of vanitie, & Schooles of Abuse'. A whole array of abuses and vices are attributed to the influence of poetry (even Virgil is taken to task for showing Dido's 'lust') and, above all, of drama. While poets, for Gosson, are dishonest salesmen, the theatre leads to prostitution because it is a meeting place for 'the wanton and his paramour'; it also disturbs the social order because it allows 'the hyerlings of some of our Players to dress in the silks only allowed by law to their betters'. Despite some positive comments on the role of ancient poetry as an incentive to martial bravery, the overall theme of this tirade is that man should put his trust in reason, knowledge and the contemplation of God's creation of nature, and should avoid the pleasure of 'poets, Pypers and players'. Yet, although Gosson condemns the effects of art throughout, his own composition exemplifies the organized argument, balanced syntax and witty figures of humanist rhetoric.[53]

Ironically, the tract was dedicated to Sidney, who later responded to Gosson's polemic with *An Apologie for Poetrie* (1595). Drawing on Aristotle's *Rhetoric*, Sidney acknowledged the moral ambiguity of poetry, but he also argued that poetry was a potential vehicle for virtue rather than a source of corruption.[54] Sidney's defence of poetry was partly based on the humanist concept of imitation. He interpreted the term in at least two senses. The first is familiar from Ascham and Spenser: imitation as a guide to virtue. The manner in which Sidney expresses this notion – 'the skill of the artificer standeth in that *Idea* or fore-conceit of the work, and not in the work itself' – is reminiscent of Seneca's statement (*Epistulae* LXV.7) that one of the causes of art is 'the pattern which [Plato] himself calls the idea'. Sidney insists that this perfect Platonic idea of the work also has a practical moral application. In his view, the art of poetry is in some respects greater than nature because while nature can create the 'particular excellency' of Cyrus only once, poetry can create many Cyruses if readers 'will learn aright why and how that maker made him'. The other sense of imitation Sidney uses to defend poetry is based on Aristotle's *Poetics*: 'Poesy therefore is an art of imitation, for so Aristotle termeth it in his word *mimesis*, that is to say, a representing, counterfeiting, or figuring forth – to speak metaphorically, a speaking picture – with this end, to teach and delight'.[55] His intermediary sources for this view of *mimesis* were Plutarch's 'How the young man should study poetry' (*Moralia* 17F–18A), Horace's *Ars poetica* and Julius Caesar Scaliger's *Poetices libri septem* (1561); but Sidney's emphasis on the psychological power of poetry to move its readers through delight and so better instruct them in virtue casts this function in a new light, influenced by his Augustinian-Calvinist belief in the weakness and needs of the human will.[56]

In contrast to Sidney's defence, George Puttenham's *The Arte of English*

Poesie (1589) is less a philosophical justification of the aesthetics and morals of poetry and more a guide to the nuts and bolts of the poetic craft. In the first book, Puttenham defines art as 'a certaine order of rules prescribed by reason, and gathered by experience'. The next two books proceed to set out these rules, the second dealing with the rules of versification, the third with rhetorical figures. Puttenham defines poetry as 'a metricall speach corrected and reformed by discreet iudgements'; poetry is written in accordance with decorum, which is exemplified by the manners of court life. While Sidney allows poetry both a rhetorically persuasive role in politics and an imaginatively creative role in aesthetics, Puttenham sees poetry as circumscribed by power. He expresses this view metaphorically in his poems on the 'Roundell', in which the perfect image of the circle is identified with God's creation and the queen's authority.[57]

For all their differences, the two defences of poetry are alike in commenting on some of the major works of English sixteenth-century humanist literature. Both Sidney and Puttenham, for instance, mention More's *Utopia*. Puttenham likens it to the commonwealth of Plato 'resting all in devise, but never put in execution, and easier to be wished then to be performed'. Sidney's criticism of More is part of a larger discussion of the relative merits of poetry and imaginative literature, on the one hand, and philosophy, on the other:

> ... even in the most excellent determination of goodness what philosopher's counsel can so readily direct a prince, as the feigned Cyrus in Xenophon; or a virtuous man in all fortunes, as Aeneas in Virgil; or a whole commonwealth, as the way of Sir Thomas More's *Utopia*. I say the way, because where Sir Thomas More erred, it was the fault of the man and not of the poet, for that way of patterning a commonwealth was most absolute ... For the question is, whether the feigned image of poesy or the regular instruction of philosophy hath the more force in teaching.

While Puttenham calls poets 'the first Philosophers, the first Astronomers and Historiographers and Oratours and Musitiens of the world', Sidney comes to the conclusion that 'the philosopher teacheth, but he teacheth obscurely, so as the learned only can understand him; that is to say, he teacheth them that are already taught. But the poet is the food for the tenderest stomachs, the poet is indeed the right popular philosopher.'[58] Puttenham regards Surrey and Wyatt as the 'two chieftaines' of English lyric verse; and Sidney finds 'in the Earl of Surrey's lyrics many things tasting of a noble birth, and worthy of a noble mind'.[59] As for tragedy, Puttenham comments on its historical context in classical Rome, while Sidney describes Seneca as the perfect model (his style is 'full of notable morality, which it doth most delightfully teach, and so obtain the very end of Poesy') and *Gorboduc* as a successful English interpretation of the form.[60]

In the end, Puttenham's work is essentially an application of the humanist rhetoric taught in grammar schools to the writing of English poetry. Sidney's treatise, on the other hand, invents a new justification for poetry as an education in virtue. This was a principle which would not only influence the teaching of both classical and vernacular literature for centuries but would also give a humanist slant to later English poets' understanding of the imaginative capacities and responsibilities of their art.

The increasing prominence of humanism in the cultural life of the nation had an effect not only on the theory and practice of English poetry but also on English prose writing. In the vernacular version of More's *Richard III*, as we have seen, it is possible discern the impact of classical authors on his prose style; More's finest and most important works, however, were composed in Latin. The first English humanist to display a wholehearted commitment to writing in the vernacular was Sir Thomas Elyot. Compiler of the first Latin-English dictionary (1538) to be based on humanist principles and an accomplished scholar in both classical languages, Elyot believed in the importance of making ancient learning available for the benefit of his fellow countrymen. Having translated Isocrates and Plutarch with the aim of seeing whether 'our Englisshe tunge mought receiue the quicke propre sentences pronounced by the grekes',[61] he came to the conclusion that it was appropriate to use the vernacular for the transmission of classical erudition. *The Castle of Health* (1534) is a book of remedies (many of them taken from ancient authors such as Galen) which he wrote in English in order to challenge the medical profession of his day, whose chief motive for using Latin, he believed, was to guard the secrets of their trade. In the third edition of this very popular work, Elyot responded to the outcry he had provoked: 'If phisitions be angry, that I haue wryten phisike in englyshe, let theym remembre, that the grekes wrate in greke, the Romanes in latyne … whiche were their owne propre maternal tonges.'[62]

Elyot's *The Boke named the Gouernour* (1531) spans several genres: it is part pedagogical treatise, part courtesy book, part ethical handbook and part political tract. In it he presents a humanist programme designed to lead the sons of English nobleman to acquire the intellectual and moral qualities necessary for them to become effective administrators of the realm. In the preface, addressed to Henry VIII, Elyot announces: 'I have nowe enterprised to describe in our vulgare tunge the fourme of a iuste publike weale: whiche mater I have gathered as well of the sayenges of moste noble autours (grekes and latynes) as by myne owne experience.'[63] Of the classical sources which

Elyot conveys to an English-reading public, Plato is by far the most important: the treatise is in many respects a reworking of the *Republic*, adapted to the needs and customs of Renaissance England; and just as Plato describes the sort of education required to train the guardians of his ideal state, so Elyot sets out in Book I of *The Gouernour* 'the lernynge and studie wherby noble men may attayne to be worthy to have authorite in a publike weale'.[64] The syllabus he recommends clearly reflects humanist pedagogical practice. The student is to begin, at the age of seven, by reading Aesop's *Fables* in Greek and then move on to some 'quicke and mery dialogues' of Lucian, the comic author popularized by More and Erasmus earlier in the century; the tutor must be careful to select only those dialogues 'whiche be without ribawdry', for 'it were better that a childe shuld neuer rede any parte of Luciane than all Luciane'.[65] Homer, Virgil, Ovid (the *Metamorphoses* and *Fasti*), Horace and other Latin poets follow. When the young man reaches the age of fourteen, he should begin to grapple with logic by studying the topics, either in the version presented in the *Topica* of Cicero or else in Rudolph Agricola's *De inventione dialectica*, a work which 'prepareth inuention, tellynge the places from whens an argument for the profe of any mater may be taken with litle studie'.[66] At this stage he is also to study rhetoric 'either in greke, out of Hermogines, or of Quintilian in latine', supplemented by Cicero's *De partitione oratoria* and Erasmus's *De copia*. For training in the practicalities of oratory, apart from Demosthenes and Cicero, Isocrates 'is euery where wonderfull profitable, hauynge as many wyse sentences as he hath wordes: and with that is so swete and delectable to rede, that after him, almost all other seme unsauery and tedious'.[67] Next on the curriculum come cosmography and geography (Strabo, Solinus and Pomponius Mela) and history (Livy, Caesar, Sallust and Tacitus). Finally, having reached the age of seventeen, the student embarks on moral philosophy, beginning with the *Nicomachean Ethics* ('to be lerned in greke; for the translations that we yet haue be but a rude and grosse shadowe of the eloquence and wisedom of Aristotell'), followed by the works of Plato and Cicero, 'wherin is ioyned grauitie with dilectation, excellent wysedom with diuine eloquence, absolute vertue with pleasure incredible'.[68]

For all his emphasis on the need to master the classical languages, Elyot was equally dedicated to improving the expressiveness and flexibility of English. This was to be achieved by increasing its vocabulary through borrowing from foreign tongues, above all Latin and Greek. Justifying his coinage of the term 'mansuetude', from the Latin *mansuetudo* ('mildness'), he makes it clear that the introduction of such neologisms into English was part of his campaign to bring the benefits of classical civilization to his own rather backward nation:

whiche terme, beinge semblably before this time unknowen in our tonge, may be by the sufferaunce of wise men nowe received by custome, wherby the terme shall be made familiare. That lyke as the Romanes translated the wisedom of Grecia in to their citie, we may, if we liste, bringe the lernynges and wisedomes of them both in to this realme of Englande, by the translation of their warkes; sens lyke entreprise hath hen taken by frenche men, Italiuus, and Germanes, to our no litle reproche for our negligence and slouth.[69]

The fact that England lagged behind the Continent in the assimilation of humanist ideals and practices, a situation which was to remain true until well into the next century,[70] provoked the diplomat Sir Thomas Hoby to a similar lament. In the preface to his translation of Baldesar Castiglione's *The Book of the Courtier* (1561), he expressed the heartfelt wish that 'profound learned men in the Greek and Latin' languages should follow his example, so that 'wee alone of the world may not be still counted barbarous in our tongue, as in time out of mind we have beene in our maners'.[71] Hoby took a more cautious attitude than Elyot towards the introduction of foreign loan words into English, submitting his prose to be vetted by Sir John Cheke, a Greek scholar of considerable eminence, who was of the 'opinion that our own tung shold be written cleane and pure, unmixt and unmangeled with borowing of other tunges'. Admitting, however, that English, 'being unperfight', had to augment its vocabulary, Cheke recommended forming new words 'from the mould of our own tung' or reviving obsolete terms before resorting to loans from other languages.[72] He put these ideas into practice in his partial translation of the New Testament, in which he shunned Latinate terms such as 'lunatic' and 'crucified' in favour of the solidly English, if somewhat eccentric, 'moond' and 'crossed', and replaced the Greek-derived 'parable' with the native 'biword'.[73]

Though Cheke and Elyot differed in their views on how to improve English, both agreed that it was in need of improvement and that it was inferior to other languages, especially Greek and Latin. This attitude was shared by Ascham, a self-professed disciple of Cheke and a follower, though he never identifies himself as such, of Elyot. Defending the decision to write his treatise on the longbow, *Toxophilus, the Schole of Shootinge* (1545), in his native language, he explained that he had 'written this Englishe matter in the Englishe tongue, for Englishe men', even though 'to haue written it in an other tonge, had bene bothe more profitable for my study, and also more honest for my name'. Moreover, 'as for ye Latin or greke tonge, euery thynge is so excellently done in them, that none can do better: In the Englysh tonge contrary, euery thinge in a maner so meanly, bothe for the matter and handelynge, that no man can do worse'.[74] In 1568, writing in Latin to the Strasbourg humanist Jean Sturm, Ascham gave a similar account of the reason for composing his educational treatise in the vernacular: 'since my *Scholemaster* was not summoned from Greece or Italy but rather born on this barbarous island, he speaks barbarously, that is, in English ... I write for Englishmen, not for foreigners.'[75] In the treatise itself, he states that 'bicause the prouidence of God hath left vnto vs in no other tong, saue onelie in the *Greke* and *Latin* tong, the trew preceptes, and perfite examples of eloquence, therefore must we seeke in the Authors onelie of those two tonges, the trewe Paterne of Eloquence'.[76] Though Ascham was primarily concerned to teach young gentleman to produce elegant and decorous Latin prose, he regarded classical authors as appropriate models for vernacular writing as well: '*Lysias, Xenophon, Plato*, and *Isocrates*' were, he maintained, 'the purest and playnest writers, that euer wrote in any tong, and best examples for any man to follow whether he write Latin, Italian, French, or English'.[77]

It was through imitation of the perspicuous and natural prose style of such classical authors, rather than by an expansion of vocabulary, that Ascham hoped to enrich English. And just as the models to be followed were drawn from antiquity, so were those to be avoided, above all, Sallust, whose writing was 'artificiall and darke' and who failed to 'expresse the matter liuely and naturally with common speach'; his predilection for Greek words and constructions resulted in a 'strange and grekish kind of writing', as did his habit of imitating Thucydides, 'of whom *Salust* hath taken the greatest part of his darknesse'.[78] Caesar and Cicero were able to write in a manner which was 'naturall and plaine' not only because of their own God-given talent but also because they were 'daylie orators [amongst] the common people ... and therefore gaue themselues to vse soch speach as the meanest should well vnderstand'. Sallust, by contrast, was a bookish author, too much given to reading uplifting works by Cato, for 'by gathering troth out of *Cato*, [he] smelleth moch of the roughnes of his style: euen as a man that eateth garlike for helth, shall cary away with him the sauor of it also, whether he will or not'.[79] Ascham's fondness for such homespun metaphors, along with the clarity and balance of his sentences, made his own style a good advertisement for the sort of sprightly natural-ness he was promoting.

Many of the lessons which Ascham had learned from classical orators such as Isocrates and Cicero were lost on the English prose writers who followed soon after him. With the publication of John Lyly's *Euphues, the Anatomy of Wit* (1578) and its sequel *Euphues and his England* (1580), a style of writing known as 'euphuism' came into vogue, characterized by perpetual straining after antithesis and alliteration, far-fetched similes and elaborate word play.[80] The extreme mannerism and artificiality of euphuism was accentuated by an excessive display of recondite classical learning, producing an effect very different from the imitation of 'common speach' recommended by Ascham; yet both prose styles were part of the legacy of humanism to English literature.

NOTES

1 Poggio Bracciolini, *Two Renaissance Book Hunters: The Letters of Poggius Bracciolini to Nicolaus de Niccolis*, trans. P. W. G. Gordan (New York, 1974), p. 48.

2 Erasmus, *Collected Works* (Toronto, 1974–), I: *Letters 1 to 141, 1484 to 1500*, pp. 235–6 (Letter 118, to Robert Fisher, 5 December [1499]).

3 R. Weiss, *Humanism in England during the Fifteenth Century*, third edition (Oxford, 1967), p. 15 n. 4.

4 P. Dean, 'Tudor humanism and the Roman past: a background to Shakespeare', *Renaissance Quarterly*, 41 (1988), 84–111, at 87; D. Pearsall, *John Lydgate* (Charlottesville, 1970), pp. 230–43.

5 W. Nelson, *John Skelton, Laureate* (New York, 1964), pp. 40–58.

6 A. Kinney, *John Skelton, Priest as Poet: Seasons of Discovery* (Chapel Hill, 1987).

7 George Puttenham, *The Arte of English Poesie*, ed. G. D. Wilcox and A. Walker (Cambridge, 1936), p. 84.

8 Weiss, *Humanism in England*, ch. 3; A. Sammut, *Unfredo, Duca di Gloucester* (Padua, 1980); see also the Bodleian Library exhibition catalogue: *Duke Humfrey's Library and the Divinity School 1488–1988* (Oxford, 1988). Works of a non-humanist character, such as Lydgate's *Fall of Princes*, were also dedicated to Humfrey.

9 R. J. Mitchell, *John Free: From Bristol to Rome in the Fifteenth Century* (London, 1955) and her *John Tiptoft (1427–70)* (London, 1938).

10 For Carbone's funeral oration see E. Garin, ed., *Prosatori latini del Quattrocento* (Milan, 1952), pp. 382–417, at 398; see also Weiss, *Humanism in England*, p. 99.

11 The 1508 statutes, drawn up by Colet, are published in J. H. Lupton, *A Life of John Colet* ..., second edition (London, 1909; reprinted Hamden CN, 1961), pp. 271–84; see also J. B. Gleason, *John Colet* (Berkeley, 1989), ch. 9.

12 Over sixty-five editions are listed in A. W. Pollard and G. R. Redgrave, *A Short-Title Catalogue of Books Printed in England, Scotland, and Ireland ... 1475–1640*, 3 vols. (London, 1976–91), II, pp. 62–4.

13 Erasmus, *Collected Works*, XXIV: *Literary and Educational Writings 2*, pp. 661–91 (*On the Method of Study*, trans. B. McGregor). See also T. W. Baldwin, *William Shakspere's Small Latine & Lesse Greeke*, 2 vols. (Urbana, 1944).

14 See the title-page of Thomas Wolsey, *Rudimenta grammatices et docendi methodus* (London, 1529).

15 P. G. Bietenholz and T. B. Deutscher, eds., *Contemporaries of Erasmus: A*

Biographical Register of the Renaissance and Reformation, 3 vols. (Toronto, 1985–7), II, pp. 135–6 (Grocyn) and 331–2 (Linacre).

16 F. Maddison, M. Pelling and C. Webster, eds., *Linacre Studies: Essays on the Life and Work of Thomas Linacre* c. 1460–1524 (Oxford, 1977).

17 J. B. Trapp, *Erasmus, Colet and More: The Early Tudor Humanists and Their Books* (London, 1991), p. 106.

18 Thomas More, *The Complete Works* (New Haven, 1963–), III.1: *Translations of Lucian*, ed. C. R. Thompson.

19 Erasmus, *Collected Works*, XXVII: *Literary and Educational Writings 5*, pp. 77–153 (*Praise of Folly*, trans. B. Radice); More, *Complete Works*, IV: *Utopia*, ed. E. Surtz and J. H. Hexter.

20 R. R. Bolgar, *The Classical Heritage and Its Beneficiaries* (Cambridge, 1954), pp. 480–1.

21 More, *Complete Works*, IV, pp. 182–5.

22 More, *Complete Works*, III.1, pp. 3, 41.

23 J. McConica, *English Humanism and Reformation Politics* (Oxford, 1965), pp. 15–16.

24 B. Bradshaw, 'More on Utopia', *The Historical Journal*, 24 (1981), 1–27.

25 More, *Complete Works*, III.2: *Latin Poems*, ed. C. H. Miller, L. Bradner, C. A. Lynch and R. P. Oliver; and II: *The History of King Richard III*, ed. R. S. Sylvester.

26 D. Hay, *Polydore Vergil: Renaissance Historian and Man of Letters* (Oxford, 1952), p. 150; T. S. Freeman, 'From Catiline to Richard III: the influence of classical historians on Polydore Vergil's *Anglica historia*', in M. A. Di Cesare, ed., *Reconsidering the Renaissance* (Binghamton, 1992), pp. 191–214; More, *Complete Works*, II, p. xcviii.

27 Erasmus, *Collected Works*, XXVII, pp. 199–288, at 252: *(The Education of a Christian Prince*, trans. N. M. Cheshire and M. J. Heath).

28 Niccolò Machiavelli, *The Discourses*, trans. L. J. Walker, 2 vols. (London, 1950), I, pp. 205–6.

29 More, *Complete Works*, II, p. 87.

30 More, *Complete Works*, II, pp. lxxxvi–xcviii.

31 More, *Complete Works*, II, p. 24.

32 Edward Halle, *The Union of the Two Noble and Illustrate Famelies of Lancastre and Yorke* (London, 1548); Raphael Holinshed, *The First and Second [and Third] Volumes of the Chronicles*, second edition (London, 1587), which was used by Shakespeare.

33 J. W. Binns, *Intellectual Culture in Elizabethan and Jacobean England: The Latin Writings of the Age* (Leeds, 1990), pp. 120–6.

34 The authors had been students at the Inner Temple, where the play was performed; the Inns of Court were centres of humanistic learning as well as drama.

35 W. Clemen, *English Tragedy before Shakespeare* (London, 1961), chs. 13–15.

36 J. W. Binns, 'Seneca and Neo-Latin tragedy in England', in C. D. N. Costa, ed., *Seneca* (London, 1974), pp. 205–34; R. S. Miola, *Shakespeare and Classical Tragedy: The Influence of Seneca* (Oxford, 1992), ch. 3.

37 See T. S. Eliot's 'Introduction' to *Seneca His Tenne Tragedies*, ed. Thomas Newton (Bloomington, 1927), pp. v–liv.

38 Shakespeare, *Richard III*, ed. A. Hammond (London, 1981), pp. 97–8, 171–5 (I.iv.1–75); H. Brooks, 'Richard III: antecedents of Clarence's dream', *Shakespeare Survey*, 32 (1979), 145–50.

39 H. Brooks, '*Richard III*, unhistorical amplifications: the women's scenes and Seneca', *Modern Language Review*, 75 (1980), 721–37.

40 Brooks, '*Richard III*, unhistorical amplifications', 734.

41 Christopher Marlowe, *The Complete Works*, ed. F. Bowers, 2 vols. (Cambridge, 1973), I, p. 218 (*Dr Faustus* V.i.1725); Shakespeare, *King Richard III*, pp. 91, 316 (V.iii.136), 319 (V.iii.201).

42 Bartolomeo Ricci, *De imitatione libri tres* (Venice, 1545), f. 43ᵛ; Roger Ascham, *The English Works*, ed. W. A. Wright (Cambridge, 1904; reprinted 1970), pp. 266–7, 272–3; see also G. W. Pigman III, 'Versions of imitation in the Renaissance', *Renaissance Quarterly*, 33 (1980), 1–32, at 3.

43 Erasmus, *Collected Works*, XXVIII: *The Ciceronian*, trans. B. I. Knott, pp. 445–6; see also Pigman, 'Imitation', 25.

44 O. B. Hardison, 'Tudor humanism and Surrey's translation of the "Aeneid"', *Studies in Philology*, 83 (1986), 237–60.

45 *Tottel's Miscellany* (1557–87), ed. H. E. Rollins, 2 vols. (Cambridge MA, 1965), I, p. 2; Ascham, *English Works*, p. 289 (*Scholemaster*).

46 D. Attridge, *Well-Weighed Syllables: Elizabethan Verse in Classical Metres* (Cambridge, 1974), pp. 165–72.

47 Henry Howard, Earl of Surrey, *Poems*, ed. E. Jones (Oxford, 1964), pp. 133–4; D. Richardson, 'Humanistic intent in Surrey's *Aeneid*', *English Literary Review*, 6 (1976), 204–19, at 205.

48 Lodovico Ariosto, *Orlando furioso*, trans. Sir John Harington, ed. R. McNulty (Oxford, 1972).

49 G. G. Smith, ed., *Elizabethan Critical Essays*, 2 vols. (Oxford, 1904), I, pp. 115–16.

50 A. Fletcher, *The Prophetic Moment: An Essay on Spenser* (Chicago, 1971).

51 Edmund Spenser, *The Works*, ed. E. Greenlaw, C. Grosvenor Osgood, F. Morgan Padelford and R. Heffner, 10 vols. (Baltimore, 1932–71), I, pp. 167–70, at 167.

52 A. Fox, *Thomas More: History and Providence* (Oxford, 1984), chs. 4–6.

53 Stephen Gosson, *The Schoole of Abuse* ..., ed. A. Freeman (New York, 1973), sigs. A3ʳ, A2ʳ, C2ʳ, C5ᵛ, A7ᵛ, D1ᵛ, D3ʳ; see also A. Kinney, 'Stephen Gosson's art of argumentation in *The Schoole of Abuse*', *Studies in English Literature*, 7 (1967), 41–54.

54 M. Ferguson, *Trials of Desire: Renaissance Defenses of Poetry* (New Haven, 1983), pp. 137–62.

55 Sir Philip Sidney, *An Apology for Poetry or the Defence of Poesy*, ed. G. Shepherd (Edinburgh, 1965), p. 101; see Aristotle, *Poetics* 1 (1447ᵃ14–15).

56 A. C. Hamilton, *Sir Philip Sidney: A Study of His Life and Works* (Cambridge, 1977), pp. 116–17.

57 Puttenham, *Arte of English Poesie*, pp. 5 (I.2), 23 (I.9), 98–100 (II.12).

58 Sidney, *Apology for Poetry*, pp. 104–14, at 108–9; Puttenham, *Art of English Poesie*, pp. 8 (I.3), 41 (I.19).

59 Puttenham, *Art of English Poesie*, p. 60 (I.31); Sidney, *Apology for Poetry*, p. 133.

60 Puttenham, *Art of English Poesie*, pp. 36–7 (I.17); Sidney, *Apology for Poetry*, pp. 133–4.

61 See the preface to his 1534 translation of Isocrates' *Ad Nicoclem*, quoted by J. M. Major, *Sir Thomas Elyot and Renaissance Humanism* (Lincoln NB, 1964), p. 82. See also Elyot's *The Education or Bringing up of Children translated out of Plutarch* (London, *c*. 1535).

62 Sir Thomas Elyot, *The Castle of Health (1541)*, ed. S. A. Tannenbaum (New York, 1937), preface.

63 Sir Thomas Elyot, *The Boke named the Gouernour*, ed. H. H. S. Croft, 2 vols. (London, 1883; reprinted New York, 1967), I, p. cxcii.

64 Elyot, *Gouernour*, I, p. 96; see also Major, *Sir Thomas Elyot*, pp. 3–8.

65 Elyot, *Gouernour*, I, pp. 56–8.

66 Elyot, *Gouernour*, I, p. 72. On Agricola and the topics, see chapter 5 above, pp. 86–8.

67 Elyot, *Gouernour*, I, pp. 72–3.

68 Elyot, *Gouernour*, I, pp. 91–4.

69 Elyot, *Gouernour*, I, pp. 268–9. See also R. F. Jones, *The Triumph of the English Language* (Stanford, 1953; reprinted 1966), pp. 79–82.

70 See chapter 14 below.

71 Baldesar Castiglione, *The Book of the Courtier*, trans. Sir Thomas Hoby, intro. J. H. Whitfield (London, 1975), pp. 1–7, at 5.

72 See his letter to Hoby dated 16 July 1557, printed in Castiglione, *The Courtier*, pp. 7–8.

73 See Jones, *Triumph*, p. 121.

74 Ascham, *English Works*, pp. x, xiv.

75 Roger Ascham, *The Whole Works*, ed. J. A. Giles, 3 vols. (London, 1864), II, pp. 174–91, at 176.

76 Ascham, *English Works*, p. 283. Ascham's favourite vernacular language was not English but Italian, 'which next the Greek and Latin tonge, I like and loue aboue all other', though he regarded contemporary Italy as a country which was so corrupt in religion and manners that 'a yong ientleman' would benefit more from studying Castiglione's *Courtier*, 'seyng it is so well translated into English by a worthie Ientleman *Syr Th. Hobbie*', 'but one yeare at home in England ... then three yeares trauell abrode spent in *Italie*': *ibid.*, pp. 218, 223.

77 Ascham, *English Works*, p. 300.

78 Ascham, *English Works*, pp. 297–9.

79 Ascham, *English Works*, p. 298.

80 For a detailed analysis of John Lyly's 'euphuism', see R. W. Bond's edition of his *Complete Prose Works*, 3 vols. (Oxford, 1902; reprinted 1967), I, pp. 120–34. For Lyly's influence on late sixteenth-century writers see P. Mack, 'Rhetoric in use: three romances by Greene and Lodge', in P. Mack, ed., *Renaissance Rhetoric* (London, 1994), pp. 119–34.

14
Humanism and seventeenth-century English literature

JOSEPH LOEWENSTEIN

Because he has 'watch'd men, manners too / Heard what times past have said, seen what ours doe', the humanist antiquary earns the praise of the humanist poet. The balanced rhythm of attention that Ben Jonson here ascribes to John Selden is an idealization of what might be called the neoclassical habit of mind, with its alternation between censorious inspection of the present and studious review of the past. Other rhythms support this central one – of collection and dissemination, exemplification and dismissal, learning and teaching:

> Which grace shall I make love to first? your skill,
> Or faith in things? or is't your wealth and will
> To instruct and teach? or your unweary'd paine
> Of Gathering? Bountie in pouring out again?
> What fables have you vext! what truth redeem'd!
> Antiquities search'd! Opinions dis-esteem'd!
> Impostures branded! and Authorities urg'd!
> What blots and errours, have you watch'd and purg'd
> Records, and Authors of! how rectified
> Times, manners, customes! ... [1]

Jonson represents Selden's classicism as an ideal personal discipline, an ethics. Oddly, however, the ethical poise asserted here is represented without perfect aesthetic poise; the poem seems a less balanced thing than its subject. It is not just the unfortunate effect of the hectic exclamation marks; it is more a matter of the Ciceronian exclamations, with their ellipses constricting the praise as much as the repetitions extend it. A good portion of the pleasure of reading this poem, and many of Jonson's other poems, has to do with the diffuse elegance of his syntax: his poems often seem to have been quite adroitly translated out of Latin. It would be unfair to say of Jonson, as he said of Spenser (and as Samuel Johnson would say of Milton), that 'in affecting the Ancients, [he] writ no Language'; yet it must be admitted that something about the language of the 'Epistle to Selden' seems not quite adequate to the balance that it is plainly intended to convey.[2] The inadequacy is hardly evidence that seventeenth-century humanism and seventeenth-century English poetry were unsuited to each other. Selden was a lawyer, someone for whom the poised, comparative alternation of attention from present to past to present was a matter of professional habit. Jonson, on the other hand, was a playwright and a translator of Horace, an actor and an historical grammarian; he had been a brick-layer and a student at Westminster School, and he experienced the humanist alternation of attention with less composure than did the antiquarian lawyer. Perhaps one hears envy in his praise.

This is not to say that Jonson's admiration and interest were not reciprocated. Both men wrote eloquently on behalf of a moderate poise ballasted by scholarship, but they also shared more particular concerns. Shortly after Jonson wrote *Bartholomew Fair*, in which he satirized the Puritan opposition to transvestite theatrical performance, Selden sent him the fruits of his researches into the Hebrew prohibition on transvestism. Selden's antiquarian writings, many of which focus on near eastern culture, are steadily informed by the desire to alienate biblical texts, to situate them in a detailed historical past, and so to resist the uncritical Puritan submission of modern English religious practice to ancient near eastern ritual and taboo. Selden's scholarship was designed to assert a sphere of state authority independent of ecclesiastical pressures; in his *Table Talk* he compares the unfounded squabbling of religious sects to 'Inigo Lanthorne, disputing with his Puppet in a Bartholomew Fair: It is so; It is not so; It is so; It is not so; crying this to one another a quarter of an Hour together.'[3] The deployment of historical scholarship against modern extremism, the use of the poet's satiric eloquence to give the antiquarian's scholarship critical force – here is Erasmian humanism firmly ensconced in English culture and only a century after its far more fragile assertion in the writings and in the life of Thomas More.

In the light of this substantial cultural achievement, the juttering cadence and slightly awkward syntax in Jonson's 'Epistle to Selden' asks for some lingering consideration. What obscurely troubles these lines is an English prosody and a Latin rhetoric imperfectly adjusted each to the other. Oddly enough, Jonson may have been seeking precisely the effects that I have here described as awkward: he claimed to have written a treatise on prosody in which he proved 'couplets to be the bravest sort of Verses, especially when they are broken, like Hexameters' – the description suggests the formal achievement to which Jonson aspired in the 'Epistle to Selden'. The poem is far less 'brave' than Dryden's *Absalom and Achitophel* or Pope's *The Rape of the Lock*: the formal success that Jonson projects, England's 'Augustan' poets would achieve. By the end of the century the couplet would be established as the English poet's normal means of going about his business in virtually all save lyric compositions; the caesura that breaks the rhythm of the 'Epistle to Selden' would inflect the rhythm and sense of the heroic couplet; above all, by the end of the century the hold of Latin syntax on English verse would loosen. In what follows I wish to account both for the unsettled classicism of the 'Epistle to Selden' and for the various classicisms that it heralded. My purpose is to show how the intellectual traditions of Continental humanism were adapted by a culture self-conscious about its belatedness, but increasingly secure in asserting the coherence of its native intellectual, political and literary traditions.

The classicist address to public life that we call humanism became routinized in seventeenth-century England – a truism, but probably true none the less. It requires much qualification, of course, the most important being that a civic classicism sputters and flares in the most admired poets of the century. Humanist syncretism has no more elaborate and imposing practitioner than Milton; the humanist aspiration to speak the dangerous language of power has no more eloquent spokesman than Dryden. Yet well before the accession of James I, seventeenth-century English classicism had become institutiona-lized in grammar schools and universities and, having gained official status, it began a slow and unsteady loss of its power to startle.[4]

Which is to say that humanist pedagogical thought, having determined educational developments in sixteenth-century England, only informed educational developments in the seventeenth century. The other chief aspects of the humanist project, philology and archaeology, had been much more difficult to import than was the pedagogical programme. During the sixteenth century, English scholars could only play catch-up to the Continent in classical philology – Sir Thomas Elyot's Latin-English dictionary, for example, is plainly derivative – while English libraries and English soil could contribute only peripherally to the archaeology of the Roman empire (though Robert Talbot's mid-century commentary on the *Antonine Itinerary* and Sir Henry Savile's turn-of-the-century treatise on Roman military science make a start). Early English humanists had, at best, adapted ingeniously to the undeniable facts of their distance from the Rome of manuscript and ruin and their belatedness with respect both to Greek studies and to the recovery of what might be called spiritualist Neoplatonism.

Indeed, belatedness is perhaps the keynote of early modern English culture. At the beginning of the seventeenth century, one of England's most brilliant scholars, Sir Henry Savile, having already translated Tacitus in

1591, cast about for another properly humanist enterprise – yet the major texts of pagan antiquity had already been edited.[5] New editions were possible, of course, and during the next decades John Bond would prepare a complete Horace (1606) and an edition of Persius' *Satires* (1614), and Thomas Farnaby would complete a sequence of essential school texts: the *Satires* of Persius and Juvenal (1612), Seneca's tragedies (1613), Martial's *Epigrams* (1615), Lucan's *Pharsalia* (1618), a complete Virgil (1634), Ovid's *Metamorphoses* (1636) and, in collaboration with Meric Casaubon, a complete Terence (1651).[6] But these were derivative editorial enterprises and would have been insufficient to Savile's ambitions; instead, he set himself the project of a massive edition of Chrysostom, which was eventually printed in types specially designed for it. Savile's was not the only great achievement of Jacobean patristic studies. Probably the most significant such effort was undertaken by Thomas James, Bodley's first librarian, although James, like Savile, was also playing catch-up. His major scholarly achievements are detailed critiques of published editions of Ambrose, Cyprian and Gregory the Great, critiques based on exhaustive and systematic collation of virtually all available manuscripts.[7] Lagging behind 125 years of *editiones principes*, seventeenth-century English humanists assert themselves within a Republic of Letters increasingly devoted to scholarly corrigenda.

Among the finest examples of seventeenth-century scholarship, solid work like James's is anything but flashy, yet it can tell us a good deal about the trajectory of European humanism. The great alliance between archival inquiry and the technology of print had dominated literary culture during the previous century and a quarter, but it was not an entirely salutary combination. The fifteenth- and sixteenth-century press must frequently take the blame for a systematic dissemination of texts based on corrupt manuscript copy and often further corrupted by careless presswork. Still, it was difficult to quarrel with the new medium; so when a scholar like James managed to muster a sceptical stance towards eminent printed texts, the scepticism is remarkable enough to demand explanation. In James's case, the motive was simply the desire to discredit the work of Catholic scholars; had it not been for his Protestant zeal, he, too, might have unwittingly deferred to the already-in-print, in all its apparent adequacy. The renewal of philological purpose in James's revisionary textual scholarship is typical: a good deal of seventeenth-century intellectual life is braced by partisanship. Indeed, the very persistence of the humanist programme in England owes much to the rejuvenating energies of an ongoing Reformation. In the late fifteenth and early sixteenth centuries the application of humanist philological methods to Christendom's most revered texts had galvanized anti-papal sentiment; in the seventeenth century the abiding traditions of hostility to the Roman Church bolstered and stimulated English philology.

By the same token, where the energies of the Reformation were most cautiously contained and managed, scholarship often suffered. This is easy to see in the case of the most influential work of seventeenth-century English prose, the King James Bible (1611). Although many of England's greatest scholars (among them not only Savile, but Lancelot Andrewes, John Overall and William Bedwell) were gathered into six teams of translators for the royal project – two assembled at Oxford, two at Cambridge and two at Westminster School – their work is a monument to consensual politics, not to scholarship.[8] To be sure, the scholar-translators were enlisted to perform a great work, but it was a work of literary conciliation: 'wee never thought from the beginning, that we should neede to make a new Translation, nor yet to make of a bad one a good one', they insist in their epistle to the reader, 'but to make a good one better' – their rendering was based closely on the Bishops' Bible of 1568 – 'or out of many good ones, one principall good one, not justly to be excepted against; that hath bene our indeavour, that our marke'.

This new vernacular Bible clearly shows the direction in which humanism had been rechannelled. The first generation of humanists had begun the work of cultural recovery by translating the Greek classics into Latin for the use of the scholarly community, but translation eventually took on a far larger function. By the sixteenth century, it had become one of the chief engines of change in European devotional life, providing the laity with relatively easy access to biblical texts.[9] Vernacularism was especially important to the nationalist piety of late Tudor England. It is therefore hardly surprising that the revision that transformed a bishops' into a king's Bible should have been prefaced with an uncompromising *apologia* for translation:

> Wee doe not deny, nay wee affirme and avow, that the very meanest translation of the Bible in English … containeth the word of God, nay, is the word of God. As the Kings Speech which hee uttered in Parliament, being translated into *French*, *Dutch*, *Italian* and *Latine*, is still the Kings Speech, though it be not interpreted by every Translator with the like grace, nor peradventure so fitly for phrase, nor so expresly for sence, every where … No cause therefore why the word translated should bee denied to be the word.[10]

This by no means dispels the mystery of the Hebrew Old Testament, nor of the Greek New Testament, nor even of the Vulgate; it is, however, a profoundly anti-classicist argument. Petrarch is reputed to have wept over a Greek manuscript of Homer, hopelessly frustrated by his belief that he could never truly read Homer because he could not read him in Greek.

Petrarch's is a philology nearly devotional in pitch; the King James Bible claims the virtual lapse of such reverence, the end of humanism as, say, Lorenzo Valla, Angelo Poliziano or even Erasmus knew it.

For all its constructive achievements, humanist philology was quite destructive of the idea of truly authoritative translation.[11] This was true, not only for Latin versions of Greek texts, or vernacular renderings of Greek or Latin texts, but – shatteringly – for the Bible, now not only accessible, but mutable. Discomfort over linguistic ramification may be observed in the embarrassed hyper-nativist slanging of many Elizabethan translations and imitations: in the exaggerated provincialism of Arthur Golding's translation of Ovid or of Spenser's Virgilian pastorals, in the obtrusively modern, obtrusively baroque figurative work of Christopher Marlowe's Musaeus, and in the constant tug of the bathetic in Shakespeare's *Venus and Adonis*. The evocations of antique milieux in many late Elizabethan texts came to seem at once awkward and studied, but the embarrassment over scriptural and classical translation would subside early in the seventeenth century, and the warm sonorities of the King James Bible, at once native and dignified, did much to ease the anxieties of linguistic belatedness. Whether or not the translators knew how successfully they had done their work, they were certainly bold in their methodological assertions: 'we have not tyed our selves to an uniformitie of phrasing, or to an identitie of words, as some peradventure would wish that we had done'. Their letter closes with powerful claims on behalf of freedom of vernacular expression – a mechanical formulary:

> we thought to savour more of curiositie then wisedome ... for is the Kingdome of God become words or syllables? why should wee be in bondage to them if we may be free, use one precisely when we may use another no lesse fit, as commodiously ... We cannot follow a better patterne for elocution then God himselfe; therefore hee using divers words, in his holy writ, and indifferently for one thing in nature: wee, if wee will not be superstitious, may use the same libertie in our English versions out of *Hebrew* or *Greeke*.

This libertarian antinominalism would be reenacted by the author of *Paradise Lost*; it would become almost libertine in the Dryden of *Absalom and Achitophel*.

If the transformation of erudite attitudes to the scriptural or classical letter had distant effects on poetics, it had more immediate effects on educational practice. During the late sixteenth and early seventeenth centuries English schoolmasters improved Latin pedagogy and gave Greek and Hebrew a more secure place in the curriculum, but, at the same time, they grew increasingly interested in the claims of the vernacular: a mid

sixteenth-century champion of linguistic nationalism such as Richard Mulcaster anticipates general trends in English schooling.[12] Although translation between the classical languages and the vernacular remained the central
grammar school exercise, the meaning of translation was subtly adjusted.
Roger Ascham had built Latin-English and English-Latin translations – the
famous routine of 'double translation' – into his educational programme,
although in Ascham's pedagogy English had the dull status of a reference,
an uninteresting standard against which renderings in Latin and constructions of Latin might be checked. Half a century later, in his *Ludus literarius*
(1612), John Brinsley would advert to Ascham's technique of the double
translation with great respect; but for Brinsley the purpose of this double
movement was to cultivate the pupil's fluency and copiousness in English.

The sway of Latinity would not lapse quickly; its persistence is easy to
observe in the continuing post-graduate interest in Latin verse composition:
Thomas May's continuation of the *Pharsalia*, the *Supplementum Lucani*,
which carries the narrative forward to the assassination of Caesar, suggests
the vitality of Anglo-Latin literary culture. But perhaps even more telling is
Sir Francis Kynaston's Latin translation of Chaucer's *Troilus and Criseyde* –
'Dolorem Troili duplicem narrare' ('The double sorrow of Troilus to tell') –
which catches the most remarkable development of English literary humanism in mid-career: that slow development by which vernacular texts
acquired the status of the Greek and Latin classics.[13] In the work of Milton
and Marvell, respectively the Latin Secretary to the Commonwealth (1649
to c. 1659) and assistant Latin Secretary (1657 to 1660), we can see traces
both of Brinsley's new pedagogy and of Ascham's older one. For most of his
life Milton's reputation rested on his achievements as a Latinist, and we
cannot speak of his having made a commitment to vernacular poetry until
relatively late in his career. He wrote his most intimate elegy, the 'Epita-
phium Damonis', in Latin, its refrain – 'Ite domum impasti, domino iam
non vacat, agni' ('Go home unfed, lambs, your shepherd has no time for
you') – a composite of two lines from Virgil; yet as the poet proceeds
towards a conventional renunciation of lament and a turn to exaltation, he
predicts a renunciation of Latin and a turn to English:

> O mihi tum si vita supersit,
> Tu procul annosa pendebis fistula pinu
> Multùm oblita mihi, aut patriis mutata camoenis
> Brittonicum strides.[14]

(Oh, if any of my life remains, you, my pipes, will hang far off, long forgotten
upon some aged pine, or, changed by some native muse, you will howl out a
British tune.)

To relinquish the language of the schoolroom in the language of the schoolroom, and to do so in such an impassioned poem, is a gesture of both delicate and uncertain valence. It is virtually impossible to gauge the relative prestige of Latin and English in Milton's career, for he published polemics in English and (naturally) drafted diplomatic correspondence for the Protectorate in Latin; he composed one great theological work in Latin, *De doctrina Christiana*, and another, *Paradise Lost*, in English. Certainly, the epic bears traces of pedagogic tradition, for Ascham had established biblical metaphrase (paraphrase from prose into verse, from verse into prose or from an original verse form into a new one) as a staple of the English humanist schoolroom.[15] Milton was not, of course, alone among English poets in elaborating this schoolboy's exercise in later literary activity, though the continuity with early literary training is clearer in the work of such Anglo-Latin poets as Walter Haddon, Thomas Drant, Henry Dethick, Patrick Adamson, William Vaughan and James Duport. What confirms the vitality of the link between Milton's education and his mature poetic activity is the way in which the epic manifests the complex linguistic braid that was the distinguishing side-effect of Tudor and Stuart grammar schooling: Milton eschews the traditional resources of English non-dramatic poetry in favour of a blank verse in which both syntax and diction yearn towards Latinity, all nominally on behalf of the antiquarian nativism so loudly asserted in the headnote prefixed to one of the 1668 issues of the poem ('ancient liberty recover'd to Heroic Poem from the troublesom and modern bondage of Rimeing'). This is perhaps to put the matter too schematically: when Milton's Adam asks Raphael the question that most stirs him and that most displays his buoyant reverence –

> Tell me, how may I know him, how adore
> From whom I have that thus I move and live,
> And feel that I am happier then I know
> *(Paradise Lost*, VIII, lines 280–2)

– a Latin syntax wells up and subsides within lines whose diction is utterly simple and utterly native.

Unlike Milton, Marvell is not remembered for his Latinity, yet his relation to humanist neoclassicism is no more settled than was Milton's. Certainly it is difficult to locate him between the poles of Ascham and Brinsley: the conjoint publication, in his *Miscellaneous Poems* (1681), of both 'On a Drop of Dew' and 'Ros', both 'Hortus' and 'The Garden', makes it difficult to assign preeminence of value, or even to argue priority of composition – in both instances, the Latin 'version' follows the English on the page, but the cultural force of the layout is almost impossible to construe. Taken singly, these poems draw on a variety of imperfectly compatible learned traditions, a tense and gnomic semantic field. But the pairings exacerbate this lively tension, for the Latin and English versions of these poems compete for semantic priority and, by their rivalry, challenge the very idea of *the* poem as singular, stable and univocal. We have here the perfect emblems of the nervously productive interplay between Latinity and Englishness within mid seventeenth-century literary culture.

To indicate the competing tugs of vernacular and Latin traditions within seventeenth-century English literary practice will not exhaust an account of how humanism shaped that practice. Perhaps it goes without saying that a self-conscious attitude to the vernacular is itself a product of late humanism. Once again, Brinsley's pedagogical writings will prove illuminating. If his *Ludus literarius* affiliates him with Aschamite translation and the more general humanist practice of classical imitation, his *Consolation for our Grammar Schools* (1622) affiliates him with yet another strain of humanist practice, for the *Consolation* contains the first plan for an EFL programme, a programme designed to help missionaries instruct indigenous peoples in the basic (English) texts of (English) Christianity; its immediate inspiration almost certainly derives from Edmund Coote's *The English Schoolmaster* (1596), the first textbook designed to teach unlettered English men and women to read the vernacular. These textbooks are just two of the many early seventeenth-century attempts to methodize pedagogy. What distinguishes these programmes is the plainness and pragmatism of their goals, their pursuit, not of Latin eloquence, but of a vernacular literacy put primarily in service of middle-class piety and mercantile advancement.

This pragmatism obviously gestures towards more pointed moments of Puritan vernacularization – towards 1642, for example, when George Snell, signing himself 'Syndicus Reipublicae Literariae', proposed a centralized school-system and vernacular regional colleges, or towards 1650, when the Rump Parliament mandated the translation of all law books into English. For all their ties to the urgencies and aspirations of their particular moments, such developments have a humanist ancestry, even as they mark a breakdown in the coherence of humanism. The shift from eloquent Latinity to practical vernacularism constitutes a separation of two strands of Erasmian pedagogical culture. Erasmus was not only the great exponent of eloquent *copia*; he was also the great exponent of systematic pedagogy, a pedagogy designed to remove as many obstacles as possible from the swift acquisition of Latin literacy. The methodization of pedagogy that he initiated was considerably advanced during the seventeenth century, as may be gleaned from the rise of the non-grammar-based pedagogies of William

Bathe, Joseph Webbe and the profoundly influential Jan Amos Comenius, or from the plan outlined in Milton's *Accedence commenc't Grammar* (1669), a textbook, written in English, designed to teach Latin in a single year.[16] Brinsley's EFL programme – like Robert Cawdrey's *Table Alphabeticall* (1602), the first English–English dictionary – obviously responds to the political exigencies of expanded trade and extended diplomacy, as well as to burgeoning missionary activity; not so obviously, the humanist analytic fix on linguistics, and specifically on language acquisition, was the necessary condition for the formulation of Brinsley's programme. Jonson was entirely the modern humanist when, in the 1620s, he began to draft a Ramist English grammar.[17]

He was not, however, a radical linguist. Jonson's grammar is informed by the assumption that the structure of English is essentially identical to that of Latin (though he does grant, as none before him had done, that the English articles had no analogue in Latin and required the invention of a new category).[18] In 1629, John Hewes effected a crucial conceptual break with his *Perfect Survey of the English Tongue*: although conceived as a text that could facilitate Latin pedagogy, the book recognizes and stresses that English is structurally different from Latin, an insight that only begins to receive sustained analysis in John Wallis's great *Grammatica linguae Anglicanae* (1653), which emphasizes the importance of word order in English and the relative simplicity of the English tense system.[19] Evidently, the trajectory of English humanism was to proceed from the analysis of classical languages to the differentiating analysis of English.

This work of differentiation was not always celebratory. We can observe Thomas Carew struggling in his elegy for Donne (1631) not only with his sense of the cultural backwardness of Renaissance England, but with a sense that the language of England, the very raw material of poetry, might be constitutively inferior to that of Greece or Rome. To the ancients, Carew writes:

> Thou shalt yield no precedence, but of time,
> And the blinde fate of language, whose tun'd chime
> More charmes the outward sense; Yet thou maiste claime
> From so great disadvantage greater fame.[20]

It is difficult to assess the depth of this linguistic fatalism: it may derive some of its profundity from the elegiac occasion. None the less, the gloomy representation of Donne's achievement as thwarted by both the structure and the history of English keeps us close to the tactics of vernacular philology. For those humanists anxious that English should attain something like the prestige of Latin, the language deserved full articulation not only of its grammar, but also of its history. Humanist classical philology was preeminently committed to the analysis of linguistic change over time; one of the ways in which English humanists contrived to shrug off their cultural belatedness was to make distinguished contributions to historical linguistics – and particularly to the historiography of the English language. In his *Restitution of Decayed Intelligence* (1605), Richard Verstegan asserted 'the great Antiquitie of our ancient English toung', and so initiated what has been called seventeenth-century England's 'Saxon craze'.[21] By 1655 the 'Caedmon' manuscript – an eleventh-century codex of poems attributed to the seventh-century English poet – had been edited and published; and by 1659 William Somner had compiled an Old English dictionary, though it took another three decades for a systematic Old English grammar, the work of George Hickes, to appear. Even before this, however, Jonson's teacher, William Camden, published a series of vernacular renderings of the Lord's Prayer in order to illustrate the evolution from Anglo-Saxon to modern English.

These are not, of course, the first important instances of vernacular exemplification, of setting forth snippets of English verse or prose as illustrations or models. Elizabethan treatises on vernacular rhetoric and poetics had already begun the work of transforming English literary practice into the object of a critical scrutiny analogous to that of the Roman rhetoricians; in a related effort, George Gascoigne, Francis Meres and George Puttenham identified canons of admired English poets and prose writers, thus proposing that England had what we now call a native tradition, a tradition analogous to that which had once been the distinguishing feature of Graeco-Roman literary culture. Milton's schoolmaster, Alexander Gill, continues this Elizabethan critical practice in his *Logonomia Anglica* (1619), adducing examples of rhetorical tropes and figures from Edmund Spenser, to whom he refers as 'our Homer'. Meres had floated this basic idea in the 1590s in that chapter of *Palladis Tamia* entitled 'A comparative discourse of our English poets with the Greeke, Latine, and Italian poets' – 'As Greece had three poets of great antiquity, Orpheus, Linus, and Musaeus, and Italy other three auncient poets, Livius Andronicus, Ennius, and Plautus: so hath England three auncient poets, Chaucer, Gower, and Lydgate ...'[22] – and Gill reasserts it – Edmund Spenser is 'Homerus noster'; John Harington, 'lepidissimus noster Martialis'; George Wither, Juvenal; Samuel Daniel, Lucan.[23] This transformation of literary culture, the simultaneous birth of English literary criticism and literary history was significantly supplemented by Camden's history of the language, which projects a linguistic continuum into a distant past. Such developments are part of the broadly diffused antiquarianism that also shows itself in late Tudor and early Stuart pageantry, law, architecture and political theory.

English scholars approached the project of making sense of the native past in many different ways. William Cartwright offers versified thanks to Kynaston for his Latin translation of *Troilus and Criseyde* thus:

> 'Tis to your Happy cares wee owe, that wee
> Read *Chaucer* now without a Dictionary; . . .
> [He] Speakes plainly now to all, being more our owne
> Eu'n hence, in that thus made to Aliens knowne.[24]

Cartwright's response is now a curiosity; seventeenth-century English antiquarianism generally leads in another direction. By the end of the century, Dryden will be translating Chaucer into modern English.

This process, which was continuous with humanist methods and ideals (if not entirely consistent with them), occasionally issued in frank promotions of English literary culture as a rival to Greek or Latin. As part of his celebration of Donne's achievement (in despite 'of time / And the blinde fate of language'), Carew denigrates imitative classicism, 'the debts of our penurious bankrupt age':

> Licentious thefts, that make poëtique rage
> A Mimique fury, when our soules must bee
> Possest, or with Anacreons Extasie,
> Or Pindars, not their owne.

Carew sees classicism as a persistent temptation to which modern 'Libertines in Poetrie', deprived of Donne's living example, will revert:

> They will repeale the goodly exil'd traine
> Of gods and goddesses, which in thy just raigne
> Was banish'd nobler Poems, now, with these
> The silenc'd tales o'th' Metamorphoses
> Shall stuffe their lines.[25]

The royalist idiom hints at how a certain species of national chauvinism shaped Carew's taste, yet his accusation was not entirely unfair. The poetasters of the early seventeenth century often turned to Ovid as an undergraduate turns to a thesaurus, and so to note Donne's disdain for Ovid is a measure of Donne's distinctiveness.

But Carew was not entirely fair either. Donne's does not exhaust the experimentalism of Jacobean poetry, and although Carew's anti-classicist lines do not do justice to that fact, they do perhaps inadvertently allude to other, classicist experimentalisms. Despite what Carew says, this is the moment when English poets first seriously opened themselves to the influence of Greek lyric – 'Anacreons Extasie / Or Pindars'. It bears remembering, after all, that Renaissance poets often broke new ground by extending the range of antique modes and genres that were made the object of emulation. Many of the stylistic breakthroughs of the 1590s, for example, derive from Donne's (and Joseph Hall's and John Marston's) novel engagement with Juvenal and Persius; indeed, Donne worked out his characteristic 'nativism' in an effort to find both a vocabulary and a rhythm of exercised conversation that were answerable to his models.[26] In the seventeenth century, Greek lyric and dramatic models became more accessible and the work of assimilating and, then, competing with them was lively and absorbing. Carew's much-admired Jonson spliced together his most enduring lyric, 'Drink to me, only, with thine eyes', out of the letters of Philostratus.[27] But the ecstasies of Anacreon and Pindar were still novelties in 1631: although the poems attributed to Anacreon were first published in the middle of the sixteenth century, it was many decades before they excited much English attention.[28]

Robert Herrick, who initiated his oddly sustaining relation with Anacreon in the early 1630s, seems at first glance to be particularly vulnerable to Carew's criticism, yet his imitative practice carries more than a little personal vanity and cultural chauvinism. In one of the poems of *Hesperides*, Herrick's mistress promises that, in Elysium,

> Ile bring thee *Herrick* to *Anacreon*,
> Quaffing his full-crown'd bowles of burning Wine,
> And in his Raptures speaking Lines of Thine.[29]

One might ask whose ecstasy is possessing whom. This is a genial cultural rivalry, more modest than that of an anonymous piece of mid-century flattery, which gives us swagger and smirk –

> And then *Flaccus Horace*,
> He was but a sowr-ass,
>   And good for nothing but *Lyrick*:
> There's but One to be found
> In all English ground
>   Writes as well: who is hight *Robert Herrick*[30]

– which seems to recall the blustering mock-classicism of the Elizabethan epyllion. Here the native, alehouse eloquence (the rhymes are excellent, but 'hight' is the best touch) seems nicely attuned to Herrick's continuing campaign to cut Horace down to Anacreontic size, a campaign to dismiss the moral – the Jonsonian – Horace. The campaign is not always so swaggering: when Herrick bids farewell to Sack, the friend of poets ancient and modern, he performs the same operation with unfussy efficiency:

> Horace, Anacreon both had lost their fame,
> Had'st thou not filled them with thy fire and flame.[31]

Here is a poetry that can quite casually subject the antique canon to modern re-evaluation, to a rivalrous modernity neither mimic nor furious. Jonson presents a very different case:

> Where art thou, *Genius?* I should use
> Thy present Aide: Arise Invention,
> Wake, and put on the wings of *Pindars* Muse,
> To towre with my intention
> High ...
> ... heat my braine
> With *Delphick* fire:
> That I may sing my thoughts, in some unvulgar straine.[32]

Here in the 'Ode to Iames, Earle of Desmond', Jonson is so intent on achieving Pindaric altitude that he achieves little else: the poem keeps missing its human subject. Jonson published the poem with an uncharacteristic subtitling note: '(writ in Queene Elizabeth's time, since lost, and recovered)'; the fastidious dating has the double function of elaborately claiming Jonson's priority in attempting an English Pindaric ode and passing the attempt off as novice work, at once amplifying the poem's protestations of audacity and apologizing for them. Neither he nor anyone else would attempt the form again until 1629 (only a few years before Carew wrote his elegy for Donne) when Jonson composed 'On the Death of Sir Henry Morison', and Milton wrote 'On the Morning of Christ's Nativity'.

In neither poem is the relation to Pindar easy or unselfconscious. (Not until Abraham Cowley took up 'Pindar's Unnavigable Song' again at mid-century would there be a hearty commitment to Pindar's bravado.) Following Julius Caesar Scaliger and Antonio Minturno,[33] Jonson makes an ethical and cosmological allegory of form, the stanzaic alternation of *strophe, antistrophe* and *epode* that provides the formal matrix of the Pindaric ode: out of his own (Horatian) convictions – and perhaps out of nervous, knowing respect for the demands of the Pindaric mode – he systematically assesses and dismisses Pindaric excess and triumph for poise and transcendence. In the 'Nativity Ode', Milton similarly reassesses his classical model, ceremoniously relinquishing Pindar's tremendousness, as the 'horrid clang', 'Cymbals' ring' and 'Timbrel'd Anthems' (lines 157, 208, 219) of paganism give way to the glowing hush of angels serviceably ordered around the sleeping *infans.* Milton's relation to antiquity was notoriously scrupulous and the master-trope of his later career, the negative simile, characteristically invoked the prestige of classicism in order to bridle it.

This is not the only anti-classicism to voice itself during the first half of the century. Perhaps the most famous and, ultimately, the most influential, was Francis Bacon's. He felt the need for intellectual reform, and specifically educational reform, with such urgency that it provoked him to a remarkable historical revisionism:

> Martin Luther, conducted (no doubt) by an higher Providence, but in discourse of reason finding what a province he had undertaken against the Bishop of Rome and the degenerate tradition of the church, and finding his own solitude, being no ways aided by the opinions of his own time, was enforced to awake all antiquity, and to call former times to his succours to make a party against the present time; so that the ancient authors, both in divinity and humanity, which had long slept in libraries, began generally to be read and revolved.

In Bacon's account, what we customarily call 'humanist education' and trace to a fourteenth-century shift in Italian pedagogy was recast as a stratagem engineered by sixteenth-century religious reformers, a stratagem that went awry:

> This by consequence did draw on a necessity of a more exquisite travail in the languages original wherein those authors did write, for the better understanding of those authors and the better advantage of pressing and applying their words. And thereof grew again a delight in their manner of style and phrase.

Bacon attacks the anti-scientific, but alluring artistry of ancient 'eloquence and variety of discourse' which, he tells us, had been cultivated

> as the fittest and forciblest access in to the capacity of the vulgar sort. So that these four causes concurring, the admiration of ancient authors, the hate of the schoolmen, the exact study of languages, and the efficacy of preaching, did bring in an affectionate study of eloquence and copie of speech, which then began to flourish. This grew speedily to an excess; for men began to hunt more after words than matter; and more after the choiceness of phrase, and the round and clean composition of the sentence, and the sweet falling of the clauses, and the varying and illustration of their works with tropes and figures, than after the weight of matter, worth of subject, soundness of argument, life of invention, or depth of judgement ... In sum, the whole inclination and bent of those times was rather towards copie than weight.[34]

This by no means devolves into a Neoscholasticism: the next stage in the argument is an attack on the scholastic passion for minute distinction, the 'monstrous altercations' of medieval intellectual practice.

The story of Bacon's 'methodical' but otherwise 'anti-humanist' influence on seventeenth-century prose and, thence, on late seventeenth-century poetry has often been told. Certainly, his assault on humanist rhetoric was, together with a Puritan emphasis on a plain sermonic style, one of the important forces galvanizing seventeenth-century educational reform. In its most extreme expression, Baconian reformism issued, at mid-century, in attempts to develop a universal grammar and to construct an ideal 'philosophical' language, a programme that has been described as 'debabelization'. Such reform was one of the organizing concerns of that great Baconian institution, the Royal Society, which established a 'committee for improving the English language' in 1664.

Besides the linguistic radicalism he unleashed, Bacon also became the exponent of important modulations *within* the humanist rhetorical tradition. He was one of the leading importers of an anti-Ciceronianism that originated on the Continent during the late sixteenth century, in the work of Marc-Antoine Muret, Justus Lipsius and Michel de Montaigne. These men, by precept and example, promoted a shift from Cicero to Silver Latin prose models: to Tacitus for his tense condensations and to Seneca for his casual, non-compulsive symmetries and to both for their shortened periods. The interest in brevity and point has many analogues in other areas of late Renaissance aesthetic practice – in the vogue for emblems, in the poetry of wit with its demotion of scheme and promotion of trope (and its preference for metaphor over simile), in the generalized social practice of the gnomic remark, in the enthusiasm for epigrams (often closely indebted, as in Jonson, to Martial), in a flourishing culture of *impresa* and trinket – and Bacon, perhaps the most scrupulously self-regulating thinker of the century, eventually intervened against an over-commitment to 'pointed' stylistics:

> The labour here is altogether, That words may be aculeate, sentences concise, and the whole contexture of the speech and discourse, rather rounding into it selfe, than spread and dilated: So that it comes to passe by this Artifice, that every passage seemes more witty and waighty than indeed it is. Such a stile as this we finde more excessively in Seneca, more moderately in Tacitus and Plinius Secundus; and of late it hath bin very pleasing unto the eares of our time ... neverthelesse, by the more exact judgements, it hath bin deservedly despised, and may be set down as a distemper of Learning, seeing it is nothing else but a hunting after words.[35]

The Baconian aesthetic was, above all, prosaic.

It is surprising only at first glance that Thomas Sprat, one of the leading figures of the movement for Baconian linguistic reform, should have written an appreciative *Account of the Life and Writings of Mr. Abraham Cowley*

(1668). Sprat was not much interested in Cowley's Anacreontic poems, but he endorsed his Pindaric poetry: 'this loose and unconfin'd measure has all the Grace and Harmony of the most Confin'd. And withal it is so large and free, that the practice of it will only exalt, not corrupt our Prose, which is certainly the most useful kind of Writing of all others, for it is the style of business and conversation.'[36] We are rather far from Jonson's Pindar, praised for his *un*vulgar strain.

The radicalism of the Royal Society does not close the literary history of classicism. As Sprat's approving account of Cowley makes clear, new trends in public intellectual culture – and particularly the development of a rigorous urban intellectual culture relatively independent of traditions of schooling and professional training – might produce new aesthetic principles, but those principles were still often articulated by reference to an ancient canon. If rational conversation was newly esteemed, if artificial schemes were generally devalued, then the shrewd, ambulatory scepticism of Horace's *Satires* could be adopted as a model: hence Alexander Brome's and Thomas Flatman's colloquial translations of Horace, hence the Earl of Rochester's urbane verse essay in criticism, 'An allusion to the tenth Satire of the first book of Horace', hence – and most important – Cowley's, Thomas Sprat's and John Oldham's sustained imitations of Horace and, much later, those of Alexander Pope. 'This mode of imitation', Dr Johnson tells us:

> in which the ancients are familiarised, by adapting their sentiments to modern topics, by making Horace say of Shakespeare what he originally said of Ennius, and accommodating his satires on Pantolabus and Nomentanus to the flatterers and prodigals of our own time, was first practised in the reign of Charles the Second ... It is a kind of middle composition between translation and original design, which pleases when the thoughts are unexpectedly applicable, and the parallels lucky.[37]

The objects of such imitations were by no means confined to the *Satires* of Horace. In the works of Oldham, Rochester, John Hughes, Thomas Wood and others we find Pindar, Juvenal, Ovid and Martial similarly 'familiarised'.[38] These poems have a complicated appeal, some of which partakes of the mischievous pleasures of the schoolroom – misquoting or twisting the antiquated lesson so that it serves an entirely local and sometimes obscene new purpose. Democratized education meant that a growing portion of the population would enjoy the tang of such misbehaviour: this was not only the age of the 'familiarised' imitation, but also a great age of classical parody, the age of Charles Cotton's *Scarronides* and James Scudamore's

Homer A la Mode (both of 1664), of John Phillips's *Maronides* (1673), of Thomas Burnet's and George Duckett's *Homerides* (1716), and of Pope's *Rape of the Lock* (1712) and *Dunciad* (1728).

But the familiarized imitation did more than snicker: an equally important part of the appeal of these poems was, precisely, the defamiliarization that came from not knowing how fully to credit the analogy of past and present, of feeling the reference of an entire poetic narrative strain and bend as it does in Dryden's great imitation of Juvenal's *Satire* X. There the *voces populi* exultantly puzzle over Sejanus, who is being dragged through the streets:

> But say, how came his Monstrous Crimes to Light?
> What is the Charge, and who the Evidence
> (The Savior of the Nation and the Prince?)
> Nothing of this; but our Old *Caesar* sent
> A Noisie Letter to his parliament:
> Nay Sirs, if *Caesar* writ, I ask no more;
> He's Guilty; and the Question's out of Door.[39]

Dr Johnson would take this further, changing Sejanus to Cardinal Wolsey and so increasing one's sense of secular typology, the repetitive configurations of politics in time. Dryden's handling of the lines is less striking and more uneasy, since it keeps alive the question of typology, indefinitely querying the resemblance of Parliament and Senate, Roman and English mob, Tiberius and William III – and Juvenal and Dryden. Here in what Johnson calls a middle composition, the truth-claims of poetry burn underground.

Translation and imitation were among Dryden's favourite forms of expression: again and again, classicism enabled him to create for his poems a strangely-lit atmosphere of – how to put this? – secret boldness. His preface to the 1693 *Satires* is a careful comparative review of the achievements of Persius, Juvenal and Horace as satirists. 'Let the *Manes* of *Juvenal* forgive me', he decides, 'if I say, that this way of *Horace* was the best, for amending Manners', and the volume includes no imitations of Horace: is the volume less interested in amending manners than it should be? Is this a world beyond reform? '*Juvenal* has rail'd more wittily than *Horace* has rally'd. *Horace* means to make his Reader Laugh; but he is not sure of his Experiment. *Juvenal* always intends to move your Indignation; and he always brings about his purpose.' The bulk of the volume is made up of imitations of Juvenal: in what way is our indignation intended? 'In *Persius* the difficulty is to find a Meaning; in *Juvenal*, to chuse a meaning.' Within a Restoration culture that has been characterized as permeated and defined by disguise, Dryden's classicism is an exercise in slyness.[40]

Perhaps the greatest instance of Dryden's secret boldness is his dedication to the 1697 *Aeneis*. There he describes a Virgil beset by enemies and evokes, in a vocabulary that firmly but deniably points to the tumultuous history of seventeenth-century England, the political circumstances in which the epic was composed:

> The Commonwealth had receiv'd a deadly Wound in the former Civil Wars betwixt *Marius* and *Sylla*. The Commons, while the first prevail'd, had almost shaken off the Yoke of the Nobility; and *Marius* and *Cinna*, like the Captains of the Mobb, under the specious Pretence of the Publick Good, and of doing Justice on the Oppressours of their Liberty, reveng'd themselves, without Form of Law, on their private Enemies. *Sylla*, in his turn, proscrib'd the Heads of the adverse Party: He too had nothing but Liberty and Reformation in his Mouth ... Thus the *Roman* People were grossly gull'd twice or thrice over and as often enslav'd in one Century, and under the same pretence of Reformation.[41]

Later, Dryden would offer a disquisition on the fragility of Aeneas' claim as Priam's heir (Helenus and Priamus were both still living; '*Aeneas* had only Married *Creusa, Priam's* Daughter'): the terms keep before us the problem of William's legitimacy, without 'chusing a meaning' as to the *pietas* of England's new king. The translation itself is constantly being turned towards the 1690s, but not in order to insist upon specific parallels.[42] Virgil's great achievement was to expose the grief, imposture, desecration and loss within his tale of political origins; Dryden's is to propose how the Revolution Settlement might yield to such exposure. *Absalom and Achitophel*, a defamiliarizing familiarization of the Bible, is the great political poem of Dryden's mid-career; *Virgil's Aeneis* is the great political poem of his latter years.

Perhaps because of the unstable semantic power latent and enduring within the classical text, the century ended with a celebrated skirmish, a quarrel over the relative merits of the most ancient texts and the most modern. That the twentieth-century reader is likely to have encountered a reference to 'The Battle of the Ancients and the Moderns' only in an introduction to Jonathan Swift's *Tale of a Tub* (1704) is telling, and *what* our current vagueness tells us is that the haunted and meticulous measuring of Now against Then that was the central activity of Renaissance humanism has lost its centrality to the educated imagination. 'The Battle of the Books' is something of a watershed in English cultural history, for subsequent literary culture is virtually unshakeable in its modernism; thenceforth, Greek and Latin literature would be felt to be 'academic' and, in most cases (one might except Shelley, for example), an author's engagement with literary antiquity had to be hedged with some form of irony in order to protect the engagement from satiric reception. Swift is perhaps the last great satirist who could assume that his readers' nostalgia would hover over some phase of classical antiquity.

Comparative defence of ancient or modern arts and sciences was already a tired subject of erudite activity in France by 1690, when Sir William Temple imported it. Temple asserted the superiority of antique learning in the amiable and rather general terms that had come to characterize the French *querelle*, whereas the defence of contemporary intellectual culture mounted by Temple's first English respondent, the young prodigy, William Wotton, was detailed and vigorous. A junior member of the Royal Society, Wotton was a far better classicist than Temple, and his scholarly superiority lends his *Reflections Upon Ancient and Modern Learning* (1694) a fine polemical cunning. He praises Polybius, for example, 'as an Instance that a History may be incomparable that has not Rhetorical Ornaments to set it off'.[43] The Baconianism that deploys the antique example against the vestiges of a (humanist) cult of (an eloquent) antiquity is unmistakable: Wotton had been educated outside the normal grammar school system and his anti-rhetorical modernism compromises, in almost off-handed fashion, the founding assumptions of humanist education.

Wotton's paradoxical use of classical learning to batter away at the cult of antiquity is particularly intriguing, for it indicates what one scholar has described as the 'fissure [that] opened up between imitation and scholarship, rhetoric and philology, literature and history' late in the seventeenth century.[44] If we can see that fissure beginning to open in Wotton's *Reflections*, we can see it gaping in the *Dissertation Upon the Epistles of Phalaris* which Richard Bentley appended to the second edition of the *Reflections* (1697) and expanded in 1699. Temple had argued simply that the older a text was, the better, and he had taken what he believed to be the most ancient works of Greek prose, Aesop's *Fables* and Phalaris' *Epistles*, as his preeminent examples. Bentley attacked both of Temple's claims on behalf of the *Epistles*, condemning them as tediously commonplace and meticulously demonstrating, by arguments chronological, philological and even numismatical, that the *Epistles* were written by a sophist, perhaps as late as the second century AD. Bentley's argument is one of the finest expressions of that critical historiography which humanism had elaborated, and it might therefore seem perverse to find in his discrediting of Phalaris a significant assault on the cult of antiquity, yet it was certainly received that way. Bentley applied a methodically constructed demystifying grid to the entire documentary past, and he operated as if no mysteriously authoritative cultural fountainhead lay outside that grid. This was not the most damaging assault on ancient textual prestige to have been mounted during the century, for it substantially repeats the procedures of Thomas Hobbes's attack on the absolute authority of the Bible in chapter 33 of *Leviathan* (1651). In arguments heavily indebted to Protestant critical analysis of the Bible, and particularly to Thomas James's *Treatise of the Corruptions of Scripture* (1612), Hobbes had confounded biblical authority by describing the historical occasions on which – and for which – individual books of the Bible were composed. Bentley's argument was less outrageous than Hobbes's, but it was outrageous enough to provoke atavistic lampoon: according to Swift, Bentley had sought to demonstrate 'that the noblest Discoveries those *Antients* ever made, of Art or of Nature, have all been produced by the transcending Genius of the present Age'.[45] Bentley's modern classicism denigrates the cult of antiquity on behalf of the cult of method – an epochal shift within the history of humanism. It was no longer possible to maintain a fruitful accord between a reverence for antiquity and a critical knowledge of its traces.

That accord is what Jonson had praised in Selden: at the beginning of the seventeenth century antiquary and poet had seemed useful and inspiring to each other. When Pope signed the contract for a translation of the *Iliad* – exactly a century after Jonson wrote the 'Epistle to Selden' – he could only provoke the scholarly community to fury. Richard Bentley's nephew, Thomas, published a letter to Pope in which he bluntly alleges that 'as for the Greek Language, everybody that knows it and has compared your Version with the Original, as I have done in many Places, must know that you know nothing of it', and the modern consensus is that Bentley was not far from the truth.[46] Pope claimed a passion for Homer, claimed that reading Homer in his youth had 'made me catch the itch of poetry'; but, knowing himself to be inadequate to the task of fully annotating the poem, he was obliged to appeal to his friend, Thomas Parnell, for legitimizing assistance.[47] In what would be a failing effort to restore the accord of humanism and literature, the wit appeals to the scholar: 'You are a Grecian and bred at the University, I a poor Englishman of my own Educating.'[48] We are a far cry from Jonson and Selden, farther still from Petrarch, weeping over a Greek manuscript of Homer that he could not read. Pope could consult the English translations of Chapman and Hobbes (he would *rely* on Dacier's French rendering); he could draw on a wealth of printed commentary, philological, archaeological and philosophical; he could consult friends who had studied at least a smattering of Greek as adolescents: in this sense, both the research project and the pedagogical mission of humanism had been achieved. But Pope wrote in anxious contempt of scholarship; Bentley's opinion of the poet's effort is now famous: 'Tis a pretty poem Mr Pope, but it is not Homer.'[49]

NOTES

My thanks to Christiane Auston, Ted Munter, Lynne Tatlock and Steven Zwicker for their assistance and wise suggestions.

1   Ben Jonson, 'An Epistle to Master Iohn Selden', in the edition of his works ed. C. H. Herford and P. Simpson, 11 vols. (Oxford, 1925–52), VIII, pp. 158-61, lines 33–44.

2   Jonson, *Discoveries*, in ed. Herford and Simpson, VIII, p. 618.

3   John Selden, *Table Talk* (London, 1890), p. 144; quoted in D. Riggs, *Ben Jonson: A Life* (Cambridge MA, 1989), pp. 198–9.

4   Again, the qualification – a description of Virgil's political circumstances written in 1696 *is* startling: 'we are to consider him as writing his Poem in a time when the Old Form of Government was subverted, and a new one just Established by Octavius Caesar: In effect by force of Arms, but seemingly by the Consent of the *Roman* People': John Dryden, *The Works*, ed. H. T. Swedenberg, E. N. Hooker and A. Roper (Berkeley, 1956–), V, p. 279. The audacious force of Dryden's Jacobite complaint depends upon the routinized, one-to-one correspondence between Augustan Rome and the England of the Revolution Settlement. And yet for all the power of this normative idiom, other dialects – of science, of utility, or of gallantry – were now competing with those associated with antiquity. At the end of his career, Dryden began to check the hypotactic habits that had so firmly anchored the classicism of his youth. His late *style* betrays a fading confidence in an alien Latinity as the anchor and centre of culture.

5   R. R. Bolgar, *The Classical Heritage and Its Beneficiaries* (Cambridge, 1958), pp. 375–7.

6   In the late seventeenth and early eighteenth century, important editions would follow: Thomas Gale's *Opuscula mythologica, ethica et physica* (1670/1), his Iamblichus (1678, which includes the Greek *editio princeps* of *De mysteriis*) and Herodotus (1679); Thomas Creech's Lucretius (1695); John Hudson's Thucydides (1696) and Josephus (1720); Joshua Barnes's Euripides (1694) and Anacreon (1705); and Thomas Stanley's Aeschylus (1663), which many scholars regard as the most distinguished English editorial achievement of the century.

7   L. D. Reynolds and N. G. Wilson, *Scribes and Scholars*, third edition (Oxford, 1991), p. 169. There were other responses to belatedness. Once the primary editorial work had been done, works of secondary scholarship could proceed: the early seventeenth century gives us Thomas Gataker's study of lots (1618); Andrew Downes's work on Demosthenes (1621); Thomas Dempster's on Etrurian culture (posthumously published, 1723–4); Sir Henry Savile on military science (1601); John Evelyn on medals (1697); Selden's work on naval law (1652), on ancient calendrical systems (1644), on tithes (1618) and, of course, *De dis Syris* (1617). This is also the great period of encyclopedic synthesis, of which Richard Burton's *Anatomy of Melancholy* (first edition, 1621) is both an early and a distinguished example. Among the others are Gataker's general treatise on Stoicism, which accompanies his edition of Marcus Aurelius' *Meditations* (1652); Thomas Stanley's history of ancient philosophy (1655–62); and Theophilus Gale's substantial improvement on Stanley, *The Court of the Gentiles* (1669–77).

8   A cautious revision of the Bishops' Bible (1568), the new version was designed to absorb and neutralize the competing claims of both the Geneva Bible (1560), still the Bible of choice for home use, and the more scholarly, but Catholic, Rheims New Testament of 1582.

9   E. Eisenstein, *The Printing Press as an Agent of Change*, 2 vols. (Cambridge, 1979), I, pp. 330–56; *The Cambridge History of the Bible*, 3 vols. (Cambridge, 1963–70), III.

10 *The English Bible Translated Out of the Original Tongues by the Commandment of King James the First*, ed. W. E. Henley, 6 vols. (London, 1903), I, p. 21.

11 See C. B. Schmitt, *Aristotle and the Renaissance* (Cambridge MA, 1983), p. 66.

12 Mulcaster's two great treatises are *Positions* (1581) and *The Elementarie* (1582). Of course, the pedagogical revolution cannot be explained simply as a development intrinsic to the logic of humanism: social pressures impinged. Between 1550 and 1650, education became substantially more popular. Philanthropic Elizabethan merchants founded many new grammar schools, but the merchants of Stuart England founded many more; see W. K. Jordan, *The Charities of Rural England, 1480-1660* (London, 1961), pp. 25 and 283. By 1640, 2.5 per cent of the adult male population was university educated, a figure not exceeded until the 1930s and with the enlarged clientele came a shift in pedagogical emphasis; see L. Stone, 'The educational revolution in England, 1560–1640', *Past and Present*, 28 (1964), 41–80, at 68–9.

13 Geoffrey Chaucer, *Amorum Troili et Creseidae libri duo priores Anglico-Latini*, trans. F. Kynaston (Oxford, 1635), sig. *2ᵛ. It remained necessary for many years to render English texts in Latin if one wished to secure the widest possible Continental readership: Dryden's *Absalom and Achitophel*, for example, would be translated into Latin as late as 1682.

14 John Milton, *Works*, ed. F. A. Patterson, 18 vols. (New York, 1931–8), I, p. 312, lines 168–71.

15 Perhaps nothing written in the seventeenth century bears the marks of its author's schooling so strongly as Jonson's *Catiline*, organized around a staging (one could not quite say 'dramatization') of those great school texts, Cicero's orations against Catiline.

16 The educational goal of a community committed to Bible-reading was to make Latin, Greek and Hebrew literacy as easy to attain as possible. In 1626 William Webbe secured a royal patent in a new method of language instruction built around Latin texts in parallel Latin–English editions, with equivalent clauses numbered: the idea was to teach Latin 'without Rules'. What is perhaps most striking about seventeenth-century developments is that the methodization of Latin pedagogy was extended beyond the scriptural languages to English (Comenius urged that children between the ages of six and twelve be enrolled in vernacular schools), to the Continental vernaculars and to the languages of the New World and the Orient.

17 On Ramism, see chapter 5 above, p. 89.

18 Alexander Gill's important *Logonomia Anglica* (London, 1619) – radically Ramist in conception and the first really thorough English grammar – is similarly shackled to the Latin grammatical categories of Priscian, though he does remark on the non-inflected character of the English adjective. It is worth remembering here that vernacular grammars, like the orthographic handbooks

that precede them, are intended to be normative, not merely descriptive: languages are being made as part of the large cultural work of nation-building.

19 England lags behind Italy by approximately a century in making this conceptual break; see L. Kukenheim, *Contributions à l'histoire de la grammaire italienne, espagnole, et française à l'époque de la Renaissance* (Amsterdam, 1932), p. 140. To an important extent the major contributions of seventeenth-century English scholars to the development of modern linguistics were made in the very different area of phonetics. England's increasing commercial prestige stimulated unprecedented foreign interest in English pronunciation, an interest to which such scholars as Robert Robinson, George Mason, John Wallis, William Holder and John Wilkins eagerly responded.

20 Thomas Carew, *Poems*, ed. R. Dunlap (Oxford, 1949), pp. 71–4, at 72–3, lines 45–8.

21 I cite Verstegan from V. Salmon, 'Effort and achievement in seventeenth-century British linguistics', in T. Bynon and F. R. Palmer, eds., *Studies in the History of Western Linguistics* (Cambridge, 1986), pp. 69–95, at 70–1; on the Saxon craze, see R. F. Jones, *The Seventeenth Century* (Stanford, 1951), p. 270.

22 G. G. Smith, ed., *Elizabethan Critical Essays*, 2 vols. (London, 1904), II, p. 314.

23 Gill, *Logonomia Anglica*, sigs. P4^v, N4^v, M3$^{r–v}$.

24 Chaucer, *Amorum Troili et Creseidae libri duo*, sig. **1^r.

25 Carew, *Poems*, pp. 72, lines 29–33, 73, lines 63–7.

26 In this inventiveness he remains unchallenged for half a century, despite the fact that many Englishmen translated from the satirists – Barten Holyday's 1616 Persius, W. B.'s Juvenal in 1617, Sir John Beaumont's Juvenal [n.d.], George Chapman's translation of Juvenal V in 1629, John Biddle's Juvenal I and II in 1634, Robert Stapleton's 1644 Juvenal, Henry Vaughan's Juvenal X in 1646, Alexander Brome's 1666 Horace, including Richard Fanshawe's renderings first published in 1652. Brome is the first to equal Donne's arch contemporaneity.

27 G. Braden, *The Classics and English Renaissance Poetry* (New Haven, 1978), pp. 166–70; Braden's account culminates with useful reflections on the relation between humanist textual scholarship and literary creativity.

28 Interest in one particular Anacreontic motif, the bee-stung Cupid, bubbles up in the poems that conclude Spenser's *Amoretti*, but Spenser's work in these poems suggests neither deep familiarity nor attentive assimilation. The full English encounter with the Anacreontea begins, deftly, with Jonson's 'Celebration of Charis'.

29 Robert Herrick, *The Poetical Works*, ed. L. C. Martin (Oxford, 1956), pp. 205–7, at 206, lines 32–4 ('The Apparition of his Mistresse calling him to *Elizium*').

30 *Naps upon Parnassus* (London, 1658), sig. A3^v.

31 Herrick, *Poetical Works*, pp. 45–6, at 45, lines 31–2 ('His fare-well to Sack').

32 Jonson, *The Under-wood* XXV, in ed. Herford and Simpson, VIII, pp. 176–80, lines 1–5, 11–13.

33 See Book I, chapter 9 of Julius Caesar Scaliger's *Poetices libri septem* (Lyons, 1561) and Book III of Antonio Minturno's *L'arte poetica* (Venice, 1564).

34 Francis Bacon, *The Advancement of Learning, Book I*, ed. W. A. Armstrong (London, 1975), pp. 70–1.

35 Francis Bacon, *De augmentis scientiarum* (1623), trans. G. Wats (Oxford,

1640), sig. D3^r. The objectifying drive of Bacon's semiotics, the pressure to subordinate words to things, produced, in the ideologues of the Royal Society, a complex set of stylistic prejudices – an anti-Ciceronian distrust of symmetry, checked by a (Ramist, scientific) respect for the analytic utility of binary structures; a resistance to elaboration, checked by a hostility to gnomic compression.

36 J. F. Spingarn, ed., *Critical Essays of the Seventeenth Century*, 3 vols. (Oxford, 1908–9), II, p. 132.

37 Samuel Johnson, 'The life of Pope', in his *The Lives of the Poets*, cited from Samuel Johnson, *Selected Poetry and Prose*, ed. F. Brady and W. K. Wimsatt (Berkeley, 1977), p. 523.

38 Henry Higden, prefacing his own rendering of Juvenal's *Satire XIII*, tries to name the form: 'A Modern Essay *Let it be: for as a Translation I could not, and as a Paraphrase I would not own it ... I have equipped them Al-a-mode* [sic]': *A Modern Essay on the Thirteenth Satire of Juvenal* (London, 1686), sig. b2^r. In 'Translation and parody: towards the genealogy of the Augustan imitation', *English Literary History*, 33 (1966), 434–47, at 436–7, H. Weinbrot identifies Sir John Denham's poem 'To Richard Fanshawe upon his Translation of Pastor Fido' (1648) as the first attempt to give a theoretical description of the form.

39 Dryden, *Works*, IV, p. 213, lines 105–11.

40 S. Zwicker, *Politics and Language in Dryden's Poetry: The Arts of Disguise* (Princeton, 1984), pp. 3–34; the Dryden quotations are taken from his *Works*, IV, pp. 71–3.

41 Dryden, *Works*, V, pp. 267–341, at 278–80.

42 Zwicker, *Politics and Language*, pp. 184–5.

43 William Wotton, *Reflections Upon Ancient and Modern Learning*, third edition (London, 1705), p. 495.

44 J. M. Levine, *The Battle of the Books: History and Literature in the Augustan Age* (Ithaca NY, 1991), p. 2; for a restatement, see pp. 45–6.

45 'Concerning critics', the first digression in Jonathan Swift, *The Tale of a Tub*, ed. H. Davis (Oxford, 1957), p. 59.

46 Thomas Bentley, *A Letter to Mr. Pope Occasioned by Sober Advice from Horace* (London, 1735), p. 14.

47 Alexander Pope, *Correspondence*, ed. G. Sherburn, 5 vols. (Oxford, 1956), I, p. 298.

48 Pope, *Correspondence*, I, p. 225.

49 Cited in various forms from various sources in Levine, *Battle of the Books*, p. 222; Levine concedes that the story of Bentley's remark to Pope may be apocryphal.

A GUIDE TO FURTHER READING IN ENGLISH

For more detailed bibliographies, including material in foreign languages, see the notes to the individual chapters.

GENERAL

Bentley, J. H., *Politics and Culture in Renaissance Naples* (Princeton, 1987)
Bolgar, R. R., *The Classical Heritage and Its Beneficiaries* (Cambridge, 1954)
Burke, P., *The Italian Renaissance: Culture and Society in Italy* (Oxford, 1987)
D'Amico, J. F., *Renaissance Humanism in Papal Rome: Humanists and Churchmen on the Eve of the Reformation* (Baltimore, 1983)
Di Cesare, M. A., ed., *Reconsidering the Renaissance* (Binghamton, 1992)
Field, J. V. and James, F. A. J. L., eds., *Renaissance and Revolution: Humanists, Scholars, Craftsmen and Natural Philosophers in Early Modern Europe* (Cambridge, 1993)
Goodman, A. and Mackay, A., eds., *The Impact of Humanism on Western Europe* (London, 1990)
IJsewijn, J., *Companion to Neo-Latin Studies*, second edition (Louvain, 1990), I: *History and Diffusion of Neo-Latin Literature*
Kelley, D. R., *Renaissance Humanism* (Boston, 1991)
King, M. L., *Venetian Humanism in an Age of Patrician Dominance* (Princeton, 1986)
Kristeller, P. O., *Renaissance Thought*, 2 vols. (New York, 1961–5)
  Renaissance Thought and Its Sources, ed. M. Mooney (New York, 1979)
  Studies in Renaissance Thought and Letters, 3 vols. (Rome, 1956–93)
Rabil, A., ed., *Renaissance Humanism: Foundations, Forms, and Legacy*, 3 vols. (Philadelphia, 1988)
Stinger, C. L., *The Renaissance in Rome* (Bloomington, 1985)
Trinkaus, C., *The Scope of Renaissance Humanism* (Ann Arbor, 1983)
Ullman, B. L., *Studies in the Italian Renaissance*, second edition (Rome, 1973)

ORIGINS OF HUMANISM

Benson, R. L. and Constable, G., eds., *Renaissance and Renewal in the Twelfth Century* (Oxford, 1982)
Bishop, M., *Petrarch and His World* (Bloomington, 1963)
Brooke, C., *The Twelfth Century Renaissance* (London, 1969)

Ferguson, W. K., *The Renaissance in Historical Thought: Five Centuries of Interpretation* (Cambridge MA, 1948)

Haskins, C. H., *The Renaissance of the Twelfth Century* (Cambridge MA, 1927)

Kohl, B. G., 'The changing concept of the *studia humanitatis* in the early Renaissance', *Renaissance Studies*, 6 (1992), 185–209

McLaughlin, M., 'Humanist concepts of Renaissance and Middle Ages', *Renaissance Studies*, 2 (1988), 131–42

Mann, N., *Petrarch* (Oxford, 1984)

Petrarch, *Lyric Poems*, ed. and trans. R. M. Durling (Cambridge MA, 1976)

Letters on Familiar Matters. Rerum familiarium libri I–XXIV, trans. A. S. Bernardo, 3 vols. (Albany NY, 1975; Baltimore, 1982–5)

Letters of Old Age. Rerum senilium libri I–IX, trans. A. S. Bernardo, S. Levin and R. A. Bernardo, 2 vols. (Baltimore, 1992)

Remedies for Fortune Fair and Foul. A Modern English Translation of De remediis utriusque fortune, trans. C. H. Rawski, 5 vols. (Bloomington, 1991)

Seigel, J. E., *Rhetoric and Philosophy in Renaissance Humanism* (Princeton, 1968)

Siraisi, N. G., *Arts and Sciences at Padua: The Studium of Padua before 1350* (Toronto, 1973)

Weiss, R., *The Dawn of Humanism in Italy* (London, 1947)

Wilkins, E. H., *Life of Petrarch* (Chicago, 1961)

The Making of the Canzoniere and Other Petrarchan Studies (Rome, 1951)

Studies in the Life and Works of Petrarch (Cambridge MA, 1955)

CLASSICAL SCHOLARSHIP

Billanovich, Giuseppe, 'Petrarch and the textual tradition of Livy', *Journal of the Warburg and Courtauld Institutes*, 14 (1951), 137–208

Branca, V., 'Ermolao Barbaro and late quattrocento Venetian humanism', in *Renaissance Venice*, ed. J. R. Hale (London, 1973), pp. 218–43

Butrica, J. L., *The Manuscript Tradition of Propertius* (Toronto, 1984)

De la Mare, A. C., 'The return of Petronius to Italy', in J. J. G. Alexander and M. T. Gibson, eds., *Medieval Learning and Literature: Essays Presented to Richard William Hunt* (Oxford, 1976), pp. 220–54

Diller, A., *Studies in Greek Manuscript Tradition* (Amsterdam, 1983)

Dionisotti, A. C., 'Polybius and the Royal Professor', in E. Gabba, ed., *Tria corda: scritti in onore di Arnaldo Momigliano* (Como, 1983), pp. 179–99

Dionisotti, A. C., Grafton, A. and Kraye, J., eds., *The Uses of Greek and Latin: Historical Essays* (London, 1988)

Dover, K. J., ed., *Perceptions of the Ancient Greeks* (Oxford, 1992): ch. 5, 'The medieval west', by A. C. Dionisotti; and ch. 6, 'The Renaissance', by P. Burke

Fryde, E. B., *Humanism and Renaissance Historiography* (London, 1983)

Gaisser, J. H., *Catullus and His Renaissance Readers* (Oxford, 1993)

Grafton, A. T., 'On the scholarship of Politian and its context', *Journal of the Warburg and Courtauld Institutes*, 40 (1977), 150–88

Defenders of the Text: The Traditions of Scholarship in an Age of Science, 1450–1800 (Cambridge MA, 1991)

Grafton, A. T., ed., *Rome Reborn: The Vatican Library and Renaissance Culture* (Washington DC, 1993)

Griffiths, G., Hankins, J. and Thompson, D., trans., *The Humanism of Leonardi Bruni: Selected Texts* (Binghamton, 1987)

Hay, D., 'Flavio Biondo and the Middle Ages', *Proceedings of the British Academy*, 45 (1959), 97–125

Kenney, E. J., *The Classical Text: Aspects of Editing in the Age of the Printed Book* (Berkeley CA, 1974)

Pfeiffer, R., *History of Classical Scholarship from 1300 to 1850* (Oxford, 1976)

Phillips, M. M., *The 'Adages' of Erasmus: A Study with Translations* (Cambridge, 1964)

Reeve, M. D., 'Statius's *Silvae* in the fifteenth century', *Classical Quarterly*, 71 (1977), 202–25

'The Italian tradition of Lucretius', *Italia medioevale e umanistica*, 23 (1980), 27–48

'The rediscovery of classical texts in the Renaissance', in O. Pecere, ed., *Itinerari dei testi antichi* (Rome, 1991), pp. 115–57

Reynolds, L. D., ed., *Texts and Transmission: A Survey of the Latin Classics* (Oxford, 1983)

Reynolds, L. D. and Wilson, N. G., *Scribes and Scholars: A Guide to the Transmission of Greek and Latin Literature*, third edition (Oxford, 1991)

Sandys, J. E., *Harvard Lectures on the Revival of Learning* (Cambridge, 1905)

Stadter, P. A., 'Niccolò Niccoli: winning back the knowledge of the ancients', in R. Avesani, M. Ferrari, T. Foffano, G. Frasso and A. Sottili, eds., *Vestigia: studi in onore di Giuseppe Billanovich*, 2 vols. (Rome, 1984), II, pp. 747–64

Tigerstedt, N., 'Observations on the reception of the Aristotelian *Poetics* in the Latin west', *Studies in the Renaissance*, 15 (1968), 7–24

Ullman, B. L., *The Humanism of Coluccio Salutati* (Padua, 1963)

Ullman, B. L. and Stadter, P. A., *The Public Library of Renaissance Florence* (Padua, 1972)

Valla, Lorenzo, *The Treatise on the Donation of Constantine*, trans. C. B. Coleman (New Haven, 1922)

Wilson, N. G., *From Byzantium to Italy: Greek Studies in the Italian Renaissance* (London, 1992)

Witt, R. G., *Hercules at the Crossroads: The Life, Works, and Thought of Coluccio Salutati* (Durham NC, 1983)

MANUSCRIPTS AND PRINTING

Alexander, J. J. G., ed., *The Painted Page: Italian Renaissance Book Illumination* (London, 1994)

Ames-Lewis, F., *The Library and Manuscripts of Piero di Cosimo de' Medici* (New York, 1984)

Bühler, C. F., *The Fifteenth-Century Book* (Philadelphia, 1960)

Davies, M., *Aldus Manutius, Printer and Publisher of Renaissance Venice* (London, 1995)

De la Mare, A. C., ed., *The Handwriting of the Italian Humanists* (Oxford, 1973–)

'Humanistic script: the first ten years', in F. Krafft and D. Wuttke, eds., *Das Verhältnis der Humanisten zum Buch* (Boppard, 1977), pp. 89–108

Eisenstein, E., *The Printing Press as an Agent of Change*, 2 vols. (Cambridge, 1979)

Hall, E., *Sweynheym and Pannartz and the Origins of Printing in Italy* (McMinnville, 1991)

Hindman, S., ed., *Printing the Written Word: The Social History of Books,* circa *1450–1520* (Ithaca NY, 1991)

Lowry, M., *The World of Aldus Manutius* (Oxford, 1979)

Nicholas Jenson and the Rise of Venetian Publishing in Renaissance Europe (Oxford, 1991)

Poggio Bracciolini, *Two Renaissance Book Hunters: The Letters of Poggius Bracciolini to Nicolaus de Niccolis,* trans. P. W. G. Gordan (New York, 1974)

Ullman, B. L., *The Origin and Development of Humanistic Script* (Rome, 1960)

Vespasiano da Bisticci, *Memoirs: Lives of Illustrious Men of the XVth Century,* trans. W. George and E. Waters (London, 1926)

LATIN AND LATIN EDUCATION

Black, R., 'Humanism and education in Renaissance Arezzo', *I Tatti Studies,* 2 (1987), 171–237

Erasmus, *The Colloquies,* trans C. R. Thompson (Chicago, 1965)

Collected Works (Toronto, 1974–), vol. XXVIII: *The Ciceronian,* trans. B. I. Knott

Fisher, A., 'The project of humanism and Valla's imperial metaphor', *Journal of Medieval and Renaissance Studies,* 23 (1993), 301–22

Gehl, P. F., *A Moral Art: Grammar, Society, and Culture in Trecento Florence* (Ithaca NY, 1993)

Grafton, A. T. and Jardine, L., *From Humanism to the Humanities: Education and the Liberal Arts in Fifteenth- and Sixteenth-Century Europe* (London, 1986)

Grendler, P., *Schooling in Renaissance Italy: Literacy and Learning, 1300–1600* (Baltimore, 1989)

Jensen, K., *Rhetorical Philosophy and Philosophical Grammar: Julius Caesar Scaliger's Theory of Language* (Munich, 1990)

Marsh, D., 'Grammar, method and polemic in Lorenzo Valla's *Elegantiae*', *Rinascimento,* 19 (1979), 91–116

Nichols, F. J., trans., *An Anthology of Neo-Latin Poetry* (New Haven, 1979)

Padley, G. A., *Grammatical Theory in Western Europe 1500–1700: The Latin Tradition* (Cambridge, 1976)

RHETORIC AND DIALECTIC

Cave, T., *The Cornucopian Text: Problems of Writing in the French Renaissance* (Oxford, 1979)

Erasmus, *Collected Works* (Toronto, 1974–), XXIV: *Literary and Educational Writings 2,* pp. 279–659 (*Copia: Foundations of the Abundant Style,* trans. B. I. Knott) and pp. 661–91 (*On the Method of Study,* trans. B. McGregor); XXV: *Literary and Educational Writings 3,* pp. 1–254 (*On the Writing of Letters,* trans. C. Fantazzi)

Mack, P., *Renaissance Argument: Valla and Agricola in the Traditions of Rhetoric and Dialectic* (Leiden, 1993)

Mack, P., ed., *Renaissance Rhetoric* (London, 1994)

Montaigne, Michel de, *The Complete Essays*, trans. M. A. Screech (London, 1993)
Murphy, J. J., ed., *Renaissance Eloquence* (Berkeley, 1983)
Sidney, Sir Philip, *The Poems*, ed. W. A. Ringler (Oxford, 1962)
The Old Arcadia, ed. J. Robertson (Oxford, 1973)
Vickers, B., *In Defence of Rhetoric* (Oxford, 1988)

BIBLICAL STUDIES

Augustijn, C., *Erasmus: His Life, Works, and Influence* (Toronto, 1992)
Bentley, J. H., *Humanists and Holy Writ: New Testament Scholarship in the Renaissance* (Princeton, 1983)
The Cambridge History of the Bible, 3 vols. (Cambridge, 1963–70), II
Jonge, H. J. de, 'The study of the New Testament', in T. H. Lunsingh Scheurleer and G. H. M. Posthumus Meyjes, eds., *Leiden University in the Seventeenth Century: An Exchange of Learning* (Leiden, 1975), pp. 65–109
Stinger, C. L., *Humanism and Church Fathers: Ambrogio Traversari and Christian Antiquity in the Italian Renaissance* (Albany, 1977)
Trinkaus, C., *In Our Image and Likeness: Humanity and Divinity in Italian Humanist Thought*, 2 vols. (London, 1970)

POLITICAL THOUGHT

Black, R., 'The political thought of the Florentine chancellors', *The Historical Journal*, 29 (1986), 991–1,003
Blythe, J. M., *Ideal Government and the Mixed Constitution in the Middle Ages* (Princeton, 1992)
Bock, G., Skinner, Q. and Viroli, M., eds., *Machiavelli and Republicanism* (Cambridge, 1990)
Burns, J. H., ed., *The Cambridge History of Political Thought 1450–1700* (Cambridge, 1991)
Gilmore, M., ed., *Studies on Machiavelli* (Florence, 1972)
Machiavelli, Niccolò, *The Prince*, ed. Q. Skinner, trans. R. Price (Cambridge, 1988)
More, Thomas, *The Complete Works* (New Haven, 1963–), IV: *Utopia*, ed. E. Surtz and J. H. Hexter
Pagden, A., ed., *The Languages of Political Theory in Early Modern Europe* (Cambridge, 1987)
Rubinstein, N., 'Political theories in the Renaissance', in *The Renaissance: Essays in Interpretation* (London, 1982), pp. 153–200
Skinner, Q., *The Foundations of Modern Political Thought*, 2 vols. (Cambridge, 1978)

PHILOSOPHY

Allen, M. J. B., *Marsilio Ficino and the Phaedran Charioteer* (Berkeley, 1981)
Icastes: Marsilio Ficino's Interpretation of Plato's Sophist (Berkeley, 1989)
Baldwin, A. and Hutton, S., eds., *Platonism and the English Imagination* (Cambridge, 1994)
Cassirer, E., Kristeller, P. O. and Randall, J. H., Jr., trans., *The Renaissance Philosophy of Man* (Chicago, 1948)

Copenhaver, B. P. and Schmitt, C. B., *Renaissance Philosophy* (Oxford, 1992)
Hankins, J., *Plato in the Italian Renaissance*, 2 vols. (Leiden, 1990)
Jones, H., *The Epicurean Tradition* (London, 1989)
Kristeller, P. O., *Eight Philosophers of the Italian Renaissance* (Stanford, 1964)
Lipsius, Justus, *Two Books of Constancie*, trans. Sir John Stradling (1594), ed. R. Kirk (New Brunswick NJ, 1939)
Morford, M., *Stoics and Neostoics: Rubens and the Circle of Lipsius* (Princeton, 1991)
Osler, M. J., ed., *Atoms, Pneuma, and Tranquillity: Epicurean and Stoic Themes in European Thought* (Cambridge, 1991)
Popkin, R. H., *The History of Scepticism from Erasmus to Spinoza* (Berkeley, 1979)
Routledge History of Philosophy (London, 1993–), IV: G. H. R. Parkinson, ed., *The Renaissance and Seventeenth-Century Rationalism*
Schmitt, C. B., *Aristotle and the Renaissance* (Cambridge MA, 1983)
Schmitt, C. B., Skinner, Q. and Kessler, E., eds., *The Cambridge History of Renaissance Philosophy* (Cambridge, 1988)
Sorell, T., ed., *The Rise of Modern Philosophy: The Tension between the New and Traditional Philosophies from Machiavelli to Leibniz* (Oxford, 1993)

ART

Alberti, Leon Battista, *On Painting and On Sculpture*, ed. and trans. C. Grayson (London, 1972)
Baxandall, M., *Giotto and the Orators: Humanist Observers of Painting in Italy and the Discovery of Pictorial Composition 1350–1650* (Oxford, 1988)
Bober, P. and Rubinstein, R., *Renaissance Artists and Antique Sculpture* (London, 1986)
Hope, C., 'Artists, patrons and advisers in the Italian Renaissance', in G. Lytle and S. Orgel, eds., *Patronage in the Renaissance* (Princeton, 1981), pp. 293–343
Muller, E. and Noël, J. M., 'Humanist views on art and morality', in *Saints and She-Devils: Images of Women in the 15th and 16th Centuries* (London, 1987), pp. 128–59
Panofsky, E., *Renaissance and Renascences in Western Art* (Stockholm, 1960)
'Erasmus and the visual arts', *Journal of the Warburg and Courtauld Institutes*, 32 (1969), 200–27
Rubens, Peter Paul, *The Letters*, trans. R. S. Magurn (Cambridge MA, 1955)
Saxl, F., 'The classical inscription in Renaissance art and politics', *Journal of the Warburg and Courtauld Institutes*, 4 (1940–1), 19–46
Seznec, J., *The Survival of the Pagan Gods* (New York, 1961)
Vasari, Giorgio, *Lives of the Artists*, trans. G. Bull, 2 vols. (Harmondsworth, 1987)
Weiss, R., *The Renaissance Discovery of Classical Antiquity*, second edition (Oxford, 1988)

VERNACULAR HUMANISM IN THE SIXTEENTH CENTURY

Ariosto, Lodovico, *Orlando furioso*, trans. Sir John Harington, ed. R. McNulty (Oxford, 1972)

Birrell, T. A., *English Monarchs and Their Books: From Henry VII to Charles II* (London, 1987)

Fraunce, Abraham, *The Arcadian Rhetoric [1588]* (Menston, 1969)

Montaigne, Michel de, *Essays*, trans. John Florio, 3 vols. (London, 1910)

Patterson, A. M., *Censorship and Interpretation: The Conditions of Writing and Reading in Early Modern England* (Madison WI, 1984)

Pastoral and Ideology: Virgil to Valéry (Oxford, 1988)

Starkey, D., ed., *Henry VIII: A European Court in England* (London, 1991)

SCIENCE AND HUMANISM IN THE SEVENTEENTH CENTURY

Baron, F., *Joachim Camerarius (1500–1574) . . . Essays on the History of Humanism during the Reformation* (Munich, 1978)

Croll, M., *Style, Rhetoric and Rhythm: Essays*, ed. J. M. Patrick and R. O. Evans (Princeton, 1966)

Donaldson, P. S., *Machiavelli and Mystery of State* (Cambridge, 1988)

Evans, R. J. W., *The Making of the Habsburg Monarchy 1550–1700* (Oxford, 1979)

Findlen, P., *Possessing Nature* (Berkeley, 1994)

Grafton, A. T., *Joseph Scaliger*, 2 vols. (Oxford, 1983–93)

'The world of the polyhistors: humanism and encyclopedism', *Central European History*, 18 (1985), 31–47

Junius, Franciscus, *De pictura veterum: The Painting of the Ancients*, ed. K. Aldrich, P. Fehl and R. Fehl, 2 vols. (Berkeley, 1991)

Kaufmann, T. DaC., *The Mastery of Nature* (Princeton, 1993)

Levine, J. M., *Humanism and History: Origins of Modern English Historiography* (Ithaca NY, 1987)

Maclean, I., *Interpretation and Meaning in the Renaissance: The Case of Law* (Cambridge, 1992)

Shearman, W., *John Dee: The Politics of Reading and Writing in the English Renaissance* (Amherst, 1995)

Stopp, F., *The Emblems of the Altdorf Academy: Medals and Medal Orations, 1577–1626* (London, 1974)

Vickers, B., ed., *Occult and Scientific Mentalities in the Renaissance* (Cambridge, 1984)

ITALIAN LITERATURE

Alberti, Leon Battista, *The Family in Renaissance Florence: A Translation of 'I libri della famiglia'*, trans. R. N. Watkins (Columbia SC, 1969)

Cox, V., *The Renaissance Dialogue: Literary Dialogue in its Social and Political Contexts, Castiglione to Galileo* (Cambridge, 1992)

Dempsey, C., *The Portrayal of Love. Botticelli's 'Primavera' and Humanist Culture at the Time of Lorenzo the Magnificent* (Princeton, 1992)

Greene, T. M., *The Light in Troy: Imitation and Discovery in Renaissance Poetry* (New Haven, 1982)

Hainsworth, P., *Petrarch the Poet* (London, 1988)

Jacoff, R., ed., *The Cambridge Companion to Dante* (Cambridge, 1993)

Marsh, D., *The Quattrocento Dialogue: Classical Tradition and Humanist Innovation* (Cambridge MA, 1980)

Medici, Lorenzo de', *Selected Poems and Prose*, trans. J. Thiem (University Park PN, 1991)

The Autobiography: A Commentary on My Sonnets, trans. J. W. Cook (Binghamton, 1995)

Poliziano, Angelo, *Stanze*, trans. D. Quint (Amherst, 1979)

ENGLISH LITERATURE

Ascham, Roger, *English Works*, ed. W. A. Wright (Cambridge, 1904; reprinted 1970)

Attridge, D., *Well-Weighed Syllables: Elizabethan Verse in Classical Metres* (Cambridge, 1974)

Bacon, Francis, *The Advancement of Learning and New Atlantis*, ed. A. Johnston (Oxford, 1974)

The Essayes or Counsels, Civill and Morall, ed. M. Kiernan (Oxford, 1985)

Baldwin, T. W., *William Shakspere's Small Latine & Lesse Greeke*, 2 vols. (Urbana, 1944)

Binns, J. W., *Intellectual Culture in Elizabethan and Jacobean England: The Latin Writings of the Age* (Leeds, 1990)

Braden, G., *The Classics and English Renaissance Poetry* (New Haven, 1978)

Renaissance Tragedy and the Senecan Tradition: Anger's Privilege (New Haven, 1985)

Brink, C. O., *English Classical Scholarship: Historical Reflections on Bentley, Porson and Housman* (Cambridge, 1986)

Carew, Thomas, *Poems*, ed. R. Dunlap (Oxford, 1949)

Carlson, D. R., *English Humanist Books: Writers and Patrons, Manuscript and Print* (Toronto, 1993)

Dryden, John, *The Works*, ed. H. T. Swedenberg, E. N. Hooker and A. Roper (Berkeley, 1956–)

Elyot, Sir Thomas, *The Boke named the Gouernour*, ed. H. H. S. Croft, 2 vols. (London, 1883; reprinted New York, 1967)

Ferguson, M., *Trials of Desire: Renaissance Defenses of Poetry* (New Haven, 1983)

Gosson, Stephen, *The Schoole of Abuse . . .*, ed. A. Freeman (New York, 1973)

Hay, D., 'England and the humanities in the fifteenth century', in H. A. Oberman and T. A. Brady, Jr., eds., *Itinerarium Italicum: The Profile of the Italian Renaissance in the Mirror of Its European Transformations* (Leiden, 1975), pp. 305–67

Herrick, Robert, *The Poetical Works*, ed. L. C. Martin (Oxford, 1956)

Howard, Henry, Earl of Surrey, *Poems*, ed. E. Jones (Oxford, 1964)

Jones, R. F., *The Triumph of the English Language* (Stanford, 1953; reprinted 1966)

Jonson, Ben, ed. C. H. Herford and P. Simpson, 11 vols. (Oxford, 1925–52)

Kinney, A. F., *Humanist Poetics: Thought, Rhetoric, and Fiction in Sixteenth-Century England* (Amherst, 1986)

Levine, J. M., *The Battle of the Books: History and Literature in the Augustan Age* (Ithaca NY, 1991)

Lyly, John, *The Complete Works*, ed. R. W. Bond, 3 vols. (Oxford, 1902; reprinted 1967)

McConica, J., *English Humanism and Reformation Politics* (Oxford, 1965)

Major, J. M., *Sir Thomas Elyot and Renaissance Humanism* (Lincoln NB, 1964)

Mason, H. A., *Humanism and Poetry in the Early Tudor Period* (London, 1959)

Miola, R. S., *Shakespeare and Classical Tragedy: The Influence of Seneca* (Oxford, 1992)

Shakespeare and Classical Comedy: The Influence of Plautus and Terence (Oxford, 1994)

More, Thomas, *The Complete Works* (New Haven, 1963–), II: *The History of King Richard III*, ed. R. S. Sylvester

Puttenham, George, *The Arte of English Poesie*, ed. G. D. Wilcox and A. Walker (Cambridge, 1936)

Riehle, W., *Shakespeare, Plautus and the Humanist Tradition* (Bury St Edmunds, 1990)

Ryan, L. V., *Roger Ascham* (Stanford, 1963)

Salmon, V., 'Effort and achievement in seventeenth-century British linguistics', in T. Bynon and F. R. Palmer, eds., *Studies in the History of Western Linguistics* (Cambridge, 1986), pp. 69–95

Shakespeare, William, *King Richard III*, ed. A. Hammond, The Arden Edition (London, 1981)

Sidney, Sir Philip, *An Apology for Poetry or the Defence of Poesy*, ed. G. Shepherd (Edinburgh, 1965)

Swift, Jonathan, *The Tale of a Tub*, ed. H. Davis (Oxford, 1957)

Trapp, J. B., *Erasmus, Colet and More: The Early Tudor Humanists and Their Books* (London, 1991)

Weiss, R., *Humanism in England during the Fifteenth Century*, third edition (Oxford, 1967)

Williamson, G., *The Senecan Amble: Prose from Bacon to Collier* (London, 1951)

Zwicker, S., *Politics and Language in Dryden's Poetry: The Arts of Disguise* (Princeton, 1984)

BIOGRAPHICAL INDEX

In addition to providing page references, this index gives dates and a brief description of the figures mentioned in the volume. For Italians, an indication of the city or province where they were born or were active is provided; for other Europeans, normally only their nationality is specified.

Biographical index

Chrysoloras, Manuel (Byzantine humanist
c. 1350–1414), 16–17, 33–4, 119, 164
Chrysostom, John, St (Greek Church Father
and bishop of Constantinople;
c. 347–407), 101, 110–11, 272
Cicero (Roman orator, statesman and
philosopher; 106–43 BC), 1, 3, 9–10,
12–14, 20–35, 38–40, 58, 64, 67, 73–6,
82–5, 87, 89, 91, 100, 118–19, 121,
126, 136, 153, 160 n. 57, 164, 189, 199,
207–10, 214, 216, 219, 227, 229–33,
235, 239, 243 nn. 25 and 39, 247, 249,
258, 262, 264, 284
Cimabue (Florentine painter; c. 1240–1302),
161
Cinna (Roman politician; fl. 87–84 BC), 287
Ciriagio, Gherardo del (Florentine scribe;
d. 1472), 50
Clapmarius, Arnold (German scholar;
1574–1604), 208–9, 218
Claudian (Roman (b. Alexandria) poet;
d. c. 404 AD), 236
Cleland, James (English educational writer;
d. 1627), 201 n. 25
Clement VII (Giulio de' Medici; Florentine
pope; 1479–1534), 113
Cochlaeus, Johannes (Johann Dobneck;
Roman Catholic controversialist;
1479–1552), 80 n. 17
Cola di Rienzo (Roman notary and
revolutionary; 1313–54), 11
Colet, John (English humanist, educator and
dean of St Paul's; 1467–1519), 74, 109,
249–50
Colmán (Irish scholar; ninth century), 25
Colonna, Francesco (Venetian Dominican
author; 1433–1527), 238–40
Colonna, Landolfo (Italian (b. Gallicano)
cleric and chronicler; c. 1250–1331),
9 10
Columella (Roman agricultural author; first
century AD) 244 n. 40
Comenius (Komensky), Jan Amos (Czech
educational theorist; 1592–1670), 212,
278, 291 n. 16
Constantine (Roman emperor; d. 337), 23,
32, 40, 104, 163
Coote, Edmund (English grammarian; fl.
1597), 277
Cope, Sir Anthony (English author and
translator; d. 1551), 194
Coronel, Pablo (Spanish converso biblical
scholar; d. 1534), 107

Cortesi, Paolo (Roman humanist, papal
secretary and Ciceronian; 1465–1510),
237
Corvinus, Matthias (King of Hungary;
1440–90), 59, 132–3
Cotton, Charles (English poet and prose
author; 1630–87), 285
Cowley, Abraham (English poet and prose
author; 1618–67), 282, 284–5
Creech, Thomas (English classical scholar
and translator; 1659–1700), 290 n. 6
Creusa (legendary Trojan, daughter of
Priam), 287
Cromwell, Thomas, Earl of Essex (English
statesman; c. 1485–1540), 191, 194
Cudworth, Ralph (English cleric and
Platonist; 1617–88), 151
Cuffe, Henry (English author and politician;
1583–1601), 210–11
Cupid (Roman god of love), 197, 258, 292
n. 28
Cyclops (mythological Greek giant), 32
Cyprian, St (Latin Church Father and bishop
of Carthage; d. 258), 111, 272
Cyriac of Ancona (Italian humanist and
antiquarian; c. 1390–1455), 36, 40
Cyrus (Persian emperor; sixth century BC),
259–60

Dacier, Anne Lefèbvre (French classical
scholar and translator; 1651/4–1720),
289
Dale, Valentine (English diplomat; d. 1589),
192, 194, 198
Daniel, Samuel (English poet; 1562–1619),
196, 198, 201 n. 31, 279
Dante Alighieri (Florentine poet and prose
author; 1265–1321), 8–9, 24, 119,
161, 167, 204, 215, 224–32, 236, 240,
245
Daphne (mythological daughter of a river-
god), 226
Dati, Agostino (Sienese humanist and
teacher; 1420–78), 79 n. 14
Dati, Leonardo (Florentine papal secretary
and bishop of Massa Marittima;
1408–72), 61 n. 13
Davanzati, Bernardo (Florentine translator;
1529–1606), 190
David (Old Testament king and putative
author of Psalms), 213
Decembrio, Angelo (Milanese humanist;
c. 1415–c. 1466), 39–40, 168